ISBN 978-1-5277-8339-3
PIBN 10894643

1 MONTH OF
FREE
READING

at

www.ForgottenBooks.com

By purchasing this book you are eligible for one month membership to ForgottenBooks.com, giving you unlimited access to our entire collection of over 700,000 titles via our web site and mobile apps.

To claim your free month visit:

www.forgottenbooks.com/free894643

SOLDIER AND BRAVE

*Historic Places Associated with Indian Affairs and
the Indian Wars in the Trans-Mississippi West*

NEW EDITION

ROBERT G. FERRIS *Series Editor*

UNITED STATES DEPARTMENT OF THE INTERIOR
NATIONAL PARK SERVICE   *Washington, D.C. 1971*

This volume was prepared in the Office of Archeology and Historic Preservation (Ernest A. Connally, Chief), Division of History, National Park Service, under the general supervision of the Chief Historian, Robert M. Utley. One of a series designed to make available to the public the studies of the National Survey of Historic Sites and Buildings, directed by Horace J. Sheely, it incorporates survey and evaluation reports prepared by the following National Park Service historians and archeologists: Edwin C. Bearss, William E. Brown, William C. Everhart, Olaf T. Hagen, Edward A. Hummel, John A. Hussey, John D. McDermott, Merrill J. Mattes, Ray H. Mattison, Charles S. Pope, Frank B. Sarles, Jr., Albert H. Schroeder, Paul J. F. Schumacher, Charles W. Snell, Erwin N. Thompson, and Robert M. Utley. These reports were reviewed by the Advisory Board on National Parks, Historic Sites, Buildings, and Monuments and the Consulting Committee for the National Survey of Historic Sites and Buildings. Members of these groups are listed in the Acknowledgments. The following Northeastern University students, employed under a cooperative agreement with their institution, provided invaluable research assistance: James H. Charleton, Richard E. Dean, Jr., and Julia Schlinski. Assistant editor for this volume was Richard E. Morris.

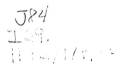

As the Nation's principal conservation agency, the Department of the Interior has basic responsibilities for water, fish, wildlife, mineral, land, park, and recreational resources. Indian and Territorial affairs are other major concerns of America's "Department of Natural Resources." The Department works to assure the wisest choice in managing all our resources so each will make its full contribution to a better United States—now and in the future.

LIBRARY OF CONGRESS CATALOG CARD NUMBER: 70-600864

For sale by the Superintendent of Documents, U.S. Government Printing Office
Washington, D.C. 20402 · Price $4.00

FOREWORD

Americans take great pride in their historic monuments. Although these monuments reflect the good and the bad, triumph and tragedy, joy and despair, all of them are part of our treasured national heritage.

Historic monuments strengthen our appreciation for the effort of our ancestors of all races that led to a Nation that attaches great importance to individual freedoms and democratic institutions.

The monuments described in this volume helped shape America as we know it today. They poignantly reflect how this Nation's ideals were forged from an amalgamation of successes and failures. They accurately mirror the growth of America.

ROGERS C. B. MORTON
Secretary of the Interior

PREFACE

The enthusiastic response of the public to this series of volumes has been heartwarming to me. It reveals a widespread interest in historic sites and buildings. At the same time, it underscores the need for continued vigilance on the part of historic preservationists.

Sites and buildings associated with Indian affairs and the Indian wars are well represented in the National Park System and in State parks. Historical societies, other organizations, county and municipal agencies, corporations, and private individuals maintain and preserve numerous other sites. But the momentum must be maintained. Increasing urbanization and the burgeoning of population in the West represent new threats to historic preservation. They must not be allowed to widen the swath of the bulldozer.

This is one of a series of books designed to make available to Americans the findings of the National Survey of Historic Sites and Buildings, a nationwide program conducted by the National Park Service of the U.S. Department of the Interior under authority of the Historic Sites Act of 1935. The Survey's purpose is to identify historic and prehistoric places of significance to the Nation.

Such places are studied and evaluated by Service field historians and archeologists, screened by a Consulting Committee of outside scholars, and final selections recommended to the Secretary of the Interior by the Advisory Board on National Parks, Historic Sites, Buildings, and Monuments. When approved by the Secretary, sites and buildings judged of national significance are eligible for designation as National Historic Landmarks.

Upon application, their owners are provided with a certificate and a bronze plaque attesting to the distinction.

Credit for the preparation of this volume is shared widely by persons both in and out of the National Park Service. In particular, the work of the Service in the general field of historic preservation has benefited inestimably from the assistance provided by the National Trust for Historic Preservation in the United States, a cosponsor of the Survey.

The sites and buildings described in this volume represent a colorful phase of American history. Yet, it was a tragic era. It has also been distorted in the popular mind by television and motion picture presentations. Visits to pertinent historic sites will do much to dispel the myths associated with the period and contribute to better understanding of its complexities.

GEORGE B. HARTZOG, JR.
Director
National Park Service

CONTENTS

x

All photographs and maps are indexed.

SOLDIER AND BRAVE

SOLDIER AND BRAVE

PART I

SOLDIER AND BRAVE:
HISTORICAL BACKGROUND

As the 19th century opened, the Indians of the trans-Mississippi West unknowingly stood on the threshold of ethnic disaster. An alien tide rolled westward. Within a century it would engulf all tribes, appropriate all but a tiny fraction of their vast domain, and leave the survivors a way of life often grotesque in its mixture of the old and the new. The tribes east of the Mississippi were already suffering this experience. They were being pushed ever westward by the advancing frontier; or left in isolated pockets surrounded by hostile conquerors; or simply annihilated; or, in rare instances, absorbed by the newcomers. A few western tribes, notably in Spanish New Mexico and California, had experienced something of what was to come. Of the rest, only the occasional visit of a French or Spanish trader kept them from forgetting that white men even existed.

Even so, the western Indian had already received two significant gifts from the white man. The horse, filtering up through successive tribes from the Spanish borderlands, revolutionized an older way of life and gave a new mobility to many nomadic and seminomadic hunting groups. This gift caused important changes not only in their economy but also in their social, ceremonial, and material organization. The Indians who confronted the 19th-century American had inhabited the West for centuries; their culture, because of the horse, had only recently taken the shape known to frontiersmen. The second gift, the gun, had by 1800 demonstrated its utility in war and the hunt to a few northern tribes bordering the French frontier but had yet to find its way into the hands of very many warriors. For horses the Indians were now beholden to no alien race; for guns they were soon to become dependent on the white man.

Not all tribes felt these influences equally. On the Great Plains the impact of horse and gun produced its highest cultural expression among the Sioux, Cheyenne, Arapaho, Crow, Kiowa, Comanche, Pawnee, and lesser-known tribes. In the Rocky Mountains, Nez Perces, Flatheads, Utes, Shoshonis, Bannocks, and others conformed only slightly less exactly to the prototype. By contrast the Pueblos of the Rio Grande drainage remained agriculturalists living in fixed dwellings. The Navajos became superb horsemen but also cultivated crops and tended herds of sheep—a legacy of Spanish times. Their neighbors, the Apaches and Yavapais, traveled their mountain-and-desert homeland by foot as often as by horse and mule; they also planted crops. The Paiutes and Western Shoshonis of the Great Basin displayed similar patterns. In the mountains of the Far West and along the Pacific coast, a woodland and marine environment, traditional hunting, gathering, and fishing customs made only minor accommodations to European technology.

As the trickle of western migration swelled to a flood in the first half of the 19th century, the western Indians, as had their eastern brethren earlier, only dimly sensed the alternative responses open to them. [Indian affairs east of the Mississippi and pertinent sites are discussed in *Founders and Frontiersmen,* Volume VII in this series; those in Alaska, in *Pioneer and Sourdough,* planned Volume XIII.] They could unite in a desperate war to turn back the invaders. They could submit, borrowing from the invaders what seemed best and rejecting the rest. Or they could give up the old and adopt the new. The first choice

4

Trappers' rendezvous on the Green River in Wyoming. The fur traders introduced the Indians to the white man's ways. William H. Jackson painting.

usually proved impossible because of traditional intertribal animosities and the independence of thought and action that characterized Indian society. The last was rarely considered seriously. Sooner or later most of the tribes turned to the second, but few succeeded. For most groups, instead, the old culture simply disintegrated under the foreign onslaught—sometimes with, sometimes without, armed resistance—and left a void imperfectly and unhappily filled by parts of the conqueror's way of life.

In the wake of the official Government explorers—Meriwether Lewis and William Clark, Zebulon Pike, Stephen H. Long—came the roving fur trappers. [The fur trade and associated sites are treated in *Trappers, Traders, and Explorers,* planned Volume IX in this series.] Spreading through the wilderness, they afforded the Indian his first sustained view of the whites. Generally he liked what he saw, for many of the trappers in fact "went Indian," adopting many Indian tools, techniques, customs, and values. But the trappers also presented only a blurred glimpse of the manners and customs of the white men. Free and company trappers roamed the West until the early 1840's, but the fur business came

5

As time went on, traders came to rely on fixed trading posts, to which the Indians brought their furs. Interior view of Fort William (Fort Laramie), Wyo., about 1837. Watercolor by Alfred Jacob Miller.

to be dominated by the fixed trading post, which relied on the Indian to do the actual fur gathering.

At Fort Union on the upper Missouri, at Bent's Fort on the Arkansas, at Fort Laramie on the North Platte, at Fort Vancouver on the Columbia, and at a host of lesser fur posts sprinkled over the West, Indian and white met on the latter's own ground. There the Indian acquired a fondness for alcohol that made it the chief tool of competition between rival companies, and there he contracted diseases such as smallpox and cholera that decimated tribe after tribe. There, too, the white man's trade goods—guns, kettles, pans, cloth, knives, hatchets, and a whole range of other useful items—fundamentally affected the Indian's material culture and thus bound him to the newcomers. Thereafter, even in time of war with the whites, he looked to them for a large variety of manufactures that had come to be regarded as essential.

6

Despite occasional armed clashes, the trapper-traders and the Indians usually dwelt compatibly side by side. Neither was bent on dispossessing or remaking the other. By the early 1840's, however, the Indian observed, coming from the East, other kinds of white men—miners, farmers, stockmen, adventurers of every breed—who did pose a threat to all he treasured.

The Oregon country, its ownership disputed between Great Britain and the United States, attracted some; Mexican California others. Then in the Mexican War (1846–48) the United States seized California and the Southwest from Mexico and extended its dominion to the Pacific. Texas, independent of Mexico since 1836, joined the Union in 1845. Settlement of the Oregon controversy in 1846 added the Pacific Northwest.

Territorial expansion stimulated emigration. The dramatic discovery of gold in California in 1848 opened the floodgates. Bound for the new possessions, few emigrants stopped to make their homes in the Indian country, but they pierced it from north to south with a tier of overland highways—the Oregon-California Trail, the Santa Fe Trail, the Gila Trail, the Smoky Hill Trail, and a multitude of alternate and feeder trails.

The overland trails destroyed a dream cherished by statesmen since the 1820's. They hoped to solve the Indian problem by erecting a "Permanent Indian Frontier," beyond which all tribes could enjoy security from invasion. To define the frontier, the Army laid out a chain of posts, running from Fort Snelling, Minn. (1819), on the north, to Fort Jesup, La. (1822), on the south. Roughly paralleling the eastern boundary of the second tier of States west of the Mississippi, it eventually extended through Forts Atkinson (1819), Leavenworth (1827), Scott (1842), Gibson (1824), Smith (1817), Towson (1824), and Washita (1842). Most of the eastern Indians were moved to new lands west of the frontier. Congress enacted a comprehensive body of legislation, the Indian Trade and Intercourse Act of 1834, to regulate relations with both immigrant and resident tribes. In 1838 Indian Territory—roughly modern Oklahoma—was established as a permanent home for the dispossessed easterners.

But in the 1840's the western trails breached the "permanent frontier" and bore streams of travelers across it. They demanded

7

protection. By 1850 the "permanent frontier" had vanished and the Federal Government had moved west to confront the Indian. Along the trails and among the settlements at trail's end, the Army built forts. The Indians met new types of men—soldiers, agents, peace commissioners—who turned out to be not nearly so agreeable as the trappers and traders.

The agents and peace commissioners represented the Government Agency charged with Indian relations: the Indian Bureau, transferred in 1849 from the War Department to the newly created Department of the Interior. They negotiated treaties, disbursed annuity goods according to treaty obligations, mediated between Indians and whites, and tried to influence the tribes to accommodate themselves to Government policies. Some of the officials, such as Tom Fitzpatrick and "Kit" Carson, were men of ability and dedication. Many, however, appointed as a reward for political services, were not only innocent of knowledge and understanding of Indians but frequently incompetent and dishonest as well.

Only dimly did the Indians perceive the implications of the first, seemingly harmless, requests of the Government's emissaries. The latter asked the guarantee of safe passage to emigrants and withdrawal from the trails. In return, once a year the Great Father in Washington would send generous presents. Most tribes, still regarded under U.S. law as "domestic dependent nations," signed treaties committing the exchange of promises to paper, and they came at specified times to centrally located agencies to receive presents from an agent appointed for the purpose. The Treaty of Fort Laramie (1851), with the Sioux, Cheyenne, Arapaho, Crow, and other tribes of the northern Plains, and the Treaty of Fort Atkinson (1853), with the Kiowas and Comanches of the southern Plains, set the pattern for others that followed. The Upper Platte and Upper Arkansas Agencies represented the tentative and rather informal beginnings of management institutions that in four decades would bend the western tribes to the Government's will.

The treaty system contained serious flaws that doomed it as an instrument for regulating relations between the two races. The signatory chiefs seldom represented all the groups whose interests were affected and could not enforce compliance by those they did

8

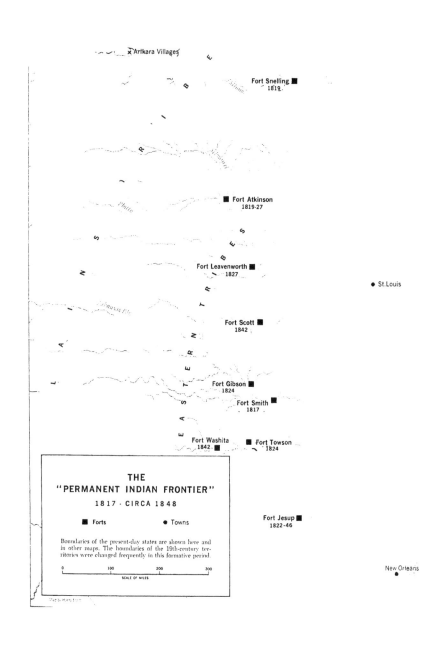

x Arikara Villages

Fort Snelling ■
1819

Fort Atkinson ■
1819-27

Fort Leavenworth ■
1827

● St.Louis

Fort Scott ■
1842

Fort Gibson ■
1824

Fort Smith ■
1817

Fort Washita ■
1842

Fort Towson ■
1824

THE
"PERMANENT INDIAN FRONTIER"
1817 · CIRCA 1848

■ Forts   ● Towns

Boundaries of the present-day states are shown here and
in other maps. The boundaries of the 19th-century territories were changed frequently in this formative period.

0   100   200   300
SCALE OF MILES

Fort Jesup ■
1822-46

New Orleans
●

Buffalo were vital to the way of life of the Plains Indians. After white hunters slaughtered the animals, troops forced the Indians onto reservations. "Indians Hunting the Bison," Charles Vogel lithograph from Karl Bodmer sketch.

represent. The white emissaries did represent the United States, but no less than the chiefs could they compel emigrants and settlers to respect the pacts. Moreover, because of cultural and language barriers, the two sides usually had sharply different understandings of what had been agreed upon. Sometimes, one or both sides lacked any serious intention to abide by a compact anyway.

And even the best of faith yielded to tensions. The Indian saw his buffalo and other game slaughtered, his timber cut, his patterns of seasonal migration disturbed, and in places ranges that had been held and cherished for generations appropriated—all by interlopers who also offered tempting targets to a people who set high value on distinction in warfare. The whites, on the other hand, saw the Indian as the possessor of an empire rich in natural resources that he had no means or ability of exploiting and that "natural law" commanded the "higher" civilization to exploit. Many whites saw him, too, as a savage who slaughtered their fellow citizens for mere plunder and the gratification of blood-lust.

Inevitably, friction occurred—along the Oregon, Santa Fe, and

9

Southern Transcontinental Trails; on the expanding Texas frontier and the static New Mexico frontier; and in California and Oregon, where miners and settlers dispossessed the aboriginal occupants of lands coveted for mining or agriculture. For many of the tribes, the decade of the 1850's brought intermittent warfare with the soldiers, whose forts spread in increasing numbers.

Like the Indian Bureau, the Army emerged as a major influence in Indian relations. Indeed, the Indian problem had been a dominant factor in bringing about the creation of the Regular Army in 1789 and provided its main occupation for a century. Its mission was to guard travel routes and settlements, keep watch on peaceful tribes, and wage war on those regarded as hostile. It was inglorious duty. Long periods of boredom, isolation, and stagnation were varied only by occasional campaigns, characterized by fatigue, exposure, frustration, and an occasional indecisive skir-

The Indians did not at first foresee the ultimate consequences of the web of trails that began to thread through their homeland. Curiosity and petty harassment usually characterized Indian reaction during early trail days. "Intercepted Wagon Train," Charles M. Russell.

*Indian elusiveness and guerilla tactics often prevented
the use of advanced Army weapons. Artillerymen
with Gatling guns at Fort Abraham Lincoln, N. Dak.*

*Soldier life during the Indian wars was often hard
and unrewarding, but it was far preferable to the
anguish of capture. "Missing," Frederic Remington.*

11

· absence of a clearly
Indians. Seldom could
l hostile. More often the
men raided. When these
ic ted against people who
il military sense. The im-
i peaceful and combatant
ed the Army to charges—
t—of warring on peaceful
n.

led to another: the impossi-
·esponsibilities of the Army
Almost every campaign in-
i arms of Government over
iich were not. Furthermore,
i mismanagement as a prime
s resented a system that forced
ill power to prevent.

iis, the Army contributed sub-
est. Soldiers conducted explora-
iind scientific knowledge of fron-
emigrants, settlers, miners, and
t gave rise to towns and cities and
cal goods and services. Soldiers built
Soldiers surveyed railroad routes,
and provided a major source of busi-
n laid.

iflict with the Indian that history chiefly
century the Army fought the woodland
e middle 19th century it had moved West
and organization suited to the new en-
nge tribes of plain, mountain, and desert.

i, serious trouble with the Sioux broke out
Army officer at Fort Laramie converted a
major confrontation. He and his detach-

13

*Commerce and trade followed the Army. Sutlers'
stores satisfied material needs of troops, civilians, and
sometimes Indians. The stores also enriched social life
at lonely outposts. Theodore R. Davis' sketch of the
sutler's store at Fort Dodge, Kansas, from* Harper's
Weekly *(May 25, 1867).*

*Black troops, often ex-slaves serving under white
officers in special regiments formed after the Civil
War, distinguished themselves during the Indian wars.
Pictured here in 1883 at Fort Snelling, Minn., is
Company I, 25th Infantry.*

mish. The stirring battles of motion pictures and television were rare. Undermanned, underpaid, widely unappreciated when not actively assailed by the press and public figures, the Army found little reward on the frontier.

Much of the frustration sprang from the absence of a clearly drawn line between peaceful and hostile Indians. Seldom could an entire tribe or band be validly branded hostile. More often the leaders professed peace while the young men raided. When these conditions led to war, it had to be conducted against people who were not all enemies in the conventional military sense. The impossibility of separating hostile from peaceful and combatant from noncombatant repeatedly exposed the Army to charges—sometimes groundless, sometimes not—of warring on peaceful Indians and killing women and children.

This ambiguity in the Army's task led to another: the impossibility of separating the powers and responsibilities of the Army from those of the Indian Bureau. Almost every campaign involved a controversy between the two arms of Government over which Indians were hostile and which were not. Furthermore, most officers regarded Indian Bureau mismanagement as a prime cause of outbreaks, and they bitterly resented a system that forced them to punish while denying them all power to prevent.

Besides its role in Indian relations, the Army contributed substantially to the opening of the West. Soldiers conducted explorations that enriched geographical and scientific knowledge of frontier lands. Soldiers protected emigrants, settlers, miners, and ranchers. Soldiers built forts that gave rise to towns and cities and that afforded markets for local goods and services. Soldiers built roads and telegraph lines. Soldiers surveyed railroad routes, guarded construction crews, and provided a major source of business once the rails had been laid.

But it is the Army's conflict with the Indian that history chiefly remembers. For half a century the Army fought the woodland tribes of the East. By the middle 19th century it had moved West and evolved techniques and organization suited to the new environment and the strange tribes of plain, mountain, and desert.

On the northern Plains, serious trouble with the Sioux broke out in 1854 when a young Army officer at Fort Laramie converted a minor incident into a major confrontation. He and his detach-

*Comanche family. Fierce, warlike, and expert horse-
men, the Comanches won the epithet of "Lords of the
South Plains." Following the Great Comanche War
Trail, they terrorized the southern Plains and
northern Mexico.*

ment were annihilated. The Army responded with a sharp campaign in 1855–56. Gen. William S. Harney's attack on a Sioux village at the Battle of Blue Water and subsequent march through
the Sioux homeland restored an uneasy calm to the Oregon-California Trail. On the southern Plains the Cheyennes, provoked by
traffic on the Smoky Hill Trail to newly discovered mines in the
Rocky Mountains, brought on a similar response from Col. Edwin
V. Sumner in 1857.

Kiowas and Comanches occasionally harassed the Santa Fe Trail, but they directed their principal aggressions at the Texas frontier. The Army established an elaborate defense system to deflect these raids. It erected two lines of posts extending from the Red River to the Rio Grande, a third down the Rio Grande to the Gulf of Mexico, and a fourth along the road from San Antonio to El Paso. Neither the forts nor offensive operations north of the Red River in the years 1858–60 noticeably diminished the destruction. These Indians had raided the Texas frontier and deep into Mexico for a century; raids were a basic economic and social pursuit, difficult to replace and not lightly surrendered.

Similarly, Apaches, Navajos, and Utes had plagued the Rio Grande settlements of New Mexico since the earliest years of Spanish rule. Now, because of the growing competition with settlers for the meager agricultural and game resources of the region, they had still greater incentive. The new network of forts disturbed the routine only slightly. Military offensives against the Utes and Jicarilla Apaches in 1854 and 1855 neutralized the menace from

Captives and plunder lured Kiowa and Comanche raiders. Quaker Indian Agent Lawrie Tatum poses at Fort Sill, Okla., about 1872 with a group of freed Mexican children.

15

Red Cloud, Oglala Sioux.

Geronimo, Chiricahua Apache.

Sitting Bull, Hunkpapa Sioux.

Victorio, Warm Springs Apache.

Satanta, Kiowa.

Satank, Kiowa.

Joseph, Nez Perce.

Big Tree, Kiowa.

17

the north. But similar campaigns between 1857 and 1861 against the Gila and the Western Apaches in the south and the Navajos to the west gave no relief to the settlements.

On the Pacific coast, a large population of semisedentary Indians occupied the rich mountains that had set off the California gold rush. Overrun by miners, some groups simply disappeared—if they were not exterminated, scattered, and destroyed as identifiable cultural entities. Others, principally in northern California and southern Oregon, fought back. In a succession of so-called "Rogue River Wars" between 1850 and 1856, the Army crushed them and placed the survivors on reservations.

North of the Columbia, in present Washington, the chieftain Kamiakin in 1855–56 briefly united the Yakima and allied tribes east of the North Cascade Mountains with Puget Sound groups to the west. The Yakimas were angered by an invasion of their lands by gold seekers headed for the newly discovered Colville diggings, and all resented land-cession treaties recently thrust upon them. As in California and Oregon, the operations of Regular and Volunteer troops, commanded by Gen. John E. Wool and Col. George Wright, ended organized resistance. The disaffection, however, spread eastward to the Spokan, Palouse, Walla Walla, and associated tribes. After a combined army of warriors mauled a command under Lt. Col. Edward J. Steptoe in the spring of 1858, Colonel Wright set forth at the head of a formidable column. He won clear victories at the Battles of Four Lakes and Spokane Plain in September, and in subsequent negotiations brought the war to a close.

Except for the tribes of California and the Pacific Northwest, the pressures of the 1850's did not fundamentally disturb the bulk of the western Indians. The forts represented a permanent encroachment on their domain. So did the handful of mining camps that appeared in the intermountain West toward the close of the decade. But soldiers and miners produced only local disruptions, causing but slight shifts in tribal ranges and alliances. Even the military campaigns—again excepting those in the Northwest—proved mainly an annoyance. They demanded constant vigilance, occasional flight, and, rarely, a skirmish or battle that involved loss of life and property. This was nothing new to a people who had always regarded intertribal warfare as a condition of life.

18

*Catholic and Protestant missionaries brought the word
of God to the Indians, but few were able to bridge
the wide cultural gap. Left, Rev. Henry H. Spalding,
Protestant. Right, Father Pierre Jean De Smet,
Catholic.*

Growing numbers of trading posts represented an encroachment,
too, but as an integral part of Indian life for almost half a century
they were not regarded with antagonism.

For three decades prior to 1860, missionaries had been filtering
into the West to try converting the natives to Christianity. Some,
like Father Pierre Jean De Smet, wandered from tribe to tribe.
Others, like the Spaldings, the Whitmans, and the Lees, established fixed missions. The Indians usually liked the missionaries.
A few even embraced Christianity. But they did so without surrendering old spiritual beliefs. Most of them found nothing in-
consistent in the adoption of at least the outward forms of as
many different religions as promised to be of some value. Aside
from enormous changes in material culture, therefore, the Indian's basic values, beliefs, customs, and habitat remained largely intact in 1860.

To this generalization there was one important exception. The
Five Civilized Tribes of Indian Territory (later Oklahoma) —   19

Authors and journalists usually portrayed Indians in
evil terms. This illustration, from Frances F. Victor's
River of the West *(Hartford, 1870), presents an*
imaginative interpretation of the Whitman Massacre.

Cherokee, Creek, Choctaw, Chickasaw, and Seminole—had resolved, even before their forced migration from the East in the
1830's, to pattern their material culture after the white man.
They retained their Indian identity, but by 1860 very much resembled him in economic, political, religious, and social forms.
Even though land remained in tribal ownership, they had become
sedentary farmers and businessmen. They were literate, and they
saw important benefits in schools and Christian churches. And
they had devised a political system based on U.S. constitutional
principles. Like the Pueblos of the Southwest, the Civilized
Tribes, after removal from the East, were not an effective part of
the Indian barrier to westward expansion.

At first the Civil War, draining off the Regulars for service in the
East, relaxed the military pressure on the western tribes. The
bloody uprising of the Minnesota Sioux in 1862, however, horri-
fied the Nation, and the opening of mining areas in Montana,
Idaho, and Arizona disturbed resident tribes. By the closing years
of the war, therefore, the Indians found themselves confronted by
more soldiers than ever before. Most were Volunteers, enlisted to

fight for the Union. Some even were "Galvanized Yankees"—Confederate prisoners clothed in blue to help guard the frontier.

The abundance of troops permitted large-scale offensive operations. In some areas they succeeded. California Volunteers extinguished the last flickers of resistance in the mountains of northern California and ruthlessly dealt with Paiute troubles in Nevada and Shoshoni troubles in Utah. Other Californians, under Gen. James H. Carleton, joined with New Mexican troops to defeat the Mescalero Apaches and to subjugate the powerful Navajos. Both groups were confined on an inhospitable reservation, Bosque Redondo, on the Pecos River of eastern New Mexico. The Mescaleros fled in 1865. For the Navajos the experience proved shattering; allowed to return to their homeland in 1868, they never again challenged U.S. rule by force of arms.

Elsewhere the operations of the Volunteers only intensified the spirit of resistance. Such was the case with the Northern Paiutes, or Snakes, of eastern Oregon and western Idaho, and with the Western Apaches of Arizona, against whom General Carleton failed as dramatically as he had succeeded against the Navajos. So,

Robert Lindneux's dramatic version of the Trail of Tears captures the poignancy and suffering of the forced removal of the Cherokees from Southeastern United States to Indian Territory.

21

too, with the Sioux. After suppressing the Minnesota outbreak of 1862, the next year Gen. Henry Hastings Sibley led a large column against the Sioux of Dakota, while Gen. Alfred Sully and another column marched up the Missouri River to cooperate. Again in 1864 and 1865, Sully, aided by expeditions from Minnesota, continued the offensive. And in 1865 still other columns, under Gen. Patrick E. Connor, moved into Sioux country from bases on the Platte. Despite victories at Big Mound, Dead Buffalo Lake, Stony Lake, Whitestone Hill, Killdeer Mountain, and Tongue River, these expeditions only provoked more determined opposition. And to the south, at Sand Creek, Colo., other Volunteers set off unprecedented hostility. Col. John M. Chivington's barbarous attack in November 1864 on Black Kettle's Cheyennes, who thought they were under military protection, spread anger and distrust among all the Plains tribes and led to a major uprising.

The 1862 uprising of the Santee Sioux in Minnesota ended in defeat. In December the Army publicly executed 38 warriors in Mankato, recorded in this panorama by John Stevens.

ATTENTION!
INDIAN
FIGHTERS

Having been authorized by the Governor to raise a Company of 100 day

U. S. VOL CAVALRY!

For immediate service against hostile Indians. I call upon all who wish to engage in such service to call at my office and enroll their names immediately.

Pay and Rations the same as other U. S. Volunteer Cavalry.

Parties furnishing their own horses will receive 40c per day, and rations for the same, while in the service.

The Company will also be entitled to all horses and other plunder taken from the Indians.

Office first door East of Recorder's Office.

HAL. SAYR.

Central City, Aug. 13, '64.

Emotions peaked and violence reigned on both sides during the Colorado hostilities in 1864. This poster promises to reward recruits with "all horses and other plunder taken from the Indians."

The extension of the railroad network westward,
facilitating settlement and enhancing Army mobility,
hastened the end of the Indian wars. Union Pacific
supply trains at the end of the track near present
Archer, Wyo.

The close of the Civil War released America's energies to the westward movement. Thousands of emigrants and settlers pushed into the Indian domain with scant regard for the sanctity of hunting grounds or treaty agreements. Railroads supplanted the trails. The Union Pacific and Central Pacific, joined in 1869, were succeeded to the north and south by other transcontinental railroads, and a network of feeder lines reached into many remote corners of the West. Miners spread up and down the mountain chains of Colorado, Montana, Idaho, Nevada, and Arizona. Steamers, sailing up the Missouri River, carried passengers and freight to Fort Benton, Mont., for the land journey to the gold mines of western Montana. Stockmen moved onto the grasslands. Dirt farmers, attracted by the liberal provisions of the Homestead Act of 1862, followed. Towns and cities sprang up everywhere. The once huge herds of buffalo dwindled to the brink of extinction, a process

Gen. George Crook.

Gen. Nelson A. Miles.

Gen. William T. Sherman.

Gen. Philip H. Sheridan.

25

Gen. William S. Harney.

Gen. Oliver O. Howard.

Gen. John E. Wool.

Gen. Winfield S. Hancock.

hastened by professional hunters interested only in the hides. Other game diminished similarly. Forts multiplied, and the soldiers came back in numbers unprecedented before the war. In a matter of two decades, 1865 to 1885, the Indian was progressively denied the two things essential to his traditional way of life—land and game. Often he fought back, and this period of history featured the last—and most intense—of the wars between the United States and its aboriginal peoples.

Nearly continuous hostilities swept the Great Plains for more than a decade after the Civil War as the flow of travelers, the advance of the railroads, and the spread of settlement ate into the traditional ranges of the Plains tribes. Red Cloud led the Sioux in opposing the Bozeman Trail, a new emigrant road that cut through their Powder River hunting domain to the Montana goldfields. The Army strengthened Fort Reno and erected Forts Phil Kearny and C. F. Smith along the trail but could not provide security. In December 1866 the Sioux wiped out an 80-man force from Fort Phil Kearny under Capt. William J. Fetterman. They tried to triumph again the following August but in the Wagon Box and Hayfield Fights were beaten back. When the Union Pa-

Peace commissioners meeting at Fort Laramie, Wyo., with Sioux chiefs. The Treaty of Fort Laramie (1868) brought temporary peace on the northern Plains— until miners invaded the Black Hills in 1874–75.

*Charles M. Russell's "Indian Hunters Return"
portrays winter life among the Indians. Recognizing
their immobility and vulnerability at that time of
the year, Gen. Philip H. Sheridan launched a hard-
hitting winter campaign in 1868–69.*

cific Railroad reached far enough west to provide another route to
Montana, in the Fort Laramie Treaty (1868) the Government reluctantly yielded to the Sioux and withdrew from the Bozeman
Trail. To the south, in Kansas, Gen. Winfield S. Hancock led an
abortive expedition against the Cheyennes and Arapahos in 1867
and, instead of pacifying, aroused a people who had not yet for-
gotten Sand Creek. Kiowas and Comanches continued to terrorize
the Texas frontier.

Despite the Medicine Lodge Treaties of 1867, which were designed to bring peace to the southern Plains, war broke out once
more in August 1868. Gen. Philip H. Sheridan organized a winter
campaign, in which columns converged on Indian Territory from
three directions. One, under Lt. Col. George A. Custer, struck the
Cheyenne camp of Black Kettle—the same chief who had suffered
so grievously at Sand Creek 4 years earlier. At the Battle of the
Washita, November 27, 1868, Custer decimated the band. Black
Kettle fell in the first charge. On Christmas Day another of the
commands, under Maj. Andrew W. Evans, attacked a Comanche

*In the Battle of the Washita, Okla., and in other
instances the Army surprised the Indians by attacking
their sleeping villages at dawn. Such an attack is
portrayed in Charles Schreyvogel's "Attack at Dawn."*

camp at Soldier Spring, on the north fork of the Red River. Custer, Evans, and Maj. Eugene A. Carr, leader of the third column, demonstrated that the Army could operate during the winter months, when the Indian was most vulnerable. Most of the tribes yielded and gathered at newly established agencies in Indian Territory. The Battle of Summit Springs, Colo., the following July brought the last holdouts to terms.

Coincident with the Plains wars of the late 1860's, a growing sentiment for the reform of Indian policy spread through eastern humanitarian and philanthropic circles and found advocates among Government officials and lawmakers. This sentiment held that the Indian should be conquered and removed from the paths of expansion by kindness rather than by military force. By treating him justly, honorably, and generously, it was contended, by setting aside reservations to be held inviolate against intrusion as his permanent home, by assisting him to learn new means of supporting himself, and by providing for his wants while he was learning, 29 the bloody warfare of the past could be avoided and more humane relationships established.

Responding to these sentiments, Congress created the Peace Commission of 1867. In treaties concluded that year and the following year with the Plains tribes at Medicine Lodge Creek, Kans., and Fort Laramie, Wyo., and with the Navajos at Fort Sumner, N. Mex., the commission planted the seeds of the new philosophy. They flowered in the Peace Policy that President Grant inaugurated shortly after taking office in 1869.

The Peace Policy did not open an era of harmony. The Indians saw nothing humane in exchanging their territory and freedom for reservations and confinement; no matter how engineered, the exchange was still compulsory. Moreover, the Government proved unable to keep whites off the reservations. Settlers, cattlemen, miners, and railroads all intruded, and a succession of "agreements"—the treaty system was discontinued in 1871—opened especially coveted tracts to settlement. Nor were the authors of the Peace Policy able to improve the management of the reservations, even though church groups now nominated the agents and superintendents. Finally, graft and corruption, a source of great irritation to the Indians, continued to diminish the quantity and quality of issue goods and rations, in poor supply anyway because of inadequate appropriations. And so the fighting went on.

In northern California an attempt to place a Modoc band on an Oregon reservation precipitated the Modoc War (1872–73). The Modoc leader, Captain Jack, took his followers into the natural fortress of the lava beds bordering Tule Lake and held off a besieging force for 5 months. During a peace conference in April 1873, the Modocs killed Gen. Edward R. S. Canby and another emissary. Not until late May did Captain Jack surrender. He and three others died on the gallows.

From Indian Territory, where the southern Plains tribes had been given reservations, Kiowas and Comanches continued to raid in Texas. The Army chafed under Peace Policy restrictions that barred them from punishing Indians on their reservations. When the Government finally lifted this ban in 1874, Kiowas, Comanches, Cheyennes, and a few Arapahos fled westward to the Staked Plains of the Texas Panhandle. General Sheridan loosed

*Despite courageous resistance, Captain Jack, right,
and his people lost the Modoc War (1872–73).
Schonchin, chained to Jack, was one of three
lieutenants who died with him on the gallows.*

*The Custer Expedition, shown here on its way to the
Black Hills in 1874, confirmed rumors of gold there
and spawned a wild rush onto the Great Sioux
Reservation that the Government could not control.
New warfare broke out on the northern Plains.*

columns on this area from Fort Bascom, N. Mex., Forts Concho
and Griffin, Tex., Fort Sill, Okla., and Fort Hays, Kans.

The resulting Red River War lasted through the autumn and
winter of 1874–75 and involved 14 engagements. The most notable were the Battle of Palo Duro Canyon, Tex., in which Col.
Ranald S. Mackenzie smashed a Comanche camp; and the Battle
of McClellan Creek, Tex., in which Col. Nelson A. Miles routed a
Cheyenne force. But it was sustained military pressure during the
winter months, rather than clashes of arms, that disheartened the
fugitives and led them, in the spring of 1875, to straggle back to
their agencies and surrender—for the final time.

The Sioux and Cheyennes had been settled on a huge reservation west of the Missouri River in Dakota. But, as a price for the
peace arranged in 1868, they had retained the Powder River country to the west as unceded hunting grounds. There, comfortably
distant from the agencies, many Sioux and Cheyennes continued
to enjoy their traditional life. Occasionally they raided settlements in Montana and along the Union Pacific Railroad. In 1873
the Northern Pacific Railroad survey up the Yellowstone River
Valley raised the specter of another railroad along the fringe of

the unceded hunting grounds. In 1874 discovery of gold in the Black Hills, a part of the Great Sioux Reservation, set off an invasion of miners and a Government effort to buy the hills from the Sioux. These events led to the Sioux War of 1876–77, a scarcely disguised attempt to clear the unceded territory of Indians and to frighten them into ceding the Black Hills.

Again General Sheridan sent converging columns—under Gen. George Crook, Gen. Alfred H. Terry, and Col. John Gibbon—into the Indian country. Crook suffered two reverses, at the Battle of Powder River, Mont., on March 17, 1876, and at the Battle of the Rosebud, Mont., on June 17. Terry and Gibbon joined on the Yellowstone and designed their own convergence. They suspected that the enemy was in the Little Bighorn Valley. They did not suspect that Sitting Bull and other chiefs had brought together an unprecedented gathering of Sioux and Cheyennes, numbering perhaps 3,000 to 5,000 fighting men. Terry's subordinate, Custer, attacked this aggregation on June 25. He and more than 200 officers and men were wiped out. The balance of the regiment endured a 2-day siege before the approach of Terry and Gibbon caused the Indians to withdraw.

In this stunning victory, however, lay the roots of Indian defeat. The Nation demanded that Custer's death be avenged, and the Army poured troops into the Sioux country. The alliance of tribes fragmented, and through the winter General Crook and Colonel Miles hounded them across the frozen land. By spring, after several battles and great suffering, most of the Sioux and Cheyennes had returned to their agencies. Only Sitting Bull scorned surrender. He and some diehard followers took refuge in Canada. They held firm until 1881, when hunger at last compelled their capitulation.

The mountain tribes—Nez Perce, Ute, and Bannock—also attempted to resist the reservation system. The Nez Perces in particular caught the imagination and sympathy of the Nation. After years of procrastination, the nontreaty portion of the tribe, one of whose spokesmen was the statesmanlike Chief Joseph, acquiesced in the Government's attempt to place them on the Idaho reservation accepted by the rest of the tribe in 1863. But en route a few angry warriors killed some settlers, and the war was on. At White Bird Canyon and Clearwater in June and July 1877, the Nez

MASSACRED

GEN. CUSTER AND 261 MEN THE VICTIMS.

NO OFFICER OR MAN OF 5 COMPANIES LEFT TO TELL THE TALE.

---

3 Days Desperate Fighting by Maj. Reno and the Remainder of the Seventh.

Full Details of the Battle.

LIST OF KILLED AND WOUNDED.

THE BISMARCK TRIBUNE'S SPECIAL CORRESPONDENT SLAIN.

Squaws Mutilate and Rob the Dead

Victims Captured Alive Tortured in a Most Fiendish Manner.

What Will Congress Do About It?

Shall This Be the Beginning of the
d ?

Headlines such as these, from the Bismarck Tribune *Extra July 6, 1876) carrying the first newspaper account of the Custer debacle, appalled the Nation and generated retaliatory campaigns that virtually ended Indian opposition on the northern Plains.*

Perces threw back Gen. Oliver O. Howard's soldiers. Then they turned eastward, over the Bitterroot Mountains. In 2½ months, burdened with their families, they traveled 1,700 miles and confounded 2,000 soldiers. At Big Hole, Clark's Fork, and Canyon Creek, they beat off attacks. But at the Bear Paw Mountains, only 40 miles from the Canadian refuge at which they aimed, Colonel Miles cut them off and after a costly 6-day siege compelled them to surrender. More than 400 captives were ultimately sent to a reservation in Indian Territory.

One of the most violent expressions of Indian resentment against the reservation system occurred at Colorado's White River Agency in September 1879. Agent Nathan C. Meeker's zealous efforts to make farmers out of his Ute charges brought them to the brink of rebellion. When he called for military help, the Utes killed him and part of his staff, burned the agency, and set forth to meet the troops. At Milk Creek they ambushed a cavalry command en route to the agency. The commander, Maj. Thomas T. Thornburgh, died and in a weeklong siege the 150-man force suffered heavy casualties. A relief column drove off the Utes, and the revolt collapsed.

Geronimo surrendering to Gen. George Crook at Cañon de los Embudos, Mexico, in March 1886. Before reaching Fort Bowie, Ariz., however, most of the Chiricahua Apaches fled. Geronimo is third from the left, and General Crook second from right.

35

*Frederic Remington's portrayal of Capt. Henry W.
Lawton's command pursuing Geronimo in the rugged
wilds of Mexico's Sierra Madre during 1886.*

By 1880 peace had come to the Great Plains, the Rocky Mountains, the Great Basin, and the Pacific slope. Only in the Apache
country of the Southwest did fighting continue. Since Spanish and

Mexican times, the Apaches had regularly raided the settlements of the Rio Grande Valley of New Mexico as well as those of the Mexican states of Coahuila, Chihuahua, and Sonora. Americans who began arriving in the Southwest after the Mexican War found that the Apaches seldom discriminated. Military operations of the 1850's and 1860's in western Texas, New Mexico, and Arizona seemed only to aggravate the chronic menace.

The Apaches had cause to remember two military acts for years. In 1861, in Arizona's Apache Pass, a young lieutenant attempted to arrest Cochise for an offense he probably had not committed and drove him to implacable hostility. And in 1863 some of General Carleton's troops induced the equally renowned Mangas Coloradas to surrender, then murdered him.

After a decade of fearful bloodshed, in 1872 Gen. Oliver O. Howard, acting as a Peace Policy emissary, persuaded Cochise to call off the war he had loosed in retribution for the Apache Pass affair. General Crook's Tonto Basin campaign (1872–73) brought a period of calm to central Arizona. However, Crook's reassignment in 1875, coupled with a movement to consolidate all Apaches on the San Carlos Reservation, spread unrest. Among the more determined in their opposition were Victorio and Geronimo. But, after 2 years of warfare that swept across southern New Mexico, western Texas, and northern Mexico in 1879–80, Victorio was slain in a battle with Mexican troops. Geronimo proved more elusive.

The Apaches made especially formidable antagonists because, besides their unusual skill at guerilla warfare, they could take refuge from U.S. troops in the mountains of northern Mexico. To cope with this situation, the Army reassigned General Crook to Arizona in September 1882. Two months earlier Geronimo and 75 followers had fled the San Carlos Reservation. From bases high in the Sierra Madre they were terrorizing Arizona settlements. Crook, an advocate of unconventional methods, organized units of Apache scouts and, under the cloak of a diplomatic agreement with the Mexican Government, sent them into the mountain recesses that hid the fugitives. Months of exhausting campaigning followed, but by the spring of 1884 most of them had been coaxed back to the reservation.

Once more, however, in May 1885 Geronimo led an exodus to

37

Mexico. Again Crook sent his scouts south of the border. Again persistence won out. Geronimo met him in council in March 1886 and agreed to surrender. En route to Fort Bowie, however, he and his followers broke for the mountains. Discouraged, his methods questioned by higher authority, Crook asked to be relieved. Gen. Nelson A. Miles took his place. Using much the same approach as Crook, Miles' officers again maneuvered Geronimo into a council, and in September 1886 he formally surrendered to Miles at Skeleton Canyon, Ariz. To insure an end to Apache outbreaks, he and his people were imprisoned in Florida.

With the collapse of the Apaches, all the western tribes had yielded to the realities of their condition and settled on reserva-

Geronimo, Natchez, and followers en route in 1886 from Fort Bowie, Ariz., to Fort Pickens, Fla., for imprisonment. Geronimo is third from right, bottom row; Natchez, fourth from right.

The ultimate humiliation for the Indians, once a proud people, was the reservation dole. Distribution of rations about 1892 at San Carlos Agency, Ariz.

tions. Military action had hastened the process, but the absence of any acceptable alternative for the Indians, given the loss of their land and traditional means of livelihood, provided the most powerful incentive. At first the reservation was simply an expedient. The problem was to clear the paths of expansion. The solution was to corral the Indians on a parcel of land that—as yet—no one else wanted, and keep them reasonably content by regular issues of food and clothing. But during the decade of the 1880's the reservation system assumed a different shape. Abolition of the treaty system in 1871 had deprived the tribes of even the small comfort of theoretical sovereignty. Thus when they came to the reservation, fresh from military conquest and dependent on Government largess, they were undeniably wards of the Government and subject to its will.

In the 1880's this will derived largely from the theories of a growing number of Indian reform organizations that exerted increasingly awesome influence on national legislators and administrators. The reformers expressed the widespread conviction that solution of the Indian problem lay in transforming the Indian, as rapidly as possible and by compulsion if necessary, into a God-fearing tiller of the soil enjoying the blessings of Christianity, education, individual instead of tribal ownership of land, and national citizenship. Reformers and like-minded officials used the reservation system as the instrument for attempting this program. Thus, in the end, the reservation system wrought with terrible swiftness the ethnic disaster that had been foreshadowed by the collapse of the "Permanent Indian Frontier."

On the reservation the Indian found himself suddenly overwhelmed by the civilizing process. It took the form of a concerted campaign to root out the old and inculcate the new. Indian policemen and Indian courts, controlled by the agent, ironically provided the compulsion. When they failed, withholding of rations ordinarily produced a surface illusion of the desired conformity.

All facets of Indian life came under fire. Because tribal communalism stood in the way of progress, the attack centered on basic social, economic, religious, and political institutions. Many of these, indeed, had already lost much of their pertinence in the transition from nomadic to sedentary life. "Every man a chief," announced the Government, and urged the people to abandon their camps, throw away their lodges, spread out over the reserva-

Reading the Declaration of Independence at Rosebud Agency, S. Dak., on the Fourth of July 1897. Those few Indians who understood the significance of the occasion must have recognized the terrible irony involved for their people.

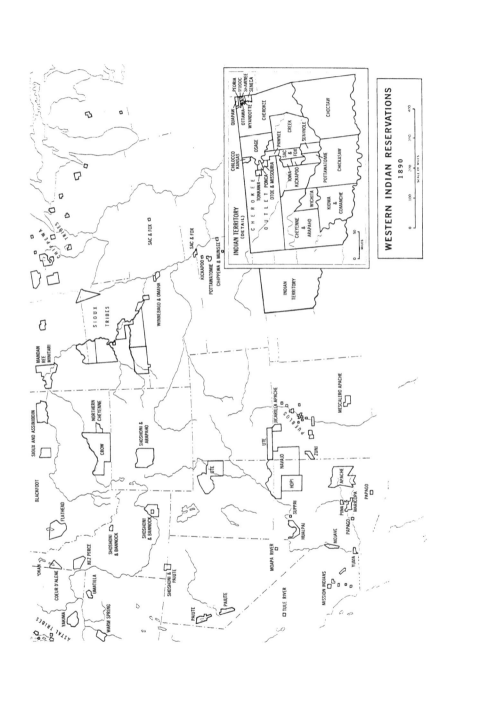

WESTERN INDIAN RESERVATIONS
1890

tion, build cabins, and ignore the traditional leaders. A list of "Indian Offenses," promulgated by the Indian Bureau, outlawed fundamental social and religious customs. These included the Sun Dance, the foundation upon which the Plains Indian had built his whole theological edifice, and the practices of the medicine man.

Other whites helped the agent. They were a different breed than the easy-going fun-loving trappers of earlier times. The "practical farmer" tried to teach farming to a people who did not want to farm, on land that for the most part was not suitable for farming anyway, using techniques that were ill adapted to the soil and climate and to the background of the trainees. The schoolteacher tried to teach unwilling children of unwilling parents the "useful arts of civilization," but these arts had little real meaning in the reservation environment. Off-reservation boarding schools, patterned after the military model of Carlisle Indian School in Pennsylvania, proved much more effective—until the child returned to the reservation and found no place for himself either in white or Indian society. Missionaries tried to substitute a frequently irrelevant Christianity for religious patterns that had proved rich and satisfying and that were a functional part of Indian culture. The Indians were often receptive to Christian teachings but also unwilling to surrender the old beliefs. They found that the trader was frequently the only entirely agreeable white man on the reservation. He provided them useful manufactures without eternally carping about their "barbarous" habits.

Central to the reform program was the severalty movement. Give the Indian individual title to the soil, reformers held, and virtually all other problems would automatically solve themselves. The Indian would become a responsible, self-supporting citizen just like all other citizens. The severalty movement culminated in the Dawes Act of 1887, which provided for the allotment of reservation lands, usually in 160-acre parcels, to individual natives. The Dawes Act gave eastern reformers and western land "boomers" common ground, for it provided that all reservation lands not needed for allotment could be thrown open to white settlement. Because the majority of western Indians at first resisted allotment, vast tracts of "surplus" reservation land were released for settlement before many Indians received allotments.

Educational programs for the Indians in the 19th century stressed remaking them in the white man's image. Chiricahua Apache students, 4 months after entering Carlisle Indian School, Pa., in 1887.

Loss of reservation land created deep resentment. Worse, after the Indian finally bowed to the inevitable and accepted allotment, he found himself imprisoned by a vicious and unfamiliar system that forced him ever lower on the economic scale. Eastern land patterns dictated 160-acre allotments. In the arid West these were too small for economic efficiency, especially when devoted to crop raising. Even these were severely reduced. Despite legal safeguards, patented land found its way, through one subterfuge or another, into white ownership. And the rest was endlessly subdivided through inheritance into tiny patches, on which the heirs eked out the barest subsistence.

Yet the policies of the 1880's, founded on the idealistic dreams of the severalty advocates, prevailed until well beyond the turn of the century.

Already, however, the "civilization" program and the beginnings of the severalty movement had produced severe emotional stresses among the tribes. A decade of exposure to reservation policies served mainly to blend twisted remnants of the old life with a few frayed strands of the new. Bleak prospects for the future combined with nostalgic memory of the past to induce a state of mind particularly susceptible to the Messianic fervor that swept the western reservations in 1889 and 1890. A strange mixture of Christian and traditional beliefs, the Ghost Dance religion promised a return of the previous order and the disappearance of the white race. The disastrous clash of arms at Wounded Knee Creek, S. Dak., December 29, 1890, shattered this dream and marked the final collapse of the Indian barrier.

In little more than a century the white man had reorganized the culture of the western Indians. But the forces of change flowed in both directions. Because he won the contest, the white man did not have to bow to a conqueror's will; thus his way of life underwent no such cataclysmic change as that of the Indian. Yet his experience with the Indian, an experience not confined to the West and in fact spanning five centuries and a continent, left him in the 20th century with a culture decidedly influenced and enriched, in some ways profoundly, by the very culture he almost destroyed.

Phillips D. Carleton observed that the whites "conquered the Indian but he was the hammer that beat out a new race on the anvil of the continent." And D. H. Lawrence added, "Not that the Red Indian will ever possess the broadlands of America. But his ghost will."

PART II

SOLDIER AND BRAVE:
SURVEY OF HISTORIC SITES
AND BUILDINGS

The recent surge of popular interest in the West, inspired by television, motion pictures, books, and magazine articles, has heightened the attraction of historic sites and buildings associated with the Indian and the Army. As a result, they are prominent in the itineraries of vacationing Americans and foreign visitors. A profusion of such places exists. In fact, among the various phases of western history, only the miner's frontier has bequeathed more tangible remains.

Army forts predominate. Of the hundreds that once speckled the landscape west of the Mississippi River, the remains of scores have survived. Because the Plains Indians posed one of the greatest barriers to the westward movement in the 19th century, most of the forts are in the Plains region. Logically, they are also concentrated along historic routes of transportation and communication such as the Missouri, Yellowstone, Platte, Arkansas, Columbia, and Gila Rivers, and the Rio Grande; the Oregon-California, Santa Fe, Southern Overland, Smoky Hill, and Bozeman Trails; and the Northern Pacific, Union Pacific, Kansas Pacific, Santa Fe, and Southern Pacific Railroads.

Only mounds of earth or foundations mark some fort sites. In other cases the remains are extensive and well preserved. Between these extremes are scores of adobe, frame, and stone ruins in varying stages of disintegration, as well as numerous reconstructions. But even the best preserved fort is a far cry from the Hollywood and literary protoype—palisaded log fortresses with corner blockhouses and massive gates. The real forts were another matter. Few had stockades. Utilitarian, often simple or even crude in construction, and sometimes only tent cities or a motley collection of sod huts or dugouts, the posts were usually constructed of more durable materials. But, to facilitate Army mobility, they were often semipermanent.

Battlefields where Indians and soldiers clashed are also numerous. The sites of almost 50 major engagements, mostly in the Plains States, may be identified. At many the natural setting remains unscarred, facilitating visualization. Farming and ranching operations have destroyed a few sites, but most have been marked by Federal, State, and local agencies, or private individuals. Many have been set aside as historical monuments.

Exemplifying other aspects of Indian affairs than the military are agencies, missions, reservation trading posts, and fur posts. Scattered about the West are the remains of numerous agencies, most dating from the late 19th century; some of the best examples are in Oklahoma, the Dakotas, and Montana. Fine Indian missions may be seen in Kansas, Idaho, Montana, and the Pacific Northwest. A superb example of a reservation trading post, where the ritual of Indian trading is displayed, is Hubbell Trading Post National Historic Site, Ariz. Time has ravaged most fur posts, but the National Park Service plans to reconstruct Bent's Old Fort, Colo., and is exploring the feasibility of reconstructing part of Fort Union, N. Dak., two outstanding posts.

Many factors have hampered historic preservation in the West. Foremost is the damage done by flood control and irrigation programs. In most of these instances the National Park Service and

Coulee Dam National
Recreation Area ⊞

W A S H I N G T O N

⚠ Cataldo Mission   Fort Benton ⚠

Nez Perce National
Historical Park ⊞   M O N T A N A

⊞ Whitman Mission   ⌇Lolo Trail
National Historic Site

⊞ Big Hole National
Battlefield

O R E G O N   Custe
                                                         Natio ⊞

                                          Bighorn Cany
                                          ⊞ Recrea

                    I D A H O

⊞ Lava Beds   Fort Hall ⚠
National Monument
                                                    W Y O M I

                                                        Fo
                                                  National

        Fort Ruby ⚠

        N E V A D A
    ⚠ Fort Churchill

⚠Presidio of San Francisco   C O L O

        ⌒   U T A H

                                                    Be
                                                National

                Pipe Spring
                National Monument ⊞

                    Canyon de Chelly
                    National Monument ⊞   Kit Carson Hoι

                Hubbell Trading Post
                National Historic Site ⊞   Fort ι
                                                   National

I F O R N I   A R I Z O N A

                                                N E W M

            ⚠Yuma Crossing

                    Fort Bowie
                    National Historic Site
                    Chiricahua ⊞   Guadal
                    National Monument   N

SOLDIER AND BRAVE

HISTORIC SITES OF NATIONAL SIGNIFICANCE

⊞ Sites in the National Park System

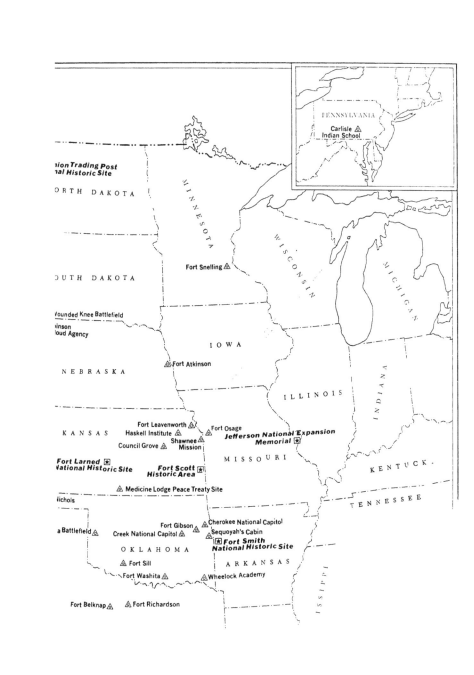

Union Trading Post
National Historic Site

ORTH DAKOTA

MINNESOTA

WISCONSIN

MICHIGAN

PENNSYLVANIA
Carlisle
Indian School

Fort Snelling

OUTH DAKOTA

Wounded Knee Battlefield

inson
loud Agency

IOWA

Fort Atkinson

NEBRASKA

ILLINOIS

INDIANA

KANSAS

Fort Leavenworth
Haskell Institute
Council Grove
Shawnee
Mission

Fort Osage

Jefferson National Expansion
Memorial

MISSOURI

KENTUCK

Fort Larned
National Historic Site

Fort Scott
Historic Area

Medicine Lodge Peace Treaty Site

TENNESSEE

lichols

a Battlefield

Fort Gibson
Creek National Capitol

Cherokee National Capitol
Sequoyah's Cabin
Fort Smith
National Historic Site

OKLAHOMA

Fort Sill

ARKANSAS

Fort Washita

Wheelock Academy

ISSIPPI

Fort Belknap

Fort Richardson

the Smithsonian Institution initiated advance historical and archeological studies and salvaged the maximum possible data and artifacts from inundated areas. Other adverse considerations are the increasing westward shift of population and the activities of vandals and "pot hunters." Weathering and aging processes have taken their toll, especially on log and frame structures.

Particularly destructive to forts was the dismantling done by settlers seeking building materials after the Army moved out. Adobe walls, deprived of roofs, doors, and windows, were left exposed to the elements. Today, as a result, at many sites adobe ruins are rapidly melting away. Stone forts are less vulnerable to the eroding influences of wind and rain, but they too provided ranchers and farmers with building materials—stone blocks already quarried and shaped. Nevertheless, the ruins of stone forts are usually more imposing than those of adobe.

Among the conditions tending to protect western sites from man and nature have been aridity and, until recently, sparsity of population. Continuous use by the Army or Bureau of Indian Affairs and the establishment of Veterans' Administration or State hospitals and institutions have also saved many forts and Indian agencies from destruction. Cities have sometimes grown up around forts, and the buildings have become private residences or business establishments.

But the most effective antidote to the loss of sites has been the vigilance of Federal, State, and local preservationists. The National Park Service preserves and interprets many of the most significant places. The U.S. Army commemorates the history of active forts. Most Western States maintain historical societies or other agencies that have taken a leading role in protecting, maintaining, surveying, and marking sites. Tribal councils, corporations, and private individuals have also done much commendable work.

Described in the following pages are some of the more significant sites and buildings illustrating Indian affairs and the Indian wars in the 19th century. They are divided into three categories: National Park Service Areas, National Historic Landmarks, and Other Sites Considered.

The principal aim of the National Survey of Historic Sites and

Buildings is to identify nationally important sites that are not *National Park Service Areas*, but no survey of historic places would be complete without including them. Further information about a particular area may be obtained by writing directly to the park superintendent at the address listed immediately following the location.

National Historic Landmarks are those sites judged by the Advisory Board on National Parks, Historic Sites, Buildings, and Monuments to meet the criteria of national significance in commemorating the history of the United States (pp. 395–397). As historic sites of national significance, they have been declared by the Secretary of the Interior to be eligible for designation as National Historic Landmarks. Some have already been so designated and others will be when the owners apply.

Other Sites Considered consist of those sites deemed by the Advisory Board to possess noteworthy historical value but not national significance. The list of sites treated in this category does not purport to be exhaustive; it is merely a representative sampling, all that is possible because of space limitations.

As time goes on, many sites in the Other Sites Considered category in all phases of history will be listed on the National Register of Historic Places, maintained by the National Park Service's Office of Archeology and Historic Preservation. This register consists not only of sites in the National Park System and National Historic Landmarks but also those of State and local significance nominated through appropriate channels by the various States. The register will be published biennially and distributed by the Superintendent of Documents, U.S. Government Printing Office, Washington, D.C. 20402. The first volume was *The National Register of Historic Places, 1969,* price $5.25.

For the convenience of the users of this volume, sites and buildings are listed alphabetically by State. The following code indicates site categories:

Site Categories

⊞ NATIONAL PARK SERVICE AREAS
△ NATIONAL HISTORIC LANDMARKS
⊗ OTHER SITES CONSIDERED

NOTE: Before visiting any site or building, inquiry should be made as to dates and hours of operation and admission costs, usually nominal. In those numerous instances where sites are privately owned, the owner's permission should be obtained for visits and his rights respected.

Big Dry Wash Battlefield, Arizona ⊗

Location: Coconino County, in Coconino National Forest, on a rough trail road, about 7 miles north of General Springs, which is located on Mogollon Rim Road. Make local inquiry.

At this site on July 17, 1882, a column of the 6th Cavalry from Fort Whipple led by Capt. Adna R. Chaffee mauled a party of 54 White Mountain Apaches under Nantiatish. The warriors, aroused by the death of their medicine man, Nakaidoklini, the year before in the Battle of Cibecue Creek and resenting the intrusion of settlers and miners, had fled the White Mountain (Fort Apache) Reservation. They raided the San Carlos Agency, plundered settlements in the Tonto Basin, and for some time evaded the 14 cavalry troops from various Arizona forts who were giving pursuit. Spying Chaffee's force from the Mogollon Rim, the Indians planned an ambush in a canyon 7 miles to the north. Chaffee, forewarned by scouts, dismounted and formed a skirmish line with part of his force at the brink of the canyon to pin down his opponents, on the opposite rim. He then deployed two parties that surprised them on the flanks.

The trail road from Mogollon Rim passes along Chaffee's approach route and terminates at the canyon brink where the fighting began. A stone monument at the southern edge of the canyon describes the action and lists the names of the soldier participants. The heavy pine forests and rugged canyon are unchanged from 1882. A marker describing the battle is located at General Springs.

Gen. George Crook, master tactician and military
innovator, wore down Arizona's Chiricahua Apaches
but was reassigned before their final surrender.

Chiricahua leaders Geronimo and Natchez (wearing hat) are on horseback in this photograph. Geronimo's son stands by his side.

Camp Verde, Arizona ⊗

Location: Yavapai County, town of Camp Verde.

Protector of settlers in the Verde Valley of central Arizona, this fort (1866–91) was also Gen. George Crook's major base during his Tonto Basin campaign (1872–73) against the Yavapais, or Apache-Mojaves, and the scene of their formal surrender. In 1871, the same year Crook arrived in Arizona to assume command of Army forces, President Grant's peace representatives established a reservation for the Yavapais near Camp Verde. But by the next year most of them had fled into the mountains. Defeated by Crook in 1872–73, they returned to the reservation for 2 years, and were then moved to the San Carlos Reservation.

No remains are extant at the fort's first location, on the east bank of the Verde River, but a few adobe buildings border the parade ground at the second, on the west bank of the river in the northern part of the town of Camp Verde. The Camp Verde Improvement Association, a local civic group, owns and has restored two of the three sets of officers' quarters and the administration building. One of the officers' quarters is a private residence. The administration building houses a museum. When this volume went to press, plans were being made to transfer the buildings and the entire fort site to the State for historical park purposes.

Canyon de Chelly National Monument, Arizona ☒

Location: Apache County, park headquarters located about 1 mile southeast of Chinle; address: P.O. Box 588, Chinle, Ariz. 86503.

Typifying the colorful Indian country of the Southwest, this national monument is of outstanding archeological and historical significance. Embracing more than 130 square miles, it consists of awesome steep-walled canyons and sheer 1,000-foot-high red sandstone cliffs that have sheltered the prehistoric Pueblo and historic Navajo Indians for thousands of years.

Tucked away in the recesses of Canyon de Chelly, nestled below towering cliffs or perched on high ledges, are the ruins of several hundred ancient villages. Dating from A.D. 350 to 1300, the ruins include Basketmaker (350–700) circular pithouses; aboveground Pueblo (700–1300) stone rectangular dwellings con-

Canyon de Chelly National Monument, historic Navajo stronghold. Spider Rock in foreground.

53

Indian Prisoners and a soldier

Camp Verde. Arizona ⊕

Canyon de Chelly National Monument, Arizona ☒

Location: Apache County, park headquarters located about 1 mile southwest of Chinle; address: P.O. Box 588, Chinle, Ariz. 86503.

Typifying the colorful Indian country of the Southwest, this national monument is of outstanding archeological and historical significance. Embracing more than 130 square miles, it consists of awesome steep-walled canyons and sheer 1,000-foot-high red sandstone cliffs that have sheltered the prehistoric Pueblo and historic Navajo Indians for thousands of years.

Tucked away in the recesses of Canyon de Chelly, nestled below towering cliffs or perched on high ledges, are the ruins of several hundred ancient villages. Dating from A.D. 350 to 1300, the ruins include Basketmaker (350–700) circular pithouses; aboveground Pueblo (70 1300) stone rectangular dwellings con-

Canyon de Chelly National Monument, historic Navajo stronghold. Spider Rock in foreground.

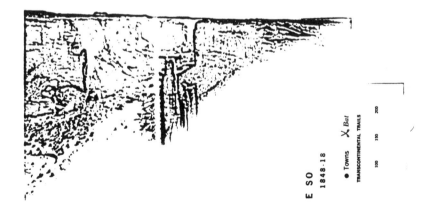

nected into compact villages; and Pueblo cliff houses, most dating from the 1100–1300 era.

About 1300 climatic and perhaps other adverse factors forced the bulk of the Pueblo occupants, as well as those residing in the Four Corners region of Arizona, Utah, Colorado, and New Mexico, to disperse to other parts of the Southwest. Some of the present-day Pueblo Indians of Arizona and New Mexico are descendants of these prehistoric peoples. The canyons continued to be sporadically occupied by the Hopi Indians, also Puebloan.

About 1700 the Navajo Indians, an aggressive people who were culturally and linguistically related to the Apaches, began to emigrate from northern New Mexico to northeastern Arizona around Canyon de Chelly. For a century and a half they raided the Pueblo villages and Spanish settlements along the upper Rio Grande Valley. As the various governments of New Mexico— Spanish, Mexican, and American—intensified reprisals, Canyon de Chelly became a major Navajo stronghold.

In 1863–64 Col. "Kit" Carson, under the direction of Gen. James H. Carleton of the California Volunteers, who occupied Arizona and New Mexico during the Civil War, conducted a full-scale campaign against the Navajos following his roundup of the Mescalero Apaches. Proceeding from Fort Wingate, N. Mex., Carson established Fort Canby, Ariz., as a base of operations. Harrying the Navajos and killing their sheep, he reduced them to near starvation. They took refuge in the supposedly impregnable fortress of Canyon de Chelly. There Carson's cavalrymen completed the subjugation. Under military escort about 8,000 half-starved people made the "Long Walk" to the Bosque Redondo Reservation in eastern New Mexico, where they joined the Mescaleros. The Navajos endured great suffering before the Government allowed them in 1868 to return to their ancestral homeland in northeastern Arizona.

Today within the national monument some Navajo families, scattered in hogans on the canyon floors, live a simple pastoral life much as they did in Carson's time. Flocks of sheep graze in the canyon and on the rims, though sheepherding has declined. The majority of the tribe are now salaried employees. Many prehistoric pictographs are visible on the cliff faces and in rock shelters. National Park Service personnel provide guided tours of the na-

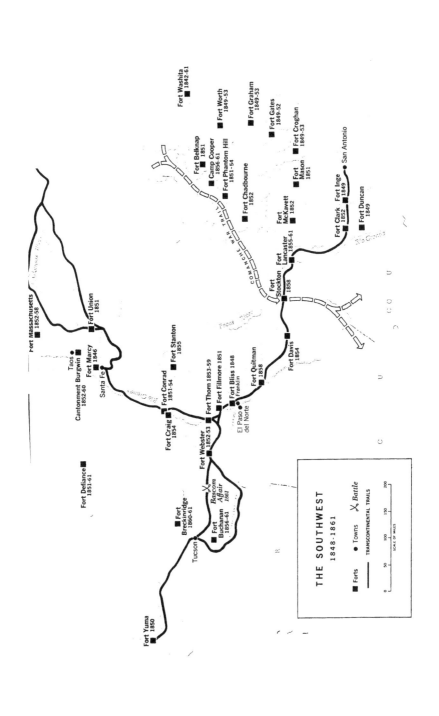

THE SOUTHWEST
1848-1861

■ Forts ● Towns ✕ Battle
TRANSCONTINENTAL TRAILS

SCALE OF MILES
0   50   100   150   200

Fort Yuma
1850

Fort Defiance
1851-61

Fort
Breckinridge
1860-61

Fort
Buchanan
1856-61

Bascom
Affair
1861

Tucson

Fort Massachusetts
1852-58

Taos
Cantonment Burgwin
1852-60
Fort Marcy
1846
Santa Fe

Fort Union
1851

Fort Stanton
1855

Fort Craig
1854

Fort Conrad
1851-54

Fort Webster
1852-53

Fort Thorn 1853-59

Fort Fillmore 1851
Fort Bliss 1848
Franklin

El Paso
del Norte

Fort Quitman
1858

Fort Davis
1854

Fort
Stockton
1858

Fort
Lancaster
1855-61

Fort Belknap
1851

Camp Cooper
1856-61

Fort Phantom Hill
1851-54

Fort Chadbourne
1852

Fort
McKavett
1852

Fort
Mason
1851

Fort Clark Fort Inge
1852   1849

Fort Duncan
1849

San Antonio

Fort Washita
1842-61

Fort Worth
1849-53

Fort Graham
1849-53

Fort Gates
1849-52

Fort Croghan
1849-53

COMANCHE WAR TRAIL

Rio Grande

Pecos River

Rio Grande

Canadian River

M E X I C O

tional monument, and visitors may avail themselves of various self-guided tours.

Chiricahua National Monument, Arizona ⊠

Location: Cochise County, accessible via Ariz. 186 and Ariz. 181, about 36 miles southeast of Willcox; address: Dos Cabezas Star Route, Willcox, Ariz. 85643.

This national monument on the western flank of the Chiricahua Mountains · is a 17-square-mile wonderland of pinnacles, ridges, canyons, and unique volcanic rock formations. The mountains, rising sharply from the dry grasslands of southeastern Arizona and southwestern New Mexico, are a verdant island of trees, plants, and wildlife in a sea of brown desert. Although primarily significant for its geological features, Chiricahua National Monument is located in an area that was the haunt of the Chiricahua Apaches and is also pertinent to the phases of history discussed in this volume.

The mountain ranges of the Southwest were the home of the nomadic Apaches and earlier men. Following the coming of the Spaniards to the Southwest in the 16th century, the Apaches moved into the Chiricahua Mountains and the Dragoon Mountains to the west and descended to plunder cattle, horses, and grain. Beginning in 1693 the Spaniards sent punitive expeditions into the mountains, but as the Spanish frontier receded and in 1821 passed into the possession of Mexico the Chiricahua Apaches felt less pressure.

After the U.S. acquisition of the Southwest in 1848, gold seekers, settlers, and troops became a new threat. The Chiricahuas, led by Cochise, Natchez, and Geronimo, courageously resisted until late in the 19th century. They clashed regularly with troops from Fort Bowie, about 15 miles to the northwest of the present national monument, and attacked wagon trains and stagecoaches passing through Apache Pass. Patrols from the fort fought many battles in the Chiricahua Mountains, near which the agency for the Chiricahua Reservation (1872–76) was situated at several different sites. But various bands of Chiricahuas escaped from the reservation and the White Mountain (Fort Apache) Reservation, 55

Upper Rhyolite Canyon, Chiricahua National Monument. From haunts in the Chiricahua and Dragoon Mountains, the Chiricahuas lashed at the invaders of their homeland.

56

some 125 miles north of Fort Bowie, to which the Chiricahuas were relocated in 1876. Often hiding in the Chiricahua Mountains, they terrorized settlers and eluded troops in Arizona, New Mexico, and Mexico until Geronimo's surrender in 1886 ended the Apache wars. "Big Foot" Massai, however, staged several one-man escapades in later years.

Exhibits at the monument headquarters, about a mile east of the entrance, interpret the natural history and history of the area. Cochise Head, Massai Point, and Massai Canyon immortalize the names of the Chiricahua Apache leaders. Massai Point Exhibit Building, at the far eastern side of the monument, presents geological exhibits. More than 15 miles of trail, many self-guiding, provide access by foot or horseback to unusual natural features.

Cibecue Creek Battlefield, Arizona ⊗

Location: Navajo County, on an unimproved road, about 2½ miles south of Cibecue.

Indicative of the strife that prevailed on Arizona reservations in the 1870's and 1880's, the battle fought at this site in 1881 was fomented by Indian resentment at the invasion of settlers and miners, aggravated by the doctrines of the medicine man Nakaidoklini. His mystical teachings and prophecies, which blended Christian and native elements and foreshadowed the Ghost Dance religion that was to sweep through the western tribes in the years 1889–91, gained him many adherents and stirred up the White Mountain (Fort Apache) Reservation. The alarmed Indian agent appealed to the nearby fort for aid.

On August 30, 1881, Col. Eugene A. Carr, the commander, and 85 men and 23 Apache scouts arrested the medicine man at his camp on Cibecue Creek. They then moved 2½ miles down the creek and made camp. Late in the afternoon a hundred of Nakaidoklini's followers attacked. Some of the Apache scouts, sympathetic with the new religion, revolted, shot a captain and six men, and joined the attackers. During the struggle, Nakaidoklini's guard killed him. Carr's men repulsed the assailants but the next morning, while the troops were still in the field warding off a force of about 500 Indians, they joined other disaffected bands

some 125 miles nort of Fort Bowie, to which the Chiricahuas were relocated in 17i. Often hiding in the Chiricahua Mountains, they terrorizecs ttlers and eluded troops in Arizona, New Mexico, and Mexico ntil Geronimo's surrender in 1886 ended the Apache wars. "Big Foot" Massai, however, staged several one-man escapades in late ears.

Exhibits at the mon ment headquarters, about a mile east of the entrance. interprc he natural history and history of the area. Cochise Head. Massa Point, and Massai Canyon immortalize the names of the Chirich ia Apache leaders. Massai Point Exhibit Building, at the far estern side of the monument, presents geological exhibits Mor han 15 miles of trail, many self-guiding, provide access by foc or horseback to unusual natural features.

Cibecue Creek Battlefield, Arizona ⊗

Location: Navajo County, on an unimproved road, about 21, miles south of Cibecue

Indicative of the strife hat prevailed on Arizona reservations in the 1870's and 1880's, the battle fought at this site in 1881 was fomented by Indian resentment at the invasion of settlers and miners, aggravated by the doctrines of the medicine man Nakaidokini. His mystical teachings and prophecies, which blended Christian and native elements and foreshadowed the Ghost Dance religion that was to sweep through the western tribes in the years 1889–91, gained him many adherents and stirred up the White Mountain (Fort Apache) Reservation. The alarmed Indian agent appealed to the nearby fort for aid.

On August 30, 1881 Col. Eugene A. Carr, the commander, and 5 men and 23 Apache scouts arrested the medicine man at his camp on Cibecue Creek. They then moved 2½ miles down the creek and made camp. Late in the afternoon a hundred of Nakaidoklini's followers attacked. Some of the Apache scouts, sympathetic with the new religion, revolted, shot a captain and six men, and joined the attackers. During the strug Nakaidokli ard killed him. Carr' men repulsed the ts but th orning, while the troops were still in d war ce of about 500 Indians, they joine disap s and assaulted Fort Apache. The garrison held out, and the Indians later surrendered.

Meantime, worried about the prospect of another general Apache war, the Army rushed in reinforcements. This caused the Chiricahuas residing on the reservation, innocent of any wrongdoing, to grow apprehensive. They became thoroughly frightened when the agency police began to arrest the leaders of the Cibecue revolt. On September 30 Geronimo and Natchez and 75 of the Chiricahuas fled the reservation to the Sierra Madre of Mexico. There they joined Nana and the remnants of Victorio's Warm Springs band. Hostilities did not end until Geronimo gave up in 1886.

The battle site is on the Fort Apache Indian Reservation. The wide and open creek valley, through which Cibecue Creek meanders, contrasts with the broken, wooded terrain on both sides. Except for an occasional Indian cornfield and scattered Apache dwellings, neither of which is out of character, the natural scene is unimpaired.

Col. Eugene A. Carr, commander of Fort Apache, fought the Battle of Cibecue Creek and other engagements in the Indian wars.

Fort Apache in 1883.

Fort Apache, Arizona ⊗

Location: Navajo County, at the Fort Apache Indian Reservation headquarters, adjacent to the town of Fort Apache.

From its founding in 1870 until the capitulation of Geronimo in 1886, this fort was closely involved in the Apache wars (1861–86). Gen. George Crook, arriving in Arizona for his first tour of duty in 1871, organized there his first company of Apache scouts, one of his tactical innovations, before moving on to Camp Verde to conduct his Tonto Basin campaign.

Situated on the White Mountain (Fort Apache) Reservation, which adjoined the San Carlos Reservation, the fort guarded the Fort Apache Agency, while Fort Thomas watched over the San Carlos Agency. The two reservations were the focus of Apache unrest, especially after troops moved the troublesome Chiricahuas in 1876 from Fort Bowie to the White Mountain Reservation. In constant turmoil, the reservations were noted for their unhealthful location, overcrowded conditions, and dissatisfied inhabitants. Sparking the discontent were inefficient and corrupt agents, friction between civil and military authorities, feeble attempts to make farmers of the nomadic Indians, and encroachment on the reservations by settlers and miners.

59

*Lt. Charles B. Gatewood and company of Apache
scouts at Fort Apache in 1880, at the end of the
Victorio campaign. Sam Bowman, civilian scout,
stands behind Gatewood.*

For a decade, until Geronimo laid down his arms, the resentful
Apaches alternately fled into Mexico, returned to the reservations
to enlist recruits, and raided along the Mexican boundary. Fort
Apache troops spent much of their time in pursuit. In 1881, at the
Battle of Cibecue Creek, a group of White Mountain Apaches defeated a force from the fort and then besieged it for a while before they surrendered. After 1886 Fort Apache ceased to be a significant frontier post, but it remained active until 1924.

Many fort buildings remain. The Fort Apache post office occupies the adobe adjutant's building. A log building, one of the
oldest structures and reputedly the residence of General Crook, as
well as the stone officers' quarters, are today the residences of
teachers and other Bureau of Indian Affairs employees. The sutler's store and commissary building, cavalry barns, and guardhouse have not been significantly altered. One of the original four
barracks, an adobe building in bad disrepair, houses the farm
shop for the Indian school. The parade ground provides a recreational area. The cemetery no longer contains soldier dead, but
does contain the bodies of Indian scouts.

Fort Bowie National Historic Site, Arizona ⊠

*Location: Cochise County, on a secondary road running
south from I-10, about 13 miles south of Bowie; address:
c/o Chiricahua National Monument, Dos Cabezas Star
Route, Willcox, Ariz. 85643.*

Few western forts have a more dramatic history than Fort Bowie
(1862–94). Its eroding adobe walls today commemorate the soldiers who for over two decades endured the hardships and dangers
of campaigns that rank among the most arduous and frustrating
in military history; and Chiricahua warriors, masters of guerilla
tactics and for two centuries obstinate defenders of their homeland against the Spaniards, Mexicans, and Americans. The hub of
military operations against the Chiricahuas, Fort Bowie was the
base of the numerous expeditions fielded by Gens. George Crook
and Nelson A. Miles that finally smashed the power of Cochise,
Mangas Coloradas, Natchez, and Geronimo. Climate and topogra-
phy aided the Indians, skilled at avoiding engagements where the
odds were not overwhelmingly in their favor. For the soldiers, the
Apache wars (1861–86) consisted chiefly of endless marches under
the desert sun and only rare chances to come to grips with the foe.

Located in the Chiricahua Mountains near the eastern entrance
of strategic Apache Pass, through which wound one of the major
transcontinental trails, the post protected military and civilian
traffic. The pass, whose history is closely interwoven with that of
the fort, was a twisting defile between the rocky foothills of the

Fort Bowie about 1890.

61

Dos Cabezas and the Chiricahua Mountains. Its spring, a rarity in the semidesert country, enhanced its attractiveness as a route. Traveling by at various times were California-bound gold seekers, other emigrants, explorers, Mexican boundary commissioners, railroad surveyors, and troops.

Long before Americans began entering the region in the mid-19th century, the Indians and Spaniards had used the pass. In 1857 San Antonio-San Diego mail coaches temporarily traversed it. The following year the Butterfield Overland Mail, fixing its route between St. Louis and San Francisco via the pass, built a stone relay station and corral just west of the spring near the future site of the fort. The company's picturesque Concord stages operated through the pass until the outbreak of the Civil War, when the route was moved northward.

When the Americans arrived in the Apache Pass region, the Chiricahua Indians were residing there. Since the 17th century their homeland had been the Chiricahua Mountains just to the south and the Dragoon Mountains to the west. One of their chiefs was the youthful Cochise. Apart from occasional stage raids, he and his people were relatively amicable until February 1861. That month a young lieutenant, George N. Bascom, from Fort Buchanan, Ariz., attempted to arrest Cochise in the pass for a depredation he probably was not guilty of and caused blood to be spilled on both sides. The Bascom Affair enraged Cochise, who launched an all-out war on the Americans.

The alienation was untimely, for a few months later the outbreak of the Civil War brought about the withdrawal of many troops from the frontier. New Mexico and Arizona lay open not only to Indian attacks but also to Confederate invasion from Texas. When the Texans arrived in the summer of 1861, they learned that the Apaches did not distinguish between blue and gray. The Indians harassed the southerners until the following year, when Gen. James H. Carleton's California Volunteers drove the Confederates out of Arizona and New Mexico.

The Volunteers swiftly received an introduction to Apache warfare. In July 1862 about 500 Chiricahuas and Gilas, led by Cochise and Mangas Coloradas, ambushed a detachment in the pass. Only by employing artillery could the troops rout the braves from
stone breastworks commanding the waterhole. To meet such

Indian police in front of the San Carlos Agency guardhouse in 1880.

threats to his line of communications through the pass with Tucson and California, Carleton ordered Fort Bowie built on a hill overlooking the spring and dominating the eastern entrance to the pass. The post consisted of hastily built breastworks enclosing a group of tents and a stone guardhouse. Although Carleton's aggressive policy decreased Indian hostilities in New Mexico, it did not intimidate Arizona's Apaches. Despite the frequent patrols sent out from the beleaguered Fort Bowie and other forts, by the close of the Civil War most of the ranches in the Tucson area and the town of Tubac had been deserted. Everywhere Apaches lurked in ambush. For 6 bloody years they continued to ravage southern Arizona.

In 1866, the same year the Government restored mail service between Tucson and Mesilla, N. Mex., Regulars replaced the Volunteers at Fort Bowie, and 2 years later moved it onto a plateau to the southeast of the original location.

To breathe new life into the Apache campaign, in 1871 General Crook assumed command of the Department of Arizona and stopped at Fort Bowie before proceeding to Fort Apache. But he was forced to suspend operations in southern Arizona while emissaries of President Grant's Peace Policy tried a conciliatory approach. One of them, Gen. Oliver O. Howard, succeeded the following year. At Cochise's Stronghold, in the Dragoon Mountains, he persuaded the Chiricahuas to settle on a newly created reservation at Sulphur Springs, whose agency was moved in quick succession from there to San Simon and Pinery Canyon and in 1875 to Fort Bowie. Meantime Crook, ignoring the Peace Policy, had

63

crushed the Yavapais, or Apache-Mojaves, of central Arizona in the Tonto Basin campaign (1872–73), for which he used Camp Verde as a base. Whether coincidentally or not, peace with the Chiricahuas prevailed until Crook was reassigned in 1875, the year after illness took the life of Cochise.

Geronimo soon resumed raiding. In 1876, alarmed by the rash of hostilities, the Indian Bureau abolished the Chiricahua Reservation. Troops from Fort Bowie moved 325 Chiricahuas to the White Mountain (Fort Apache) Reservation, on the north of San Carlos, where the Apaches were being concentrated. But Geronimo and a group of recalcitrants, refusing assignment there, conducted a 3-year reign of terror. While the Chiricahuas were at peace in 1880 and 1881, Fort Bowie troops aided the drive against the Warm Springs Apache Victorio and his successor, Nana, in New Mexico. During the fall of 1881, however, a series of clashes occurred between Fort Apache troops, reinforced by those from Fort Bowie, and the White Mountain Apaches, who were aggravated by an influx of settlers and miners onto reservation lands. The Chiricahuas feared the Army would make no distinction between the innocent and the guilty. Geronimo, Natchez, and 75 warriors, avoiding pursuing columns, fled to Mexico's Sierra Madre and began 2 years of raiding on both sides of the border. Their numbers, swelled by newly recruited allies from the San Carlos Reservation, rose to 700. The U.S. Army and the Mexican troops guarded the waterholes and trusted that diligent pursuit and hardship would discourage the raiders.

In September 1882 Crook reassumed command in Arizona. Maintaining his field headquarters at Fort Bowie, he tightened discipline and reformed reservation management. Taking advantage of the agreement made by Mexico and the United States to permit their troops to follow Apaches across the international boundary, Crook employed large numbers of his Apache scouts, led by white officers, to ferret the Apaches out of the Sierra Madre. Convinced that the mountains no longer afforded sanctuary, in 1883–84 Geronimo and more than 300 of his followers returned to the San Carlos Reservation. But it continued to simmer with unrest, intensified by Indian Bureau-Army friction over reservation management.

64   After 2 years of comparative peace, in May 1885 Geronimo,

Natchez, Nana, and 190 men once again fled into Mexico. The persistent Crook, though winning no major victories, eventually wore them down and in March 1886 they surrendered to him at Cañon de los Embudos, Mexico. En route to Fort Bowie, however, most of them escaped to the Sierra Madre. Stung by the storm of public and official criticism that greeted this defection, General Crook asked to be relieved.

General Miles took over the next month. He revamped the supply system and, to improve communications, erected 27 heliograph stations on high peaks in Arizona and New Mexico, one on Bowie Peak. His newly organized "pursuing commands," possibly because of large reinforcements, quickly crushed Geronimo. His final surrender in September at Skeleton Canyon, Ariz., brought an end to the long and bitter Apache wars. At Fort Bowie special precautions were required to protect Geronimo and his fellow prisoners from the wrath of local settlers until they were moved to Fort Pickens, Fla. Their fellow Chiricahuas and some Warm Springs Apaches, including many scouts who had served Crook with distinction, had preceded them earlier in the year and had been sent to Fort Marion, Fla.

Until Fort Bowie was inactivated in 1894, the garrison merely rounded up Apaches who wandered from the reservation and investigated reports of depredations. Stagecoach service through Apache Pass had ceased with the advent of the railroad in the region in 1881.

Ruins of Fort Bowie.

Fort Bowie National Historic Site was authorized by Congress in 1964. An extensive restoration and interpretive program is planned. Today only rock foundations and adobe remnants mark the site of the original fort. Wall fragments and rock foundations of more than 40 buildings of the second dot the slope below Bowie Peak. The stone corrals are essentially intact, and remains of the water system are prominent. Well preserved traces of the stage route may be seen at various points in the pass, and a pile of rock rubble north of the fort cemetery and about 700 yards west of the spring marks the site of the Butterfield stage station. The historical setting of the fort and pass has been only slightly impaired by roads and ranching activity.

Fort Breckinridge (Old Camp Grant), Arizona ⊗

Location: Pinal County, just southeast of the junction of Ariz. 77 and an unimproved road, about 10 miles north of Mammoth.

This was the second military post in the area of the Gadsden Purchase (1853). Troops from Fort Buchanan, the first, founded it in 1860 to assist in watching over emigrants and settlers. The next February the garrison reinforced Fort Buchanan troops during the hostilities associated with the Bascom Affair. In July, faced by a Confederate invasion of New Mexico from Texas, the Army abandoned Fort Breckinridge, as well as other posts in southern Arizona, and put it to the torch. In 1862 California Volunteers temporarily occupied the site, known as Fort Stanford. Five years later Regulars built a new post, Camp Grant.

Despite the forceful measures of the California Volunteers, when the Civil War ended Arizona Territory was still besieged by Apaches. Arizonans frantically petitioned the U.S. Government for more troops. Incensed at all Indians and embittered at governmental neglect, a mob of 54 Tucson citizens, aided by 92 Papago Indians, old enemies of the Apaches, took matters into their own hands. They blamed raids in the vicinity on a group of 300 Aravaipa Apaches, led by Eskiminzin, who had surrendered at Camp Grant and were residing about 4 miles away under its protection. On April 30, 1871, the mob descended on them; killed 118 people, mostly women; and captured 27 children, some of whom became slaves of the Papagos or servants in Tucson homes.

The massacre and the acquittal in December of 108 persons charged with being involved, though receiving the approbation of many westerners, created indignation in the East and did much to hamper Grant's Peace Policy in Arizona. The desert tribes soon learned of it, and peace emissaries found them more reluctant than ever to trade their freedom for the apparent insecurity of reservation life. Gen. George Crook, who had taken over the Department of Arizona in June 1871, soon led expeditions against the Apaches out of Old Camp Grant and Forts McDowell and Apache in his Tonto Basin campaign (1872–73). Late in 1872 Camp Grant was relocated 50 miles to the southeast and became known as Fort Grant (New Camp Grant).

The barren site of Fort Breckinridge (Old Camp Grant), on privately owned land, is covered with mesquite and cactus and a scattering of rubble and ruins.

Fort Buchanan (Camp Crittenden), Arizona ⊗

Location: Santa Cruz County, just west of Ariz. 82, about 1 mile west of Sonoita.

Supplementing a number of other military posts established in the territory acquired from Mexico in 1848, Fort Buchanan (1856–61) was the first within the bounds of the Gadsden Purchase (1853). About 22 miles east of Tubac, it protected settlers and stages from Chiricahua Apaches. A detachment from the post, led by Lt. George N. Bascom, was involved in the episode with Cochise at Apache Pass that precipitated the Apache wars (1861–86). At the beginning of the Civil War, Regulars evacuated and destroyed it. The following year, General Carleton's California Volunteers occasionally camped at the site. To aid in the renewed effort against the Apaches, the post was reactivated as Camp Crittenden (1868–73) on a hill about one-half mile to the east.

The privately owned sites of Fort Buchanan and Camp Crittenden are used for grazing. The only remains are scattered rocks, mounds of earth, and fragmented adobe ruins.

Fort Defiance, Arizona ⊗

Location: Apache County, town of Fort Defiance.

The name of this fort (1851–61) typifies the attitude of its garrison and that of the Navajos it sought to control. Only 3 miles west of the Arizona-New Mexico boundary, it was the first Army post in Arizona and one of many established within the Mexican Cession (1848). After the failure of several treaties with the restive Navajos, who had terrorized residents of the Southwest since Spanish times, Fort Defiance was founded to quiet them. In 1858, until which time only intermittent skirmishing had occurred, hostilities became intense. Two years later 1,000 Navajos besieged the fort but were unable to capture it.

In 1868 Fort Defiance became the Navajo Indian Agency, today at Window Rock. A Navajo tribal school and hospital, around which the town of Fort Defiance has grown up, now occupies the fort site. Modern construction has altered it considerably, but the fort outlines are visible.

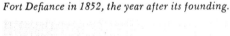

Fort Defiance in 1852, the year after its founding.

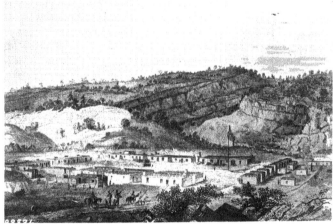

Fort Grant (New Camp Grant), Arizona ⊗

Location: Graham County, town of Fort Grant.

The successor of Old Camp Grant, this fort (1872–1905) was founded along a route employed by Apaches fleeing into Mexico from the San Carlos Reservation. Until the surrender of Geron.

Bands boosted troop morale. First Infantry band at Fort Grant in 1882.

Officers and wives at Fort Grant officers' quarters in 1885.

69

Military officials often had disciplinary problems.
Guardhouse prisoners laboring at Fort Grant
in the mid-1880's. Target range and Graham
Mountains in background.

imo in 1886, its troops and those from other forts in the region
tried to intercept these roving bands and pursued raiding parties
along the international boundary. In 1911 the State acquired the
fort for use as a reform school, today called the State Industrial
School.

An extensive construction program has destroyed much of the
historic setting, and a large swimming pool takes up part of the
old parade ground. Several of the original adobe officers' quarters, most of which have been modernized, are still used.

Fort Huachuca, Arizona ⊗

> Location: Cochise County, on the Fort Huachuca Mili-
> tary Reservation, town of Fort Huachuca.

Fort Huachuca (1877–present), one of a chain of forts established
to guard southern Arizona against the Chiricahua Apaches, figured prominently in the campaigns that finally pacified them. At
this fort Capt. Henry W. Lawton, General Miles' protege, and
Acting Assistant Surgeon Leonard Wood organized the elite striking force that chased Geronimo and his followers through the

wilds of Mexico's Sierra Madre during the summer of 1886. The campaign, though it involved no decisive engagements, proved instrumental in Geronimo's surrender later in the year.

Construction at modern Fort Huachuca, which houses the Army Strategic Communications Command, has encroached only slightly on the historic scene. The large adobe houses on officers' row, built in the 1880's, have been remodeled but still serve their original function. Several other residences dating from the same period have also been renovated and are occupied by offices. Three large frame barracks accommodate classrooms and offices. A row of eight adobe huts, a half mile north of the parade ground, was built around 1900 to house Apache scouts. The Fort Huachuca Post Museum interprets the history of the post.

Fort Lowell, Arizona ⊗

Location: Pima County, on Craycroft Road, in the northeastern part of Tucson.

A part of the system of forts guarding southern Arizona during the years of Apache hostilities, this one served more as a supply depot and administrative center than as a combat base. It occupied two sites. The first post, essentially a tent city, was established in May 1862 just east of Tucson by California Volunteers who had captured the town from the Confederates. In 1873 the post was relocated 7 miles northeast of town, where permanent adobe construction began. The garrison remained until 1891.

The Santa Rita Hotel is located on the first site. The extensive surviving adobe ruins at the second, standing 7 feet high, represent an excellent specimen of the typical southwestern fort of the 19th century. Pima County owns the eastern part of the fort grounds and commemorates them in Fort Lowell Park. Noteworthy remains are those of the hospital and one cavalry and two infantry barracks. These have been stabilized by the Arizona Pioneers' Historical Society. It has also reconstructed the commanding officer's house and furnished it in period style, and plans to restore the hospital and establish there a museum on Army medical history in the Southwest. Outside the park, about 200 yards to the west on Fort Lowell Road, is the sutler's store, now a private

Column leaving an unidentified southwestern post, probably in Arizona sometime in the 1880's.

residence; and three officers' quarters, in varying condition, on privately owned land. Immediately to the east are the ruins of the guardhouse.

Fort McDowell, Arizona ⊗
Location: Maricopa County, town of Fort McDowell.

Founded by California Volunteers on the west bank of the Verde River in the midst of Indian country and along travel routes, this isolated post (1865–91) was ever on the alert for the Apaches who roamed the Salt and Gila River Valleys and was a key base in General Crook's Tonto Basin campaign. Columns from Fort McDowell and Old Camp Grant won the Battle of Salt River Canyon, Ariz., instrumental in bringing that campaign to a close.

The site of the fort, just west of the Fort McDowell Indian Agency, is overgrown with vegetation. The only original building is the officers' quarters. Low earth mounds and adobe remnants mark the location of other structures.

Canyon de Chelly ⚔ *1864*

▲ Navajo Agency 1868
(Fort Defiance)

Fort Wingate ■
1868

Fort Wingate ■ ... Albuquerque
1862-68

Camp Verde ■   ⚔ *Big Dry Wash*
1866   *1882*

Salt River
Fort McDowell ■ *Canyon* ⚔   *Cibecue* ⚔   Fort Apache 1870
1865   *1872*   *Creek*   ■ ▲ Fort Apache Agency
                         1881   1872

Fort Craig ■
1854-84

■ Fort Yuma   ▲ San Carlos Agency
1850-82   1873

                          ■ Fort Thomas
                             1876-90

Camp Grant   ■ Fort Bayard
1867 ■   1866   Fort Selden
                                                    ■ 1865-
Fort Lowell   ■ Fort Grant
■ 1862   1872   Fort Cummings ■
Tucson ●   1863-86
        Apache Pass ⚔ ■ Fort Bowie
                    1862   1862

          Camp Crittenden
Tubac ■ 1868-73   Fort E
 ●   1
Fort Huachuca ■ 1877   Skeleton Canyon   El Pas
                             o

Canyon de los Embudos o

THE SOUTHWEST AND
THE SOUTHERN PLAINS
1862-1890

■ Forts   ▲ Agencies

● Towns   ⚔ *Battles*

        o Sites

0   25   50   76   100   125   150
          SCALE OF MILES

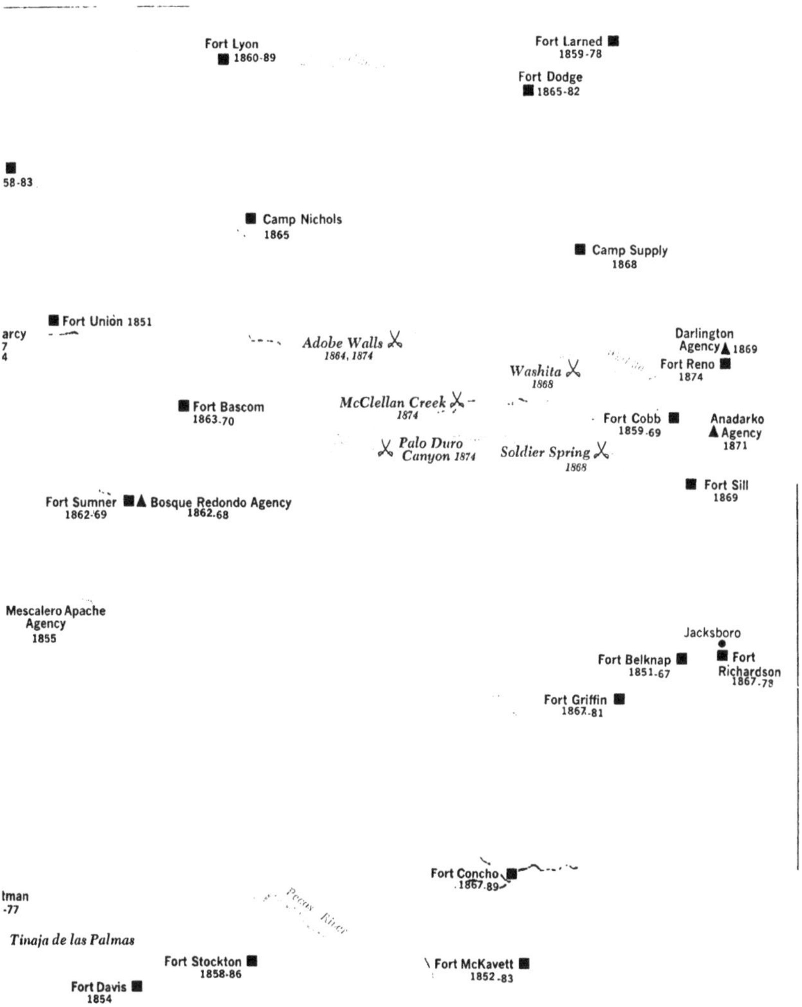

Fort Lyon
■ 1860-89

Fort Larned ■
1859-78

Fort Dodge
■ 1865-82

■
58-83

■ Camp Nichols
1865

■ Camp Supply
1868

arcy
7
4

■ Fort Union 1851

Adobe Walls ✂
1864, 1874

Darlington
Agency ▲ 1869
Fort Reno ■
1874

Washita ✂
1868

■ Fort Bascom
1863-70

McClellan Creek ✂
1874

· Fort Cobb ■
1859-69

Anadarko
▲ Agency
1871

✂ Palo Duro
Canyon 1874

Soldier Spring ✂
1868

■ Fort Sill
1869

Fort Sumner ■▲ Bosque Redondo Agency
1862-69   1862-68

Mescalero Apache
Agency
1855

Jacksboro
•
Fort Belknap ■ ■ Fort
1851-67   Richardson
1867-78

Fort Griffin ■
1867-81

Fort Concho ■
.1867-89

tman
-77

Pecos River

Tinaja de las Palmas

Fort Stockton ■
1858-86

\ Fort McKavett ■
1852-83

Fort Davis ■
1854

Fort Mohave, Arizona ⊗

*Location: Mohave County, on the west fork of an unim-
proved road, about 5 miles south of Roger's Landing.*

Active in the years 1859–90, this hardship post was founded near
the head of the Mohave Valley on the east bank of the Colorado
River at Beale's Crossing, which had been forded in 1857 by Edward F. Beale's camel caravan en route to California. The destruction by the Mohave Indians of an emigrant train trying Beale's
route the next spring resulted in the activation of the fort by an
expedition that came up the Colorado from Fort Yuma, Calif.,
and faced immediate Indian attacks. Until the garrison burned
the post and departed at the beginning of the Civil War, it kept
watch over the restless Indians and protected stages and the sel-
dom-used emigrant road. The clamor of settlers for security from
hostile Mohaves and Paiutes resulted in the reactivation of the
fort in 1863.

The site, on the Fort Mohave Indian Reservation, is privately
owned. The only recognizable remains are sidewalks; remnants of
drainage ditches and the water system; and the littered cemetery,
which no longer contains soldier burials.

Apache scouts, somewhere in Arizona. Date unknown.

73

Fort Whipple, Arizona ⊗

Location: Yavapai County, at the junction of U.S. 89 and Ariz. 69, about 1 mile east of Prescott.

Centrally located in Arizona, this fort was the nerve center of the early campaigns that sought to quell the Apaches. It served as the residence and main headquarters of department commanders George Crook and George Stoneman, who maintained field headquarters nearer the scene of the action. The garrison's outstanding achievement was its victory in the Battle of the Big Dry Wash (1882). Occupying two different sites, the post was known at various times and sometimes simultaneously as Camp and Fort Whipple, Camp Clark, Whipple Depot, Prescott Barracks, and Whipple Barracks. In December 1863 California Volunteers founded it as Fort Whipple, 24 miles northeast of the site of Prescott, to protect miners. The following month, when governmental officials arrived, it became the temporary capital of newly created Arizona Territory.

The next May the fort, along with the Territorial government, moved southward to Granite Creek, east of future Prescott, which grew up as the Territorial capital. In 1870 Whipple Depot, a quartermaster installation that had been established adjacent to the fort, became a separate command. In 1879 Fort Whipple was redesignated as Whipple Barracks, which was garrisoned until 1898 and in the 1902–22 period. The Public Health Service then acquired it for hospital purposes.

A Veterans' Administration hospital today, Fort Whipple consists of a large number of brick and stone buildings, most dating from 1904, that are used as staff residences, offices, and patients' quarters. The site of the original stockade is marked.

Hubbell Trading Post National Historic Site, Arizona ⊠

Location: Apache County, on Ariz. 264, about 1 mile west of Ganado; address: P.O. Box 298, Ganado, Ariz. 86505.

This national historic site preserves the Hubbell Trading Post, still an active trading post after serving the Navajo Indians for more than 90 years, as a living example of a reservation trading

Hubbell Trading Post National Historic Site.

post of yesterday. It typifies the role of such posts in Indian life and their contributions to the acculturative process.

The reservation trading post was the final manifestation of the Indian trade, a dominant factor in shaping the history of the North American Continent. From the earliest times, when the trade provided a motive for European colonization and influenced the course of subsequent colonial expansion, the trader achieved an importance among the Indian tribes unequaled by any other white man. After the American Revolution, large fur companies, operating out of isolated frontier outposts, gained the ascendancy over independent fur traders and triumphed over the Government's "factory" system. The companies dominated the trade for more than half a century until the advance of settlement and the beginning of the Indian wars destroyed their pattern of operations. Roving traders, often unscrupulous men bartering arms, ammunition, and liquor for Indian furs and goods, came to predominate. Gradually, between 1840 and 1890, as one tribe after another capitulated to the Army and were confined on reservations, the roving traders vanished.

Perhaps even more influential than his predecessors was the reservation trader, who was licensed by the Government and set up permanent posts on reservations amid newly conquered tribes. Not only did he supply the Indians with the white man's goods, but he helped them adapt their economy to reservation life, transmitted to them aspects of white civilization and material culture, and aided them in adjusting to their new way of life. In carrying out these activities, he also helped the U.S. Government fulfill its objectives in setting up reservations—to control and "civilize" the Indians.

The owner of Hubbell Trading Post for more than 50 years, John Lorenzo Hubbell, the "King of Northern Arizona," epitomized the reservation trader. The son of a Connecticut Yankee who had married into a New Mexico family of Spanish descent, Hubbell was born in Pajarito, N. Mex., in 1853. In the early 1870's he traveled throughout northern Arizona and southeastern Utah and became familiar with the customs and language of the Navajos. He worked for a time as a clerk in a Mormon trading post and in 1874 as an interpreter at the Navajo Agency at Fort Defiance, Ariz. In 1878, 2 years after he began trading in Arizona, he purchased William Leonard's trading post west of Ganado, the site of the present post. A shrewd businessman and beyond question the dean of the Navajo traders, Hubbell eventually built up a trading empire that included 14 trading posts, a wholesale house in Winslow, Ariz., and a stage and freight line. The hospitality of "Lorenzo the Magnificent," as Theodore Roosevelt dubbed him, was legendary throughout the Southwest and nearly everyone of importance who passed through northeastern Arizona visited him at his post. He was also active in county, State, and national politics.

But the most important aspect of Hubbell's personality and career was his friendship with the Navajo people. Coming to the reservation at a critical time in the history of the Navajos, when the suffering of the "Long Walk" and confinement at Fort Sumner, N. Mex., was still fresh in their minds, more than any other man he helped them adjust to reservation life. From the beginning they flocked to the post, where he was not only their merchant, but was also their teacher in understanding the ways of the white man and often their spokesman and contact with the outside world. He translated and wrote letters for them, arbitrated family quarrels, explained Government policy, and cared for the sick. Once he dined 300 Navajos in his hacienda. One of his most significant achievements was encouraging them to develop craftwork, especially silversmithing and blanket and rug weaving, into profitable industries that provided the basis for a sound economy. Although a devout Roman Catholic, Hubbell was instrumental in persuading the Presbyterian Church to establish in 1901 a mission and school in Ganado and even took the missionaries into his home for a year while the mission was being built.

Hubbell's death in 1930 was mourned by the Navajos probably more than that of any other white man they had known. He was buried on Hubbell Hill, overlooking the trading post, next to his wife and his closest Navajo Friend, Many Horses. Members of his family continued to operate the post. Shortly after World War II, trading posts on the Navajo Reservation began to decline as the customs of the inhabitants modernized.

In the National Park System since 1965, Hubbell Trading Post,

John Lorenzo Hubbell trading for a Navajo blanket about 1905.

surrounded by the Navajo Reservation, is still operated as an active trading post by the Southwestern Monuments Association under an agreement with the National Park Service. Barely changed since Hubbell completed the present post about 1900 to replace an earlier, smaller structure, it helps the visitor to visualize and understand the pattern of Navajo trade, the type of man who conducted it, and the kind of life he lived. The long, stone trading post, with its wareroom, storeroom, office, and rugroom, appears much as it did in Hubbell's time and resembles other Navajo trading posts. The original massive counters still dominate the storeroom; the office furniture is more than half a century old; and the rugroom contains antique firearms, Indian craftwork, paintings, and a variety of rugs. Hubbell's rambling adobe hacienda retains all its charm and portrays the manner in which reservation traders lived. The barn and utility buildings, most of stone construction, round out the picture of a trading post of yesteryear.

Pipe Spring National Monument, Arizona ☒

Location: Mohave County, on Ariz. 389, about 15 miles southwest of Fredonia; address: c/o Southern Utah Group, National Park Service, P.O. Box 749, Cedar City, Utah 84720.

The Mormon extension southward from the Salt Lake Basin and the achievements of the southwestern pioneers are exemplified in this national monument. In the 1850's the Mormons began dispersing from the basin to locations in southern Utah and northern Arizona that provided water. As centers of defense against Indian attacks and way stations for travelers, they established at strategic locations a series of forts, such as Pipe Spring in Arizona and Cove Fort and Fort Deseret in Utah. Pipe Spring National Monument contains probably the best remaining example of such a fort.

Although the Domínguez-Escalante Expedition of 1776 passed nearby, the first white men known to have visited Pipe Spring were members of the Jacob Hamblin party, who camped there in 1858. They had been sent out by Brigham Young to explore and

Pipe Spring National Monument.

report on the Colorado River country and to try to negotiate a treaty of peace with the Navajos living on the south side of the river. Between 1863 and 1865 Pipe Spring was the headquarters of a cattle ranch run by a Mormon, but some marauding Navajos killed the inhabitants.

In 1869 the Mormon Church acquired the property. Within a couple of years Bishop Anson P. Winsor built a fort that became known as "Winsor Castle." It consisted of two redstone buildings, two stories high, facing each other across a courtyard. Sandstone walls and heavy gates enclosed its sides. The firing platform just below the top of one wall and the associated loopholes remaining today were designed to withstand Indian attacks. A continuous flow of water was insured, for one of the buildings stood directly over a spring. Bishop Winsor left Pipe Spring about 1875. The place became important as a cattle ranch and as the starting point for cattle drives to the railroad at Lund, Utah, about 100 miles away.

Park rangers conduct tours of the fort and outbuildings. Exhibits feature pioneer tools and furnishings.

Salt River Canyon (Skeleton Cave) Battlefield, Arizona ⊗

Location: Maricopa County, in Salt River Canyon, near Horse Mesa Dam. The dam is bounded on the east by Apache Lake and on the southwest by Canyon Lake (Salt River). The site is accessible only with great difficulty and the aid of guides, by boat from Canyon Lake or by unimproved road from the town of Horse Mesa.

The Army won its most striking victory in the long history of Apache warfare at this site, where Gen. George Crook also tasted triumph in his Tonto Basin campaign. At dawn on December 28, 1872, a 130-man force, consisting of about two companies of the 5th Cavalry from Fort McDowell and Old Camp Grant and 30 Apache scouts under the command of Capt. William H. Brown, surprised a band of more than a hundred Yavapais as they tried to emerge from a cave deep in the recesses of Salt River Canyon. The trapped Indians refused to surrender. Some of Brown's men shot at the roof of the cave and deflected a deadly fire into the defenders. Other soldiers completed the destruction by rolling boulders over the cliffs above. About 75 Indians died, and most of the rest were captured. This victory, along with Crook's other aggressive measures, so lowered the morale of the Yavapais that on April 6, 1873, they made peace at Camp Verde.

The natural setting is unimpaired. The cave lies on the north wall of the canyon in the angle of a sharp turn to the south. Access is gained by climbing a steep mountainside, crossing a lava bed, and descending from the rim of the gorge by a trail on the face of the cliff. The cave is an elliptical undercut about 65 by 25 feet, situated at the base of a cliff 170 feet high and at the top of a steep slope falling away some 1,200 feet to the water below. The cave's ceiling is blackened from the smoke of Indian fires and scarred by carbine bullets. The U.S. Bureau of Reclamation has jurisdiction over the site.

Skeleton Canyon, Arizona ⊗

Location: Cochise County, on an unimproved road, about 8 miles southeast of the hamlet of Apache.

In this canyon, a favorite Apache haunt in southeastern Arizona, the Chiricahuas Geronimo and Natchez, son of Cochise and hereditary chief of the tribe, surrendered to Gen. Nelson A. Miles on September 3, 1886. Lasting peace had come to the Southwest. For all practical purposes the Apache wars had ended and, except for the Sioux outbreak of 1890, so had the Indian wars. The weary warriors, after being harried throughout the Sierra Madre all summer by Capt. Henry W. Lawton's picked troops, were receptive to peace overtures. Lt. Charles B. Gatewood, who had befriended Geronimo, and two Chiricahua Apache scouts set out from Fort Bowie. Meeting with Geronimo and Natchez near Fronteras, Mexico, they induced them to surrender to General Miles. Lawton's command escorted them northward to Skeleton Canyon, 35 miles southeast of Fort Bowie, where the ceremony occurred. Lawton then took the captives to the fort, from where they were shipped to Florida for imprisonment.

A cairn of rocks, 6 feet high, overgrown with mesquite, marks the surrender site. The cairn stands on a bench just south of the creek that flows out of Skeleton Canyon, 100 yards east of a privately owned ranch and barn and immediately above a stock pond and corral. The ranch facilities constitute a minor intrusion, but the desert character of the terrain is little changed from the historic period. A large stone monument on U.S. 80 at Apache commemorates the site.

Yuma Crossing, Arizona-California ⚠

> *Location: Yuma County, Ariz., and Imperial County, Calif. The crossing is between the U.S. 80 and old highway bridges over the Colorado River in the vicinity of two small islands at a point directly below the proposed I-8 bridge. Other associated sites are in the city of Yuma, Ariz., and in Imperial County, Calif., in the vicinity of the city of Winterhaven.*

From historic times to the present this crossing near the mouth of the Gila River, the only natural crossing of the Colorado River in the southern desert region, has been a major entry route—for covered wagons, railroads, and automobiles—into California from the southeast and one of the most strategic transportation-com-

*George H. Baker's lithograph of Yuma Crossing in
its heyday, about 1870. Ferry masts are in foreground.
Fort Yuma stands on hill across the river.*

munication gateways in the West. During the last half of the
19th century, Fort Yuma and the Yuma Quartermaster Depot
were situated adjacent to it.

Prehistoric Indian trails converged at the crossing, over which
passed many Spanish explorers beginning in 1540. In 1774 it became a stopping point on a newly pioneered route from Tubac,
Ariz., to Los Angeles. In 1779 Father Francisco Garcés founded a
mission on the California side of the river. Two years later the
Spaniards added a presidio and colony, but that same year the
Yuma Indians destroyed the settlement. The extreme hostility of
the Yumas, Mohaves, Apaches, and other Indians in the region
prevented much further Spanish or Mexican (1821–48) use of the
crossing, though after 1826 it was on a Sonora (Mexico)-Califor-
nia route used by Mexican traders and mail carriers. Gen. Stephen W. Kearny's Army of the West, en route to California in
1846, forded at the crossing, as did Lt. Col. Philip St. George
Cooke's Mormon Battalion the next year.

Traffic over the crossing boomed following the discovery of
gold in California in 1848, the same year the United States acquired the Southwest from Mexico. Thousands of prospectors and
other emigrants moved over the Southern Transcontinental Trail

in covered wagons and stages. The flow of traffic fostered the operation of various ferries across the river, the most important being that of Louis J. F. Jaeger (or Yager). He conducted his business from 1850 until 1877, when the Southern Pacific Railroad bridged the river and brought an end to most trail traffic and ferry operation.

Meantime, in 1850, the Army had also reacted to the emigration by establishing Fort Yuma on the California side of the river to protect travelers. For the first 4 months the fort was located about one-half mile below the mouth of the Gila, but it was then moved to its permanent site on a bluff overlooking the junction of the Gila and Colorado. Yuma Indian attacks in 1850–51 and supply problems caused the fort's abandonment, but it was reoccupied the next year. Its garrison, serving at a post that had the reputation as the hottest in the West, mainly escorted emigrants. Situated on the Mexican border, it was also involved in customs and immigration matters. In 1858–61 it was a stopping point of the Butterfield Overland Mail, which established a stage station on the California edge of the river.

Soon after the founding of the fort, the town of Colorado City grew up across the river in Arizona. Later renamed Arizona City and then Yuma, it became a major way station on the overland trail and a terminal point for the busy steamboat traffic that supplied Fort Yuma beginning in 1852, when steamboats were successfully introduced on the Colorado River. Ships from California ports rounded Lower California and sailed up the Gulf of California to the mouth of the river, from where flat-bottomed river steamers took the cargoes upriver to Yuma. Jaeger's Ferry Landing, on the south bank, became the steamboat landing.

For these reasons in 1864 the Army established the Yuma Quartermaster Depot, Ariz., adjacent to Jaeger's Landing. The depot distributed supplies, received on ships from California, by freight wagon to Arizona forts. It was also a quartering place for mules, sometimes as many as 900 being on hand. Destroyed by fire in 1867, the depot was immediately rebuilt and functioned until the late 1880's. From 1908 until 1954 it served as a customs house and immigration checkpoint. Fort Yuma's importance had diminished following the Civil War, during which California Volunteers replaced the Regular troops. After the war, the fort was mainly a supply and personnel depot. The Army evacuated it in 1882, and 2 years later the Indian Bureau assumed jurisdiction.

In the years 1876–1909 the Arizona Territorial Prison, a symbol of harsh frontier justice, stood atop a barren cliff overlooking the river just east of Jaeger's Landing. Housing notorious frontier desperadoes and a peak population of 376 prisoners, the prison enjoyed a reputation paralleling that of Alcatraz in later times. The Territorial prison's adobe walls were 18 feet high and 8 feet thick at the base. The stone cell blocks, naked to the desert heat, were guarded at two corners by towers mounting Gatling guns, which prevented several escapes.

Modern structures on both sides of the river and powerlines crossing it have impaired the natural setting of historic Yuma Crossing. On the California side of the river where the old highway and railroad bridges cross, about a dozen adobe buildings from the late military period are grouped around the parade ground at Fort Yuma, a registered State historical landmark that is today the agency headquarters of the Fort Yuma (Quechan)

Modern view of barracks at Fort Yuma, Calif.

84

Indian Reservation. Many of the structures have been altered and some are in poor condition, but they are all of considerable architectural interest. Surrounding and linking them are verandas, designed to preclude the need to walk in the sun.

About a quarter of a mile west of the historic crossing in Arizona are several adobe and plaster buildings that were once part of the Yuma Quartermaster Depot. Owned by the city of Yuma, some are unoccupied and the U.S. Bureau of Reclamation uses others. Just east of the crossing at the south end of the old railroad and old highway bridges directly opposite Fort Yuma is another interesting complex, the Arizona Territorial Prison, a unit of the Arizona park system. Originally constructed of adobe and stone, much of it is now in partial ruins. One restored building serves as a museum. Of special interest are the guard tower, several banks of cell blocks, and the entrance gate.

Fort Smith National Historic Site, Arkansas ⊠

Location: Sebastian County. The visitor center is located on Rogers Avenue between Second and Third Streets, city of Fort Smith. Address: P.O. Box 1406, Fort Smith, Ark. 72901.

Fort Smith, one of the first U.S. military posts in the area of the Louisiana Purchase, was one of those making up the "Permanent Indian Frontier" in the first half of the 19th century. For nearly fourscore years, from 1817 to 1890—first as a military post and then as the seat of a Federal district court—it was a center of law and order for a wide expanse of untamed western frontier. At the fort, soldier, Indian, lawman, and outlaw played their parts in the drama that changed the face of the Indian country; blue-clad troopers marched out to carry the U.S. flag westward; and U.S. deputy marshals, the men who "rode for Judge Parker," crossed the Poteau River to bring justice to the lawless lands of Indian Territory beyond. Fort Smith National Historic Site preserves the site of the small first Fort Smith (1817–33), the remains of the enlarged second fort (1839–71), and the building that housed the Federal district court (1872–90)—all reminders of the day when civilization and security ended on the banks of the Arkansas and

Poteau Rivers and when men were carving the Nation out of the wilderness.

Fort Smith was one of a series of forts founded along the frontier by the U.S. Government after the War of 1812 (1812–14), when the normal pattern of westward expansion resumed, to protect settlers, control the Indians, and foster the growth of the fur trade. The first Fort Smith was established in 1817 in Missouri Territory, which at that time included present Arkansas, on a rocky bluff at Belle Point—which French traders had named *La Belle Pointe*—at the junction of the Poteau and Arkansas Rivers. Completed in 1822, the first fort was a simple wooden stockaded structure with two two-story blockhouses.

The fort's primary mission was to keep peace between the Osage and Cherokee Indians and to prevent white encroachment on Indian lands. The restless Cherokees, who in 1808 had begun crossing the Mississippi River and moving into present northwestern Arkansas, had penetrated Osage hunting grounds. A threat of war continually existed between the two tribes, but the Fort Smith troops were able to control the situation. In 1819, only 2 years after the post's founding, it was the scene of a peace meeting between Osages and Cherokees, and a bloody war was averted

Sketch of Fort Smith in 1865, from the October 7 edition of Frank Leslie's Illustrated Newspaper.

when the Army insisted that the Cherokees return some hostages. In 1824, by which time the frontier had shifted farther westward, the garrison departed and moved 80 miles up the Arkansas River to the mouth of the Grand River, where it founded Fort Gibson, Okla. Small detachments returned sporadically to Fort Smith until 1833 to aid in the construction of military roads and to attempt to curb the illegal liquor traffic into Indian country, but the fort rapidly deteriorated.

In 1836 Arkansas became a State and the demands of its citizens for protection against possible Indian uprisings caused Congress 2 years later to authorize the War Department to build a second Fort Smith, a larger and more impressive installation adjacent to the earlier fort. Construction began in 1839 but because of the opposition of Col. Zachary Taylor, appointed the departmental commander in 1841, and other military officials, work proceeded slowly. The Army ultimately modified its plans and made the fort a supply depot. Completed and garrisoned in May 1846, the second Fort Smith equipped and provisioned other forts to the west in Indian Territory.

Fort Smith was also the base for the first two of Capt. Randolph B. Marcy's exploration and military reconnaissance expeditions. In 1849 he escorted a party of gold seekers over the Fort Smith-Santa Fe Route and on the return trip pioneered the El Paso-Fort Smith Route, which came to be known as the Butterfield Route and replaced the more northerly Fort Smith-Santa Fe segment of the Southern Overland Trail. In 1850–51 he reconnoitered the Texas-Oklahoma frontier to select sites for an outer string of military posts to safeguard the advance of settlement and protect the Choctaws and Chickasaws from depredations by Plains Indians. This led to the founding of Fort Arbuckle, Okla., and Forts Belknap and Phantom Hill, Tex., the first links in a chain of posts that eventually stretched from the Red River to El Paso. Fort Smith also provided minor logistical support for Marcy's third expedition, along the Canadian and Red Rivers, from Fort Belknap. During the Civil War both the North and South used Fort Smith's supply and hospital facilities, but in 1871 the War Department abandoned it.

That same year the U.S. Court for the Western District of Arkansas moved from Van Buren to the town of Fort Smith, which 87

*Old Commissary Building, Fort Smith National
Historic Site.*

had grown up adjacent to the fort. The next year it occupied the
abandoned barracks building and subsequently added a second
story and jail wing. For the next 25 years, the town of Fort Smith
was a center of law and order on the frontier. The court had jurisdiction over part of Arkansas, where State courts shared its
sphere of authority, but its primary influence and authority were
felt in Indian Territory. Although the Indians had their own
tribal courts, these had no jurisdiction over white men and no
other system of law existed. Thus the area was a sanctuary from arrest or extradition for the most desperate class of criminals from
all over the United States. Disorder ruled, and reputable men—
white and Indian—urgently appealed to the Federal Government
for relief.

In 1875 the youthful and vigorous Judge Isaac C. Parker, who
came to be known as the "Hangin' Judge," arrived at Fort Smith
and tackled the problem of crime in Indian Territory. For 21
years he dispensed swift justice with an iron hand. Gradually,
however, judicial authority in Indian Territory was divided

among Parker's court and other Federal courts at Paris, Tex., and at Wichita and Fort Scott, Kans. In 1896 it received its own judicial districts and courts. That same year, 6 years after Parker had moved his court to a new building near the fort, his court was dissolved. The passing of the Parker court followed closely on the vanishing of the frontier.

No surface remains of the first Fort Smith are extant, though archeological excavation has revealed its exact location and stone foundations of one blockhouse and the walls. Visible at Belle Point are the quarries that were the source of stone for the second fort. The only significant remains of this post are the old commissary building and the altered barracks building that later housed the Federal district court and is now the Fort Smith Visitor Center. The former, used by the Army until 1871 and now housing a museum, was built of stone between 1839 and 1846. Originally intended as the north bastion of the fort, before completion it was converted into a commissary. Except for minor alterations, it appears much as it originally did. Soldiers erected half of the second building in the early 1850's for a barracks, on the foundations of a larger barracks building that had been destroyed by fire in 1849. In 1872 the Federal district court occupied it. The other half of the two-story brick building is a later addition.

Of special interest is Judge Parker's courtroom, in the visitor center, which has been restored to its original appearance. In nearby Fort Smith National Cemetery, established during the Civil War, rest a number of Federal and Confederate dead from Civil War battlefields of northwestern Arkansas, as well as the remains of Judge Parker.

Benicia Barracks and Arsenal, California ⊗
Location: Solano County, eastern edge of Benicia.

Until inactivated in 1963 the modern Army installation known as Benicia Arsenal included what were once two separate posts, Benicia Barracks (1849–1908) and Benicia Arsenal (1851–1963). The barracks, established at the western end of Suisun Bay as an infantry base in 1849, was one of the first military posts in California. Two years later, to support troops scattered along the Pacific coast

Arsenal ("Clocktower") Building (1859), Benicia
Arsenal, as it appears today.

conducting exploration and combating Indians, the Army founded adjacent to the barracks an ordnance supply depot, the first in the Far West, for the Pacific Division. The next year, 1852, the depot was officially designated an arsenal. It soon had a quartermaster depot associated with it. The barracks remained a garrisoned infantry post until 1898, when its troops departed for duty in the Philippines. In 1908 the arsenal absorbed it.

Throughout its existence the barracks-arsenal was a primary staging area and logistical support center for the Western United States and the Pacific area—in the Indian wars, Civil War, Spanish-American War, World Wars I and II, and the Korean conflict. For slightly more than 3 years during two separate periods in the 1850's Benicia was the headquarters of the Army's Department of the Pacific, before and after that time located at the Presidio of San Francisco. William T. Sherman, George Crook, and Ulysses S. Grant served at the arsenal as young lieutenants; Col. James W. Benét, father of the poets William Rose and Stephen Vincent, was commanding officer. And the Army's camel experiment in

California ended at the arsenal, where the camels were assembled in 1863 and sold at public auction the next year.

The old barracks and arsenal are both registered State historical landmarks. In 1965, or 2 years after the Army inactivated the arsenal, it conveyed the installation to the city of Benicia. The city has leased it to a corporation, which has modified some of the buildings. All of them are open to exterior inspection, but may not be entered except by permission. To facilitate a walking tour, the corporation has published a brochure on the history of the buildings. The barracks and arsenal sites are situated about one-quarter mile apart. Extant on 252 acres of the 2,200 acres that comprised the military reservation are 21 one- and two-story structures, four of frame and 17 of brick and sandstone, that were constructed between 1854 and 1884. One of these, the hospital, believed to be the first military hospital on the Pacific coast, in which Indian war casualties were treated, is at the barracks; and the remainder at the arsenal. Three other buildings date from 1900, 1909, and 1911.

Practically all the structures were used for modern arsenal purposes. They are all in excellent condition, have been little altered, and suffer only from minor intrusions. As a whole they provide an outstanding example of military architecture, especially of arsenals, in the last half of the 19th century. Buildings of historical interest, besides the hospital, include the arsenal; headquarters building; the commanding officer's quarters; various shops and warehouses, among them those that housed the camels in 1863–64; various officers' quarters; barracks; powder magazines; and guardhouse. Burials in the post cemetery date from the 1850's.

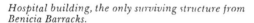

Hospital building, the only surviving structure from Benicia Barracks.

91

Fort Bidwell, California ⊗

Location: Modoc County, town of Fort Bidwell.

Tucked into the extreme northeastern corner of California, Fort Bidwell (1865–93) was founded by Volunteer troops to protect settlers and emigrants from the Indians of northern California, southern Oregon, and western Nevada. In the 1890's the log post spread slightly to the south of its original location, and a town grew up around it. Its garrison fought with Gen. George Crook at the nearby Battle of Infernal Caverns in September 1867, during his 1866–68 Snake campaign, and in the wars against the Modocs (1872–73), Nez Perces (1877), and Bannocks (1878). The Indian Bureau succeeded the Army at the post and utilized it for a boarding school, which was operated until 1930. In that year the original two-story barracks, later a school dormitory, was razed.

All that remains, in varying states of preservation, are the stable; a school, now a private residence; a few other buildings; a graveyard; and the parade ground. The site, headquarters of the Fort Bidwell Indian Reservation and a registered State historical landmark, is marked by a monument.

Fort Bragg, California ⊗

Location: Mendocino County, Main Street, town of Fort Bragg.

The major mission of the small garrison assigned to this coastal fort, established in 1857 on the Mendocino Indian Reservation, was control of the reservation. When the post was but a year old, its troops took part in the campaign in eastern Washington. At the beginning of the Civil War, California Volunteers replaced the Regulars and in 1864, by which time most of the Indians had departed from the reservation, abandoned it. Three years later the Government opened the lands to settlement, and the town of Fort Bragg grew up around the site.

A State marker commemorating the fort, a registered State historical landmark, is located near the hospital site, at 321 Main Street. Main Street bisects the site of the parade ground, bounded on the north by Laurel Street between Franklin and McPherson and on the south at a point about 100 feet south of Redwood Street.

Fort Humboldt, California ⊗

Location: Humboldt County, just off U.S. 101, southern edge of Eureka.

This fort, active in the years 1853–67 and located on a bluff overlooking Humboldt Bay and the Pacific, was the Army headquarters and logistics base for northern California and one of the few posts in the area. Lt. George Crook arrived with the first detachment, and Capt. Ulysses S. Grant served at the post during the years 1853–54. The garrison served in the second Rogue River War (1855–56), in Oregon.

Nothing remains of Fort Humboldt on the actual fort site. The only extant structure of any sort is the remodeled hospital, which has been shifted slightly from its original location. State offices now occupy it. Markers indicate officers' row. A bronze tablet on a boulder, placed by the Daughters of the American Revolution, marks the site. It is a registered State historical landmark and State historical monument.

Fort Jones, California ⊗

Location: Siskiyou County, East Side Road, about one-half mile south of the town of Fort Jones.

Fort Jones (1852–58), a small post in the Scott River Valley of north-central California, was founded to protect gold miners from the Indians. Two young officers who served there were Lt. George Crook and Capt. Ulysses S. Grant. The troops participated in the 1858 campaign in eastern Washington; the first (1853) and second (1855–56) Rogue River Wars, in Oregon; and the 1857 campaign against the Pit River Indians, in the northeastern part of California.

All traces of the post, originally of log and later of frame, have disappeared. A flagpole and commemorative marker, erected by Siskiyou County, indicate the site, a registered State historical landmark.

93

Fort Tejon, California ⊗

Location: Kern County, on I-5 (Calif. 99), about 38 miles south of Bakersfield.

Near Tejon Pass along one of the routes running north from Los Angeles to the northern goldfields. Fort Tejon (1854–64) protected travelers and settlers; was a station on the Butterfield Overland Mail (1858–59); patrolled the area for cattle rustlers and horse thieves; served as a social and political center for a large area in central California; and controlled the Indians living on the Tejon (Sebastian) Indian Reservation. The reservation, founded in 1853 about 20 miles to the north by Edward F. Beale, Superintendent of Indian Affairs for California and Nevada (1852–56), was a governmental experiment he conceived in Indian management. It was the first of a series of small but well-defined reservations where Indians were to be concentrated and taught farming and trades so they could become self-sufficient. Beale's successors established a few other reservations, but mismanagement weakened practically all of them. The Fort Tejon Reservation was disbanded in 1863.

Meantime Fort Tejon had entered a new era in 1857 when Beale, while surveying for the Army a proposed wagon road across the Southwest, brought a 25-camel caravan from Camp Verde, Tex., to the scene of his earlier reservation experiment. The camels were later also quartered at Drum Barracks (Camp Drum), at present Wilmington, Calif., and other installations in southern California. They transported supplies between Fort Tejon and Drum Barracks, as well as between other posts. The outbreak of the Civil War and other factors ended the experiment. In 1861 the Army inactivated Fort Tejon, the camels temporarily went to other posts, and in 1863 were transported to Benicia Arsenal, Calif., and sold there the next year at public auction.

The year before, Volunteers from Camp Independence, Calif., had regarrisoned Fort Tejon to control 1,000 Indians they had removed from the Owens River Valley. By the middle of 1864, dissatisfied with conditions, most of the latter had returned to the valley. Evacuated that same year by the Army, Fort Tejon became part of the Rancho Castac and 2 years later part of Rancho El

Tejon, owned by Beale, who used its buildings as residences and stables.

Fort Tejon State Historical Park is also a registered State historical landmark. It features three restored adobe buildings: a barracks, an officers' quarters, and a building that probably was an orderly's residence. Adobe ruins mark the sites of other buildings. A visitor center displays exhibits.

Lava Beds National Monument, California ⊞

Location: Siskiyou and Modoc Counties, accessible via Calif. 139 and secondary roads; address: P.O. Box 867, Tulelake, Calif. 96134.

This national monument, consisting of more than 46,000 acres of solidified lava flow, is geologically as well as historically interesting. The major events of the Modoc War (1872–73), one of the

Journalists often accompanied troops on the Indian frontier. Here a San Francisco Bulletin *correspondent poses with soldiers in California's lava beds during the Modoc War.*

95

last Indian-soldier clashes in the Pacific Northwest, occurred within its boundaries.

The Modocs, aroused by the intrusion of emigrants, settlers, and ranchers into their homeland on the Lost River along the California-Oregon boundary north of Tule Lake, reacted by a series of assaults on the newcomers. Public demand for their removal heightened. In 1864 they agreed to relocate to the newly opened Klamath Indian Reservation, on Oregon's Upper Klamath Lake. Spurred by repeated conflicts with the Klamath Indians, the following year Captain Jack and most of the Modocs fled to their home country, about 35 miles southeastward. There they resided for 4 years in uneasy coexistence with the settlers and ranchers. In 1869 U.S. officials convinced them to return to the reservation. Still unable to reconcile intertribal differences, the next year they again headed tor the Lost River. For 2 years, U.S. representatives pressured Captain Jack to move back onto the reservation.

Finally, late in November 1872, troops from Fort Klamath, Oreg., proceeded to Captain Jack's village, on the west side of the Lost River near its mouth, at the northwestern corner of Tule Lake, to coerce the band. But, before any discussion could take place, firing broke out on both sides. Some settlers then attacked a second Modoc village, on the east bank of the river. Captain Jack's group retreated southward across Tule Lake in canoes, and the other band traveled by horseback around the eastern side of the lake. Uniting in the north-central region of the lava beds they took cover in a natural fortress of caves, crevices, and twisted masses of lava rock that came to be known as Captain Jack's Stronghold. They managed to exist by eating a herd of cattle they discovered and found other ways to keep alive. On January 17, 1873, about 300 Regular and Volunteer troops opened an attack. Yet the Indians, numbering only 70 or so, repelled them.

Late that month the Secretary of War halted military operations to allow a Department of the Interior peace commission, which included the military department commander, Brig. Gen. Edward R. S. Canby, to try negotiation. At the third truce meeting, on April 11, after a brief exchange of words, the Modocs killed General Canby and another commissioner, the Reverend Eleasar Thomas, both of whom were strong advocates of fair treat-

*Gen. Edward R. S. Canby,
who died with Rev.
Eleasar Thomas at the
hands of the Modocs
while serving as a peace
commissioner.*

*Assassination of the Modoc War peace commissioners,
a sketch originally appearing in the* London Times
and reprinted in Harper's Weekly *(June 28, 1873).*

ment of the Modocs. The rest of the party managed to escape, but the eastern humanitarians whose prodding had brought about the peacemaking attempt, as well as President Grant's Peace Policy, suffered setbacks.

On April 15 about 650 soldiers launched a second assault on the stronghold. When they captured it 2 days later, they found it deserted. For weeks they pursued the band throughout the lava beds and the surrounding region, clashed with it several times, and took a few captives. Eventually the harassed Modocs surrendered. The soldiers apprehended Captain Jack on June 1 and transported him to Fort Klamath, where he and five others stood trial and were convicted of murder. President Grant commuted the sentences of two of them to life imprisonment. In October Captain Jack and three other leaders died on the gallows. Troops escorted the surviving Modocs to a reservation in Indian Territory, and the Pacific Northwest gained several years of peace—but only at the expense of a campaign that had been prolonged beyond all expectations and proved very costly to the military, which suffered 126 casualties.

Museum exhibits, markers, and self-guiding trails interpret the park's geology and history. Noteworthy sites are those of Captain Jack's Stronghold, the Army base camp, the place of Canby's death, and the principal engagements. The terrain is essentially unchanged since the time of the Modoc War.

Presidio of San Francisco, California ⚑

> Location: San Francisco County, below the southern end
> of the Golden Gate Bridge, San Francisco.

The colorful history of this presidio, for almost two centuries the guardian of the finest harbor on the Pacific coast, spans the Spanish, Mexican, and American periods in California, from 1776 to the present. During all the wars and conflicts since the Mexican War—Indian, Civil, Spanish-Amercan, World Wars I and II, Korea, and Vietnam—the post has been a major coastal defense base and, except for a 3-year period in the 1850's, command headquarters for the Western United States and the Pacific area. It was in the latter capacity, particularly, that the presidio was involved with the Indian wars, though troops also fanned out from it to serve in the various campaigns.

The presidio's importance transcends the military and enters the realms of politics, economics, and diplomacy. Used by the Spaniards as a base for exploration and conquest, it figured prominently in their extension of settlement into northern California. The northern bastion of Spain's New World Empire, it was for many decades the chief barrier against British, Russian, and American expansion in California. Between 1821 and 1836, under Mexican rule, the presidio continued to be the military headquarters of northern California, but its strength gradually declined. In 1836, the year after the Mexican Government established Yerba Buena Pueblo (San Francisco) not far away and transferred the headquarters to Sonoma, it withdrew the garrison. The buildings disintegrated rapidly.

U.S. forces seized California in 1846· Early the following year troops garrisoned the presidio, repairing the remaining buildings and adding new ones. The next April it became a permanent post. By 1890, when it accommodated six artillery batteries, one cavalry troop, and two infantry companies, it had been permanently constructed of brick.

Two installations associated with the presidio are Fort Point (Fort Winfield Scott) and Fort Mason. The story of Fort Point traces back to the Spaniards, who established a castillo, or fort, on the site. During the years 1853–61 the U.S. Army razed the disintegrating castillo, lowered the face of the cliff on which it stood some 90 feet so that the new batteries could more easily fire on ships, and erected and immediately garrisoned the largest fortification of its kind on the Pacific coast, Fort Point.

During the years 1865–78 Fort Point was a subpost of the presidio and for a decade after 1868 was not garrisoned. The Army redesignated it Fort Winfield Scott in 1882, and 4 years later it again became a presidio subpost. In 1897 all the guns were removed. Seriously damaged by the San Francisco earthquake of 1906 and declared unsafe, the fort was abandoned by the Army in 1914, though it received some use during World Wars I and II. The modern Fort Winfield Scott Reservation, on the western side of the presidio, includes Fort Point.

The second major installation whose history merges with that

*Modern view of the Presidio of San Francisco and
Golden Gate Bridge.*

of the presidio, in Spanish times as today outside its boundaries, is
Fort Mason. Originally the site of a Spanish battery, it was later a
Civil War defense emplacement and the residence of prominent
generals.

In addition to sites and buildings associated with the Spanish-
Mexican period, various old Army buildings are extant at the
presidio. The oldest remaining structure is the hospital, built in
1854. The brick stables now serve as offices and storehouses. A
stone magazine dates from 1863. Fort Point is dwarfed by the
Golden Gate Bridge. Changed but slightly since the time of its
construction, it is one of the outstanding historical structures at
the presidio and a prime example of a 19th-century coastal fort.
The Fort Point Museum Association maintains a two-room museum. The modern headquarters building of Fort Winfield Scott
was completed in 1912, after the old brick fort was condemned.
The presidio is a registered State historical landmark.

The present 69-acre Fort Mason Reservation, under the jurisdiction of the General Services Administration and the Army, is
bounded by Van Ness Avenue and Bay and Lacuna Streets. Of

special interest is McDowell Hall (Brooks House No. 1), on the north side of MacArthur Avenue. A large two-story framehouse erected in 1855 and 9 years later converted into a duplex, it was the residence of 38 commanding generals of the Army's western headquarters from 1865 until 1943, including Gens. Irvin McDowell, Edward O. C. Ord, John Pope, Nelson A. Miles, and Arthur MacArthur. It is now an officers' mess.

Beecher's Island Battlefield, Colorado ⊗

Location: Yuma County, adjacent to the town of Beecher Island.

In an indecisive but bitterly fought battle at this site, a force of about 50 frontiersmen under Maj. George A. Forsyth engaged more than 1,000 Sioux and Cheyennes, led by Roman Nose, Pawnee Killer, and other chiefs. Pursued all the way from Fort Wallace, Kans., on September 16, 1868, the Indians turned on the troops, who entrenched themselves on a small sandy island in the Arikaree River. During the 9-day siege and the repeated Indian charges that followed, volunteers worked their way through enemy lines to obtain reinforcements from Fort Wallace, 125

Frederic Remington's version of the Battle of
Beecher's Island.

miles away, who drove off the Indians. Casualties were heavy on both sides. Half the soldiers were wounded, Forsyth four times. The dead included Roman Nose and Lt. Frederick W. Beecher, after whom the island came to be named. Immediately after this battle, Maj. Gen. Philip H. Sheridan began his 1868–69 winter campaign.

The island has long since disappeared because of shifting river channels, but a large monument near the post office at the town of Beecher Island commemorates the battle.

Bent's New Fort, Colorado ⊗

> *Location: Bent County, on a secondary road about 1½ miles south of U.S, 50, some 7 miles west of Lamar. Make local inquiry.*

William Bent abandoned Bent's Old Fort in 1849 and moved 38 miles down the Arkansas River to the Big Timbers locality, a favorite Cheyenne and Arapaho campground. There he erected a temporary log stockade on the north bank of the river and resumed trading. In 1852–53 he replaced the stockade with a permanent stone structure that came to be known as Bent's New Fort. Resembling Bent's Old Fort, but smaller, it consisted of 12 rooms surrounding a central courtyard. It had parapets but no bastions, and cannon were placed on the corners of the roof. The walls were 16 feet high. The fort was never a success, for by the time of its founding the Indian trade was rapidly decreasing. Emigrants, gold seekers, and increased freight traffic had made the Arkansas River a main-traveled highway. They felled the cottonwoods at Big Timbers and frightened away the game.

In 1860 troops began construction of Fort Wise (Fort Lyon No. 1) a mile southwest of Bent's post. Bent leased it to the Army and moved upriver to the mouth of the Purgatoire River, where he built a wooden stockade and lived until his death in 1869. The Army, which used Bent's New Fort as a commissary warehouse, erected extensive earthworks around it and diamond-shaped gun emplacements at the corners. In 1867 soldiers built Fort Lyon No. 2 near present Las Animas, Colo., and abandoned Fort Lyon No. 1 and Bent's New Fort.

The buildings of Bent's New Fort disintegrated many years ago, but their outlines are visible. Earthwork remains are substantial. A marker indicates the site, in private ownership.

Bent's Old Fort National Historic Site, Colorado ⊠

Location: Otero County, on Colo. 194, about 8 miles northeast of La Junta; address: P.O. Box 581, La Junta, Colo. 81050.

Bent's Old Fort, on the north bank of the Arkansas River in southeastern Colorado, was one of the most significant outposts on the Santa Fe Trail and as the principal outpost of American civilization on the southwestern Plains was instrumental in shaping national destiny there. In the heart of Indian country and buffalo hunting grounds and at the crossroads of key overland routes, it was a fur trading center and rendezvous for traders and Indians; a way station and supply center for emigrants and caravans; and the chief point of contact and cultural transmission between whites and Indians of the southern Plains. In the 1840's, when traffic on the Santa Fe Trail was at its height, Bent's Old Fort, on the Mountain Branch, resembled a great Oriental caravansary and an Occidental mercantile house. In its later years it was a military staging base for the U.S. conquest of New Mexico.

Among the earliest western fur traders were the brothers William and Charles Bent and Céran St. Vrain, all of whom in the 1820's began to engage in the Mexican and Indian trade. In 1831 or 1832 Charles Bent and St. Vrain formed a partnership, which in time became Bent, St. Vrain, and Co., and entered the Santa Fe trade. In the late 1820's or early 1830's William Bent, who had apparently been trading independently, erected a large adobe fort on the north bank of the Arkansas River, 12 miles west of the mouth of the Purgatoire. At first named Fort William, it was also known as Bent's Fort and finally as Bent's Old Fort. Elaborately constructed, it was eventually a massive adobe structure of quadrangular shape having 24 rooms lining the walls, supported by poles. Two 30-foot cylindrical bastions, equipped with cannon, flanked the southwest and northeast corners. The walls were 15 feet high and 2 feet thick and extended 4 feet above the building

William Bent, prominent fur trader, won the respect of the Indians.

roofs to serve as a banquette and were pierced with loopholes. On the south side was a cattleyard, enclosed by a high wall. A self-sufficient institution, the fort was operated by about 60 persons of many nationalities and vocations, including blacksmiths, trappers and traders, carpenters, mechanics, wheelwrights, gunsmiths, cooks, cattle herders, hunters, clerks, teamsters, and laborers.

The fort was the headquarters of Bent, St. Vrain, and Co. and the great crossroads station of the Southwest, for it was located at the junction of the north-south route between the Platte River and Santa Fe and the east-west route up the Arkansas River to the mountains. Mountain men stopped by to exchange their beaver skins, obtain supplies and traps, and visit with one another. Traders forwarded their fur shipments and obtained goods. For 16 years Bent, St. Vrain, and Co. managed a highly profitable trading empire stretching from Texas to Wyoming and from the Rockies to Kansas, as well as participating in the Santa Fe trade.

In 1835 William Bent, who acted as resident manager at the fort, married the daughter of a prominent Southern Cheyenne and became especially influential with that tribe. Besides encouraging intertribal peace, he required his employees to trade fairly with the Indians and restricted the use of whisky in trade. His influence helped the Arapahos and Southern Cheyennes remain friendly to the United States until well after the War with Mexico. Because of its reputation as a neutral area in Indian country, the post was a natural meetingplace for southern Plains tribes and U.S. officials, as well as for intertribal councils.

In 1835 Col. Henry Dodge met at the fort with the chiefs of several tribes to discuss depredations on the Santa Fe Trail. Five years later, at a major peace council held 3 miles to the east, William Bent served as mediator among several tribes, including the Cheyennes and Comanches, who made a peace pact. Taking advantage of the fort's location and Bent's singular influence, the Government in 1846 designated it as the Upper Platte and Arkansas Indian Agency. The agent was Tom Fitzpatrick. His activities among the Indians inhabiting a huge area, running eastward from the Rockies and from the Arkansas River on the south to the Missouri River on the north, helped bring about treaties at Forts Laramie (1851) and Atkinson (1853) that temporarily brought a degree of peace to the Plains.

Powerful as the Bents and St. Vrain were, as the War with Mexico (1846–48) approached, events beyond their control were destined to destroy the company and the trade. In 1846 the U.S. Army decided to use their post as a staging base for the conquest of New Mexico. That summer Gen. Stephen W. Kearny and his Army of the West, consisting of about 1,650 dragoons and Missouri Volunteers·from Fort Leavenworth, Kans., followed by some

Lt. James W. Abert made this sketch of Bent's Old Fort in the mid-1840's.

300 to 400 wagons of Santa Fe traders, rested at the fort before proceeding to occupy New Mexico.

When Kearny departed, Government wagon trains congregated in ever-increasing numbers. Horses and mules overgrazed nearby pastures. Quartermaster stores piled up at the fort, and soldiers, teamsters, and artisans in Government employ occupied the rooms. Not only did the Government fail to compensate the company adequately, but trade also suffered because the Indians were reluctant to come near when so many whites were present. Following the soldiers into New Mexico were scores of settlers, gold seekers, and other adventurers who slaughtered the buffalo, fouled the watering places, destroyed scarce forage, and used up precious wood. The company was caught between the millstones of resentful Indians and invading whites.

Several other factors accelerated the company's demise. In 1847 Charles Bent, who the year before had been appointed the first Governor of New Mexico Territory, was assassinated by Taos Indians during a revolt. The following year St. Vrain sold his interest in the company to William Bent. The final blow was a cholera epidemic, which in 1849 spread from emigrant wagons and decimated the Plains tribes. That same year the disillusioned William Bent abandoned the fort, moved 38 miles down the Arkansas, and founded Bent's New Fort in an ill-fated attempt to restore his trading business.

Bent may have partially blown up and burned Bent's Old Fort at the time he departed. By 1861, at the end of more than a decade of disuse, the fort's rehabilitated walls sheltered a stage station on the Barlow and Sanderson route between Kansas City and Santa Fe. When the railroads replaced stagecoaches, the buildings served as cattle corrals and gradually collapsed and disintegrated. Yet as late as 1915 parts of the old walls were still standing.

Early in the 1950's the State Historical Society of Colorado acquired Bent's Old Fort from the Colorado chapter of the Daughters of the American Revolution. The society arranged with Trinidad (Colo.) State Junior College to perform the initial archeological investigation and determine the fort's general outlines. The society then erected a low wall, about 3 to 4 feet high, delineating them. After the National Park Service activated Bent's Old Fort National Historic Site in 1963, it tore down the wall

Fort Garland, Colorado ⊗
Location: Costilla County, town of Fort Garland.

In southern Colorado near La Veta Pass and an Indian trail running between the Rio Grande and the Arkansas River Valley, this fort (1858–83) replaced Fort Massachusetts, 6 miles to the north. The new post protected settlers in the San Luis Valley and warded off Ute and Apache attacks on the roads running south to Taos. During the Civil War, the fort was an assembly point for Colorado Volunteers; and the garrison participated in the Battle of Glorieta Pass, N. Mex. (1862), which turned back the Confederate invasion from Texas. In 1866–67 Col. "Kit" Carson was the commander. In the former year, accompanied by Lt. Gen. William T. Sherman, he held a council with the Ute chief Ouray. This, along with concessions that Carson gained for the tribe in an 1868 treaty, was instrumental in keeping it peaceful, even during the

Restored barracks at Fort Garland State Historical Monument.

107

*Southern Ute chiefs and Government officials in
Washington, D.C., about 1874. Chief Ouray is second
from right, front row.*

Ute uprising of 1879 in western Colorado. Nonetheless, at that
time reinforcements arrived at Fort Garland, and 2 years later
troops removed the local Utes to Utah.

Today a State historical monument, Fort Garland features
seven restored buildings: five officers' quarters, the cavalry barracks, and the infantry barracks. Of adobe construction, they have
flat, earth-covered roofs and viga ceilings. A large museum is divided among the buildings. An eighth structure, the sutler's store,
not owned by the State, is a private residence.

Fort Lyon No. 1 (Fort Wise), Colorado ⊗

> *Location: Bent County, on a secondary road about 1½
> miles south of U.S. 50, some 8 miles west of Lamar. Make
> local inquiry.*

Established by Colorado Volunteers in 1860 on the north bank of
the Arkansas River a mile upstream from Bent's New Fort, Fort
Lyon No. 1 was known as Fort Wise until 1862. Two years after
its founding the garrison marched into New Mexico and helped
defeat a Confederate force from Texas in the Battle of Glorieta

Pass. During the rest of the Civil War the post was the principal guardian of the Mountain Branch of the Santa Fe Trail. Cooperating with detachments from Fort Larned, Kans., and Fort Union, N. Mex., its troops escorted traffic along the upper reaches of the Arkansas to Raton Pass.

The fort was also involved with the uprising of Southern Cheyennes and Arapahos in Colorado that reached a climax in 1864. Three years before, a few chiefs, pacified by Col. Edwin V. Sumner's 1857 campaign, had concluded the Treaty of Fort Wise. Guaranteeing peace along the Santa Fe Trail and in the region, they relinquished all the territory assigned to their tribes by the Fort Laramie Treaty (1851) and promised to settle on a reservation in the area of the upper Arkansas. But most of the other chiefs, refusing to be bound by the treaty, kept on hunting buffalo between the Platte and the Arkansas. Miners and settlers continued to flow into Colorado, whose Regular garrisons were serving in the Civil War. In the spring of 1864 the predictable collision occurred. Throughout the summer, warriors raided roads and settlements and practically halted traffic on the Santa Fe Trail. Coloradans obtained their revenge at Sand Creek, only 40 miles down the Arkansas from Fort Lyon No. 1, where a group of peaceful Indians who thought they were under the post's protection were slaughtered. Infuriated, the Plains Indians launched a full-scale war.

During the summer of 1867, because of floods, unhealthful conditions, and the decreasing supply of timber, the Army relocated the fort 20 miles upstream and redesignated it as Fort Lyon No. 2. For a time, however, a Kansas City-Santa Fe line used the dirt-roofed stone buildings at the first Fort Lyon as a stage station.

All that remains at the site, in private ownership but indicated by a stone marker, are traces of the building outlines.

Fort Lyon No. 2, Colorado ⊗

Location: Bent County, on County 183, about 5 miles northeast of Las Animas.

The successor of Fort Lyon No. 1, this fort (1867–89) was also located on the Arkansas River, on a bluff about 2 miles below the

109

mouth of the Purgatoire. By the time of its activation the need for protection of the Mountain Branch of the Santa Fe Trail had lessened, the Confederate threat ended, and the focus in the Indian campaigns shifted to Kansas and Indian Territory. Troops from the fort, however, did play a small part in General Sheridan's 1868–69 campaign. One of the three participating columns, led by Maj. Eugene A. Carr, moved southeastward in brutal weather, founded a supply base on the North Canadian River some 100 miles west of Camp Supply, Okla., reached the Canadian River, and turned back without ever having seen any Indians.

The Navy utilized the fort in the 1906–22 period, and since 1934 it has been a Veterans' Administration hospital. Various adobe and stone structures, some remodeled and used by the Veterans' Administration but all in good condition, date from the 1860's. Among them are the commissary building, several officers' quarters, storehouses, and the commanding officer's residence. The building where "Kit" Carson died has been altered and now serves as a chapel.

Fort Sedgwick and Julesburg, Colorado ⊗

Location: Sedgwick County. The site of Fort Sedgwick is just off an unimproved road slightly north of I–80 and south of U.S. 138, about 1½ miles southeast of Ovid. The site of the original Julesburg is about 1 mile to the east of the fort site.

Early in 1865 this fort (1864–71) and town on the south bank of the South Platte felt the wrath generated among the southern Plains Indians by the Sand Creek Massacre (November 1864). The fort had been founded during the Indian uprisings in Colorado that peaked in the summer of 1864 and was responsible for protecting settlers, emigrants, and the overland route to Denver. The town of Julesburg, just to the east, was a stage and freight station. On January 7, 1865, a thousand Cheyennes, Arapahos, and Sioux attacked the weakly garrisoned post, but failed to take it and sacked the town. A few weeks later, on February 18, they again pillaged the town, this time burning it to the ground. Thereafter the focus of hostilities shifted north of the Platte. No attempt was made to rebuild Julesburg, and it subsequently occupied three different sites nearby, including that of the present town.

The privately owned sites of the adobe fort and the first Julesburg are located in plowed fields. No remains of either are extant. A stone monument marks the original Julesburg site. The modern town contains the Julesburg Historical Museum, operated by the Fort Sedgwick Historical Society. It interprets the history of the fort and the towns.

Meeker (Nathan C.) Home, Colorado ⊗

> *Location: Weld County, 9th Avenue at 13th Street, city of Greeley.*

This was the residence of Nathan C. Meeker, idealistic founder of the city of Greeley, who later died a martyr's death as an Indian agent. Born in 1817 in Euclid, Ohio, he early became a wanderer around the East. Changing vocations often, he worked as a journalist, author, social reformer, teacher, and businessman. In 1865

Nathan C. Meeker, idealistic Indian agent, killed in 1879 by his rebellious Ute charges.

111

Nathan C. Meeker Home.

he joined Horace Greeley's *New York Tribune,* eventually becoming its agricultural editor. Like Greeley, Meeker had a deep interest in the West, expressed in his book *Life in the West* (1866). While on a newspaper trip to the Rocky Mountain region in 1869, he evolved a plan to organize an agricultural colony there. On his return to the East later that year, supported by Greeley, he launched his Union Colony of Colorado and recruited 200 colonists.

The next year Meeker set out to found Greeley, an experimental cooperative community, in northeastern Colorado. After several false starts, it succeeded. Despite his wanderlust, Meeker stayed there for 8 years. To repay debts he had incurred and to confirm his belief that agriculture could bring self-sufficiency and prosperity to the Indians, as well as a better adjustment to the ways of the whites, at the age of 60 he enthusiastically obtained a position as Indian agent at the White River Agency, Colo. But the next year his Ute charges murdered him, and his family returned to their home in Greeley.

The two-story home, completed in the year 1871 and a city-operated museum since 1929, is still essentially in its original condition, except for the addition of a kitchen. In 1959 extensive restoration took place. At that time the house was equipped with furnishings, some of them dating to the 1870's and belonging to the Meeker family.

Meeker Massacre Site, Colorado ⊗

Location: Rio Blanco County, just off Colo. 64, about 3 miles west of Meeker.

The Ute uprising of 1879 began at this site, the location of the White River Agency and the scene of the Meeker Massacre. With the possible exception of the Ghost Dance outbreak of the Sioux in 1890, the massacre was probably the most violent expression of Indian resentment toward the reservation system. The agency had been founded in 1873 for several bands of Utes, who had agreed in a treaty that year to settle on a reservation. Five years later Nathan C. Meeker, founder of the city of Greeley, assumed the duties of Indian agent. Resisting his undiplomatic and stubborn efforts to make them farm, raise stock, discontinue their pony rac-

The Meeker Massacre, rendered by an unknown artist.

ing and hunting forays, and send their children to school, as well as resenting settler encroachment on their reservation and Indian Bureau mismanagement, the nomadic Utes revolted. Assaulted by a subchief during a petty quarrel, Meeker called for troops. On September 29, 1879, before they arrived, the Indians attacked the agency, burned the buildings, and killed Meeker and nine of his employees. Meeker's wife, daughter, and another girl were held as captives for 23 days. After the massacre, relief columns from Forts Fred Steele and D. A. Russell, Wyo., defeated the Utes in the Battle of Milk Creek, Colo., and ended the uprising.

The site, indicated by a wooden marker on the south side of the highway, is in a privately owned meadow on the north side of the White River. A few traces of building foundations reveal the location of the Indian agency. A monument indicates the spot where Meeker died.

Milk Creek Battlefield, Colorado ⊗

Location: Moffat County, on an unimproved road, about 20 miles northeast of Meeker.

Following the Meeker Massacre, the Utes ambushed a column of 150 troops under Maj. Thomas T. Thornburgh at this site on the northern edge of the White River Reservation, approximately 18 miles from the Indian agency. The soldiers had marched south from Fort Fred Steele, Wyo., in answer to Meeker's plea for help. Forming a wagon corral and sending out a messenger with a call for aid, they held out from September 29 until October 5, 1879. During that time, 35 black cavalrymen, based at Fort Lewis, Colo., broke through the Indian line to reinforce their comrades-in-arms. A relief expedition of 350 men led by Col. Wesley Merritt from Fort D. A. Russell, Wyo., finally lifted the siege and rounded up the hostiles. Army casualties were 13 dead, including Major Thornburgh, and 43 wounded. The Government imprisoned several of the Ute leaders, and placed the tribe on a new reservation, in Utah.

The battlefield, situated in a brush-lined canyon, appears today much as it did in 1879. A monument bears the names of the dead soldiers.

Sand Creek Massacre Site, Colorado ⊗

Location: Kiowa County, on an unimproved road, about 9 miles northeast of Chivington.

At this site occurred the tragic Sand Creek, or Chivington, Massacre, one of the results of the Indian-white conflict that boiled in Colorado during the Civil War. The Southern Cheyennes and Arapahos, resenting the mounting invasion of settlers and miners and taking advantage of the absence of Regular troops, took to the warpath. Both Indians and whites committed savage killings. By the spring of 1864 Coloradans were screaming for revenge. As a prelude to military action, that summer Territorial officials extended vague promises of sanctuary to Indian groups reporting to Army forts. One of those that did so, at Fort Lyon, Colo., in October, was led by Black Kettle. Believing themselves to be under the protection of the fort, he and about 500 Cheyennes and a handful of Arapahos camped at Sand Creek, 40 miles down the Arkansas River.

On November 29 Col. John M. Chivington, a strong advocate of Indian extermination, and 700 Colorado Volunteers appeared at the camp without warning, following a march through bitter cold and snow from Fort Lyon. Although Black Kettle hastily

Coloradans applauded and Congress denounced Col. John M. Chivington ("The Fighting Parson") for the butchery at Sand Creek. Portrait from Frank Leslie's Illustrated Newspaper *(December 19, 1863).*

115

*Robert Lindneux's version of the Sand
Creek Massacre.*

raised the U.S. and white flags to confirm his peaceful intent, the
troops swooped down on his poorly armed people and indiscriminately killed and mutilated 200 of them, nearly two-thirds
women and children, though Black Kettle managed to escape.
Most Denverites approved of Chivington's actions, but a congressional investigation denounced him for the wanton slaughter and
he resigned. The word of the massacre spread swiftly among the
Plains Indians. By the following summer practically all the tribes
between Canada and the Red River were at war, and the weak
Army garrisons were forced to stand by impotently.

The natural features of the site, privately owned rangeland,
have not changed essentially since 1864. A stone marker is located
on a ridge overlooking the bottomland where Black Kettle's village stood.

Summit Springs Battlefield, Colorado ⊗

> *Location: Straddling the Logan-Washington county line,
> on an unimproved road, about 10 miles southeast of At-
> wood.*

The Battle of Summit Springs represented the culmination of
General Sheridan's 1868–69 campaign. Maj. Eugene A. Carr, com-

manding five companies of the 5th Cavalry from Fort McPherson, Nebr., and 150 Pawnee scouts under Maj. Frank North and Capt. Luther North, guided by "Buffalo Bill" Cody, were pursuing Chief Tall Bull and his Cheyenne "Dog Soldiers," who had been plundering settlements in Kansas and eastern Colorado. On July 11, 1869, the troops surprised the Cheyennes at Summit Springs, killed 50 of them, including Tall Bull, and captured 117. Only one cavalryman was wounded.

The battlefield, privately owned pastureland, is indicated by a stone marker near the springs from which the battle took its name.

Castillo de San Marcos (Fort Marion) National Monument, Florida ☒

Location: St. Johns County, eastern part of St. Augustine; address: 1 Castillo Drive, St. Augustine, Fla. 32084.

The well-preserved Castillo de San Marcos, constructed by the Spaniards in the years 1672–96, commemorates primarily the Anglo-Spanish struggle for the present Southeastern United States during the 17th and 18th centuries, a topic outside the scope of this volume. For most of the 19th century, however, the post was known as Fort Marion, a U.S. Army base and military prison where Seminoles and Indians from the Southwest were incarcerated and where Lt. Richard H. Pratt conducted an educational program for some of them that resulted in his founding the Carlisle Indian School, Pa.

In 1821, when the United States officially acquired Florida from Spain, it occupied the castillo and designated it as the Post of St. Augustine, renamed 4 years later as Fort Marion. It was a logistical base during the Second Seminole War (1835–43), fought because of the tribe's opposition to relocation west of the Mississippi. During the war, some of the captured chiefs and their followers were imprisoned at the fort.

Later in the century the post again served as a prison for Indians, this time for those from the West. At the end of the Red River War (1874–75), the Government transported more than 70 tribal leaders—mainly Kiowas, Comanches, and Southern Chey-

Fort Marion about the time of the Civil War.

ennes, but including two Arapahos, and one Caddo—from Fort
Sill, Okla., to Fort Marion for indefinite imprisonment. The antagonism of frontiersmen toward the Indians dictated against
holding a civil trial in the West; and the U.S. Attorney General
contended that, as wards of the Government, they could not be
tried before a military court in peacetime.

Lieutenant Pratt, a cavalry officer, escorted the prisoners and
supervised them after their arrival at Fort Marion in the spring of
1875. Several incidents had marred the train trip to Florida.
Throngs of curious onlookers gathered at every major depot along
the way to jeer at the captives. A Cheyenne chief escaped through
a train window; in the process of recapturing him, a soldier shot
and killed him. Another Cheyenne tried but failed to commit suicide on board the train, but managed to starve himself to death
after reaching Florida.

At first the Indians were shackled and confined in the casemates
of Fort Marion, though several times a day soldiers conducted
them to the roof for air and exercise. Within a few months, however, Pratt ordered the shackles removed and allowed the prisoners to build a huge shed for quarters on one of the terrepleins.

Dressing them in military uniforms, he conducted daily drills. As time went on, he allowed his charges considerable freedom of egress from the fort and welcomed visitors. For employment, they polished "sea bean" shells, which they sold to curio dealers and others along with handcrafted items. The prisoners also found jobs in nearby orange groves and packinghouses, and occasionally worked in the local sawmill and railroad depot.

The most significant aspect of prison life was Pratt's educational experiment. Convinced that the Indians should be assimilated into American society, Pratt provided the younger ones with academic instruction. When they learned to read and write English, he began to contact various vocational schools, hoping to secure their acceptance for training under Government sponsorship. The only response came from Hampton Institute, Va., a black school. By early 1878, when the War Department released the prisoners, Pratt had arranged for the education of 17 at the insti-

Lt. Richard H. Pratt's wards at Fort Marion received military training. Here is a group of Indian guards, who replaced the Army guards.

tute and five others by private citizens. The rest returned to Indian Territory. The next year Pratt, enthused over his educational program, established the Carlisle Indian School.

Fort Marion played a prison-type role once again in 1886–87. In 1886 some 500 Chiricahuas and Warm Springs Apaches, who had been terrorizing the Southwest, arrived from Arizona. Not rigidly confined but quartered in a tent city atop the wide fort walls, they suffered from extremely crowded conditions. Removed from their natural habitat, they began dying in alarming numbers. In 1887, largely because of the pleas of the Indian Rights Association and Generals Crook and Howard, the Army moved the Indians to a 2,100-acre reservation at Mount Vernon Barracks, Ala. In 1888, they were joined by Geronimo, Natchez, and 26 other tribal leaders who had been imprisoned for 2 years at Fort Pickens, Fla., where their wives and families had joined them from Fort Marion in 1887. In 1894 all of them were again relocated, to Fort Sill, Okla.

Included in Castillo de San Marcos National Monument are the castillo-fort, surrounded by moat and outworks, and a gate that was once part of the wall around the city of St. Augustine. Each evening from December 1 through Labor Day a sound and light program telling the history of the castillo is presented. Fort Marion's role is interpreted as part of the park's overall program.

Camp Lyon, Idaho ⊗

> *Location: Owyhee County, on an unimproved road that branches off from U.S. 95 at the northern edge of Sheaville, Oreg., about 10 miles northwest of De Lamar, Idaho.*

This crude post near the Oregon-Idaho boundary was active only from 1865 until 1869. In January 1867 its troops, serving in General Crook's drive against the Snakes (1866–68), accompanied him on a scout along the Owyhee River that culminated in a victory at Steens Mountain. The garrison also protected miners, settlers, travelers, and stages on the Ruby City-Owyhee Crossing Road.

The site, marked by a sign, is privately owned. No remains of the eight or so log-walled huts, roofed with dirt-covered poles, that made up the fort are extant. The cabin atop the hill over-looking the site and other ranch buildings, however, may incorporate some of the fort's lumber.

Cataldo (Sacred Heart) Mission, Idaho ⚠

Location: Kootenai County, on I–90 (U.S. 10), about 28 miles east of Coeur d'Alene.

The Cataldo Mission commemorates Roman Catholic missionary activities among the Indians of the Oregon country. Built during the period 1848–53 by Indian laborers using primitive methods, it is the oldest extant structure in Idaho. Reflecting the Greek Revival style, it is also of considerable architectural interest.

Reacting to reports that a Nez Perce and Flathead Indian delegation had visited governmental officials at St. Louis seeking to learn about the white man's religion, in 1840 the Bishop of St. Louis authorized Jesuit Father Pierre Jean De Smet to travel west and select mission sites. That year he journeyed with a fur caravan from St. Louis to Montana's Three Forks of the Missouri, investigating sites and preaching among the Flatheads. From then until 1846 he traveled extensively in the region between St. Louis and the Pacific Northwest and even into Canada. He and his colleagues founded at least eight missions in western Montana, northern Idaho, and eastern Washington.

After 1842 De Smet worked in conjunction with Canadian missionaries, who had preceded him by 2 years in the Oregon country. Late in 1838 the first Canadian priests had arrived at the Hudson's Bay Co. station of Fort Vancouver, Wash. At first the company restricted them from the area south of the Columbia River. By 1842 they had established a number of missions and mission stations in Washington and Oregon along the lower Columbia River and in the Willamette Valley. Both they and De Smet, who concentrated his efforts to the east, laid the foundations for later missionaries of their faith.

The first mission founded by Father De Smet, in 1841, was St. Mary's, at present Stevensville, Mont., replaced in 1850 by an agricultural settlement and trading post known as Fort Owen. Late in 1842 or early in 1843 Father Nicholas Point set out from St.

Mary's and founded among the Coeur d'Alene Indians the Mission of the Sacred Heart (Coeur d'Alene), on the St. Joe River near the southern tip of Idaho's Coeur d'Alene Lake. Because of recurrent flooding, in 1846 the mission was moved to its present location, on a low hill adjacent to the Coeur d'Alene River.

There, at a site chosen by Father De Smet, Father Joseph Joset, who had assisted Father Point at the first mission site, erected a temporary bark chapel. In 1848 Father Anthony Ravalli, an Italian-born priest, came from St. Mary's and began constructing the present mission building. He drew plans for a structure 90 feet long, 40 feet wide, and 30 feet high. Its construction was a remarkable feat of skill and ingenuity. The workmen were two priests and a band of Indians. Apart from several broadaxes, an auger, some rope and pulleys, and a pocketknife, they had no tools. Yet they followed the plans faithfully.

The work crew sawed trees with an improvised whipsaw. Harnessed to crude trucks, they hauled rocks for the foundation and logs for uprights and rafters. They joined the latter with wooden pegs, fitted into auger holes, and laced beams together with willow saplings for walls. The completed walls, covered with mud

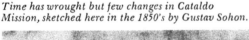

Time has wrought but few changes in Cataldo Mission, sketched here in the 1850's by Gustav Sohon.

from the riverbank, were 8 inches thick. The church was in use by 1849 and formally opened in the early 1850's. The outstanding architectural feature, typical of the Greek Revival style, was the porch. It consisted of six tall classical columns, each cut from a single pine tree, supporting a wide roof. Inside the building, three altars and a baptismal font were erected. The workmen carved statues from logs and used Indian dyes for decoration.

The missionaries greatly influenced the life of the Coeur d'Alene Indians, originally organized in small, nomadic bands that utilized horses to hunt buffalo on the Plains. Under Jesuit guidance, many of the Indians settled near the mission and became farmers, though in 1858 some of them fought against the Army in eastern Washington. In 1861–62 Lt. John Mullan used the mission as a base camp for labor crews building the Mullan Road, connecting the Missouri and the Columbia. Because of Indian hostilities along the route, he urged the Jesuits not to abandon the mission, which he considered a moderating influence. When the road was completed, the mission served as a resting point for travelers. In 1877, when the Coeur d'Alene Indians in the vicinity were relocated about 45 miles southwestward because of a redefinition of their reservation boundaries, originally established in 1855, the missionaries at Cataldo moved to Desmet, Idaho.

In 1865 clapboard was applied to the walls of the mission. Otherwise it remained unaltered over the years, though it fell into disrepair and all the outbuildings disappeared. In 1928–30 civic organizations in Kellogg, Coeur d'Alene, and Spokane repaired and restored it as nearly as possible to its original condition, but did not remove the clapboard. Once each year a special Mass is celebrated in the mission building, which is still a consecrated church, owned and administered by the Boise Diocese. At other times a resident caretaker opens the church for visitors.

Fort Boise (Boise Barracks), Idaho ⊗
Location: Ada County, 5th and Fort Streets, Boise.

Known after 1879 as Boise Barracks, this post was founded by Oregon and Washington Volunteers in 1863 along the Oregon Trail

123

Commanding officer's quarters, Fort Boise,
as it appears today.

in the Boise River Valley to guard the trail, protect miners, and aid law enforcement in the mining camps. Beginning in 1860 thousands of prospectors, ignoring warnings of Indian massacres, swarmed into Idaho and eastern Oregon. Infuriated, the Northern Paiutes (Snakes) of the Snake River region preyed on stagecoaches, wagon trains, miners, and ranchers. Civil War Volunteers could not quell them, and negotiations to place them on reservations ended in failure. The progress of the Regulars who inherited the difficult task at the end of the war was not sufficient to quiet the public uproar. In December 1866 a new district commander, Gen. George Crook, arrived at Fort Boise. Immediately tightening discipline and bolstering morale, he organized a group of Indian scouts, moved promptly into the field, and launched a hard-hitting campaign (1866–68). It crushed the Snakes, perfected his combat techniques, and helped propel him to the fore of the Indian-fighting generals.

Centrally located as it was, Fort Boise also participated in other northwest campaigns. Its garrison bore the brunt of the Bannock War (1878), fought in Idaho and eastern Oregon against the Bannocks who had fled westward from the Fort Hall Reservation, Idaho, and their newly recruited Paiute, Umatilla, and Cayuse allies. In July Gen. Oliver O. Howard defeated them at Birch Creek, Oreg., and returned them to the reservation.

In 1919, some 6 years after its inactivation, the post passed into the hands of the Public Health Service; and in 1938 to the Veterans' Administration. Today a city park occupies part of the site. Several 19th-century buildings, a few considerably altered and most of them used by the Veterans' Administration, are still standing. The oldest (1863) is one of a group of officers' quarters; the rest date from the 1890's. Other structures are a paymaster's office (1864) and an unidentified building (1870).

Fort Hall [Fur Trading Post], Idaho ⚠
Location: Bannock County, just off an unimproved road, about 11 miles west of the town of Fort Hall. Make local inquiry.

The Fort Hall fur trading post, not to be confused with the later Army fort of the same name at a different location, was particularly noteworthy in the history of the fur trade, transportation-communications, and overland emigration. Its significance in these fields is discussed in detail in the appropriate volumes of this series. The fur trading post, however, also had associations with military-Indian affairs.

The post was founded by Nathaniel J. Wyeth, an opportunistic New England businessman who dreamed of exploiting the natural resources of the Oregon country. After an exploratory expedition there in 1832–33, he returned the next year. Near the confluence of the Snake and Portneuf Rivers in southeastern Idaho, he built Fort Hall, a stockade of cottonwood logs with two blockhouses. But he found he could not compete with the powerful Hudson's Bay Co., which the same year built a rival post, Old Fort Boise (Snake Fort), Idaho, 260 miles to the west at the confluence of the Boise and Snake Rivers.

Interior view of Fort Hall trading post, in 1849.

Around 1837 the Hudson's Bay Co. purchased Fort Hall from Wyeth, reconstructed it with adobe, and enlarged it considerably. It became a center of the Rocky Mountain fur trade and was such a lucrative enterprise that the Hudson's Bay Co. maintained it until approximately 1856, or a decade after the United States acquired full rights to the Oregon country from Great Britain. The post served an acculturative role among the intermountain tribes similar to that of Fort Union Trading Post, N. Dak., Fort Laramie, Wyo., and Bent's Old Fort, Colo., among the Plains Indians.

Occupying a prime location only 50 miles northeast of the point where the Oregon-California Trail forked to Oregon and California, Fort Hall in 1842–43 became a major way station and supply point for emigrants and travelers. Dr. Marcus Whitman, Rev. Henry H. Spalding, and Father Pierre Jean De Smet stopped there at various times. So did the explorer John C. Frémont in 1843, while probing the Far West. He recommended establishment of a permanent military post at the spot to supply emigrants and protect them from the Indians. The Army never acted on his proposal, but troops later frequently camped at the fur post site or its vicinity.

In 1849 the Loring Expedition of Mounted Riflemen from Fort Leavenworth, Kans., establishing posts along the Oregon Trail, founded Cantonment Loring, often incorrectly known as Fort Hall, apparently 3 miles up the Snake River from the fur trading post. Loring left two companies to erect a permanent post and proceeded to Fort Vancouver, Wash. A shortage of forage and provisions, however, caused the abandonment of the cantonment the next May.

A decline in trade and increasing Indian hostilities led the Hudson's Bay Co. to discontinue operations at Fort Hall sometime around 1856. For a few years itinerant traders sometimes lived in the crumbling buildings. In 1859–60 and 1863 Regulars and Oregon Volunteers camped there while patrolling the trail. A flood in the latter year destroyed much of the fort. During the 1860's and 1870's overland stage and mail lines used the site, a key road junction, as a base. So, too, did freighters hauling supplies to mining camps in Oregon, Washington, Idaho, and Montana.

In 1865–66, slightly to the north of the Fort Hall site, Oregon Volunteers protecting the Oregon Trail maintained temporary Camp Lander. For materials, they may have utilized log and adobe scraps from the old fort. Federal troops returned to the area in 1870, but they established a new post, also named Fort Hall, 25 miles to the northeast.

The fur post site is on the Fort Hall Indian Reservation. A small monument stands about 50 yards from the edge of American Falls Reservoir. The only surface remains are low earth mounds outlining the fort's walls. Except for the waters of the reservoir, the natural scene is relatively unchanged. The sites of the nearby posts of Cantonment Loring and Camp Lander, often confused with Fort Hall, have not been ascertained.

Fort Hall [U.S. Army Post], Idaho ⊗

Location: Bingham County, along an unimproved road, about 12 miles southeast of Blackfoot. Make local inquiry.

This fort was established in 1870 between the Snake and Portneut Rivers about 25 miles northeast of its namesake, the old fur trading post, to control and protect the Shoshonis and Bannocks who resided on the Fort Hall Indian Reservation, founded 3 years before. The Bannocks, angered by the invasion of settlers, chafing at restriction to the reservation, and resenting the inadequacy of food and other annuities, began plundering white settlements and

127

ranches and set off the Bannock War (1878). Fort Boise, Idaho, however, conducted the principal military operations against them and the allies they acquired as they fled westward in Idaho and into Oregon. Fort Hall remained active until 1883, by which time the area was more densely populated and the completion of a railroad through the region made it possible to bring any needed troops northward from Fort Douglas, Utah. The Indian Bureau took over the military reservation.

The site is located along Lincoln Creek on the Fort Hall Indian Reservation. No remains have survived of the log and frame post.

Lolo Trail, Idaho-Montana ⚠

Location: Clearwater and Idaho Counties, Idaho, and Missoula County, Mont. The trail extends from Weippe Prairie, near Weippe, Idaho, to the vicinity of the junction of U.S. 12 and U.S. 93, near Lolo, Mont.

Ever a dim track through a primeval land, this trail across the Bitterroot Mountains of Idaho and Montana is in wilderness country even today. Being interpreted in conjunction with Nez Perce National Historical Park, Idaho, under a cooperative agreement between the U.S. Forest Service and the National Park Service, it is a National Historic Landmark primarily because of its relations with the Lewis and Clark Expedition (1804–6). Long before that time, however, the Nez Perce Indians followed it en route from Idaho to their buffalo hunting grounds in Montana; and in 1877 the nontreaty Nez Perces traveled over it on their eastward flight during the Nez Perce War.

The trail extended eastward across some 150 miles of rugged terrain from Weippe Prairie, Idaho, through Lolo Pass into the Bitterroot River Valley of western Montana to the junction of Lolo Creek and the Bitterroot River. For most of its distance, the trail passed along the high backbone of the mountain mass between the north fork of the Clearwater River and its middle fork, the Lochsa River. Along the stream courses, cascades and rapids made the river gorges impassable, and the steep rock walls of the gorges prevented the establishment of a practical foot trail along

128

View from the Lolo Trail in Idaho.

the streams. U.S. 12, known as the Lewis and Clark Highway, parallels the route today but for the most part runs south of it.

The eastern part of the trail is in the Lolo National Forest of Idaho and the Bitterroot National Forest of Montana; its middle and western parts in Clearwater National Forest, Idaho. A dirt fire-access road constructed by the U.S. Forest Service in 1939, ordinarily suitable only for trucks and four-wheel-powered vehicles, generally follows a large portion of the trail. The road runs from the vicinity of Powell Ranger Station, on U.S. 12 about 12 miles southwest of Lolo Pass, to Pierce, Idaho. Its western portion runs north of the trail, but its central and eastern portions closely conform to it.

The trail was the traditional route of the Nez Perce Indians from their homeland along the Clearwater River, in north-central Idaho, to their buffalo hunting grounds in Montana. For this reason, the trail is sometimes known as the Nez Perce Buffalo Road. In September 1805 Lewis and Clark moved over it, the most arduous and critical portion of their 4,000-mile journey to the Pacific. Hampered by sleet and snow, dense underbrush, dangerous terrain, lack of food, and exhaustion, the men found the crossing to be a terrible ordeal. The lateness of the season threatened to strand them in the midst of the Rocky Mountains for the winter. On their return trip in June 1806 they once again followed the trail. The other dramatic incident involving it occurred in 1877, when about 700 nontreaty Nez Perces crossed it after the Battle of the Clearwater, Idaho. Resisting confinement to an Idaho reservation, they moved into Montana, pursued by Gen. Oliver O. Howard's slow-moving Army, but were finally vanquished at the Battle of Bear Paw Mountains, Mont.

The U.S. Forest Service has placed historical markers along the trail at sites associated with the Lewis and Clark Expedition and the Nez Perce War.

Nez Perce National Historical Park, Idaho ☒

Location: Clearwater, Idaho, Lewis, and Nez Perce Counties; headquarters at the Spalding park unit, in Nez Perce County, about 10 miles east of Lewiston; address: P.O. Box 93, Spalding, Idaho 83551.

Situated in the ruggedly beautiful Nez Perce country, which encompasses 12,000 square miles of northern Idaho, this new and unique park allows today's traveler to see the land almost as Lewis and Clark described it well over a century and a half ago. Scene of many colorful and significant events in the history of the Rocky Mountain frontier, the park interprets the prehistory, history, and culture of the Nez Perce Indians, including their religion; missionary efforts among them; the Lewis and Clark Expedition; the invasion of fur traders, miners, and settlers; and the Nez Perce War (1877).

Meriwether Lewis and William Clark, on their westward journey in 1805, were the first white men to contact the hospitable Nez Perces. In 1811 they also aided a small group of Astorians, a section of the overland party, who passed through the area on their way to found a fur post near the mouth of the Columbia River. The next year, personnel from Fort Astoria established trade relations with the Nez Perces, and other American and British traders soon visited them.

In 1836 the Reverend and Mrs. Henry H. (Eliza) Spalding, the first U.S. missionaries to the Nez Perces, arrived. On Lapwai Creek they founded a sister mission to the Whitman (Wai-ilatpu) Mission. The latter had been established the same year among the Cayuse Indians, about 110 miles farther west, in present Washington, by their fellow American Board missionaries Marcus and Narcissa Whitman. Two years later the Spaldings moved their mission about 2 miles down the creek to its juncture with the Clearwater River.

The Spaldings made only limited progress in converting their charges to Christianity and persuading them to abandon nomadic hunting in favor of sedentary farming. Jeopardizing their efforts was Spalding's defensively critical attitude toward the other missionaries, especially the Whitmans. The personalities of the two men clashed, and Spalding's philosophy of missionary work resulted in arguments with his fellow workers.

Spalding nevertheless built the first white home, church, school, flour mill, sawmill, blacksmith shop, and loom in Idaho. In 1839 the mission received the first printing press in the Pacific Northwest, donated by American Board missionaries in Honolulu. This press, today in the museum of the Oregon Historical Society, printed the first books in the Nez Perce language, as well as one in the Spokan tongue. For this purpose, the missionaries devised phonetic renderings of the languages.

At the time of the massacre at the Whitman Mission, in November 1847, Spalding closed his mission and he and his wife moved to the Willamette Valley. In later years they returned to the Nez Perce country, where he taught school and preached until he died in 1874.

Despite the Cayuse animosity, relations between the Americans and the Nez Perces remained good until the 1860's, when miners and settlers poured into their ancestral homeland of north-central Idaho, northeastern Oregon, and southeastern Washington. In 1863 most of them reluctantly agreed to a major reduction in their reservation, to north-central Idaho. But for years several bands, known as the nontreaty Nez Perces, lived outside the reservation and resisted Army and Indian Bureau attempts to confine them with their acquiescent brethren. In 1876 a committee appointed by the Secretary of the Interior met with representatives of the two factions at the Lapwai Agency, Idaho, and later recommended to the Government the use of force if necessary to move the recalcitrants onto the reservation. Finally, under duress, in 1877 they began to migrate there. En route in June a few revengeful warriors murdered some settlers along the Salmon River south of the reservation. Brig. Gen. Oliver O. Howard, in charge of the relocation, sent two companies of cavalry under Capt. David Perry, from Fort Lapwai, Idaho, to restore order.

The warriors who had committed the murders belonged to a group camped on Camas Prairie, who subsequently moved to White Bird Canyon. As the troops rode down the canyon on June 17 toward the camp, about 60 or 70 of the Indians took cover at a point between the camp and the approaching soldiers, and the Battle of White Bird Canyon broke out. Assaulted vigorously on the flanks, Perry's men retreated in disorder up the canyon. Thirty-four of them died, but not a single one of their opponents. The victory here proved to be the Indians' undoing, for it emboldened them to follow a course of defiance that eventually resulted in the destruction of their power. A series of skirmishes ensued between troopers and various Nez Perce bands that culminated in the Battle of the Clearwater, on July 11–12.

That battle was indecisive, but it marked the beginning of an epic fighting retreat by the Indians in an effort to find a haven in Montana or, as they knew Sitting Bull had done, in Canada. The episode is one of the more dramatic in the long struggle of the U.S. Government to force the Indians off lands coveted by white settlers and confine them to ever-diminishing reservations.

The leaders of the march were Chief Joseph, later the statesman-diplomat of his people; Frog (Ollokot), his brother; Chief White Bird; Chief Looking Glass; Chief Sound (Toohoolhoolzote); and Chief Rainbow. They guided 700 people with their possessions, transported by thousands of horses, across the Bitterroot Mountains over the Lolo Trail, the route of their past annual treks to the buffalo range in Montana. In 2½ months they were to travel 1,700 miles, trying to avoid conflict whenever possible, either dodging or fending off the 2,000 troops trying to catch them. Although impeded by many women and children, they evaded General Howard's pursuing party of cavalry and hopelessly outdistanced his slow-moving infantry and artillery. Once across the trail, the Indians headed southward and then slightly eastward. Losing men and resources at the Battle of the Big Hole, Mont., they passed through Yellowstone National Park and turned northward but met disaster at the Battle of Bear Paw Mountains, Mont., in the fall of 1877.

During the campaign about 120 Indians had died and 88 had been wounded. They killed about 180 whites and wounded 150. Confined at Fort Leavenworth, Kans., between November 1877 and July 1878 and enduring much suffering because of the abysmal conditions, the Nez Perces were then exiled to a reservation in Indian Territory and not allowed to return to the Pacific Northwest until 1885.

Nez Perce National Historical Park, authorized by Congress in 1965 and in the initial phase of development when this volume went to press, represents a new concept in a national park. It is a joint venture of the National Park Service, other governmental agencies, the State of Idaho, the Nez Perce Tribal Executive Committee, private organizations, and individuals. Of the 24 sites involved, 20 will remain in the hands of their present owners or under a protective scenic easement. Folders available to visitors at National Park Service units give exact locations of all sites and routing information.

The National Park Service administers four major sites: Spalding, East Kamiah, White Bird Battlefield, and Canoe Camp. At Spalding are a Nez Perce campsite of archeological significance; the remains of the Spalding (Lapwai) Mission (1838–47), consisting of traces of the millrace and ruins of two chimneys; site of the original Lapwai Indian Agency (1855–84) for the Nez Perces; a Nez Perce cemetery, where a large tombstone marks the graves of Henry and Eliza Spalding; and Watson's Store, a typical general store of the 1910–15 period that served the Nez Perces until only a few years ago. Extensive archeological excavation is planned at Spalding.

A prominent feature at East Kamiah is the "Heart of the Monster," a rocky hump protruding from the level valley to a height of 50 to 60 feet that figures strongly in Nez Perce mythology. Also situated at East Kamiah is the McBeth House, a small framehouse that was the residence of missionaries Susan and Kate McBeth in the 1870's. White Bird Battlefield was the site of the first battle of the Nez Perce War, on June 17, 1877. Canoe Camp, a 3-acre road-

.osing men and sources at the Battle of the Big Hole,
y passed through Yellowstone National Park and
thward but met disaster at the Battle of Bear Paw
Mont., in the fall of 1877.

he campaign about 120 Indians had died and 88 had
led. They killed about 180 whites and wounded 150.

Fort Leavenworth, Kans., between November 1877
78 and enduring much suffering because of the abys-
ons, the Nez Perces were then exiled to a reservation
Territory and to allowed to return to the Pacific
until 1885.

National Historical Park, authorized by Congress in
the initial phase of development when this volume
s, represents a new concept in a national park. It is a
e of the National Park Service, other governmental
State of Idaho, the Nez Perce Tribal Executive Com-
ite organizations, and individuals. Of the 24 sites in-
ill remain in te hands of their present owners or
ective scenic easement. Folders available to visitors at
rk Service unit give exact locations of all sites and
mation.

onal Park Service administers four major sites: Spald-
miah, White Bird Battlefield, and Canoe Camp. At
a Nez Perce campsite of archeological significance;
of the Spalding-Lapwai Mission (1838–47), consist-
of the millrace and ruins of two chimneys; site of
Lapwai Indian Agency (1855-84) for the Nez Perces;
cemetery, where a large tombstone marks the graves
I Eliza Spalding; and Watson's Store, a typical gen-
the 1910-15 period that served the Nez Perces until
years ago. Extensive archeological excavation is
lding.

It feature at East Kamiah is the "Heart of the Mon-
hump protruding from the level valley to a height
t that figures strongly in Nez Perce mythology. Also
t Kamiah is the McBeth House, a small framehouse
esidence of missionaries Susan and Kate McBeth in
hite Bird Battlefield was the site of the   battle of
War, on June 7, 1877. Canoe   acre

Barracks at Fort Lapwai, Idaho. Date unknown.

side park along the bank of the Clearwater River, was the location of a Lewis and Clark campsite in 1805.

Many of the 20 sites among the non-Park Service group are related to the phases of history treated in this volume. Fort Lapwai, the Army's major post in Nez Perce country, was founded by Volunteers in 1862 about 3 miles south of the Clearwater River in the Lapwai Valley. The post prevented clashes between Indians and whites on the Nez Perce Reservation, and played a prominent role in the Nez Perce War. Made a subpost of Fort Walla Walla. Wash., in 1884, Fort Lapwai was abandoned the following year and bcame the headquarters of the Nez Perce Indian Agency. In recent years this agency was replaced by the Northern Idaho Indian Agency, which serves all the northern Idaho tribes. The parade ground may still be seen, as well as a frame officers' quarters on its southwestern corner, now used by the Indian agency staff, and the stables.

Two natural formations east of Lewiston, Coyote's Fishnet and Ant and Yellow Jacket, are associated with Nez Perce legend and mythology. Weippe Prairie, a National Historic Landmark because of its relationship with the Lewis and Clark Expedition, was a favorite place for the Nez Perces to gather camas roots, an important part of their food supply. At this place Lewis and Clark, descending the Bitterroots in 1805, first encountered the tribe.

At the site of the city of Pierce, a prospecting party headed by E. D. Pierce made the first significant gold discovery in Idaho in 1860. The ensuing gold rush brought thousands of miners and settlers onto Nez Perce lands and within 3 years resulted in the creation of Idaho Territory. Two engagements of the Nez Perce War are commemorated at other cooperative park units; the site of the Cottonwood Skirmishes and Clearwater Battlefield. On the steep bluffs overlooking the Clearwater River are remains of stone breastworks used by Indians and soldiers during the Battle of the Clearwater. Also associated with the Nez Perce War and Nez Perce culture is Camas Prairie, a plateau-valley in the heart of the Nez Perce country, indicated by a highway marker. Once a sea of blue-flowered camas and grass, it was the place where the warriors who murdered the settlers on the Salmon River were camped with their group before it moved to White Bird Canyon.

The Lolo Trail, Idaho-Montana, a National Historic Landmark described separately in this volume, was the traditional route of the Nez Perces across the Bitterroot Mountains to their buffalo hunting grounds in Montana and the avenue of the non-treaty faction of the tribe in 1877. It was also the westward and eastward route of Lewis and Clark in 1805 and 1806. Some other sites in the park area, much of which is located within the boundaries of the historic Nez Perce Indian Reservation, are associated with missionary activities among the tribe.

Part of White Bird Canyon Battlefield, Idaho.
View from Volunteers Knoll toward the mouth
of White Bird Creek.

Council Grove, Kansas ⚠

Location: Morris County.

The site and town of Council Grove are primarily significant in the history of the Santa Fe Trail, but they also have associations with the Osage and Kaw, or Kansa, Indians. In 1825 the U.S. Government Survey Commission, surveying the route of the Santa Fe Trail, met at the site of Council Grove and signed a treaty with the Osage Indians that granted the United States right-of-way over that portion of the Santa Fe Trail running across the tribe's lands and guaranteed the safe passage of traffic. Shortly after the commission completed its survey in 1827, the site of Council Grove became a way station on the trail.

Along the Neosho River, 150 miles west of Independence, Mo., where the rolling prairies met the Great Plains in an area of abundant timber, water, and grass, the spot was a natural resting point and rendezvous for emigrants, traders, and soldiers about to embark upon the semiarid and dangerous plains. It was a perfect place to graze stock; repair harnesses, yokes, and wagons; and cut spare axles. To insure mutual safety on the rugged trek ahead, westbound travelers organized quasi-military caravans to decrease vulnerability to Indian attack. The U.S. Army set up a wagon repair depot at the site during the War with Mexico.

In 1846 the U.S. Government negotiated a treaty with the Kaw Indians that diminished their lands to a reservation 20 miles square, including the site of Council Grove. The treaty stipulated that the Government provide $1,000 annually for educational purposes. Traders and Government agents soon moved to Council Grove and a settlement sprang up. In 1850 the Methodist Episcopal Church, South, which had maintained a mission among the Kaws for 20 years, contracted with the U.S. Government to found a mission school there. In 1850–51, utilizing Government funds, the church built the Kaw Mission, a two-story native stone structure of eight rooms that was capable of boarding 50 students, in addition to housing teachers and other mission personnel. The school, which had an average attendance of 30, was not successful. The Kaws, opposed to having their children indoctrinated in alien ways, sent only orphan boys or other tribal dependents and no girls. The teachers provided instruction in most academic sub-

136

jects and vocational training only in agriculture. In 1854, because of the excessive operational costs, the Government withdrew its support of the school and it closed. Reopened that same year, it became one of the first white schools in Kansas Territory.

The town of Council Grove incorporated in 1858. The following year the U.S. Government signed another treaty with the Kaws further reducing their reservation to an area 9 by 14 miles. Finally, in the 1870's the tribe gave up its land in Kansas and moved to a new reservation in Indian Territory (Oklahoma).

The Council Grove area today retains much of the flavor of the era of the Santa Fe trade. To the north and south of the town, the Neosho River is still shaded by giant hardwoods; to the east and west, trail tracks mark the route of the wagon caravans. Within the town are a number of historic sites and buildings, all on or near Main Street (U.S. 56). The one-story Last Chance Store (1857), so called because it provided the last chance for travelers on the trail to obtain supplies before reaching New Mexico, is privately owned and appears unchanged except for new shingles and the re-pointing of the stone. The two-story stone Kaw Methodist Mission

Kaw Methodist Mission.

(1850–51) is owned and maintained as a museum by the State historical society. Preserved under an attractive shelter on private property is the stump of Council Oak, believed to be the site of the consummation of the 1825 treaty. The Post Office Oak, also on private property, served as a post office for Santa Fe Trail travelers. The Hays Tavern (1857), a two-story frame hostel, has been considerably modernized by its private owners. Near the town, at the site of the trail crossing of the Neosho River, is Madonna of the Trail Monument Park, a favorite trail campsite.

Fort Atkinson (Fort Mann), Kansas ⊗

Location: Ford County, just off U.S. 50, about 4 miles west of Dodge City.

Fort Mann (ca. 1845–50), a crude adobe or log post on the north bank of the Arkansas River about 25 miles east of the Cimarron Crossing at the halfway point on the Santa Fe Trail between Fort Leavenworth and Santa Fe, served as a repair depot and rest stop for Army caravans and other freighters and travelers. The one-company post of Fort Atkinson (1850–54), constructed of sod, protected trail traffic and was in constant danger of Indian attack. At the fort on July 27, 1853, Indian Agent Thomas Fitzpatrick, representing the U.S. Government, signed with representatives of the Comanche, Kiowa, and Kiowa-Apache tribes the Fort Atkinson Treaty, comparable to the Fort Laramie Treaty (1851) with the northern Plains tribes. The southern Indians agreed to stop warring with one another and not to molest travelers on the Santa Fe Trail nor interfere with the construction of military posts and roads.

The evacuation of the fort in 1854 was a serious blow to the Santa Fe trade, and the New Mexico Territorial Legislature petitioned Congress to reestablish it. Not until 1859, however, the year Fort Larned, Kans., was founded, did another military post guard the central segment of the trail.

A large stone marker on the north side of U.S. 50, 4 miles west of Dodge City, commemorates the fort sites, on cultivated bottom land along the Arkansas River about half a mile to the southeast of the marker. No remains have survived.

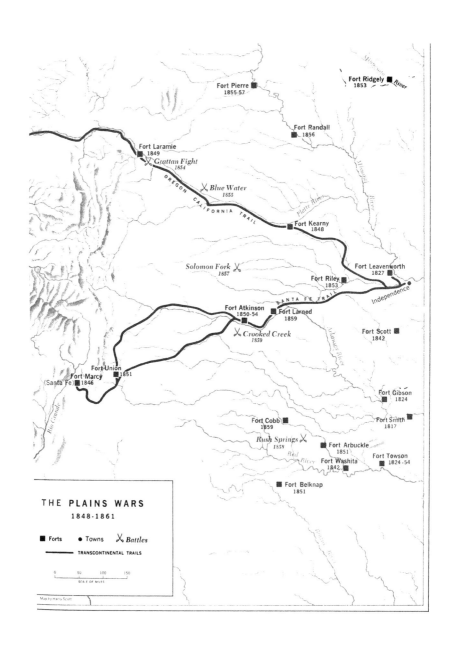

Fort Pierre
1855-57

Fort Ridgely
1853

Missouri River

Fort Randall
1856

Fort Laramie
1849

⚔ *Grattan Fight*
1854

Missouri River

OREGON CALIFORNIA TRAIL

⚔ *Blue Water*
1855

Platte River

Fort Kearny
1848

Solomon Fork ⚔
1857

Fort Leavenworth
1827

Fort Riley
1853

SANTA FE TRAIL

Independence

Fort Atkinson
1850-54

Fort Larned
1859

Fort Scott
1842

⚔ *Crooked Creek*
1859

Arkansas River

Fort Union
1851

Fort Marcy
(Santa Fe) 1846

Fort Gibson
1824

Rio Grande

Fort Cobb
1859

Fort Smith
1817

Rush Springs ⚔
1858

Fort Arbuckle
1851

Fort Towson
1824-54

Red River

Fort Washita
1842

Fort Belknap
1851

Brazos River

THE PLAINS WARS
1848-1861

■ Forts   ● Towns   ⚔ *Battles*

────── TRANSCONTINENTAL TRAILS

0   50   100   150
SCALE OF MILES

Map by Harry Scott

Fort Dodge, Kansas ⊗

Location: Ford County, town of Fort Dodge.

Founded in 1865 on the Arkansas River and Santa Fe Trail about 60 miles southwest of Fort Larned and 25 miles east of the Cimarron Crossing of the trail, Fort Dodge was the most westerly in Kansas on the trail and one of its most important guardians and stopping points in the later years. The fort also protected Santa Fe Railway survey and construction crews.

During the turbulent 1860's, the bloodiest period of Indian warfare on the southern Plains, Fort Dodge was active in military operations, especially Maj. Gen. Philip H. Sheridan's winter campaign of 1868–69. Contrary to their agreements in the Medicine Lodge Treaties of 1867, the thousands of Comanches, Kiowas, Cheyennes, and Arapahos who roamed in pursuit of the buffalo over his huge command area began a reign of terror the following spring and summer from Kansas as far south as the Texas Panhandle, raiding the Santa Fe Trail and even Fort Dodge itself. Sheridan, heading the Department of the Missouri, was stymied. His troops were unable to take effective offensive action against the swift-moving bands of warriors who lived off the land. Their intimate knowledge of the geography, especially the location of waterholes, allowed them to appear from nowhere and disappear just as suddenly. When troops pursued a war party, it dispersed in all directions and reunited at a prearranged point to continue raiding.

Sheridan, desperate by the end of the summer and barraged with demands from frontiersmen to exterminate the Indians and from eastern humanitarians to soothe them, finally decided to launch an aggressive winter campaign. He knew that the warriors preferred not to fight then, when they were immobilized and vulnerable, surrounded by women and children in their camps. Sheridan notified all friendly Indians to take refuge on the reservation set apart by the Medicine Lodge Treaties and report at Fort Cobb, Okla., which he ordered reactivated. He accumulated huge stores of supplies and winter equipment at Forts Dodge, Arbuckle (Okla.), Lyon (Colo.), and Bascom (N.Mex.); and formed wagon and pack trains to transport them. He also inaugurated a rigorous training program for the troops, and recruited white and Indian scouts.

139

The main column proceeded southward into Indian Territory from Fort Dodge and founded Camp Supply as an advance base. There Sheridan sent Lt. Col. George A. Custer and his regiment, the 7th Cavalry, on the expedition that ended in victory at the Battle of the Washita. Two other columns, which were supposed to drive the stragglers eastward toward the main column's line of advance, moved out from Fort Bascom, N. Mex., and Fort Lyon, Colo. The Fort Bascom column won the Battle of Soldier Spring, Okla. Sheridan's campaign was very successful. It broke Indian morale and marked an innovation in Army tactics.

The 1868–69 campaign did not solve the Indian problem on the southern Plains. This occurred in the Red River War (1874–75), in which Fort Dodge was again a base. In 1872 the Santa Fe Railway had arrived in the vicinity and brought a change in economy from buffalo to cattle drives. Dodge City, the prototype of the wild and lawless cowtown, grew up in the shadow of the fort. By the end of the 1870's the frontier had moved westward from Fort Dodge with the railroad. In 1882 the Army evacuated the fort.

Numerous stone buildings, dating from 1867 and 1868, remodeled and used by the State soldiers' home that now occupies the site, stand among modern structures. They include two of the three original barracks, on the eastern side of the parade ground, which were connected in modern times; the commandant's house, in which Custer, Sheridan, and Miles may have resided, now the superintendent's residence; another unidentified structure, presently used as the administration building; the hospital, which now houses residents; a building currently used as a library that was probably the commissary; and three small cottages.

Fort Harker, Kansas ⊗

Location: Ellsworth County, Kanopolis.

Many of the Indian uprisings on the central Plains that led to General Sheridan's 1868–69 campaign erupted in the vicinity of Fort Harker (1864–73). On the north bank of the Smoky Hill River and just north of the Santa Fe Trail, the post guarded the Smoky Hill Trail to Denver and crews constructing the Kansas Pacific Railroad and was a military rendezvous point. It was the starting point and major base of Maj. Gen. Winfield S. Hancock's 1,400-man expedition of 1867 that sought to intimidate the Cheyennes and other Kansas tribes but inflamed them instead and aroused the ire of eastern humanitarians. No major engagement occurred, but the belligerent Hancock burned villages and pursued the Indians relentlessly. During. the campaign, Lt. Col. George A. Custer assembled troops and replenished supplies at Fort Harker.

Kanopolis has grown up around the few stone buildings that remain at the final site, a mile east of the original location. The officers' quarters and the commanding officer's house have been modernized and are now private residences. The two-story guardhouse, with barred windows, is a town museum.

Fort Hays, Kansas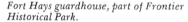

Location: Ellis County, at the intersection of Main Street (U.S. 183) and Bus. I-70 (U.S. 40), on the southern edge of Hays.

This fort (1865–89) along the Big Creek branch of the Smoky Hill River was one of the guardians of the Smoky Hill Trail and

Fort Hays guardhouse, part of Frontier Historical Park.

141

laborers working on the Kansas Pacific Railroad. In 1867, because of flooding, it was moved from its original site 15 miles to the west on Big Creek. Indians periodically burned nearby stage stations. The fort supported General Hancock's 1867 campaign and served as General Sheridan's temporary headquarters in 1868–69. Captives taken at the Battle of the Washita, Okla., were imprisoned in a stockade next to the guardhouse. Lieutenant Colonel Custer's 7th Cavalry headquartered at the fort for several summers late in the decade and camped nearby. Adjacent Hays City, established in 1867, was a wild frontier town.

The remains of the fort are exhibited in Frontier Historical Park, a State historical monument administered by the State historical society. All the original buildings were of frame except for the limestone blockhouse and guardhouse. These two structures, well preserved, are the only ones that have survived at their original sites. The two-story hexagonal blockhouse houses a museum. A frame officers' quarters, moved from the fort in 1901 into Hays, where it was altered and used as a private residence, has been relocated to the fort area. The State is conducting archeological excavations at the site.

Fort Larned National Historic Site, Kansas ☒

Location: Pawnee County, on U.S. 156, some 6 miles west of Larned; address: Route 3, Larned, Kans. 67550.

Located on the Santa Fe Trail in an area well known as an Indian rendezvous, Fort Larned was a major protector of the trail and one of the busiest posts in Kansas during the 1860's. It served as a base of operations against hostile tribes and was an Indian agency and annuity distribution point for those that were peaceful.

Settler and Army response to Indian depredations in Texas in the 1840's forced large numbers of Kiowas and Comanches to relocate farther north, especially along the Santa Fe Trail. Traffic on it boomed after the United States acquired the Southwest from Mexico in the mid-19th century. The gold rushes to California in 1849 and to the Pike's Peak region of Colorado in 1858 provided further stimulus. The Indians, angered by the invasion of their buffalo hunting grounds and the other disruptions, struck back

*View from southeastern corner of parade ground,
Fort Larned NHS. Corner of old commissary
building at left, north bachelor officers' quarters
in left center, infantry barracks at right, and
corner of new commissary building at extreme right.*

with attacks on the trail. As a link between Forts Riley and Leavenworth, Kans., on the east, and Fort Union, N. Mex., on the west, in 1859 the Army founded a temporary post called Camp Alert, or Camp on the Pawnee Fork, near Lookout (now Jenkins) Hill, about 5 miles from the Pawnee River's confluence with the Arkansas. The next year, at a site 3 miles to the west, the camp became a permanent installation, Fort Larned.

The new fort was the northern anchor of the line of forts defining the southwestern military frontier that extended south to the Rio Grande through Fort Cobb, Okla., and Forts Griffin, Concho, McKavett, Clark, and Duncan, Tex. One of Larned's prime responsibilities was defending the Kansas segment of the Santa Fe Trail, on which it was a way station, but it also cooperated with Fort Lyon, Colo., and Fort Union, N. Mex., in protecting the Cimarron Cutoff and the Mountain Branch. In 1864, when the Chivington Massacre fomented an Indian war on the Plains, at a time when most of the forts were not adequately manned because of the Civil War, the War Department prohibited travel beyond Fort Larned without armed escort. The fort furnished guard detachments for mail stages and wagon trains.

Indians conducted numerous raids in the vicinity, and the fort fielded countless expeditions and patrols. In 1867 Gen. Winfield S. Hancock visited it on his abortive campaign against the southern Plains tribes. And it provided minor support to General Sheridan's 1868–69 campaign.

The fort was also an administrative center for the U.S. Government's unsuccessful attempts to pacify the Plains tribes by peaceful means. In the treaties of Fort Wise (1861), Little Arkansas (1865), and Medicine Lodge (1867), the Government agreed to pay annuities to the Cheyennes, Arapahos, Kiowas, Kiowa-Apaches, and Comanches in return for keeping the peace and not molesting the Santa Fe Trail. From 1861 to 1868, before the tribes were relocated to Indian Territory, Fort Larned served as an Indian agency.

Ironically, Fort Larned's last important function—protecting railroad construction crews—helped end the usefulness of the trail it had so long guarded. In the 1870–72 period the arrival of the Kansas Pacific and Santa Fe lines dealt a death blow to the trail. In the summer of 1878 the garrison moved to Fort Dodge, and 4 years later the Government sold the buildings and land at public auction. The Fort Larned Historical Society initiated a program in 1957 to preserve the fort and open it to the public. Seven years later it became a national historic site.

All the remaining buildings, nine in number, date from the period 1866–68, when the original sod and adobe buildings gave way to substantial limestone structures. They were later extensively modified for farm-ranch use. The National Park Service, carrying out a comprehensive historic preservation program, plans to restore these and reconstruct others. One of the two barracks, altered by raising the walls and adding a high connecting gambrel roof, now houses a visitor center, gift shop, and museum. Two of the three renovated officers' quarters are private residences. The third, part of which has been refurnished, is open to the public. The quartermaster storehouse and old commissary building, linked at present by a stone wall, contain exhibits relating to the fort and frontier history. A long shed joins the shop-bakery building, which once housed blacksmith, wheelwright, carpenter, painter, and saddler shops, as well as the post bakery, and the new commissary building. The National Park Service plans to rebuild the hexagonal blockhouse (1865). Santa Fe Trail ruts are visible in the vicinity of the fort.

Fort Leavenworth, Kansas ⚠

Location: Leavenworth County, northern edge of Leaven-worth.

This fort on the west bank of the Missouri River, the oldest active Army post west of the Mississippi, is one of the most historic in the West and in the Nation. From the time of its founding in 1827 to the present, it has been a front-ranking military installation. Centrally located on the main westward travel routes in the 19th century, it was a troop and transportation center, supply depot, and exploration base that figured prominently in the Plains campaigns against the Indians and the Mexican and Civil Wars. A modern training center, it has also supported the wars of the 20th century.

As early as 1824 Missouri citizens petitioned Congress to activate a military post at the Arkansas Crossing of the Santa Fe Trail to protect traders. Three years later, in a more defensible and logistically supportable location, just over the western boundary of Missouri and about 300 miles northeast of the crossing, Col. Henry Leavenworth founded the fort that came to bear his name. From 1827 until 1839 it was headquarters for the Upper Missouri Indian Agency, which had jurisdiction over all the tribes in the Upper Missouri and northern Plains region, and was the scene of many conferences and treaty councils. The garrison also inspected Missouri River steamboats to prevent the smuggling of alcohol to the Indians.

Replacing Fort Atkinson, Nebr., on the "Permanent Indian Frontier," the fort guarded the Santa Fe Trail and quelled Indian disturbances. The 1st Dragoons, mounted troops activated for use on the frontier to counter the mounted tactics of the Indians, came to the fort in 1834, the year after Congress established a regiment of 10 companies on an experimental basis. The regiment proved so effective that in 1836 Congress founded a second one. For three decades prior to the Civil War, particularly, the fort's location near the eastern termini of the Santa Fe and Oregon-Cal-

Then and now view at Fort Leavenworth. The building at left, residence of the commanding officer from 1837 until 1890, is still used as an officers' quarters. The house at right was erected about 1870.

ifornia Trails made it a key frontier post and transportation mecca. The firm of Russell, Majors, and Waddell, which beginning in 1854 took over the transportation of supplies to all Army posts west of the Missouri, maintained its headquarters nearby.

Exploring expeditions that used Fort Leavenworth as a base of operations between 1829 and 1845 included Maj. Bennett Riley's 1829 reconnaissance of the Santa Fe Trail to the Mexican border; Col. Henry Dodge's peacemaking mission in 1835 among the southern Plains tribes, during which three companies of dragoons in 3½ months marched 1,600 miles to the Rockies via the Oregon-California Trail and returned via the Santa Fe Trail; and Col. Stephen W. Kearny's expedition to the southern Plains and the Rockies in 1845, which sought to impress the Indians with U.S. military prowess, gathered information on the Plains country, and escorted caravans over the Oregon-California and Santa Fe Trails.

During the Mexican War (1846–48), the fort was the base for General Kearny's Army of the West, which occupied New Mexico and California. Following the war, it was the chief supply depot for western Army posts. It was also the base of the Loring Expedition. In 1849 Lt. Col. William W. Loring led the Regiment of Mounted Riflemen westward; bought Fort Laramie, Wyo., from the American Fur Co.; founded Cantonment Loring, Idaho; and helped garrison Fort Vancouver, Wash. The year before, the regiment had helped man the second Fort Kearny, Nebr., also along the Oregon Trail. The regiment had been organized 2 years earlier specifically for Indian and Oregon-California Trail duty, but had been diverted to the Mexican War.

In October 1854 the first Territorial Governor of Kansas, Andrew H. Reeder, was inaugurated at the fort. Preferring its protective defenses, he maintained offices there for a few months before moving to Shawnee Mission, Kans. By this time settlers had begun to push into the area, and the town of Leavenworth soon sprang up adjacent to the fort.

After the Civil War, by which time the frontier had advanced well beyond the fort, it continued as a quartermaster depot and ordnance arsenal. In 1881 it became a school for infantry and cavalry officers, reorganized in 1901 as the General Service and Staff School. During the 20th century, it remained an officers' school,

Artillery maneuvers at Fort Leavenworth in 1884.

and in World Wars I and II served as an induction and training center. Today it is the headquarters of the Command and General Staff College.

Numerous historic structures, scattered among modern ones, are practically all still in use. Marked by the Army, they include the present post headquarters, a complex of four brick buildings, two built in 1859 as arsenal shops and two in the early 1900's; the commanding general's home, constructed in 1861 as the arsenal commandant's residence and considerably remodeled since; the sutler's house (1841), a log building that has been covered with a frame exterior and altered by the addition of a second story and is today occupied by the assistant commandant of the Command and General Staff College; a stone chapel (1878); the stone buildings of the U.S. Disciplinary Barracks, a military prison founded in 1874; the "Rookery," dating from the early 1830's and enlarged in 1879, which was the first permanent post headquarters, in 1854 the temporary residence of Kansas' first Territorial Governor, and is today an officers' quarters; a double officers' quarters (1837), the home of the post commander between 1840 and 1890; the "Syracuse houses" (1855), two identical frame officers' quarters; and the present Army Bank Building, likely built in the late 1870's, once the post headquarters and later used for school purposes. Well-defined ruts of a variant route of the Oregon-California Trail run from the old fort area to the river's edge. The Army maintains a museum devoted to the post's history. The cemetery contains many burials dating from the Indian wars.

Fort Riley, Kansas ⊗

Location: Geary County, on Kans. 18, about 4 miles north-east of Junction City.

Fort Riley (1853–present) has had a diverse history. Activated at the junction of the Smoky Hill and Republican forks of the Kansas River, it was one of several forts established to guard the Smoky Hill Trail to Denver. Situated between the Santa Fe and Oregon-California Trails, it also defended them. A center for protecting settlers from the Indians, it drilled troops for frontier duty and supplied other western posts. In the 1850's and 1860's it was the base of several expeditions against the Indians—as far west as Santa Fe. At the fort in 1866 Lt. Col. George A. Custer organized the newly authorized 7th Calvary Regiment. In 1891 the post became headquarters of the School of Application for Cavalry and Light Artillery, which in 1908 became the Mounted Service School and in 1919 the Cavalry School, maintained until 1946. Fort Riley today accommodates the Army General School.

An interesting early building on the Fort Riley Military Reservation, at the now extinct town of Pawnee, is the first Kansas Territorial Capitol (1855), a two-story limestone structure restored and furnished in period style; the Kansas State Historical Society administers it. Two other structures (1855) are an officers' quarters, a stone building with a frame porch, once occupied by Custer; and the post chapel, which has undergone some alteration. A large stone marker, erected in 1893, commemorates the Battle of Wounded Knee, S. Dak. (1890), the final major engagement involving 7th Cavalry troops from Fort Riley.

Fort Scott Historic Area, Kansas ⊠

Location: Bourbon County, at the junction of U.S. 54 and U.S. 69, city of Fort Scott; address: c/o Midwest Regional Office, National Park Service, 1709 Jackson Street, Omaha, Nebr. 68102.

Fort Scott was unique among frontier forts. Its missions over the years were more variegated than most. Although towns grew up alongside many posts and enjoyed a close interrelationship, that

149

between Fort Scott and the town of the same name was unusually cohesive. Few of the towns experienced as tumultuous a life as Fort Scott. The military history of the fort and town may be divided into three distinct phases. In the period 1842–53, as one of the chain of posts on the "Permanent Indian Frontier," the fort had a broad role in Indian affairs. During the Civil War, in 1862–65, it was a key Union post in the West. During the years 1869–73, the town was the headquarters for troops protecting workers constructing a railroad through the region.

The 1st Dragoons founded the fort in 1842, only 5 miles from the Missouri border on lands ceded to but unoccupied by various New York tribes. The post was established to help control and protect the eastern Indians who were relocated to Indian Territory in the 1830's and to improve communications among forts. Situated on the Marmaton River about equidistant between Fort Leavenworth, Kans., and Fort Gibson, Okla., it sat astride the new 286-mile Fort Leavenworth-Fort Gibson Military Road. Personnel from Fort Wayne, Okla. (1838–42), discontinued because the Cherokees resented its existence on their lands, built and garrisoned Fort Scott.

The dragoons policed Indian Territory, prevented the encroachment of frontiersmen, and maintained peace in the region. In conjunction with troops from Fort Leavenworth, Kans., they took part in three major expeditions: those led by Capt. Philip St. George Cooke (1843), Maj. Clifton Wharton (1844), and Col. Stephen W. Kearny (1845). Ranging the northern Plains and the Rocky Mountains, the dragoons marched as far as New Mexico, Colorado, and Wyoming. Their goals included general exploration and reconnaissance, protection of the Oregon-California and Santa Fe Trails, and negotiation with and pacification of the Indians.

Many troops from the fort served in the Mexican War (1846–48). Afterwards, the post resumed patrolling the Santa Fe Trail. But in 1853, the military frontier having moved westward, the Army inactivated the post. Two years later, not owning the land, the Government sold the buildings at public auction.

The town of Fort Scott, which then grew up around the abandoned fort, was a focal point for the turmoil and violence that plagued Kansas and Missouri during the decade preceding the

Civil War. The "Free-State Hotel," a stopping point of John Brown's antislavery followers, occupied one of the former fort's officers' quarters. Directly across the parade ground, in an old barracks next to the hospital, stood the "Pro-Slavery Hotel" (in 1862 renamed the Western Hotel). Federal troops, frequently assigned to the town for the purpose of quelling disorder, resided in tent camps in the vicinity.

In 1862 the Union reactivated Fort Scott. It served as a headquarters, supply and troop depot, prisoner-of-war camp, general hospital, training center for black and Indian troops, recruiting point, and refuge for displaced Indians and Union sympathizers who fled from Arkansas. Although never directly attacked, the fort was an important link between men and supplies in the north and the battles and campaigns in Arkansas, Missouri, and Indian Territory.

The third and last military occupation of the town of Fort Scott involved a mission as unique as the earlier two. It resulted from a

Restored Officers' Quarters No. 1 and front corner of Officers' Quarters No. 2, Fort Scott.

151

land controversy concerning the building of the Missouri River, Fort Scott, and Gulf Railroad through the Cherokee Neutral Lands. These consisted of some 800,000 acres in southeastern Kansas that had been awarded the Cherokees in 1835 but reacquired by the U.S. Government in 1866 as a price for the Cherokee Nation's pro-Confederacy stance. The land claims of the squatter farmers on the neutral lands had not been confirmed, so the railroad obtained title from the Government. The settlers, contending the railroad's land title was fraudulent, attacked construction posts and workmen. The Army designated the town of Fort Scott as headquarters for the "Post of Southeast Kansas" (1869–73), but did not occupy the former fort. Troops protected construction crews from a series of camps along the right-of-way.

Fort Scott Historic Area is located in the northeastern part of the business district of the town of Fort Scott. Authorized by Congress in 1964, it is preserved by the city of Fort Scott through a cooperative agreement with the National Park Service. Although the city of Fort Scott encroaches upon the fort site, long-range plans call for removal of nonhistorical structures and restoration of the area to approximate the 1842–53 period. Museum exhibits will interpret other phases of the fort's history. The city has initiated archeological investigation and plans to restore several structures and rebuild others.

The primary extant sites and structures, dating from the 1840's, include the parade ground; 2½ two-story frame officers' quarters, in good condition; the hospital, a frame shell; the well; and some stone outbuildings, all in fair condition. One of the officers' quarters, before the Civil War the "Free-State Hotel," was restored by the Works Progress Administration (WPA) in 1939 and rebuilt after a fire in 1967. Just north of the group of officers' quarters is a squared-log blockhouse known as "Fort Blair," a Civil War fortification. Moved from its original location some five blocks distant, it has been completely reconstructed. Scheduled for reconstruction are two infantry and one dragoon barracks, the guardhouse, and the well canopy, all of frame; wooden flagpole; and the stone magazine. One of the infantry barracks was the "Pro-Slavery" (Western) Hotel. Many Fort Scott soldiers, as well as others who died in the region during the Indian wars, are buried in the national cemetery on the southern edge of the town of Fort Scott.

Fort Wallace, Kansas ⊗

Location: Wallace County, on an unimproved road, about 2 miles southeast of Wallace.

Commanding major Indian routes to and from Indian Territory and the reservations north of the Platte River, this fort (1865–82) was the westernmost on the Smoky Hill Trail in Kansas. Protection of the trail and construction crews of the Kansas Pacific Railroad were its prime responsibilities. Often besieged, it bore the brunt of Indian hostilities in the region in the 1860's and the 1870's. After several changes of site in the vicinity, it was finally located at the junction of Pond Creek with the south fork of the Smoky Hill River.

When Lt. Col. George A. Custer's 7th Cavalry, participating in General Hancock's 1867 campaign, arrived at Fort Wallace in July, they found the slender garrison exhausted, its supplies low, and travel over the Smoky Hill Trail at a standstill. Custer proceeded to Fort Harker for supplies and then traveled to Fort Riley, Kans., to visit his wife, which resulted in his court-martial and suspension for a year. While at Fort Wallace, Custer's men erected a stone monument in memory of 10 members of the 7th Cavalry and 3d Infantry who had died in battle. The next year, in September, Maj. George A. Forsyth and a small group of frontiersmen set out from the fort in pursuit of a group of marauding Indians. The chase culminated in the Battle of Beecher's Island, Colo.; the fort supplied the reinforcements that freed the besieged force.

The site, on private property, is on the south side of the road between it and the Smoky Hill River. Stone from the dismantled buildings is evident in others throughout the county. Some traces of structural outlines are visible, and the site is comparatively unspoiled. The military interments at the fort cemetery, across the road, have been relocated to national cemeteries. The Fort Wallace Memorial Association has restored the monument erected by Custer's men in 1867.

Haskell Institute, Kansas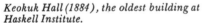

Location: Douglas County, on Kans. 10, southeastern edge of Lawrence.

Established in 1884 as the Indian Training School, Haskell Institute was one of the nonreservation Indian schools modeled after the Carlisle Indian School, Pa., and within a few years attained an importance second only to it. Of all the nonreservation schools set up in the late 19th century, when many reformers believed that Indian education should be provided at off-reservation boarding schools removed from the pervasive influence and restrictions of reservation life, Haskell is one of the few surviving today. Its history mirrors the changing governmental philosophy of education for Indians—which has ranged from vocational education and the inculcation of white values to preprofessional and precollegiate training and recognition of the richness of the Indian heritage. The major goal today is to aid students who return to their tribes to improve their own social and economic conditions as well as that of their people and to aid all students to take their place in national life.

The institute opened in 1884 with only 22 pupils, but by the end of the second year enrollment numbered 220 from 31 tribes. In the early years the educational program stressed vocational training and elementary education, for many of the students had

Keokuk Hall (1884), the oldest building at Haskell Institute.

to be taught to speak, read, and write English. By 1906, however, when enrollment numbered 921 from 60 tribes, emphasis had begun to shift toward academic training. Although agriculture, handicrafts, and home economics continued to be taught, the curriculum came more and more to resemble that of standard elementary and junior high schools. Later the program was broadened to equal a standard high school course. In 1931 enrollment reached a peak of 1,240. In 1965 the school ended its academic program, created new curricula and facilities, and became the first Indian school offering vocational and technical training exclusively at the postsecondary level.

Administered by the U.S. Bureau of Indian Affairs, Haskell Institute today resembles a typical small American college. Most of the buildings are modern structures, but several recall the school's early years: Keokuk Hall (1884), a boys' dormitory; the hospital (1886), today housing school employees; Hiawatha Hall (1898), a girls' gymnasium; Winona Hall (1899), a girls' dormitory; and Tecumseh Hall (1915), a boys' gymnasium.

Highland (Iowa, Sauk, and Fox) Mission, Kansas ⊗

Location: Doniphan County, on Kans. 136 just off U.S. 36, about 3 miles east of Highland.

This Presbyterian mission, which relocated from northwestern Missouri in 1837 with the Iowas, Sauks, and Foxes, was founded at its new location by Rev. Samuel M. Irvin and remained in operation officially until 1866, the last 7 years under the name of the Orphan Indian Institute. The first building was a one-story log structure covered with clapboards. In 1846 workmen completed a permanent three-story building of stone and brick with 32 rooms. Until 1863, when the mission became inactive, Indian children received elementary schooling and instruction in the Iowa and English tongues, in domestic arts, manual trades, and farming. The missionaries, however, had less success in converting and domesticating their adult, nomadic charges. Progress with them was especially difficult because of outbreaks of cholera and smallpox. In 1843 receipt of a printing press made possible the publication of a hymnal and grammar books in the Iowa language.

155

Highland Mission today.

When the mission building was sold in 1868, the west end was razed. In 1941 the State acquired the remaining portion, which had been preserved by the Northeast Kansas Historical Society, and operates it as a museum.

Medicine Lodge Peace Treaty Site, Kansas △

Location: Barber County, in the area just south and east of the town of Medicine Lodge.

In October 1867 U.S. peace commissioners concluded treaties with the southern Plains tribes at this site that represent milestones in Government-Indian relations. The treaties did not bring peace, but they are significant as the first such documents aimed at remaking the Plains Indians in the white man's image and absorbing them into American society rather than merely removing them from areas of settlement. Thus the treaties signaled a new era in Indian-white conflict—not only a struggle for land but also a struggle for cultural identity.

After the Civil War, when emigration surged and railroads pushed westward, the clash with the Indians intensified. Congressmen soon tired of destructive, costly, and indecisive military campaigns—such as that of General Hancock in Kansas in the spring of 1867. Also influenced by the agitation of humanitarians and Indian Bureau officials, Congress decided to seek a peaceful solution. In July 1867 it created a special Peace Commission to negotiate with the Plains tribes. Consisting of the Commissioner of Indian Affairs, three other prominent civilians, and three Army generals, it was charged with erasing the causes of war, insuring the security of frontier settlements and railroad construction, and inaugurating a program to "civilize" the Indians.

The commission originally planned to conclude a treaty with the northern Plains tribes at Fort Laramie, Wyo., before meeting with the southern Plains groups. In August the members held friendly but inconclusive councils with the Indians on a trip by steamboat up the Missouri River from Omaha, where they proceeded from St. Louis. En route by rail to Fort Laramie, they held a conference with the Sioux Chief Spotted Tail and others at North Platte, Nebr., and learned that the militant Sioux were not ready to confer. Postponing the Fort Laramie council until November, they proceeded to Fort Larned, Kans., to meet with the southern Plains tribes. Because the Southern Cheyennes refused to come near the string of posts on the Arkansas River, however, the commissioners agreed to negotiate with the Indians 70 miles south of the Arkansas near a sacred Indian site not far from a

Jack Howland's sketch of a council with Kiowas and Comanches that preceded the Medicine Lodge Treaty. Harper's Weekly *(November 16, 1867).*

small natural basin where Medicine Lodge and Elm Creeks merged.

The commission party, which arrived on October 19, presented an impressive spectacle. It consisted of a 2-mile-long caravan of nearly 100 wagons bearing supplies and gifts for the Indians. Accompanying it were State officials, Indian agents, newspaper reporters, adventurers, and an escort of 500 troops of the 7th Cavalry. Along both sides of Medicine Lodge Creek, thousands of Arapahos, Kiowas, Kiowa-Apaches, and Comanches were camped. With the Southern Cheyennes, who had not yet arrived, the total number was about 5,000. Negotiations took place beneath a specially constructed brush arbor 20 feet high in a clearing prepared for the occasion.

On October 21 the Kiowas and Comanches signed one treaty and the Kiowa-Apaches another. The Southern Cheyennes appeared on October 27, and the following day they and the Arapahos concluded a treaty. The three peace treaties were generally similar to one another and to those subsequently signed at Fort Laramie. The tribes agreed to move onto reservations set aside in Indian Territory, partly on lands the U.S. Government had forced the Five Civilized Tribes to relinquish because of their support of the Confederacy. The Kiowa, Kiowa-Apache, and Comanche reservation was to be located between the Red and Washita Rivers in southwestern Indian Territory; the Arapaho-Cheyenne reservation, to the northeast between the Cimarron and Arkansas south of the Kansas border. In 1869 these reservations were formally created, the Darlington Agency and Fort Reno supervising the Cheyenne-Arapaho Reservation and the Fort Sill Agency and Fort Sill controlling the Kiowa-Comanche Reservation.

The United States promised to provide the reservations, where the Indians would pursue farming, with educational, medical, and agricultural facilities as well as food and other annuities; and to grant hunting rights to the five tribes for an indefinite period in the area south of the Arkansas River. The Indians promised not to attack settlers or oppose railroad and military construction. They also relinquished claims to all lands outside the reservations.

Immediately after completing the Medicine Lodge treaties, the commissioners proceeded to Fort Laramie, where they arrived on

November 9, 1867. But the last of the northern Plains tribes did not sign treaties until the following November. Neither of these groups of treaties brought more than temporary peace. On the southern Plains, war broke out before a year had passed, and General Sheridan responded in his punitive winter campaign of 1868–69.

The treaties were signed in the area south and east of the modern town of Medicine Lodge. This tract, in public and private ownership, includes the swampy and heavily wooded confluence of Medicine Lodge and Elm Creeks. A dirt road, branching off South Main Street and paralleling Elm Creek, approaches within about 50 yards of the confluence of the creeks. The Indian camps were along both banks of Medicine Lodge Creek. Cultivated farmlands today line its northern side.

East of the town of Medicine Lodge is a 400-acre Memorial Peace Park, a natural amphitheater owned by the Medicine Lodge Peace Treaty Association that overlooks the Indian campgrounds and treaty-signing site. Since 1927, at 5-year intervals, Medicine Lodge citizens have presented at this park a pageant depicting the treaty signing and later settlement. The Centennial Pageant, in 1967, featured 1,200 participants, including several hundred descendants of the Plains Indians who had gathered there a century before. The northern part of the park is a city golf course.

Shawnee Mission, Kansas ⚠

> *Location: Johnson County, West 53d Street and Mission Road (35th Street), one block north of U.S. 50–69, Fairway (Kansas City suburb).*

Shawnee Mission was one of the earliest, largest, and most successful mission schools in pre-Territorial Kansas and the West. Founded in 1830 at the first of two locations and under the first of various names as the Shawnee Methodist Mission and Indian Manual Labor School to educate and provide religious instruction for Shawnee Indian children, it grew into a vocational training center for many tribes. Situated near the beginning points of the 159

Restored North Building, Shawnee Mission.

Santa Fe and Oregon-California Trails, it was an outpost of civilization and a social center on the trails. During the years 1854–55, it was also the capital of Kansas Territory.

In 1829, by which time most of the Missouri Shawnees had relocated to a tract in eastern Kansas in accordance with an 1825 treaty and 3 years before their tribesmen from Ohio joined them, the Missouri group requested missionaries. The Reverend Thomas Johnson of the Methodist Episcopal Church established a two-story log mission school near present Turner, Kans., in 1830–31. Until 1837, when emphasis shifted to vocational training and enrollment surpassed 35, he taught English and arithmetic to both sexes, home arts to the girls, and crafts to the boys. In 1834 he received the first printing press in Kansas and utilized it to advantage in his educational program. Four years later he recommended to the Methodist missionary society the establishment of a central manual labor school for the benefit of all tribes. The War Department, which administered Indian affairs, agreed to finance it but stipulated a site on Indian lands and outside the State of Missouri.

Johnson chose another location on Shawnee lands, a few miles to the southeast. Construction began in January 1839, and in October the Johnson family and the students moved from the abandoned first school to the new one and into the West Building, the first completed. Indian laborers plowed and enclosed some 400 acres of land and planted orchards and gardens that came to yield rich harvests, including grain to feed the herds of livestock. In February 1840 some 60 students from various tribes were enrolled, and others had been turned away because of lack of space. Most of the males studied agriculture, and some of them learned blacksmithing, wagonmaking, and shoemaking; the girls learned domestic arts; and all students, religion. At its peak the mission accommodated 137 pupils and consisted of about 2,240 acres and 16 brick, stone, and frame school structures, workshops, and outbuildings. Ill health forced Johnson to return East in the years 1841–47, though the school continued to operate.

The institution was renamed the Fort Leavenworth Indian Manual Training School in 1847. Yet the next year Johnson began a shift toward academic instruction by organizing a separate classical department, the "Western Academy." Offering courses in Latin and Greek, as well as in English, this 3-year experiment attracted both white and Indian students.

The year 1854 was an eventful one. On November 24 Andrew H. Reeder, first Territorial Governor of Kansas, moved his executive offices from Fort Leavenworth, where he had been inaugurated on October 7, to the mission's North Building. For a few weeks in June and July 1855 he relocated to Pawnee, Kans., adjoining the Fort Riley Military Reservation, and convened the first Territorial Legislature. The proslavery party, determined to legislate nearer home, charged him with speculating in Pawnee real estate, unseated all but two of his fellow Free Staters, and transferred the seat of government back to Shawnee Mission. There, in the East Building, the so-called "bogus legislature" adopted the proslavery statutes of the State of Missouri virtually in their entirety, but the Free Staters refused to recognize them.

In 1854, when the Shawnees ceded most of their lands in eastern Kansas to the U.S. Government, they granted portions of the mission lands and improvements to the missionary society of the Methodist Episcopal Church, South, on the condition that the church pay them $10,000 to use for the education of their children. The next year the Indian Bureau, which had taken over Indian affairs from the Army in 1849, agreed with the society to pay it $5,000 annually and credit the $10,000 due the Shawnees at the rate of $1,000 per year if it would board, clothe, and educate a certain number of Shawnee children at the school. The school was renamed the Shawnee Manual Labor School, though children from other tribes continued to attend.

The Shawnees soon became dissatisfied with the school. In 1858 the Tribal Council considered withdrawing their funds from the mission school and setting up another system of education. A joint Indian-missionary society committee recommended to the Indian Bureau that the contract be terminated at the end of the school year and that the funds be administered by a Government commissioner, who would disburse tuition to any institution of the parents' choice. Apparently the Indian Bureau took no action on the recommendations.

That same year Thomas Johnson moved to Kansas City; although he retained the superintendency of the school until 1862, his son Alexander operated it. Early in 1860 the Tribal Council again complained to the Indian Bureau. It charged school officials with poor management, the squandering of money, and physical neglect of the children. Finally, in September 1862, the Shawnee Mission closed and the contract between the Government and the Methodist Episcopal Church ended. Union troops occupied the mission during the Civil War. In 1865 Johnson's heirs acquired title.

In 1927 the State gained possession of the present 12-acre site, now a State park administered by the Kansas State Historical Society. The park consists of three of the original brick structures, in excellent condition. The West Building (1839), a two-story structure that has been extensively modified over the years and is now occupied by the custodian, originally provided classrooms and a dining hall but sometimes served as a residence for the superintendent, teachers, and their families, as well as Territorial officers. In the 2½-story East Building (1841) were a chapel, classrooms, and an attic dormitory for male students. Restoration of the two-story North Building (1845), separated from the other two buildings by 53d Street, was completed in 1942. This structure contained girls' classrooms and dormitory, but on occasion housed teachers, Territorial officials, and the superintendent. It features a piazza across most of its length. The East and North Buildings are furnished in period styles. Reverend Johnson is buried in a cemetery a short distance from the mission.

Fort Jesup, Louisiana △

Location: Sabine Parish, on La. 6, about 7 miles northeast of Many.

From its founding in 1822, when it was the most southwesterly outpost of the United States, until its inactivation in 1846, this fort was the southern anchor of the "Permanent Indian Frontier." Because of a dispute over the Texas-United States boundary, in 1806 Spain and the United States had designated as a neutral strip an area 30 to 40 miles wide extending eastward from the Sabine River and embracing most of the present western tier of parishes in Louisiana. Under the Adams-Onis Treaty of 1819, the United States acquired the strip, which had become a haven for outlaws and marauders who molested settlers emigrating to Texas, and moved swiftly to occupy and police it. Pending ratification of the treaty, which occurred in 1821, the U.S. Government in 1820 built Fort Selden, La., on the Bayou Pierre near its junction with the Red River just outside the strip on its eastern edge. The following year it made plans to set up another post nearer the Sabine.

The Army abandoned Fort Selden in 1822. Lt. Col. Zachary Taylor occupied the watershed between the Sabine and the Red

Reconstructed officers' quarters and modern visitor center, Fort Jesup State Monument.

163

Rivers and moved to a point 25 miles south-southwest of Fort Selden, where his troops built a group of log cabins that became Fort Jesup. Within a few months, it had the largest garrison in Louisiana, consisting of a battalion of the 7th Infantry under Lt. Col. James B. Many. In 1827–28 the troops helped construct a military road 262 miles northwest to Fort Towson, Okla. Gen. Henry Leavenworth commanded Fort Jesup in the years 1831–33. The next year Colonel Many reassumed command and garrisoned it with six companies of the 3d Infantry. In 1833 the Government, recognizing the enlargement and expansion of the post, created the 16,000-acre Fort Jesup Military Reservation. The following June troops from Fort Jesup participated in the ceremonies involved in the signing of the Caddo Indian Treaty at the Caddo Indian Agency headquarters, on the bluff overlooking Bayou Pierre, some 9 miles south of present Shreveport. This was the only treaty the U.S. Government ever executed with the Indians in Louisiana.

After the Texas Revolution began in 1835, reinforcements arrived at Fort Jesup. Maj. Gen. Edmund P. Gaines assembled 13 infantry companies at the fort and early in 1836 marched to the Sabine, where he founded the temporary post of Camp Sabine. From there he occupied Nacogdoches and remained until the independence of Texas was assured. In 1846, the year after President James K. Polk ordered Gen. Zachary Taylor, the Fort Jesup commander, to move a force into Texas in anticipation of a war with Mexico, the Army inactivated the fort.

Fort Jesup State Monument commemorates the fort. The only original building is one of the log kitchens, which has been repaired, reroofed, and refurnished with period reproductions of authentic kitchenware. An officers' quarters, reconstructed for use as a visitor center and park administrative office, contains historical exhibits.

Birch Coulee Battlefield, Minnesota ⊗

Location: Renville County, just off U.S. 71, about 1 mile north of Morton.

The battle at this site near the junction of Birch Coulee and the Minnesota River, about 16 miles northwest of Fort Ridgely and just opposite the Lower, or Redwood, Sioux Agency, marked the high tide of the Sioux during their 1862 revolt. After killing hundreds of settlers in the Minnesota River Valley and attacking Fort Ridgely and New Ulm, on September 2 Chief Little Crow's Santee Sioux surrounded a force of 170 Volunteers under Capt. Hiram P. Grant. Col. Henry Hastings Sibley had sent them ahead from Fort Ridgely to reconnoiter the Redwood Agency, which the Indians had attacked the previous month, and to bury the dead. Besieged for 31 hours, the soldiers lost 22 killed and 60 wounded before the arrival of Sibley and reinforcements on September 3. The Indians, who had few casualties, fled.

A marker on U.S. 71 directs the visitor to the battlefield site, which is preserved in 32-acre Birch Coulee State Memorial Park. The rolling, tree-studded battlefield is relatively unchanged.

Fort Ridgely and New Ulm, Minnesota ⊗

Location: The park commemorating the fort site is in Nicollet County, on Minn. 4, about 7 miles south of Fairfax. The city of New Ulm, on Minn. 15, is in Brown County.

This fort (1853–67) and town bore the brunt of the 1862 Minnesota Sioux uprising. They provided refuge for settlers from the Minnesota River Valley, and countered successive onslaughts. The fort also provided troops for the 1862–64 retaliatory campaigns of Gen. Henry Hastings Sibley westward into Minnesota and the Dakotas.

The Spirit Lake Massacre of 1857, when some Santee, or Eastern, Sioux killed nearly 50 settlers just across the Minnesota border in Iowa, was a significant portent of future violence arising from Indian opposition to settlement on their lands. But, although the Sioux and Cheyennes raided periodically, the big explosion did not come until 1862. In August of that year the Santees of Minnesota went on the warpath under Chief Little Crow. After killing the whites at the Lower, or Redwood, Sioux Agency, his warriors swept up and down the Minnesota River Valley and slaughtered perhaps 800 settlers and soldiers, took many captives, and inflicted immense property damage. Refugees from the valley swarmed into Fort Ridgely, about 12 miles below the agency, and   165

*Gen. Henry Hastings
Sibley led the campaign
against the Santee Sioux
of Minnesota. Engraving
by J. C. Buttre after
a photograph by J. W.
Campbell.*

New Ulm, a German settlement 15 miles farther south down the valley from the fort.

Sending a courier to Fort Snelling for reinforcements, Capt. John S. Marsh left a skeleton guard at Fort Ridgely and set out for the agency with 45 men and an interpreter. Just before he reached there, an overwhelming force of Indians struck. In a running fight back to the fort, half the soldiers died, including Marsh. More refugees poured into the fort. When about 400 Sioux attacked on August 20, and 2 days later about twice that number, the artillery and rifle fire of the 180 Volunteer and civilian defenders beat off repeated charges. Their casualties heavy, the Indians finally abandoned the effort.

While the main body of warriors was preparing to attack Fort Ridgely, on August 19 about 100 had raided New Ulm, whose normal population of 900 had been swollen to 1,500 by the influx of refugees. Judge Charles E. Flandrau, a leading citizen, organized a defense force of about 250 poorly armed men. After putting three houses to the torch, the Indians withdrew. Four days later, having failed to take Fort Ridgely, 650 warriors again moved against New Ulm. They drove the defenders from the outskirts and occupied outlying houses. Fighting raged back and forth throughout the day. Finally, Flandrau and 50 men charged, forced the Indians from the houses, and burned them. Deprived of these shelters, the Sioux departed. In New Ulm about 34 set tlers lost their lives and 60 suffered wounds; fire destroyed 190

Chief Little Crow, leader of the Minnesota Sioux uprising.

buildings. Indian losses are not known. That same month, farther west, the Sioux launched a series of attacks on settlers in the region of Fort Abercrombie, N. Dak., and the next month besieged the fort.

As soon as news of the Little Crow uprising reached St. Paul, Gov. Alexander Ramsey commissioned his predecessor, Henry Hastings Sibley, as a colonel in the State militia to put it down. Assembling all the Volunteer troops who had not been sent off to the Civil War, Sibley advanced up the Minnesota River at the head of nearly 1,500 men and on August 28 arrived at Fort Ridgely. On September 3 the command relieved a 170-man detachment that Sibley had sent on August 31 to reconnoiter the Redwood Agency and bury bodies. The detachment had been besieged for 31 hours by a large band of Sioux at Birch Coulee, about 16 miles northwest of Fort Ridgely.

On September 19 Sibley and 1,400 Volunteer troops set out from the post. Four days later they managed to escape the full brunt of an ambush and won a decisive victory over Little Crow in the ensuing Battle of Wood Lake, Minn. The Minnesota outbreak ended, though many of the Sioux, including Little Crow and another principal leader, Inkpaduta, fled westward into Dakota rather than surrender.

Sibley imprisoned 2,000 warriors and tried them before a military court. Of more than 300 sentenced to die, President Lincoln pardoned most of them. In December the Army publicly hanged 38 at Mankato. The following June, near the town of Hutchinson, settlers killed Little Crow, who had slipped back into Minnesota to steal horses.

The Santees who had eluded Sibley's troops and fled to Dakota joined forces with the Teton Sioux, belonging to the Western, or Prairie, Sioux. In the spring of 1863 Sibley, now a brigadier general, gave pursuit from Fort Ridgely. Spending the summer campaigning, he won victories in July in North Dakota at the Battles of Big Mound, Dead Buffalo Lake, and Stony Lake. Sibley followed the survivors to the Missouri River, which he reached on July 29, and then returned to Minnesota.

Brig. Gen. Alfred Sully had intended to unite with Sibley in a joint campaign, but low water delayed his journey up the Missouri River from Sioux City, Iowa. Sully nevertheless carried on

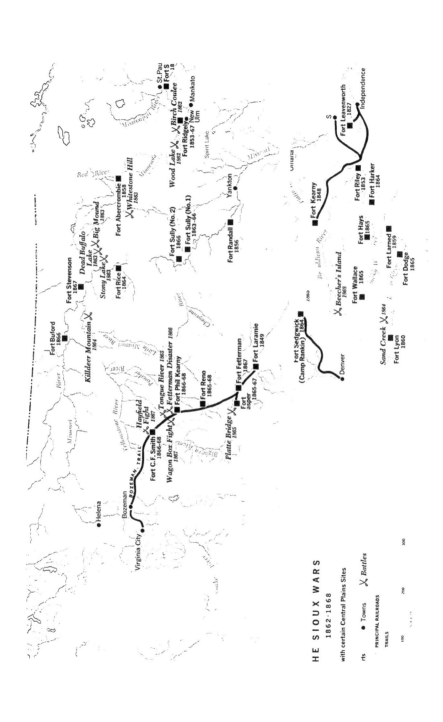

HE SIOUX WARS
1862-1868

with certain Central Plains Sites

rts   ● Towns   ✗ Battles

PRINCIPAL RAILROADS

TRAILS

100   200   300

Virginia City

● Helena

Bozeman
BOZEMAN TRAIL

Fort C.F. Smith
1866-68

Hayfield
✗ Fight
1867

Wagon Box Fight
1867

Tongue River 1865
✗ Fetterman Disaster 1866
Fort Phil Kearny
1866-68

Fort Reno
1865-68

Fort
asper
1865

Platte Bridge ✗
1865

Fort Fetterman
1867

Fort Laramie
1849

Killdeer Mountain ✗
1864

Fort Buford
1866

Fort Stevenson
1867

Dead Buffalo
Lake
1863 ✗ ✗ Big Mound
Stony Lake ✗ 1863
1863

Fort Rice
1864

Fort Abercrombie
1858
✗ Whitestone Hill
1863

Fort Sully (No.2)
1866

Fort Sully (No.1)
1863-66

Fort Randall
1856

Wood Lake ✗ ✗ Birch Coulee
1862   1862
Fort Ridgely ● New ● Mankato
1853-67 Ulm

St. Pau
Fort S
18

Yankton

Spirit Lake

Red River

Minnesota

Mississippi River

Missouri

Red River

Little Missouri River

Missouri River

Yellowstone River

Powder River

Cheyenne River

Bighorn River

Fort Sedgwick
(Camp Rankin) 1864

✗ Beecher's Island
1868

Fort Wallace
1865

Fort Hays
1865

Fort Larned
1859

Fort Dodge
1865

Sand Creek ✗ 1864

Fort Lyon
1860

● Denver

Fort Kearny
1848

Fort Riley
1853

Fort Harker
1864

Fort Leavenworth
1827

Independence

S

Omaha

Re ublican River

Arkansas

and defeated the Indians in the Battle of Whitestone Hill, N. Dak. (September 1863), and after wintering on the Missouri River near present Pierre, S. Dak., in the Battle of Killdeer Mountain, N. Dak. (July 1864). By this time the Sioux coalition, which had never been very cohesive and which had suffered heavily, had been disbanded.

Fort Ridgely State Park is surrounded by essentially unimpaired prairie and woodlands. Archeological excavations in the 1930's revealed the building foundations, some of which were stabilized and left exposed and are still preserved today. A log powder magazine has been reconstructed. A restored stone commissary building houses a small museum that interprets the history of the fort, along with various markers. The scene of the fighting in the western outskirts of the modern city of New Ulm has been completely changed by urban expansion. At the Lower Sioux Agency site, the Minnesota Historical Society is creating a center to interpret the Sioux war of 1862.

Fort Snelling, Minnesota ⚠

Location: Hennepin County, adjacent to the junction of Minn. 5 and Minn. 55, South Minneapolis.

Founded in 1819, this fort was for many years the most northwesterly military base in the United States; a key bastion on the upper Mississippi; and the northern outpost on the "Permanent Indian Frontier," which extended as far south as Fort Jesup, La. The post protected settlers from Indians, cleared the way for the settlement of the old Northwest, and promoted the growth of the fur trade. Later, from 1861 until 1946, it was essentially a training installation.

After the War of 1812 the Army, seeking to extend U.S. control over the upper Mississippi Valley, planned a fort at the confluence of the Mississippi and Minnesota Rivers, a site that had been well known to French traders, on land that Lt. Zebulon M. Pike had purchased for a pittance in 1805 from the Sioux Indians. In 1819 Lt. Col. Henry Leavenworth led a detachment up the Mississippi from Prairie du Chien, Wis., to build the fort and wintered near an Indian village at the site of Mendota, Minn. The camp, known

Fort Snelling in 1844, by J. C. Wild.

as Camp New Hope, consisted of log cabins and a stockade. In 1820 the troops moved across the Mississippi and established Camp Coldwater just north of the mouth of the Minnesota. That same year Col. Josiah Snelling succeeded Leavenworth and began constructing a permanent fort on a 100-foot-high bluff overlooking the confluence of the Minnesota and Mississippi Rivers. The fort, completed in 1823 and named Fort St. Anthony, became Fort Snelling 2 years later. Of log and stone, it was constructed in the shape of a diamond and was surrounded by a limestone wall. More medieval in appearance than most forts, it had towers commanding the four corners.

The fort, a quarter mile east of an Indian agency, guarded the region between the Great Lakes and the Missouri River. The officers cooperated with Indian Agent Lawrence Taliaferro, who served between 1819 and 1839, in preventing clashes between the Sioux and Chippewas. Later the garrison kept other Iowa, Minnesota, and Wisconsin Indians on their reservations. It also policed the Canadian border to prevent the incursions of *Métis* and French-Canadian buffalo hunters.

Once the frontier advanced to the Great Plains, Fort Snelling's importance declined and it became mainly a supply base. In 1857

the Army abandoned it. Reactivated in 1861 as a training center
for Civil War troops, it also was instrumental in putting down the
1862 Sioux uprising in the Minnesota River Valley. The focus of
conflict between Indians and soldiers subsequently shifted West,
to the Dakotas, and later to Montana and Wyoming. Playing a
supporting role in these operations, in 1881 the fort became headquarters of the Department of Dakota '(Minnesota, the Dakotas,
and Montana). In later years it was mainly a training center. In
1946 the Army departed and deeded it to the Veterans' Administration.

Modern bridges, highways, and urban expansion have impaired
the historical scene. The Veterans' Administration, other Govern-

*The Minnesota Historical Society is carrying out
an extensive restoration-reconstruction program
at Fort Snelling. The round tower, background,
is one of the structures that has been restored.*

ment Agencies, and the State have jurisdiction over various parts of the modern Fort Snelling reservation. The Minnesota Historical Society has long been active in preserving and interpreting the old fort. In 1957–58 excavations uncovered the foundations of several structures, including the powder magazine, schoolhouse, sutler's store, hospital, shops, cisterns, and a portion of the original walls. At that time, two of the original 16 buildings, constructed in the early 1820's, were still standing: a hexagonal stone tower, only slightly altered; and a round stone tower, considered the oldest building in Minnesota.

In October 1969 the State acquired from the Veterans' Administration for inclusion in Fort Snelling State Park the old fort area, a 21.25-acre tract lying to the east and north of the adjacent freeway and surrounded on three sides by the modern Fort Snelling installation. Four years before, with the permission of the Veterans' Administration, the State historical society had begun a large-scale reconstruction-restoration program. By April of 1970, it had reconstructed the guard complex, a building consisting of separate rooms that served a wide variety of functions and were separated by interior walls; pentagonal tower; 560 feet of the original wall; schoolhouse; powder magazine; sutler's store; and well house. Restorations included the old round and hexagonal towers. The society plans to furnish all the buildings in period style. When this volume went to press, it was still seeking title to a 141.39-acre tract comprising the later fort area, to the west and south of the freeway.

Lac Qui Parle Mission, Minnesota ⊗

Location: Chippewa County, on an unimproved road, about 4 miles northwest of Watson.

Established in 1835 by the Presbyterian Church among the Sioux, this mission housed one of the first Indian schools west of the Mississippi. The mission's founder, Rev. Thomas S. Williamson, and his coworkers devised a phonetic system and translated the Christian Gospels and other works into the Sioux language. They also helped Rev. Stephen R. Riggs compile the first grammar-dictionary in the tongue, published in 1852 by the Smithsonian Institution. The mission was abandoned the following year. The reconstructed log chapel and school (1835) is part of Lac Qui Parle State Park.

Sibley (Henry Hastings) House, Minnesota ⊗

Location: Dakota County, just off Main Street (Minn. 13, Sibley Memorial Highway), Mendota (Minneapolis-St. Paul suburb).

Perhaps Minnesota's most famous old house and the first in the State constructed of stone, this residence is of architectural and historical interest. Henry Hastings Sibley (1811–91), pioneer fur trader and later the first Governor and commander of Volunteer forces during the Sioux uprising of 1862, erected it in 1835. The year before, as the local *bourgeois* for the American Fur Co., he had arrived as a young man of 23 at the thriving fur trade town of

Henry Hastings Sibley House.

St. Peter's, known as Mendota after 1837. Opposite Fort Snelling at the confluence of the Mississippi and Minnesota Rivers, it was the first permanent white settlement in Minnesota and the focal point of the Red River fur trade. Marrying in 1843, Sibley brought his wife to the home, where nine children were born to them. The leader in making the town a business and cultural center, Sibley entertained many celebrities in his home, where Indians also frequently visited to trade. In time, Minneapolis and St. Paul gained the ascendancy over Mendota, and in 1860 the Sibley family moved to St. Paul.

The Daughters of the American Revolution owns the house, restored by the Sibley House Association, and several outbuildings. Of native stone with white wood cornices and trim, the large two-story home represents the colonial style and closely resembles many of the stone residences in Pennsylvania and the Western Reserve territory in Ohio. In excellent condition, it is furnished with period pieces, some of which belonged to the Sibley family.

Wood Lake Battlefield, Minnesota ⊗

Location: Yellow Medicine County, just off Minn. 274, about 7 miles south of Granite Falls.

The so-called Battle of Wood Lake, which followed the Army disaster at Birch Coulee, Minn., was the first decisive defeat of the Sioux in the Minnesota uprising of 1862 and marked the end of the campaign there. Col. Henry Hastings Sibley set out from Fort Ridgely on September 19 in command of 1,400 Volunteers. Near Wood Lake on September 23 they managed to avoid an ambush by Chief Little Crow and 700 braves, and in the ensuing battle killed 30 Indians and wounded many more. In contrast, Army casualties were seven dead and 30 wounded. Six days later Sibley won a brigadier general's star.

The State preserves an acre of the battlefield, which contains a monument. Cultivated fields dot the gently rolling prairie terrain. Lone Tree Lake, where the battle actually took place, has disappeared since 1862. Sibley's guide mistook it for Wood Lake, several miles to the west, hence the misnomer.

Fort Osage, Missouri △

Location: Jackson County, northern edge of Sibley.

Fort Osage, primarily of significance in the fur trade, was also among the first military outposts in the trans-Mississippi West. It was founded in 1808 by Gen. William Clark, Superintendent of Indian Affairs at St. Louis and later Governor of Missouri Territory, at a site he and Meriwether Lewis had noted in 1804 on their continent-spanning expedition. On the south bank of the Missouri River overlooking a river bend, it allowed an excellent view of river traffic.

One of the most successful of the 28 Indian trading posts, or Government "factories," in operation between 1795 and 1822, the fort was one of few to show a profit. It was one of three in the trans-Mississippi West; the other two were at Arkansas Post, Ark., and Natchitoches, La., but these were unsuccessful.

The idea of winning the good will of the Indians by supplying them with goods from official trading posts originated in the colonial period, when Pennsylvania and Massachusetts experimented with the idea. In 1793 Congress acted on President George Washington's recommendation that the Government establish a series of trading posts where Indians could secure goods at cost by barter. These posts were intended to strengthen military policy, promote peace on the frontier, prevent the exploitation of the Indians by private traders, and offset the influence of the British and Spanish over the former.

In 1795 the system was initiated. The Government appointed a superintendent of Indian trade, who shipped goods, obtained in open market or by bids, to factors at the trading posts. The factors bartered the goods to the Indians for furs, skins, or other items. These were shipped back East to the superintendent, who disposed of them at auction or in foreign markets. Complicated and idealistic, the system proved to be a failure. It suffered from poor administration, the extension of too much credit to the Indians, inferior trade goods and Indian products, and high freight costs. Congressional antagonism toward the system, whetted by the opposition of fur companies, grew throughout the years and, although the Army and Indian Bureau supported the program, led in 1822 to its abolition.

Restored officers' quarters, Fort Osage.

Between 1808 and 1822 Fort Osage, sometimes called Fort Clark, was the principal outpost of civilization on the Missouri River and in western Missouri. At the fort in 1808 U.S. Government officials signed a treaty with the Osages, who ceded most of their lands in present Missouri and the northern part of Arkansas. That same year George C. Sibley was appointed factor. The fort became a rendezvous for Indians and traders alike. During the trading season, as many as 5,000 Indians camped nearby. Well-known fur traders who lived at or visited the fort included Jim Bridger and Manuel Lisa. In 1811 the Astorians stopped there on their journey to the Pacific, where they helped build Fort Astoria. At the beginning of the War of 1812 the Army abandoned the post and the following year Sibley moved the trading post to the site of Arrow Rock, Mo., where he built a small fort. After the war, in 1815 or 1816, both the factor and the garrison returned to Fort Osage. The latter remained until 1819, when it moved upriver with the Army's first Yellowstone Expedition to found Fort Atkinson, Nebr.

In 1821, the same year Capt. William Becknell stopped at the fort on the pioneering expedition that marked the beginning of the Santa Fe trade, Fort Osage became the terminus of the Boone's Lick Trail, first east-west highway to extend through the newly created State of Missouri from St. Charles, Mo. After 1822, when Congress abolished the factory system, the abandoned fort served as a Government storehouse and stopping point for traders on the Santa Fe Trail. In 1825 Sibley was one of the members of a U.S. commission that began a survey of the Santa Fe Trail at the gates of Fort Osage, its eastern terminus until about 1827.

No remains of the original log fort are extant. In 1941 the County Court of Jackson County, Mo., acquired the site. Between 1948 and 1961, based on extensive archeological excavation and historical research, the Jackson County Park Department, with the technical assistance of the Native Sons of Kansas City (Mo.), completed the restoration. It includes five blockhouses, the main one containing original cannon and exhibits; officers' quarters; barracks; the factory, which is furnished with period pieces and has a museum on the second floor featuring exhibits on the factory system and military artifacts; an interpreter's house; blacksmith shop; well; and the Little Osage Village.

Jefferson Barracks, Missouri ⊗

Location: St. Louis County, northern entrance accessible from Kingston Road (Mo. 231), on the southern edge of St. Louis.

Along the west bank of the Mississippi a few miles below St. Louis, this post was the successor of Fort Belle Fontaine (1805–26), established not long after the Louisiana Purchase north of the city on the Missouri River about 4 miles from its confluence with the Mississippi. Jefferson Barracks, founded in 1826 by troops from the fort under Capt. Stephen W. Kearny and Col. Henry Leavenworth, assumed its role as the western military headquarters. At the barracks in 1826 Colonel Leavenworth founded an infantry training school, and within a few years Col. Henry Dodge organized the 1st Dragoons.

Like the city on its northern flank, the barracks enjoyed a repu-

Troops assigned to noncombat posts had considera-
ble time for recreation. Here is the Jefferson
Barracks, Mo., baseball team in the 1880's. Two
of the players later died in the Battle of Wounded
Knee, S. Dak.

tation as the "gateway to the West." It was the starting point of numerous military and exploring expeditions. Its excellent Mississippi River location facilitated the movement of personnel ordnance, and other supplies by steamboat along the Mississippi, Missouri, Ohio, Red, Arkansas, and Sabine Rivers—to frontier posts throughout the West and the Middle West and to such distant conflicts as the Black Hawk War (1832), chiefly in Wisconsin and Illinois; the second Seminole War (1835–42), in Florida; and the Mexican War (1846–48).

The barracks was originally an infantry training base, replacement center, and supply depot. During the Civil War, it served as a hospital and recuperation center. From 1894 through World War II, it functioned as an induction, training, supply, and replacement center. In 1850 an ordnance depot, a supplement to the St. Louis Arsenal, was added. In 1867, just to the south, a national cemetery was established. That same year the post became an engineer depot. In 1871 the Ordnance Department took over jurisdiction of the entire barracks for depot use, but 7 years later relinquished most of it for use in cavalry training. In 1894 the Army regarrisoned it as a regular military post.

Many of the noted military figures of the 19th century served at the post at one time or another, often as young lieutenants and sometimes as base commanders: Robert E. Lee, Ulysses S. Grant, Jefferson Davis, William T. Sherman, Philip H. Sheridan, Winfield Scott, James Longstreet, Joseph E. Johnston, Winfield S. Hancock, Henry Atkinson, John C. Frémont, Don Carlos Buell, George B. Crittenden, John B. Hood, and Zachary Taylor.

Since 1946, when the Army moved out, various Federal, State, and county agencies, as well as corporations and private individuals, have owned or leased parts of the reservation. Of primary interest is the county's Jefferson Barracks Historical Park, which covers 490 acres in the northern half of the reservation, formerly occupied by the ordnance depot. Restored limestone buildings consist of a two-story civilian laborer's house (1851), in its later

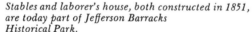

Stables and laborer's house, both constructed in 1851, are today part of Jefferson Barracks Historical Park.

years a guardhouse and barracks, now furnished to represent the 1850–65 period; a stable (1851), one story plus loft, once used as an icehouse; and a large one-story powder magazine (1857), surrounded by a stone wall, which presently houses a museum. The county plans to restore four other buildings.

The Missouri National Guard utilizes 134 acres of the parade ground area. The original gray limestone structures that lined three sides of the parade ground in the years 1827–37 were torn down in the period 1891–95 and the parade ground enlarged to its present size. Dating from the latter period are six brick barracks and a guardhouse on the south side of the parade ground and an administration building on the east end. Adjoining the parade ground and extending to the south and southwest is a 309-acre national cemetery. A Veterans' Administration hospital occupies 136 acres in the southeast corner of the reservation.

Jefferson National Expansion Memorial, Missouri ⊠

Location: St. Louis, downtown; address: 11 North 4th Street, St. Louis, Mo. 63102.

This memorial celebrates the vision of President Jefferson, the architect of westward expansion, and all aspects of that vital national movement.

St. Louis, "gateway to the West," was founded in 1764 by Frenchmen from New Orleans and became a center of French-Canadian culture and Spanish governmental control. Conveniently located in relation to the mouths of the Ohio, Missouri, and other Mississippi tributaries, it became the hub of midcontinental commerce, transportation, and culture—the point where East met West and jumping-off place to the wilderness beyond. A base of operations for traders, travelers, scientists, explorers, military leaders, Indian agents, and missionaries, it was also headquarters of the western fur trade and focus of advanced scientific and political thought in the West.

Along the St. Louis waterfront, hulking steamboats from the East and South met the riverboats that served the frontier communities and outposts on the upper Mississippi and Missouri Rivers. At this major transfer point, a small but teeming city, mercan-

Gateway Arch and Old Courthouse, Jefferson
National Expansion Memorial.

tile establishments, boatyards, saloons, and lodginghouses accommodated and supplied the westbound settlers and other frontiersmen who congregated there before setting out across the Plains. Oregon and California pioneers and gold seekers bought tools, wagons, guns, and supplies; lumbermen, planters, farmers, and fur dealers sold their products; and artisans fashioned Newell & Sutton plows, Murphy wagons for the Santa Fe trade, Grimsley dragoon saddles, Hawken "plains" rifles, and the cast-iron stoves of Filley, and Bridge & Beach.

To dramatize westward expansion and the great cultural, political, economic, and other benefits that followed in the wake of the Louisiana Purchase of 1803, an extensive development program for the memorial is being undertaken by the National Park Service and the Jefferson National Expansion Memorial Association, a nonprofit organization of public-spirited citizens. Crowded, obsolescent industrial buildings have been cleared away as part of a broad urban renewal program.

The dominant feature of the memorial—on the site of the original village of St. Louis—is a 630-foot-high stainless steel arch, designed by the noted architect Eero Saarinen, and completed in 1965. Rising from the west bank of the Mississippi River, it symbolizes the historic role of St. Louis as gateway to the West. It contains an elevator system enabling the visitor to reach an observatory at the top. Scaled to the heroic dimensions of such structures as the Washington Monument, the Eiffel Tower, and the Statue of Liberty, the arch ranks with them in size and grandeur.

An underground visitor center, featuring a Museum of Westward Expansion—temporarily located in the Old Courthouse—is planned at the base of the arch. Exhibits portraying the experiences and contributions of western explorers, fur traders, statesmen, overland emigrants, soldiers, miners, Indians, cattlemen, and farmers will present our western heritage in new dimensions. Guided, as well as self-guided, tours for visiting groups will be provided. The devices and services used in telling the story of westward expansion will be enriched through the years by continuing historical research.

Two historic buildings are preserved at the memorial. One is the Old Courthouse, constructed during the period 1839–64. It was the scene of the first trial in the famous Dred Scott case and the dominant architectural feature of the town during the years that St. Louis was "emporium of the West." Its rotunda resounded with the oratory of Thomas Hart Benton and other famed speakers of the 19th century. At the courthouse Senator Benton delivered his well-known oration, using as his theme Bishop Berkeley's poetic phrase "Westward the course of empire." The second historic structure is the Old Cathedral, built during the period 1831–34 on church property set aside at the time of the founding of St. Louis. It was at one time the seat of the archdiocese, but is now a shrine and place of worship.

Bear Paw Mountains Battlefield, Montana ⊗

Location: Blaine County, on an unimproved road, about 16 miles south of Chinook.

One of the most spectacular retreats and tribal movements in U.S. history and one of the more valiant, though futile, attempts of the

Charles M. Russell's pen drawing of the Battle of Bear Paw Mountains.

Indians to escape the imposition of the white man's civilization on their culture ended at this battlefield. The nontreaty Nez Perces, following the Battle of the Big Hole, Mont., were convinced they would no longer be safe on U.S. soil and finally turned northward to seek sanctuary in Canada. But only 40 miles from the border a column led by Col. Nelson A. Miles, after a swift march from Fort Keogh, Mont., found them camped on Snake Creek in the Bear Paw Mountains and struck on September 30, 1877. Although taken by surprise, the Nez Perces inflicted 20 percent casualties and beat off the assault. Miles then surrounded them, but they held out for 6 days. On October 5 the bulk of the group, or 418 people, surrendered, though some had already escaped to Canada. The day before, General Howard, who had been pursuing the Nez Perces all the way from Idaho, and an advance party of 17 men had arrived—too late to be of much assistance. Miles escorted the captives to Fort Keogh, from where they were sent to Fort Leavenworth, Kans., for confinement and then to a reservation in Indian Territory.

Bear Paw State Monument preserves 160 acres of slightly rolling grasslands where the fighting took place. Two monuments stand in the park. The historic scene has changed little.

Big Hole National Battlefield, Montana ⊠

Location: Beaverhead County, on Mont. 43, about 12
miles west of Wisdom; address: c/o Yellowstone National
Park, Yellowstone National Park, Wyo. 82190.

This national battlefield memorializes the courage of the Nez
Perce Indians and the soldiers who fought one of the battles of
the Nez Perce War at the site in 1877. After crossing the Lolo
Trail in their flight from Idaho, believing their tribulations over,
the nontreaty Nez Perces proceeded southward along the Bitterroot Valley. Reaching the Big Hole prairie on August 7, they
camped near the north fork of the Big Hole River.

On August 8 Col. John Gibbon, accompanied by 17 officers and
146 enlisted men of the 7th Infantry from Fort Ellis, Missoula,

Indian village site, Big Hole National Battlefield.
The tepees marking the site were erected for the
visitor center ground-breaking ceremonies in August
1967, but have since been removed.

and Shaw, Mont., and a group of civilian volunteers located the camp. That evening the troops, undetected, took a position directly across the river from it. At dawn, the tepees clearly in sight, they moved down into the willow-lined river bottom. An Indian on his way to check the horseherd, which the troops had already passed, approached the left of the line. When one of the men fired and killed him, the assault began. The troops plunged across the river to the camp. Most of the Indians, who had been sleeping, fled in panic. Some ran directly into the path of the soldiers, who fired at anyone in sight—man, woman, or child. Before the troops could destroy the camp, the Indians, infuriated at the loss of women and children, began a counterattack.

The soldiers retreated to a wooded area across the river from the upper end of the camp. They took shelter on a bluff behind logs and trees and in hastily dug rifle pits. At this point, some of the Indians besieged the troops, while others returned to the camp to pack supplies and equipment. The main body departed, continuing their retreat, while a small group of warriors maintained the siege until the next morning.

Gibbon was unable to give pursuit because of his heavy losses—29 dead and 40 wounded—and lack of supplies. His men had slain 89 Indians, including probably 50 women and children, and wounded many more. The loss of warriors, lodges, and supplies seriously handicapped the embittered Nez Perces, but they pushed on southward and eastward across Yellowstone National Park. Continually brushing aside or eluding the military forces pursuing them, they then turned northward en route to a hoped-for refuge in Canada. But less than 2 months elapsed before they met a heart-rending defeat at the Battle of Bear Paw Mountains, Mont.

Big Hole National Battlefield embraces the siege area, the site of the Indian village, a monument to the Nez Perce Chief Joseph, the place where the Indians captured a howitzer, and the area across the Big Hole River where the Nez Perces besieged the troops. The natural setting has changed little since 1877. Traces of rifle pits may still be seen. The visitor center museum displays exhibits of the battle, including the captured howitzer and a battle diorama. A self-guiding trail leads through the siege area to the howitzer-capture site.

Location: Big Horn County, on I–90 (U.S. 87), about 1
mile southeast of its junction with U.S. 212, which is some
15 miles southeast of Hardin; address: P.O. Box 416, Crow
Agency, Mont. 59022.

Of all the battles between Indians and soldiers, the best known is
"Custer's Last Stand," commemorated by this national monument. On a hot June Sunday in 1876, hordes of painted warriors
swarmed over a treeless ridge rising from the Little Bighorn Valley and wiped out a battalion of the 7th Cavalry, 220 blue-shirted
troopers led by Lt. Col. George A. Custer. When the guns fell si-
lent and the smoke and dust of the battle lifted, after probably no
more than an hour, every soldier lay dead. Four miles to the
southeast, battalions under Maj. Marcus A. Reno and Capt. Frederick W. Benteen beat off repeated assaults and held out until the
approach of reinforcements the next day caused the Indians to
withdraw. Reno and Benteen lost 47 men. All told, more than
half of the 700 men in the regiment died or received wounds;
Indian losses have never been authoritatively estimated.
Custer sustained the most spectacular defeat suffered by the

Lt. Col. George A. Custer
His death and the dev-
astating defeat inflicted
on his troops at the Battl
of the Little Bighorn
brought him enduring
fame.

186

Army in the Indian wars. His Sioux and Cheyenne opponents, making one of the last major armed efforts of the northern Plains Indians to resist white encroachment on their homeland, won one of the greatest triumphs of the American Indians in their four-century struggle against the alien tide that was finally to inundate them. Thus Custer Battlefield serves as a reminder of the long and poignant struggle for possession of the North American Continent. But more particularly it pays tribute to the courage of the soldiers and the Indians who fought in the battle—representatives of two clashing civilizations, one group believing firmly in the inevitability of its advance and the other equally as determined not to yield.

The catalyst that had generated the unified Indian response represented in the Battle of the Little Bighorn was Sioux and Cheyenne anger at the invasion of the Black Hills by miners and prospectors in 1874–75. More broadly involved was the resentment that had smoldered among the tribes since the Fort Laramie Treaty (1868). A group of Indians had subsequently elected to live in the unceded Powder River hunting grounds of Montana and Wyoming, west of the Black Hills and south of the Yellowstone River. Prominent among their leaders were the Hunkpapa medicine man Sitting Bull and the Oglala war chief Crazy Horse. They demonstrated their contempt for the treaty, as well as their fury at violations of it, by attacking isolated settlements and travelers and by contesting the advance of surveying crews mapping a route for the Northern Pacific Railroad.

The bulk of the Sioux had settled on the Great Sioux Reservation, created by the Fort Laramie Treaty in the western half of South Dakota and including the Black Hills, sacred to the Sioux. In 1874 Custer led an expedition into the hills and confirmed and publicized the already known presence of gold in paying quantities. Living up to treaty commitments, the Army barred prospectors from the hills, but many kept clandestinely slipping in. In September 1875 Government representatives, in negotiations near Fort Robinson, Nebr., tried to buy the hills from the reservation Sioux, but they refused. Foreseeing the inevitable, the Government—in direct violation of the Fort Laramie Treaty—threw the area open to anyone willing to accept the risks involved. Miners swarmed in.

*"Custer's Last Stand" has inspired almost 800
artists. Most of their renditions are more dramatic
than accurate. Here is "Custer's Last Fight,"
by W. R. Leigh.*

Incensed, hundreds of the reservation Sioux joined their non-reservation brethren in the unceded Powder River country. All vowed to resist further white advances. So long as they did not have to depend on the Government for food, they could not be fully controlled. And so long as they had access to the abundant game in the Powder River region, they would not be dependent. In December 1875 the Indian Bureau ordered them to report to the agencies by January 31, 1876, or be driven in by the Army. This ultimatum, which allowed insufficient time for compliance, precipitated another war. When the Indians did not comply, the Army was charged with enforcing the order.

In March 1876 an ineffectual campaign of Brig. Gen. George Crook north from Fort Fetterman, Wyo., was climaxed by the bitterly fought but indecisive Battle of Powder River, Mont. Maj. Gen. Philip H. Sheridan, commanding the Division of the Missouri, then decided to conduct a three-pronged summer offensive. While Brig. Gen. Alfred H. Terry, commanding the Department of Dakota, marched westward from Fort Abraham Lincoln, N. Dak., another column under Col. John Gibbon, his district commander, would travel eastward from Fort Shaw, Mont. Crook, heading the Department of the Platte, and his troops were to complete the envelopment by a northward push from Fort Fetterman. To insure success, Sheridan stripped the garrisons throughout the Departments of the Platte and Dakota.

Crook was the first to engage the foe. The Sioux and Cheyennes had united in one huge camp on the Little Bighorn River. Warned by scouts of Crook's approach northward down Rosebud Creek, Crazy Horse and his warriors engaged him in the Battle of the Rosebud, Mont. (June 17, 1876), and fought so fiercely that he decided to withdraw to present Sheridan, Wyo., to regroup and await reinforcements. Meantime Gibbon, who had acquired additional troops at Fort Ellis, and Terry, both unaware of what had happened to Crook, had met on the Yellowstone at the mouth of the Rosebud. Terry's largest contingent consisted of the flamboyant Lt. Col. George A. Custer's 7th Cavalry, eager to repeat its success of the Washita campaign. Custer, a youthful major general in the Civil War and now at 36 a plainsman with a decade of experience, had fought Sitting Bull on the Yellowstone in 1873.

View of the visitor center and national cemetery from Custer Hill, Custer Battlefield National Monument.

189

Scouting reports of an Indian trail in the Rosebud Valley convinced Terry that the quarry were camped in the Little Bighorn
Valley. Fearful lest they escape, he decided to trap them and force
a battle. He gave Custer only generalized orders and granted him
latitude to alter them if the tactical situation warranted. According to the overall plan, Custer was to move southward up the Rosebud to its head, cross over to the Little Bighorn, and proceed
northward until he reached the vicinity of the camp. He was not
to engage the enemy until June 26, by which time Gibbon's command and the rest of Terry's forces, including slow-moving infantry as well as cavalry, would have time to reach the northern end
of the Little Bighorn Valley via the Yellowstone and the Bighorn.
Custer's troopers rode off confidently on June 22.

Custer soon located and followed the trail. When it veered westward he followed it instead of proceeding to the head of the Rosebud as planned. His scouts discovered the Indian village in the
Little Bighorn Valley from the ridge dividing the valleys of the
Rosebud and Little Bighorn. On June 25, sighting two small
Indian parties as he descended to the latter, Custer decided his
regiment had been detected. He made the decision to strike immediately instead of waiting until the next day. Dividing his regiment into three battalions, he directed Captain Benteen and three
companies to reconnoiter along the base of the Wolf Mountains
to the left, or southeast, of the main force. Custer and Major
Reno, commanding five and three companies respectively, headed
down what is now Reno Creek toward the Little Bighorn River.
Near it they observed an Indian band a short distance ahead. Custer commanded Reno to give pursuit. Reno crossed the river and
passed down the valley until the camp—a huge village—came
into view. A mass of warriors rode out and gave battle. Routed,
Reno's men retreated back across the river and dug in along some
high bluffs. Benteen's battalion later joined them there.

Meanwhile, Custer, instead of following Reno, had ridden
north and then west. Possibly afraid that the entire Indian force
might get away, he may have intended to assault it from the rear.
Instead, thousands of Sioux and Cheyenne warriors under Crazy
Horse, Gall, and other leaders fell upon his battalion. The troops
apparently fought a series of uncoordinated and separate com-
pany-sized actions along the ridges lining the river across from the

■ 1867

● Helena

✗ Big Hole
  1877

✗ Fort Keogh
    1876 ■ ● Miles

Fort Ellis
■ 1867-86
Bozeman ●

River

Canyon ✗
Creek
1877

Fort Custer, ■
1877
Little Bighorn ✗ 1876   ✗ Lame
                          Deer
                          1877

Powder
River ✗
1876

✗ Rosebud 1876

✗ Wolf Mountain
      1877

● Sheridan

Yellowstone
National
Park
1872

✗ Dull Knife
    1876

■ Fort Washakie
    1869

Fort Fetterm
■ 1867

Fort Lar
   1

Fort Fred Steele ■
   1868-86

■ Fort Bridger
   1858-90

Fort D. A. R
      1867
Cheyenne

THE NORTHERN PLAINS
1868-1890

■ Forts   ▲ Agencies

● Towns   ✗ Battles

0   25   50   75   100   125   150
SCALE OF MILES

Fort Totten ■
1867-90

Fort Stevenson ■
1867-83

Fort A.Lincoln ■ ● Bismarck
1872

Fort Rice ■
1864-78

Standing Rock
Agency ▲ ■ Fort Yates
1873   1874

Fort Sisseton
■ 1864-89

Slim Buttes ✕
1876

Cheyenne River
Agency ▲ ■ Fort Bennett 1870
1868   ■ Fort Sully
          1866

Fort Meade
✕wood ● ■ 1878

● Rapid City

Pine Ridge ✕ Wounded Knee   Rosebud   Whetstone
Agency ▲   1890   ▲ Agency   Agency ▲
1878   1878   Fort Randall
et ✕   ■ 1856
k ✕ 1876 ▲ Spotted Tail Agency   Fort Niobrara   1868-73
          1874-77   1880
Robinson ■▲ Red Cloud Agency   ■
1874   1873-77

per Platte Agency—
868-72

Fort Hartsuff
■ 1874-81

Fort Omaha
1868 ■
●
Omaha

■ Fort Sidney
1867

Fort McPherson ■
1863-80

✕ Summit Springs   ■ Fort Kearny
1869   1848-71

Beecher's Island ✕ 1868

village. Finally, pinned down in terrain unsuited to mounted action, the remnants of the five companies dismounted and made separate last-ditch stands on what is now Custer Hill and in the ravine to the west near the river. Reno and Benteen withstood a siege until the approach of the columns led by Generals Terry and Gibbon on June 26 scared the Indians away.

Exactly what happened after Custer led his battalion into the Little Bighorn Valley is not certain. The enigma of its annihilation spurs students of military history to infinite speculations over exactly why and how Custer met such a catastrophe. But one thing is certain. By suffering one of the worst defeats in the history of the Indian wars, he won for himself and his regiment an immortality that no victory, however brilliant or decisive, could ever have achieved.

The Indians were to have but a short time to savor their triumph at the Little Bighorn. The Custer disaster shocked the Nation, which demanded revenge. Within 2 years, most of the Indians who had defeated Custer had been forced to surrender and the power of the northern Plains tribes broken forever.

At the visitor center, museum exhibits, literature, and National Park Service personnel interpret the battle and its significance. Near the visitor center is Custer Battlefield National Cemetery, which contains the bodies of soldiers killed in other Indian battles. A road runs from the visitor center to Custer Hill, which is dominated by a granite memorial shaft erected over the mass grave of the enlisted men killed in the battle. Custer's remains are interred at the United States Military Academy, West Point, N.Y., and those of other officers elsewhere at various locations. From the shaft the visitor is able to see most of the battlefield as well as the valley in which the Indian village was located. Interpretive signs and markers on Custer Hill and Battle Ridge describe the combat action and denote where the men of Custer's immediate command fell. In a detached section of the national monument, 4 miles to the southeast, is the site of the Reno-Benteen defense perimeter. It is accessible by a road passing through the Crow Indian Reservation. Self-guided trails lead to restored rifle pits. Reno Hill affords a fine view of the valley from which Reno retreated on the afternoon of June 25.

Fort Assinniboine, Montana ⊗

Location: Hill County, on an unimproved road, about 7 miles southwest of Havre.

The original missions of Fort Assinniboine (1879–1911), some 38 miles south of the Canadian border, were to prevent Sitting Bull and his followers, who had fled to Canada in 1876, from reentering the country and to protect area settlers from the Blackfeet Indians. Although Sitting Bull never appeared in the area and the troops took part in few regional engagements of importance, the fort accommodated a large garrison throughout its history. Of brick construction, it was one of the most elaborate posts in Montana. In 1913 the U.S. Department of Agriculture acquired it, and in 1927 tore down most of the buildings.

The remaining structures, a guardhouse and a multiplex officers' quarters, are utilized by a U.S. Agricultural Experiment Station. A commemorative marker, erected by the Daughters of the American Revolution, stands on the parade ground.

Scene at Fort Assinniboine in the 1880's.

Gustav Sohon's drawing of Fort Benton, probably sketched in the early 1860's.

Fort Benton, Montana △

Location: Chouteau County.

Growing up around a fur trading post on the Missouri River, the town of Fort Benton became the hub of traffic moving westward to the goldfields of Idaho and Montana. At the head of steamboat navigation on the Missouri, it was the eastern terminus of the Mullan Road. Between 1869 and 1881 it was also the site of a military post.

In 1847 Alexander Culbertson of the American Fur Co. established the fur trading post that was first known as Fort Lewis but 3 years later was renamed Fort Benton. It soon became the foremost establishment in Montana, but the fur trade was rapidly declining. After the arrival in 1859 of the *Chippewa*, a sternwheeler, the first steamboat to penetrate that far up the Missouri, the post became a trade-transportation center and a town grew up next to it.

Following the 1862 gold strike in Montana, Indian hostilities closed many overland routes, particularly the convenient Bozeman Trail. Prospectors sailed up the Missouri by steamboat to Fort Benton and then pushed overland to Bannack, Virginia City, Helena, and other mining camps. Sometimes as many as 30 to 40 steamboats were docked at the riverfront. Ox teams and mule pack trains carried food and other supplies, which St. Louis and Portland merchants keenly competed to furnish, to settlements in Idaho, Montana, and Canada. Much of this commerce, as well as emigrants en route to the Pacific Northwest, passed over the Mullan Road, a military road running westward from Fort Benton, Mont., to Fort Walla Walla, Wash. Constructed in 1859–62 under the supervision of Lt. John Mullan, it was the first wagon road over the northern Rockies. The town of Fort Benton remained a major transportation center until the arrival of the railroads in the region in the 1880's.

In 1869 the U.S. Army had leased and occupied the trading post from the American Fur Co., but by 1874 most of the troops were living in town. The one-company post served mainly as a supply depot for Forts Shaw and Ellis, Mont., and in 1881 the garrison was transferred to Fort Shaw.

All that remains of the early fort are a blockhouse and a portion of the adobe walls, located in a city park overlooking the Missouri River on the eastern edge of the business district. Nearby is the privately owned Fort Benton Museum, which contains historical exhibits. The riverfront, where steamboats once docked, is little changed. Several brick and stone commercial buildings of 19th-century vintage give a historic flavor to the town.

Fort Custer, Montana ⊗

Location: Big Horn County, on an unimproved road, about 1 mile west of I–90 and 2 miles southeast of Hardin.

Some of the troops that massed in the region following the Custer catastrophe, which occurred the year before only a few miles away, activated Fort Custer (1877–98). By that time most of the hostile Indians in the vicinity had been confined to reservations, but the post supplied troops for some of the Plains campaigns, the Bannock War (1878) , and an uprising at Crow Agency, Mont., in 1886. After the Army evacuated the post, the buildings were sold and became the nucleus of present Hardin.

A Daughters of the American Revolution marker designates the

*Undated photograph of 10th Cavalry parade
at Fort Custer.*

site, within the boundaries of the Crow Indian Reservation on an
abandoned golf course. All that remains are scattered cellars and
ground depressions.

Fort Ellis, Montana ⊗

> *Location: Gallatin County, on I-90, about 3½ miles east
> of Bozeman.*

Fort Ellis (1867–86) watched over miners and settlers in the Gal-
latin River Valley of western Montana and the nearby Bozeman,
Bridger, and Flathead Passes. Figuring in the 1876–81 Sioux campaigns, it was the base at which Col. John Gibbon, operating out
of Fort Shaw, Mont., acquired additional troops in 1876 before
proceeding eastward in the ill-fated operation that ended in the
Custer disaster. Gibbon also led Fort Ellis troops in the Battle of
the Big Hole, Mont.

The Montana State University's Fort Ellis Experiment Station
occupies the site, but no buildings remain. A commemorative
monument is located just off I-90.

Fort Keogh, Montana ⊗

> *Location: Custer County, on U.S. 10, southwestern edge of
> Miles City.*

Situated on the south bank of the Yellowstone River at the mouth
of the Tongue River, this post was known as the Tongue River

Weather conditions on the northern Plains created
hardships for troops in the field, but their families
could often enjoy skating. Here is a skating party
at Fort Keogh about 1890.

Cantonment for the first year or so and then relocated a mile away
and redesignated Fort Keogh. Col. Nelson A. Miles founded it in
August 1876 as a base for patrolling the Yellowstone to prevent
the escape to Canada of the Indians who had wiped out Custer.
Combining diplomacy with war, he persuaded many hostiles to
give up, and in May 1877 defeated Chief Lame Deer in the Battle
of Lame Deer, Mont. By spring of that year most of the Sioux and
Cheyennes had reported to their agencies except Sitting Bull and
his followers, who in May fled to Canada. Miles patrolled the international boundary so closely they could not pursue buffalo into
the United States and surrendered at Fort Buford, N. Dak., in
1881.

In September 1877, despite the exigencies of the Sioux-Chey-
enne campaign, Miles set out from Fort Keogh and crushed the
nontreaty Nez Perces, heading for Canada, in the Battle of Bear
Paw Mountains. The next month his troops escorted 418 captives
to the fort, from where they proceeded in November to Fort
Leavenworth, Kans. The Army garrisoned the post continuously
until 1908, reactivated it as a quartermaster depot during World
War I, and in 1924 transferred it to the Department of the
Interior.

A Range Livestock Experiment Station of the U.S. Department
of Agriculture occupies the site today. Although several officers'
quarters, barracks, and noncommissioned officers' quarters are

Fort Keogh winter scene, undated.

used by the experiment station, most of the buildings associated with the military period have given way to modern construction. The superintendent resides in Colonel Miles' residence, at the western point of the post's unusual diamond-shaped parade ground. A mile to the east, in a field on the southern side of the highway, is the site of the Tongue River Cantonment, marked by mounds of dirt, rubble, and an original wall.

Fort Logan, Montana ⊗

Location: Meagher County, on an unimproved road, about 20 miles northwest of the town of White Sulphur Springs.

Called Camp Baker until 1878, when it was renamed Fort Logan, this fort (1869–80) was established at one site in the Smith River Valley and later relocated to another 5 miles to the north. It protected miners and settlers; guarded the freight route to Fort Benton; and provided troops for many of the campaigns in western Montana, including the Nez Perce War (1877).

Traces of almost all the buildings are extant, though some have been moved and are utilized by the present ranch owners. An adobe storehouse is deteriorating. Two frame officers' quarters are in near-original condition. The blockhouse, commemorated by a Daughters of the American Revolution plaque, has been relocated to the center of the parade ground.

Fort Missoula, Montana ⊗

Location: Missoula County, just off U.S. 93, southwestern edge of Missoula.

The Army founded this fort in 1877 on the Bitterroot River to watch over settlers. Its garrison took part in only one engagement of consequence, the Battle of the Big Hole (August 1877), 90 miles to the south, in the Nez Perce War. The captives were incarcerated at Fort Missoula. During the next 2 years, when they were not countering minor Indian harassments, the troops restored a stretch of the Mullan Road, running from Fort Benton, Mont., to Fort Walla Walla, Wash. In postfrontier days the fort was not continuously active or garrisoned. Today's Fort Missoula Military Reservation serves Reserve units and various Government agencies.

The only extant buildings of the old post are the stone magazine (1878); log laundresses' quarters (1877), originally a temporary officers' quarters and today an officers' club; and a log sergeants' family quarters (1878). A stone marker and plaque commemorate the garrison's participation in the Nez Perce War.

Fort Shaw, Montana ⊗

Location: Cascade County, on Mont. 20, about one-half mile northwest of the town of Fort Shaw.

Founded in 1867, this post protected settlers, kept the road open between Fort Benton and Helena, and guarded miners in northwestern Montana. During the 1876 campaign against the Sioux and Cheyennes, Col. John Gibbon, the base commander, led the garrison up the Missouri, procured reinforcements at Fort Ellis, Mont., rendezvoused with the forces of General Terry on the Yellowstone at the mouth of the Rosebud, and subsequently relieved the survivors of Custer's regiment at the Little Bighorn. The next year troops from the fort and Forts Ellis and Missoula, again under Gibbon, defeated the nontreaty Nez Perces, retreating from Idaho to Montana, at the Battle of the Big Hole. After the Army relinquished the fort in 1891, for many years the Department of the Interior used it as an Indian school. At that time workmen covered the frame-roofed adobe buildings with wood siding and erected some new buildings. Later the U.S. Bureau of Reclamation occupied the fort. In 1926 ownership passed to the Fort Shaw School District.

Since then, a few of the buildings have been used for school and community purposes, some have been rented to private individuals, and others have deteriorated or been demolished to make way for new construction.

Lame Deer Battlefield, Montana ⊗

Location: Rosebud County, a short distance off an unimproved road, about 1⅓ miles southwest of Lame Deer. Make local inquiry.

One of the final struggles in the Army's conquest of the Sioux took place at this site on May 7, 1877. Col. Nelson A. Miles' troops, from the Tongue River Cantonment, defeated Lame Deer's band of Miniconjou Sioux, except for Sitting Bull's Hunkpapa group the last remnant of the coalition that the year before had overwhelmed Custer at the Battle of the Little Bighorn. Surprised and surrounded in his camp, Lame Deer at first attempted to surrender but a scuffle broke out in which the chief, his son, 12 warriors, and four soldiers died. The subdued Indian survivors reported to the reservation.

The battlefield, indicated by a marker, is located along Lame Deer Creek, a tributary of Rosebud Creek, on a privately owned ranch near the Northern Cheyenne Agency. Except for the unimproved road running up the valley from Lame Deer, the site is not marked by any significant modern intrusions. It is surrounded by rugged hills dotted with scrub pine.

Powder River Battlefield, Montana ⊗

Location: Powder River County, accessible via an unimproved road, about 4 miles northeast of Moorhead. Make local inquiry.

At this battlefield occurred the opening battle in the 1876 Army campaign against the Sioux and Cheyennes. In March 1876 Brig.

...troops, to the bluffs above the
...the commanding heights, and poured a deadly
...below. After burning most of the village, Reyn-
...the Indian powers and hastily retreated. That
...harassed him and captured all the ponies.
...his forces but, discouraged by the setback, the
...supplies, and the bitter cold and deep snow, he re-
...Fetterman to refit. If nothing, he had succeeded
...ing Indian resistance.

...privately owned, is used for ranching purposes. The
...was situated on the west side of the Powder River.
...river overflowed and covered the bottom land with
...of silt. The mesa and bluffs from which the Indi-
...attacked are unchanged. A marker is located near the
...of Moorhead.

...attlefield, Montana ⊗

*...cation: Big Horn County, is off an unimproved road,
...out 3 miles southwest of Kirk. Make local inquiry.*

...battle in the Army's 1876 campaign against the Sioux
...tes was fought on this battlefield. After the Battle of
...er in March 1876, General Crook retreated from
...his base at Fort Fetterman. In May, as part of a
...ed offensive, he once again advanced northward from
...d was the first of the columns to meet the enemy.
...a huge Indian camp on the Little Bighorn River re-
...k's approach northward down Rosebud Creek. Crazy
...rth about 1,500 warriors atop the 1,774 troops. On
...ok drove the attackers from the field, but the opposi-
...strong he returned to his supply depot and base on
...at present Sheridan, Wyo. to reorganize and await

The Battle of the Ro↑ ↑d, colorfully depicted by J. E. Taylor in Rm ↑d I. Dodge's Our Wild Indians *(Hartford, 18↑*

planned with the o↑↑r two columns, which were not aware of his withdrawal. One we↑ later Custer met disaster when he attacked the village on the L↑↑e Bighorn.

The battlefiel↑ ↑nsists of rugged and rolling terrain, today used for ranch purp↑es. A few grainfields are scattered about the landscape, but mo↑ f it is stock range that has not changed to any appreciable de↑↑e since 1876. A monument stands near a gravel road east of ↑e battleground. Permission to visit the site, accessible onl↑ b↑ fo↑ must be obtained from the ranch owner.

St. Ignatius Missi↑. Montana ⊗

> *Location↑l ↑ke County, on the southwestern edge of the tow·n of S Ignatius.*

Established in 1855 ↑ Father Adrien Hocken, this mission carried out the terms of a↑ 1855 treaty by which the U.S. Government agreed to provide ↑e Flathead Indians with schools, mills, and blacksmith and car↑nter shops as part of the payment for ceded lands. On the reser↑tion created by the treaty the priests taught the Indians the ru↑ments of farming, carpentry, and milling.

Gen. George Crook advanced north from Fort Fetterman. Discovering an Indian trail, he sent Col. Joseph ʝ. Reynolds and six troops of the 2d and 3d Cavalry to find the village he suspected to be at the end of the trail. At dawn on the 17th, in the Powder River Valley, Reynolds located and charged the village. The surprised inhabitants fled from their lodges to the bluffs above the valley, occupied the commanding heights, and poured a deadly fire at the troops below. After burning most of the village, Reynolds captured the Indian ponies and hastily retreated. That night the warriors harassed him and recaptured all the ponies. Crook reunited his forces but, discouraged by the setback, the shortage of supplies, and the bitter cold and deep snow, he returned to Fort Fetterman to refit. If anything, he had succeeded only in stiffening Indian resistance.

The site, privately owned, is used for ranching purposes. The Indian village was situated on the west side of the Powder River. In 1923 the river overflowed and covered the bottom land with about a foot of silt. The mesa and bluffs from which the Indians counterattacked are unchanged. A marker is located near the northern edge of Moorhead.

Rosebud Battlefield, Montana ⊗

Location: Big Horn County, just off an unimproved road, about 9 miles southwest of Kirby. Make local inquiry.

The second battle in the Army's 1876 campaign against the Sioux and Cheyennes was fought on this battlefield. After the Battle of Powder River in March 1876, General Crook retreated from Montana to his base at Fort Fetterman. In May, as part of a three-pronged offensive, he once again advanced northward from the fort, and was the first of the columns to meet the enemy. Scouts from a huge Indian camp on the Little Bighorn River reported Crook's approach northward down Rosebud Creek. Crazy Horse led forth about 1,500 warriors to stop the 1,774 troops. On June 17 Crook drove the attackers from the field, but the opposition was so strong he returned to his supply depot and base on Goose Creek at present Sheridan, Wyo., to reorganize and await reinforcements. This action prevented him from joining forces as

The Battle of the Rosebud, colorfully depicted by J. E. Taylor in Richard I. Dodge's Our Wild Indians *(Hartford, 1883).*

planned with the other two columns, which were not aware of his withdrawal. One week later Custer met disaster when he attacked the village on the Little Bighorn.

The battlefield consists of rugged and rolling terrain, today used for ranch purposes. A few grainfields are scattered about the landscape, but most of it is stock range that has not changed to any appreciable degree since 1876. A monument stands near a gravel road east of the battleground. Permission to visit the site, accessible only by foot, must be obtained from the ranch owner.

St. Ignatius Mission, Montana ⊗

> *Location: Lake County, on the southwestern edge of the town of St. Ignatius.*

Established in 1855 by Father Adrien Hoeken, this mission carried out the terms of an 1855 treaty by which the U.S. Government agreed to provide the Flathead Indians with schools, mills, and blacksmith and carpenter shops as part of the payment for ceded lands. On the reservation created by the treaty the priests taught the Indians the rudiments of farming, carpentry, and milling.

Later Sisters of Providence from Canada set up a boarding school for girls, and the priests erected a school for boys.

Surviving structures include a log cabin (1854), the first home of the missionaries; an old mill, in poor condition; a girls' dormitory built in the 1890's, not used currently; and a church (1891) of considerable architectural interest. The Society of Jesus operates the mission today.

Wolf Mountain (Tongue River) Battlefield, Montana ⊗

Location: Rosebud County, on an unimproved road, about 15 miles southwest of Birney.

The battle fought at this site climaxed Col. Nelson A. Miles' winter drive of 1876–77 in pursuit of the Sioux under Crazy Horse who had annihilated the Custer command the preceding summer on the Little Bighorn. In October Miles captured and sent 2,000 of them back to the reservation. Despite blizzards and extreme cold he remained in the field. On January 7, 1877, he camped beside the Tongue River on the southern flank of the Wolf Mountains. The next morning Crazy Horse and 800 braves made a surprise attack. Miles, his howitzers disguised as wagons, quickly repulsed it. The Indians took refuge on bluffs overlooking the camp. When the troops assaulted the bluffs, the warriors withdrew under cover of a snowstorm. Many of them surrendered with Crazy Horse and Dull Knife's Cheyennes in the spring at Fort Robinson, Nebr.

The battlefield is on the east side of the Tongue River, beneath Pyramid Butte, a spur of the Wolf Mountains. A gravel road bridges the river from the west, crosses the valley where Miles camped; ascends the bluffs just south of Pyramid Butte, the final Indian position; and continues toward the town of Birney. Except for the road, the site is unchanged since 1877.

Blue Water (Ash Hollow) Battlefield, Nebraska ⊗

Location: Garden County. The battlefield extends about 8 miles north up Blue Water Creek Valley from the U.S. 26 bridge across Blue Water Creek, about 2 miles northwest of Lewellen.

The Battle of Blue Water was the first major clash between U.S. soldiers and the Sioux Indians. In 1855, to punish the Sioux for their depredations following the Grattan Fight near Fort Laramie, Wyo., the previous year, the Army sent out Col. William S. Harney and an expedition of 600 men from Fort Leavenworth, Kans. Harney discovered the Brûlé Sioux village of Little Thunder in Blue Water Creek Valley, just above the creek's junction with the North Platte. By a circuitous route dragoons entered the valley and advanced downstream, while Harney and a force of infantrymen marched up the valley from the Platte. Attacked from two directions on September 3, the Indians scattered, but not before the troops killed 80 warriors, wounded five, and captured 70 women and children. Four soldiers met death and seven suffered wounds. The rest of the Sioux and Northern Cheyennes in the vicinity managed to avoid the troops. The latter moved northwestward to Fort Laramie and marched over the Fort Laramie-Fort Pierre Road through the heart of Sioux country to Fort Pierre, on the Missouri River. There they joined part of the expedition that had come up the Missouri and spent the winter of 1855–56. For almost a decade most of the Sioux gave no further serious trouble.

Except for patches of cultivation along Blue Water Creek, most of the valley is stock range and essentially resembles its historical appearance. The terrain near the mouth of the creek is rugged, but the site of the Indian village farther upstream is more level. Broken hills are on each side, where the Indians took refuge from Harney's troops. The site is in private ownership, but a 40-acre State historical park overlooks the battlefield.

Fort Atkinson, Nebraska ⛁

Location: Washington County, on a secondary road, about 1 mile east of the town of Fort Calhoun.

One of the first forts west of the Mississippi, the first west of the Missouri, and at the time the largest and most advanced frontier post, this fort (1819–27) had a short but important history. Next to Fort Smith (1817), it was the earliest on the "Permanent Indian Frontier." It was also an administrative center for the Indians on the upper Missouri and a base for fur traders and explorers.

The fort was founded by the first Yellowstone Expedition. The expedition was one in a series planned after the War of 1812 by Secretary of War John C. Calhoun to awe the Indians of the upper Missouri River with U.S. military power, counter British influence, and establish a chain of military posts. Col. Henry Atkinson set out from Plattsburgh, N.Y., in the spring of 1819 with 1,126 soldiers of the 6th Infantry and many women and children. He planned to proceed up the Missouri and found a post somewhere near the mouth of the Yellowstone—a goal never reached because of lack of funds. In the fall, at the end of a 2,628-mile trek, the expedition bivouacked at Council Bluffs, a site on the west bank of the Missouri River at which Lewis and Clark had camped in 1804, held their first council with the Indians, and recommended as a site for a fort. On the river bottom near the bluffs, Atkinson and his men constructed Cantonment Missouri. But, after a winter of disease and hardship and a disastrous spring flood, they moved to a site high on the top of the bluffs, where by fall a permanent brick and log fort, soon known as Fort Atkinson, had taken shape.

A quadrangular stockade, with bastions at the northwest and southeast corners, surrounded the buildings. They included barracks, officers' quarters, sutler's house and store, Indian council house, hospital, powder magazine, laundresses' quarters, and stables. Near the fort were a dairy, gristmill, limekiln, sawmill, blacksmith shop, and brickyard. Agriculture and Indian management dominated life at the fort, which more resembled a frontier village and social center than a military installation. The soldiers, supervised by a director of agriculture and a superintendent of livestock, farmed and raised stock. By 1821 they had tilled 504 acres of land. Agricultural activities embraced dairying, cheesemaking, meat curing, soapmaking, and milling. Fur traders brought news from St. Louis or the Indian country. Indians dropped in to hold councils and trade at the agency. Indian Agent Benjamin O'Fallon, who had established the Upper Missouri Indian Agency at the fort in 1819, worked to keep peace among the tribes and insure their cooperation with trappers and traders. Visitors at the fort were such explorers and mountain men as Jed Smith, Ed Rose, Hiram Scott, Jim Beckwourth, Jim Clyman, and Tom Fitzpatrick.

In 1823 news reached Fort Atkinson of an Arikara attack on William H. Ashley's fur brigade, 14 of whose 90 men had died and 11 received wounds. To punish the Indians, Col. Henry Leavenworth led 220 Regulars, 120 mountain men, and 400 to 500 Sioux allies up the Missouri to the Arikara villages and fought the first large-scale battle between U.S. troops and the Plains Indians. Although he recovered some of the goods stolen from Ashley, he mismanaged the attack and inspired the Arikaras with contempt for U.S. military prowess. Two years later the second and last Yellowstone Expedition in the 1820's had more success. Colonel Atkinson, 457 soldiers, and Indian Agent O'Fallon traveled to the mouth of the Yellowstone, negotiated treaties with 12 tribes, and accomplished much toward gaining the friendship of the Indians and promoting the fur trade.

In 1827, to afford better protection for the Santa Fe Trail, the Government replaced Fort Atkinson, distant from civilization and not on main routes of travel, with Fort Leavenworth, Kans., farther down the Missouri, and relocated the Indian agency.

Fort Atkinson State Historical Park consists of 147 acres, including a buffer strip. The cantonment site, on the river bottom, has not been exactly determined. The fort site lies on a plateau rising from the flood plain above the western edge of the Missouri River Valley. In the 1820's the river ran along the foot of the bluffs. The old channel is still evident, but the modern one is 3 miles to the east. The only visible remains at the site are low earth mounds on the eastern edge. The rest of the site has been leveled and placed in cultivation. A continuing program of archeological excavation by the Nebraska State Historical Society has yielded numerous artifacts, many of which are displayed at the Fort Calhoun Museum, and exposed several foundations.

Fort Hartsuff, Nebraska ⊗
> *Location: Valley County, on an unimproved road, about 3 miles northwest of Elyria.*

This fort (1874–81) protected settlers in the Northern Loup Valley of central Nebraska and the Pawnee Indian Reservation, in present Nance County, from the raids of roving Sioux who re- 205 sided farther north and west. The transfer of the Pawnees to Indian Territory, the Army's push of the Sioux into the Dakotas, and the ensuing influx of settlers into the region ended the need for the post.

After the Army departed, farmers utilized some of the buildings, constructed mostly of concrete and stone. Traces remain of practically all of them. Some are mere ruins or shells, but others have roofs and interior plaster. Fort Hartsuff State Historical Park has completed restoration of the guardhouse and dispensary and has begun work on the adjutant's office and the officers' quarters.

Fort Kearny, Nebraska ⊗

> *Location: Kearney County, on an unimproved road, about 7 miles southeast of Kearney.*

Forts Kearny, Nebr., and Laramie, Wyo., were the first two posts garrisoned to protect the Oregon-California Trail. The original Fort Kearny (1846–48) was a two-story log blockhouse not continuously occupied, along the west bank of the Missouri River at the eastern edge of the State on the site of Nebraska City. Because

Fort Kearny, Nebr., by William H. Jackson.

this location was too far from the Oregon-California Trail, in 1848 troops founded in its stead a new post some 200 miles westward in mid-Nebraska along the trail on the south bank of the Platte River and about halfway between Forts Leavenworth, Kans., and Laramie, Wyo. The post guarded the trail, served as an ammunition depot, and protected peaceable Indians in the area from hostiles and outlaws. In 1871, the transcontinental railroad having been completed 2 years earlier and the usefulness of the trail negated, the Army relinquished the fort.

Fort Kearny State Historical Park, primarily a recreational area, includes 40 acres of the second Fort Kearny site. There are no above-surface remains. The State is conducting archeological excavations and has placed interpretive markers at building sites. Replicas of the palisade and blacksmith-carpenter shop have been erected. An interpretive center presents audio-visual programs and museum displays. The reconstructed blockhouse of the first Fort Kearny, located on the main street of Nebraska City, Nebr., serves as a youth center.

Fort Omaha, Nebraska ⊗

Location: Douglas County, in northern Omaha, bounded approximately on the east by 30th Street (U.S. 73), on the south by Redman Avenue, on the west by 33d Street, and on the north by Laurel Avenue. The main entrance is on Fort Street, off 30th Street.

The Post of Omaha came into being in 1863 to train Civil War Volunteers. Three years later it became headquarters of the Department of the Platte. In 1868 a new post was activated 4 miles northwest of the city. Known as Sherman Barracks the first year and then as Omaha Barracks, in 1878 it was redesignated as Fort Omaha. From 1875 to 1882 and from 1886 to 1888, as commander of the Department of the Platte, Brig. Gen. George Crook was stationed at the post when he was not in the field. He directed many major campaigns on the northern Plains, serving in which were numerous troops that had passed through Fort Omaha.

The Fort Omaha garrison moved in 1896 to Fort Crook, which   207 had been activated 5 years earlier about 10 miles south of Omaha as the New Post of Fort Omaha. The first soldiers had arrived there in 1895. In 1905 the Army reactivated Fort Omaha, and during World War I used it for a balloon school. The Navy has had jurisdiction over the base since 1947, and still utilizes it along with other branches of the Armed Forces for recruiting. Reserve training, and administration.

Seven buildings from the 1870's and 1880's have survived. One of the oldest is the commanding officer's house, or Crook House, completed in 1879. Its first tenant was General Crook, and today the commander of Fort Omaha occupies it. A large two-story brick structure, asymmetrical in plan, Italianate in style, and crowned by hipped roofs, it is in good condition. A long one-story porch projects from its eastern facade. The interior has been altered over the years, but the exterior has changed little. Fort Omaha is not ordinarily open to the public.

Fort Robinson and Red Cloud Agency, Nebraska △

Location: Dawes and Sioux Counties. Fort Robinson is on U.S. 20, about 4 miles west of Crawford. The site of Red Cloud Agency is on an unimproved road, about 1½ miles east of the fort.

These two installations along the White River in northwestern Nebraska were the scene of many exciting events during the final two decades of Sioux and Cheyenne resistance on the northern Plains. The fort was founded in 1874 to protect the Red Cloud Agency, which had been moved the year before from its first location (1871–73), on the Oregon-California Trail and the North Platte River about 25 miles southeast of Fort Laramie, Wyo. The agency's mission was to control and issue food and annuities to the Sioux and Cheyennes. Among them was the recalcitrant Oglala Chief Red Cloud, who had refused to move onto the Great Sioux Reservation of western South Dakota, created by the Fort Laramie Treaty (1868), and insisted on residing in the unceded territory north of the North Platte.

Life at the agency was hectic. At times 13,000 Indians, many hostile, were camped nearby awaiting supplies. Aggravating the

Fort Robinson officers' quarters in the late 1870's.

situation were their nonreservation kin and Arapahos, residents of
the surrounding unceded hunting territory who wintered near
the agency to procure food. De facto rulers of the agency, the
Indians kept the inexperienced, and often dishonest, agents and
their staff in a virtual state of siege. The braves went on a rampage in February 1874 and killed the acting agent. The next
month, to restore peace, the Army founded Fort Robinson adjacent to the agency and Camp Sheridan near the newly established
Spotted Tail Agency, 40 miles to the northeast, which administered mainly the Upper Brûlés. Realizing the troops' daily presence generated friction, in May the commander relocated the fort
about 1½ miles west of the agency.

But the Army could not prevent corruption in agency management, which infuriated the Indians. In 1875 a special Government commission conducting hearings at various locations
throughout the Nation, including the Red Cloud and Spotted
Tail Agencies, confirmed reports that agents, other Government
employees, contractors, and freighters were profiting from traffic
in Indian food and annuities, many of them inferior. The nationwide publicity aroused the ire of eastern humanitarians.

A far stronger reason for Indian hostility was the violation of the Fort Laramie Treaty represented by the 1874–75 mining invasion of the Black Hills, for which the fort was a way station on the main route to the goldfields. In September 1875, first at the fort and then at a site 8 miles to the east, Government representatives tried to buy the hills from the reservation Sioux, but they refused. The fort supported campaigns in Wyoming and Montana the next year against the nonreservation and reservation Sioux and Cheyennes who united under Sitting Bull and other leaders and overwhelmed Custer in June at the Battle of the Little Bighorn.

Following this campaign and a victory over the Sioux in September in the Battle of Slim Buttes, S. Dak., Brig. Gen. George Crook returned via the Black Hills to Fort Laramie, Wyo. He then marched to the Red Cloud and Spotted Tail Agencies and put down a threatened uprising by disarming and dismounting Red Cloud's Oglalas and Red Leaf's Brûlés. Crook and the other generals triumphed in their retaliatory winter campaigns. Some 4,500 Sioux and Cheyennes, including the Cheyenne Dull Knife and the Oglala Sioux Crazy Horse, surrendered in the winter and spring at Fort Robinson and Camp Sheridan. As a result of a misunderstanding, in September 1877 the Fort Robinson commander attempted to arrest Crazy Horse. Resisting, in the guardhouse Crazy Horse pulled a knife, a soldier bayoneted him, and he died a short time later in the adjutant's office next door. An Indian rebellion was averted. The next month, however, the Red Cloud and Spotted Tail Agencies and their residents, in accordance with the Black Hills Treaty of 1876, moved to the Pine Ridge and Rosebud Reservations in South Dakota.

In September 1878 the Cheyenne Dull Knife and his band, who had been assigned from Fort Robinson to Darlington Agency, in Indian Territory, escaped and headed for their homeland. They were captured in the sandhills near Fort Robinson, where they were confined. They again tried to gain their freedom in January 1879, but troops killed some of them and captured the rest. In 1890, during the Ghost Dance rebellion, elements of the black 9th Cavalry and the white 8th Infantry from Fort Robinson were among the first troops on the scene at the Pine Ridge Agency, S. Dak.

During the late 1870's, ranchers had begun to move into the

*The Fort Robinson headquarters building (1905)
serves as a museum today.*

area around Fort Robinson and once the railroad arrived, in 1886, homesteaders followed. The presence of the post mitigated conflicts between the two groups. In 1890 the fort's importance increased as a result of the inactivation of Fort Laramie. Remaining active through World War II, in its final years Fort Robinson served as a cavalry base, remount depot, war-dog training center, and prisoner-of-war camp. Since 1949, or 2 years after the Army departed, it has been occupied by the Fort Robinson Beef Cattle Research Station, a joint enterprise of the U.S. Department of Agriculture and the University of Nebraska.

Fort Robinson State Park consists of the principal historic buildings: six sets of frame-covered adobe officers' quarters, built in 1874–75; and six sets of brick officers' quarters, constructed in 1887. Several miscellaneous structures—storehouses, shops, and offices—date from the period 1886–1910, but the rest of the buildings are later additions. The Nebraska State Historical Society has placed interpretive markers around the fort area and maintains a museum in the frame headquarters building (1905). The society has reconstructed the guardhouse where Crazy Horse was mortally wounded and the adjutant's office, both built in 1874.

At the Red Cloud Agency site, to the east of the fort, no remains are extant but a monument commemorates it and the State has conducted some archeological investigation. The historic scene is unimpaired by modern intrusions. During the summer months the State historical society conducts tours to the site from the Fort Robinson museum. The fort and agency sites are on lands owned by the U.S. Government and the State of Nebraska.

War Bonnet (Hat) Creek Battlefield, Nebraska ⊗

Location: Sioux County, on an unimproved road, about 17 miles northeast of Harrison. Make local inquiry.

At this site in the extreme northwestern corner of Nebraska near the Wyoming and South Dakota boundaries occurred one of the series of defeats inflicted on the Indians after the Custer debacle in 1876. The victorious Indians had scattered across eastern Montana. Soon large reinforcements poured up the Missouri. Col. Wesley Merritt, commanding the 5th Cavalry, en route from Fort Laramie, Wyo., to Goose Creek to reinforce General Crook, learned that 1,000 Cheyennes had left the Spotted Tail and Red Cloud Agencies in Nebraska to join the triumphant Sioux of Crazy Horse and Sitting Bull. Merritt delayed his movement to intercept them. On July 17, 1876, at War Bonnet (Hat) Creek, Nebr., he whipped them and drove them back to their agencies. In the battle, "Buffalo Bill" Cody reputedly killed Chief Yellow Hand, an episode that novelists and Cody publicity agents later turned into a legend.

The rolling grassland where the battle was fought has changed little since 1876. The site, in private ownership, is not designated by any monument or marker and is not open to the public.

Camp Winfield Scott, Nevada ⊗

Location: Humboldt County, on an unimproved road, about 5 miles east of the town of Paradise Valley.

This camp (1866–71) was founded near the head of Paradise Valley in northern Nevada to protect settlers and travelers from

Northern Paiute depredations. It was one of the bases used by General Crook in his 1866–68 campaign against the tribe. The garrison, however, spent most of its time patrolling and capturing Indian cattle rustlers.

The campsite is on a privately owned ranch. All the remaining buildings are adobe: two officers' quarters, now serving as ranch and bunk houses; and a barracks, used as a barn. The barracks contains remnants of a chimney, fireplace, and doorways. Behind one of the officers' quarters is a stone cellar, whose barred windows indicate use as a magazine or guardhouse.

Fort Churchill, Nevada ⚠

> *Location: Lyon County, on Nev. 2B, about 1 mile west of U.S. Alt. 95, some 7 miles south of the town of Silver Springs.*

Fort Churchill (1860–69), as guardian in west-central Nevada of the Central Overland Mail and Pony Express routes, the transcontinental telegraph line, and east-west and north-south emigrant

Ruins of officers' quarters, Fort Churchill Historic State Monument.

213

trails, was primarily significant in the history of western transportation and communication. But it also protected mining camps, ranches, and emigrants from the Indians and served as a supply depot for military operations in Nevada. Its founding, 25 miles east of Virginia City on the north bank of the Carson River adjacent to Buckland Station, a trading post that had been established in 1859, was the direct result of a Southern Paiute uprising in the spring of 1860. This had been generated by a silver rush to the region the previous year and culminated in the Battles of Pyramid Lake (May and June 1860). During the Civil War, California and Nevada Volunteers replaced the Regulars and considerably enlarged the post. The Paiutes caused no further trouble in the Carson River Valley, though at times the fort aided in quelling Indian disturbances in northeastern Nevada. In 1870, the year after the Army abandoned the fort, the Government sold the buildings at public auction.

Over the years the adobe buildings were either destroyed or fell into ruins. By 1930 the walls stood only 2 or 3 feet above ground. In 1935, after the National Park Service had supervised a program of archeological excavation and historical research, a force of Civilian Conservation Corps (CCC) laborers reconstructed a number of buildings on their original foundations. The ruins of some 15 of these structures comprise Fort Churchill Historic State Monument, which also includes a small museum and the old post cemetery. In the 1880's the soldier dead, many from the Indian wars, had been moved to Carson City and San Francisco; the graves of Samuel Buckland and several other early settlers remain.

Fort Halleck, Nevada ⊗

Location: Elko County, on Nev. 11 at Secret Canyon, about 11 miles southeast of Halleck.

The troops at Fort Halleck (1867–86), in the Humboldt River Valley of northeastern Nevada, watched over the nearby route of the Central Pacific Railroad, stage and telegraph lines, and settlers. Most of the small garrison served in the Nez Perce War (1877).

A stone marker identifies the site, which is in a privately owned meadow. All the log and adobe buildings have long since disappeared, but brush-covered earth mounds indicate the location of the guardhouse, magazine, and commissary warehouse; and traces of rock walls, either the headquarters building or the officers' quarters.

Fort McDermit, Nevada ⊗

Location: Humboldt County, on an unimproved road, about 2 miles east of U.S. 95 and McDermit.

General George Crook utilized this fort (1865–89), which had been founded by California Volunteers in a canyon of the Santa Rosa Mountains just south of the present Oregon-Nevada boundary, in his 1866–68 campaign against the Snake Indians. Its garrison also took part in the Bannock War (1878); protected settlers and ranchers from Paiute harassments; guarded the road running north into Oregon; and in the later years policed the adjacent Indian agency. The Army's successor at the fort was the Indian Bureau. It operated a school in one of the buildings, most of which were of stone.

The remaining structures, which include two officers' quarters, serve as headquarters of the Fort McDermit Indian Agency.

Fort Ruby, Nevada △

Location: White Pine County, on an unimproved road, about 8 miles south of the town of Cave Creek. Access is difficult. Make local inquiry.

Eastern Nevada's Fort Ruby (1862–69) played a major role in the history of transportation and communication, but also participated in the Indian wars. In 1859 William Rogers, an assistant Indian agent and the first white settler in Ruby Valley, built a cabin near the southern end of the valley. It became a station for stagecoaches on the Central Overland Mail route, the Pony Express, and a relay station on the transcontinental telegraph line. During the Civil War, in the fall of 1862, to protect these facilities and to control the Gosiute and Paiute Indians, who were focusing their attacks on Overland Mail stages, Col. Patrick E. Connor's California Volunteers founded Fort Douglas, Utah, near Salt Lake City, and Fort Ruby in Nevada's Ruby Valley about 3 miles west of the stage station. Troops from the fort engaged in several skirmishes during the Gosiute War (1863). The next year Nevada Volunteers replaced the California troops and garrisoned the fort until 1869, when the completion of the Central Pacific Railroad, the first transcontinental line, brought an end to stage service and thus the need for Fort Ruby.

The site is on a privately owned ranch. The only extant structures are two one-story log buildings, surrounded by more modern structures. The former are the earliest extant examples of pioneer log construction in Nevada. One of them, now used as a tool shed and in fair condition, is palisaded, a rare example of that type of construction. The other, in good condition, is constructed of round logs in a horizontal position, the ends saddle notched. The site of the overland stage and Pony Express station, 3 miles to the east, has been marked by the Forest Service, U.S. Department of Agriculture.

Pyramid Lake Battlefield, Nevada ⊗

Location: Washoe County, just off Nev. 34, about 4 miles southeast of the southern tip of Pyramid Lake and immediately south of Nixon.

Twice in 1860 Southern Paiute Indians, resenting the intrusion of miners and settlers in the Carson River Valley of western Nevada, clashed with troops at this battlefield north of the valley. In the late 1850's the fertile valley, a welcome sight to emigrants passing over the Carson Branch of the California Trail after traversing an inhospitable stretch of desert, had become the site of two trading posts, the Buckland and Williams Stations. They were Central Overland Mail and Pony Express stations and supplied miners and emigrants. On May 7, 1860, the Paiutes, aroused by the abduction of two Indian girls by traders at the Williams Station, burned it and killed five men. In retaliation the miners at Virginia City, Carson City, Genoa, and Gold Hill organized at Buckland Station a punitive expedition of 105 Nevada Volunteers, under Maj. William M. Ormsby. They marched northward into the Paiute country around Pyramid Lake. Riding carelessly up the Truckee River Valley, on May 12 they fell into an ambush just south of the lake that took the lives of 46 men.

News of the defeat threw miners and settlers into a frenzy of fear and temporarily halted stage and Pony Express service over the western end of the Central Overland Mail route. Reinforcements rushed in from California. By the end of the month 800 men, including some Regulars, were under arms in Carson Valley. This force, commanded by former Texas Ranger Col. Jack Hays, also marched northward and encountered the Paiutes on June 3, at the site of the May 12 clash. In a 3-hour battle, 25 of the Indians died and the survivors fled into the hills. The next month the Army founded Fort Churchill near Buckland Station to keep watch over the defeated Paiutes and guard stage and mail routes.

The battle site, on the Pyramid Lake Indian Reservation, is virtually unchanged from its historic appearance. It lies in the lowlands along the east bank of the Truckee River. Just above the site, on the western rim of the Truckee River Gorge, runs Nev. 34 and a railroad. A marker across the street from the Nixon Post Office commemorates the battlefield.

Wovoka ("Jack Wilson") Hut, Nevada ⊗

Location: Lyon County, on an unimproved road, along the northeastern side of Mill Ditch, Nordyke.

This hut in the Mason Valley of west-central Nevada was one of the abodes of the Paiute mystic Wovoka, or "Jack Wilson" (1858–1932), the Indian messiah who founded the Ghost Dance religion. Upon the death of his medicine-man father, when Wovoka was only 14, the rancher David Wilson took him into his family and employed him as a ranch hand. Despite the Christian training and other education he received from the Wilsons, he found assimilation into white society impossible. Entering manhood, he left the ranch. Before settling down in the Mason Valley and raising a family, he worked his way through California, Washington, and Oregon. During the trip he became fascinated with the Shaker religion, whose extensive rituals and death-like trances one of the Washington tribes practiced.

Wovoka, or "Jack Wilson," Paiute messiah and founder of the Ghost Dance religion.

As time went on, Wovoka synthesized Shaker and other Christian doctrines and his native beliefs into a religion he evolved to uplift the despairing Indians. Its revelation came to him in 1889 after a serious illness. Instead of encouraging his race's hatred of the whites, whom Wovoka believed would disappear supernaturally, he preached temporary submission, love, and brotherhood. The old order would be restored; the Indians would reinherit their lands; the buffalo, symbol of past greatness, would return; and prosperity would reign. Until the millennium came in the spring of 1891 and brought immortality and resurrection, all Indian dead would reside in a special heaven. Salvation was attainable only by adherence to a code similar to the Ten Commandments and the performance of certain rituals. The climax of these was the Ghost Dance, preceded by ceremonial purification and painting of the body. This hypnotic dance, which allowed for the expression of repressed hostility and frustration, made possible communion with the dead and promoted the coming of the millennium.

During the years 1889–91 the religion spread to some eastern and most of the western tribes, whose bitterness and impotence made practically all of them susceptible to its messianic fervor. Their bleak prospects for the future were salved only by nostalgic memories of the past. This was particularly true of the Sioux, who added aggressive and anti-white elements to Wovoka's pacifistic religion. As a result, troops crushed them at the Battle of Wounded Knee, S. Dak. The battle and the nonoccurrence of the millennium destroyed the belief of most Indians in Wovoka's teachings. Yet the Sioux incorporated some aspects of the Ghost Dance into their tribal dances, and the religion lingered for awhile among other groups, especially the Paiutes.

In the late 19th century a fire destroyed the Wilson ranchhouse. Apparently Wovoka only visited there and resided in a crude semi-subterranean hut, which has survived on the modern Nordyke Ranch just east of the ranchhouse. Of mud and wood, it measures 10 by 6 feet. It is largely intact, although some of the roof mud has collapsed. The site, used for ranching purposes, is not open to the public, but the owner has cooperated with a local civic group in protecting it. Wovoka is buried in the cemetery at Schurz, Nev., about 20 miles northeast of Nordyke.

Carson ("Kit") House, New Mexico △

Location: Taos County, Kit Carson Avenue, Taos.

Between 1843 and 1868 this was the home of Christopher ("Kit") Carson, probably the most renowned of all the mountain men—a legend in his own lifetime. Fur trapper, trader, and guide, he was a dominant figure in the fur trade, but he also served as an Indian agent and won distinction in the Indian wars.

A native of Kentucky who spent most of his youth in Missouri, Carson (1809–68) in 1826 emigrated west over the Santa Fe Trail. In the late 1820's he entered the fur trade at Taos, rendezvous and winter headquarters for many independent trappers. They operated over a large arc of territory extending from the headwaters of the Rio Grande and Arkansas River across the deserts to the San Juan, Gila, Salt, and Colorado Rivers. Reopening the old Spanish trails to California, they were among the first Americans to make a lodgment there. About 1836 Carson married, in Indian fashion, an Arapaho girl, who died bearing him a daughter.

The fur trade began to decline in the mid-1830's, and many

Col. Christopher "Kit" Carson, ex-mountain man, led New Mexico Volunteers in highly successful campaigns against the Indians of the Southwest.

"Kit" Carson House.

trappers and traders retired in Taos. Carson, returning from duty
as guide for Frémont's first expedition (1842), moved there. In
1843 he remarried. His bride was Maria Josefa Jaramillo, daughter of a prominent and wealthy local family and sister of the wife
of Charles Bent. The same year, Carson purchased what came to
be known as the Kit Carson House, which had been built in 1825.

For the next 25 years Carson resided in the home only intermittently, but apparently six of the seven children he and Maria had
were born there. His diverse activities kept him away for long
stretches of time. He was a guide for Frémont's second expedition
(1843–44). Going to California in 1845 with the third, between
then and early 1849 he took an active part in the U.S. conquest of
California. He then returned to Taos.

In 1851 Carson began managing a ranch on Rayado Creek east
of the Sangre de Cristo Mountains, where his family joined him.
The longest continuous period he lived in the Taos house was
from early 1854 until 1861, during which time he was Indian
agent, mainly for two bands of Utes. For several months in 1854,
until another building was available, he used the house as agency
headquarters.

At the outbreak of the Civil War, in 1861, Carson resigned as
Indian agent and entered a new phase of his multifaceted career. 221

Aiding in organizing the 1st New Mexico Volunteer Infantry, he was commissioned as lieutenant colonel in July and only 2 months later as colonel. For his gallantry in the Battle of Valverde, N. Mex., against a Confederate force from Texas, and for other distinguished service in New Mexico, he won a brevet of brigadier general in January 1866. Under the direction of Gen. James H. Carleton, commander of the Department of New Mexico, Carson conducted highly successful campaigns against the Mescalero Apaches (1862–63); the Navajos (1863–64); and the Kiowas and Comanches (1864–65), in which he fought his last engagement, the Battle of Adobe Walls, Tex.

In the summer of 1866 Carson assumed command of Fort Garland, Colo., taking his family with him, but he had to resign in November 1867 because of ill health. The next spring he again relocated his family, from Taos to Boggsville, Colo. But he died at nearby Fort Lyon (No. 2) in May, shortly after the birth of their seventh child took his wife's life. They were buried there, but the bodies were later moved to Taos.

The Kit Carson Memorial Foundation, Inc., administers the house on behalf of Bent Masonic Lodge #42, the owner and restorer. Four rooms of the U-shaped residence are original and three of them—the parlor, kitchen, and bedroom—are authentically refurnished in a combination of Spanish Colonial and Territorial styles. The fourth original room features displays associated with Carson's life. The remaining rooms serve as exhibit rooms and offices. The well-preserved exterior features a patio and typical Spanish mud oven. Carson and his wife are buried in Kit Carson Memorial State Park, at the end of Dragoon Lane, elsewhere in town.

Fort Bascom, New Mexico ⊗

Location: San Miguel County, accessible via unimproved roads from Logan and N. Mex. 39. Make local inquiry.

Founded on the south bank of the Canadian River in eastern New Mexico during the Civil War, Fort Bascom (1863–70) had a short but distinguished history. It helped control the Kiowas, Comanches, and other tribes inhabiting the Red and Canadian

River region; watched over the Goodnight-Loving Cattle Trail, as well as the Santa Fe Trail; and policed the activities of the "Comancheros," American and Mexican renegades who traded illegally with the Indians. The fort fielded several expeditions against the southern Plains tribes. Col. "Kit" Carson led one of them, dispatched in 1864 by General Carleton because of harassment of the Santa Fe Trail. Carson clashed with a village of Kiowas in the Battle of Adobe Walls, Tex.

Fort Bascom was also the base of one of the three columns deployed by General Sheridan in his 1868–69 campaign. In November and December 1868 troops moved down the Canadian River; established a supply depot at Monument Creek; picked up a fresh southbound trail a few miles west of the Antelope Hills; pursued it vainly to the north fork of the Red River, then turned northward; and on Christmas Day won a resounding victory in the Battle of Soldier Spring, Okla.

At the time of the fort's abandonment in 1870, when the troops and stores were transferred to Fort Union, N. Mex., the poorly constructed post was still unfinished. It consisted of a sandstone officers' quarters and a few adobe buildings. No remains have survived. Permission must be obtained from the ranch owner to visit the site.

Fort Bayard, New Mexico ⊗

> Location: Grant County, on an unimproved road, about 1 mile north of Central.

Fort Bayard (1866–1900), established by General Carleton's California Volunteers at the base of the Santa Rita Mountains in southwestern New Mexico to protect the Pinos Altos mining district from Apache depredations, was a key post in the Apache Wars (1861–86), particularly the 1879–80 campaign against Victorio. The fort was less than a year old when it suffered the first of numerous Apache attacks. In 1900, when the post's military days ended, the Army utilized it as a 'tuberculosis hospital. Between 1922 and 1965 the Veterans' Administration had jurisdiction. In the latter year, retaining control of the cemetery, it transferred

Sixth Cavalry in training at Fort Bayard.

the rest of the property to the State of New Mexico for use as a hospital.

Expansion, remodeling, and modernization by the Veterans' Administration obliterated the old fort, except for occasional overgrown foundations. Modern hospital buildings flank the former parade ground. The houses along what was once officers' row, now designated doctors' row, were built on the foundations of the officers' quarters. The only major vestige of the old post is the cemetery, on a hill overlooking the site. The burials date back to the early days of Fort Bayard.

Fort Craig, New Mexico ⊗

Location: Socorro County, on an unimproved road, about 5 miles east of the Fort Craig marker on I-25 (U.S. 85), some 4 miles south of San Marcial.

This post's predecessor was Fort Conrad (1851–54), a motley group of adobe and cottonwood huts about 9 miles to the north, also on the west bank of the Rio Grande. Troops occupied Fort Conrad while they built Fort Craig (1854–84). The mission of the forts, near the northern end of the *Jornada del Muerto* (Journey of Death), was protecting westbound miners from Navajos and Apaches and guarding the Santa Fe-El Paso Road. The garrison, almost continuously occupied with defensive actions and patrols, took part in the Navajo and Apache conflicts of the 1850's and in the Apache wars (1861–86). Supported by troop remnants from abandoned posts in Arizona and New Mexico that had marshaled at the fort, it also fought in the nearby Battle of Valverde (February 1862), the first major battle of the Civil War in the Southwest.

The walls of 17 of Fort Craig's adobe buildings, in varying stages of disintegration, and the stone guardhouse are visible, as are earth mounds representing Civil War fortifications. The military cemetery is still surrounded by a stone wall but the burials, including those who died at the Battle of Valverde, were moved to Santa Fe in 1876. Nothing is left to indicate the site of Fort Conrad, on an unimproved road running east from I-25 (U.S. 85), about 5 miles north of San Marcial.

Fort Cummings, New Mexico ⊗

Location: Luna County, on an unimproved road, about 21 miles northeast of Deming and some 6 miles northwest of N. Mex. 26. Make local inquiry.

General Carleton's California Volunteers founded this fort in 1863 to guard strategic Cooke's Spring and the road to California.

Iron-fisted Gen. James H. Carleton, Civil War commander of the Department of New Mexico, won unprecedented victories against the Indians of the Southwest.

225

From 1858 until 1861 the site had been a Butterfield Overland Mail station, attacked by Apaches during the last year. Several expeditions and many patrols set out from the fort, some even pushing into nearby Mexico, but they made few contacts with the Indians. Abandoned in 1873, the post disintegrated. Between 1880 and 1886 it was reoccupied because of renewed Apache hostilities but the troops lived in tents outside the walls.

Remains of two officers' quarters, ruins of adobe walls, and earth mounds indicating foundations are located on privately owned ranchland. A plaque at the site, erected by the Daughters of the American Revolution, commemorates the Butterfield Overland Mail.

Fort Fillmore, New Mexico ⊗

Location: Dona Ana County, on an unimproved road between I-10 (U.S. 80–85) and N. Mex. 478, about 5 miles southeast of Las Cruces.

Along the Rio Grande not far from the Mexican border and a few miles southeast of the town of Mesilla, this tiny adobe fort was founded in 1851 to control local Apaches. By the end of the 1850's it had declined and fallen into disrepair. In 1861, however, spurred by rumors of Confederate invasion of New Mexico, the Army reinforced it. During July a force of 250 Texans took Mesilla. Failing in an attempt to liberate the town, the garrison abandoned the fort and marched toward Fort Stanton, N. Mex., but was captured east of Las Cruces. The next summer, California Volunteers temporarily occupied the post before moving into Mesilla.

The site of the fort, along a one-lane ranch road among sandhills about 1¼ miles east of N. Mex. 478, has been obscured by shifting sands. A State marker is located in the vicinity but not at the actual site.

Fort McRae, New Mexico ⊗

Location: Sierra County, in McRae Canyon, about 6 miles northeast of Truth or Consequences, N. Mex., and 4 miles northeast of Elephant Butte Dam. Accessible by foot only. Make local inquiry.

This fort (1863–76) was a small adobe post about 3 miles east of the Rio Grande and 5 miles west of the boundary of the *Jornada del Muerto* (Journey of Death). The *Jornada* was a desert valley about 90 miles long and 35 miles wide on *El Camino Real* (The Royal Road), for centuries the major New Mexico-Mexico traffic artery. Near the fort was the *Ojo del Muerto* (Spring of Death), one of the two watering places in the *Jornada* area. The Apaches used the spring and frequently ambushed travelers. After the massacre of a wagon train in March 1863, New Mexico Volunteers soon arrived in the area and founded Fort McRae. Shortly thereafter, California Volunteers occupied it. They sent out patrols; pursued hostile Indians, who often rustled the fort's livestock; and protected travelers on *El Camino Real*. In July 1866 Regulars took over the post.

Only foundation traces remain. The site is located on corporation-owned ranchlands. Permission must be obtained to visit it.

Fort Selden, New Mexico ⊗

> *Location: Dona Ana County, on an unimproved road, about 15 miles northwest of Las Cruces.*

Situated on a slight rise overlooking the Rio Grande at the lower end of the *Jornada del Muerto* (Journey of Death), Fort Selden (1865–90) protected settlers in the Mesilla Valley and travelers on the El Paso-Santa Fe post road. The garrison, frequently harassed by Indians, took part in the campaigns against the Apaches until the fort's inactivation in 1877. In 1880, during the campaign against Geronimo, troops reoccupied it as a base to patrol the Mexican border.

Eroding adobe walls of some 25 buildings stand as high as 10 feet or more. A New Mexico historical marker on U.S. 85, from which the fort is visible, provides a brief sketch of its history.

Fort Stanton, New Mexico ⊗

> *Location: Lincoln County, on a secondary road, about 5 miles southeast of Capitan.*

Originally consisting of two blockhouses surrounded by an adobe wall, this fort was founded in 1855 to control the Mescalero

227

Dress parade at Fort Stanton in 1885.

Apaches, whom the Army had rounded up, and was the agency for the tribe until 1861. In that year, the Union Army abandoned the fort, temporarily occupied by Confederates, and did not return permanently until the following year. Meantime the Mescaleros, freed from military restraint, had begun to raid throughout central New Mexico. During the years 1862–64 Col. "Kit" Carson's New Mexico Volunteers, after reactivating Fort Stanton, captured the Mescaleros, as well as the Navajos, who were marauding in Arizona and New Mexico. In 1862–63 Carson placed 400 Mescaleros on the newly established Bosque Redondo Reservation, guarded by Fort Sumner, and in 1864 jammed in an additional 8,000 Navajos. The next year the Mescaleros, resenting the numerically superior Navajos, fled.

Brought under control once again in 1871, the Mescaleros were reestablished on the Fort Stanton Reservation, where the Jicarilla Apaches joined them in 1883. Many of the Mescaleros became restless because of dissatisfaction with the agents, factional quarrels among themselves, and disputes with cattlemen. They alternately fled and returned until the reservation became a virtual replacement depot for hostile Apaches. In 1879 many joined Victorio's band of about 100, formed principally with recruits from the Fort Stanton Reservation. In January 1880, when Victorio reappeared from Mexico, troops attempted to disarm the agency Mes-

228

caleros, but 50 escaped and joined Victorio. His death at the hands of Mexican troops in October brought an end to the Mescalero outbreaks.

The Army abandoned the fort in 1896, and 3 years later the U.S. Public Health Service acquired it for use as a merchant marine hospital. Today it is a State sanitarium. Many of the stone buildings, which in 1868 had replaced the original adobe, have been remodeled and are used as residences, wards, and offices. Including the commanding officer's house, officers' quarters, and barracks, they are grouped around the parade ground, whose southern end is covered with modern construction.

Fort Sumner, New Mexico ⊗

Location: De Baca County, on an unimproved road off N. Mex. 212, about 6 miles southeast of the town of Fort Sumner.

Fort Sumner was founded in 1862 at Bosque Redondo ("Round Grove of Trees") along the Pecos River in eastern New Mexico to guard the 400 Mescaleros and 8,000 Navajos conquered by Col. "Kit" Carson in 1862–64. In 1865 the Mescaleros, who detested the Navajos, fled. Three years later the U.S. Government commissioners who had earlier concluded treaties at Fort Laramie, Wyo., and Medicine Lodge, Kans., negotiated a treaty with the Navajos at Fort Sumner that allowed them to return to their ancestral homeland in northeastern Arizona. In the meantime, however, floods, drought, lack of skill, and Kiowa and Comanche raids had doomed all attempts at agriculture. Supplies and other necessities were scarce, and crowded conditions resulted in the spread of disease.

From 1866 through the early 1870's Fort Sumner was a way station on the Goodnight-Loving Cattle Trail. Herds wintered near the fort, and were sometimes purchased by the Government for issue to the reservation Indians. In 1869, the year after the Navajos departed, Fort Summer was demilitarized and put up for auction. The New Mexico cattle king Lucien Maxwell purchased it and remodeled some of the buildings for residential and ranching purposes. On his death, his son Peter inherited the property. In

229

1881 Pat Garrett shot and killed "Billy the Kid" in the house. A group of Colorado cattlemen bought the ranch in 1884, but their business collapsed a decade later.

The fort site is identifiable in a pasture on the east bank of the Pecos River, but in 1941 a flood washed away all traces of the adobe ruins. A guide is recommended, and permission to visit the site should be obtained from its private owner. A State marker is located at the junction of U.S. 60 and N. Mex. 212. A small cemetery behind a curio shop off N. Mex. 212 about a mile east of the fort site contains the grave of "Billy the Kid."

Fort Union National Monument, New Mexico ⊠

Location: Mora County, at the northern terminus of N. Mex. 477, about 7½ miles north of Watrous; address: Watrous, N. Mex. 87753.

Bustling center of frontier defense in the Southwest for four decades, Fort Union was the largest U.S. military post in the region and a base for both military and civilian ventures that molded its destiny. Astride the southern end of the Mountain Branch of the Santa Fe Trail near the point where it merged with the southern terminus of the Cimarron Cutoff, the post was one of the most important of a string established in New Mexico and southern Arizona in the area acquired from Mexico in the Mexican War (1846–48).

The fort's mission was broad. It protected the Santa Fe Trail, on which it was a resting place and refitting point and a stopping point for Independence (Mo.)-Santa Fe mail coaches; was the major Army supply depot in the Southwest; served as a transportation entrepot for civilian wagon freighters carrying military supplies; and provided a base for campaigns that penetrated the homeland of the Apaches, Utes, Navajos, Kiowas, and Comanches. Also, in a phase of history extraneous to this volume, the fort played a strong role in repelling the Confederate invasion of New Mexico from Texas in 1862; it was the prime staging area and logistical base and supported the force of Colorado Volunteers that won a victory over the southerners at the Battle of Glorieta Pass, N. Mex. (March 1862).

Ruins of Fort Union, reminders of a vanished frontier.

Three different Fort Unions existed over the years. The first, a shabby collection of log buildings, was erected in 1851, only 5 years after the U.S. conquest of New Mexico, on the west bank of Coyote Creek. The second post, begun in 1861 in preparation for the Confederate thrust from the south, was located across the creek from the first. A massive earthwork fort in a star shape, it had ditches, parapets, and bombproofs. Work continued intermittently until June 1862, by which time the need for the fortification had passed. The last fort, a large complex of adobe structures in the Territorial architectural style, was begun in 1863 and finished in 1869. It was situated in the same area as the star fort, except for the arsenal, built on the site of the first fort.

Probably the most dramatic duty of the garrison, particularly at the time of Indian uprisings, was furnishing escorts and other protection for the Santa Fe Trail. Dragoons and Mounted Riflemen focused their efforts on the Cimarron Cutoff, which extended northeastward to the Cimarron Crossing of the Arkansas River. Travel over it was risky, for it passed through Kiowa and Comanche country, but it had the advantage of being shorter than the Mountain Branch. The Civil War years were the most critical time on the trail because of the Confederate threat of invasion

t Union, reminders of a
ntier.

fferent Fort Uⁱons existed over the years. The first, a
ection of log buildings, was erected in 1851, only 5
he U.S. conquest of New Mexico, on the west bank of
ₑk. The second post, begun in 1861 in preparation for
erate thrust from the south, was located across the
the first. A massive earthwork fort in a star shape, it
ₛ, parapets, and bombproofs. Work continued inter-
ntil June 1862 y which time the need for the fortifi-
passed. The last fort, a large complex of adobe struc-
Territorial arhi tectural style, was begun in 1863 and
1869. It was sit ted in the same area as the star fort,
he arsenal, buiⁱₙ the site of the first fort.
the most dramt c duty of the garrison, particularly at
Indian uprisins was furnishing escorts and other pro-
the Santa Fe Trⁱil. Dragoons and Mounted Riflemen
ⁱir efforts on ₁⁻ Cimarron Cutoff, which extended
ird to the Cimrron Crossing of the Arkansas River.
r it was risky, fr it passed through Kiowa and **Coman-**
y, but it had tₑ advantage of being **shorter than** th
Branch. The Cvil War years were tᵣ ost criⁱ
e trail becauseₒf **the Confederate** of ir

ort Union, remirle s of a
·ontier.

lifferent Fort Ui ns existed over the years. The first, a
llection of log n ildings, was erected in 1851, only 5
the U.S conques of New Mexico, on the west bank of
eek. The second post, begun in 1861 in preparation for
derate thrust t> n the south, was located across the
n the first. A ns: ve earthwork fort in a star shape, it
es, parapets, an bombproofs. Work continued inter-
until June 1862 y which time the need for the fortifi-
passed. The la lort, a large complex of adobe struc-
e Territorial arh tectural style, was begun in 1863 and
1869. It was si ted in the same area as the star fort,
the arsenal, bui c n the site of the first fort.
y the most dramt c duty of the garrison, particularly at
f Indian uprisins was furnishing escorts and other pro-
the Santa Fe Tr il. Dragoons and Mounted Riflemen
eir efforts on 1 Cimarron Cutoff, which extended
ard to the Cimr on Crossing of the Arkansas River.
·r it was risky, fc t passed through Kiowa and Coman-
y, but it had th advantage of being shorter than the
Branch. The Cvil War years were the r t critical
ie trail because)f the Confederate thre invasion

and attacks on trail caravans, the critical need to assure a continuous flow of provisions to Union forces in New Mexico, and the mounting Indian menace occasioned partly by the withdrawal of Regular troops and their replacement by Volunteers. Nevertheless the fort—employing escorts, temporary posts, and full-scale offensive campaigns—kept the trail open.

The trail was related to the fort's mission as a supply depot. Over it, until the Santa Fe Railway arrived in the region in 1879, surged long tandem freight wagons, pulled by 12-yoke teams, carrying military supplies to the fort for distribution to posts all over the Southwest. The heavy concentration of troops in New Mexico and Arizona were scattered at farflung posts. The land was not rich enough to feed this army, and almost all provisions had to be hauled over the Santa Fe Trail from Fort Leavenworth, Kans. The need for a depot in eastern New Mexico to receive and distribute supplies and ordnance was clear.

The wagon freighting traffic grew so heavy that Fort Union became a freight destination rivaling if not exceeding Santa Fe in importance. Civilian companies performed under contract virtually all military freighting on the trail. The freight was unloaded at Fort Union, repacked, and assigned as needed to other posts. When wagons or entire trains contained shipments for one fort only, they often continued directly to their destination. Large-scale military freighting, dominated by Russell, Majors, and Waddell, continued until 1866, when the railroad moved west into Kansas. Each railhead town thereafter served briefly as the port of embarkation for freight wagons. After the rails reached Denver in 1870, wagons continued to move supplies over the Mountain Branch of the trail between Pueblo and Fort Union. The Santa Fe Railway crossed the Mora Valley in 1879 and ended the era of military freighting on the trail.

Protection of the Santa Fe Trail and logistical support of troops in the region were indirectly related to the Indian wars, but the fort was also directly involved in them. When the U.S. acquired the Southwest in the Mexican War, it also inherited the Indian problems that had plagued its people since the earliest times. The nomadic tribes of New Mexico had long fought the Spaniards and Mexicans. Now they fought the Americans, who were overrunning their lands, killing off their game, or passing over transcontinental trails on their way to the California goldfields.

From 1851 until 1875, in major offensives or patrol-type actions, sometimes meeting the enemy and sometimes not, Fort Union troops were usually in the field, skirmishing with Indians. Notable campaigns in which the garrison took part before the Civil War were those against the Jicarilla Apaches, in 1854; the Utes, in 1855, in southern Colorado, then part of New Mexico Territory; and in 1860 the Kiowas and Comanches menacing the eastern borders of New Mexico. The Indians were especially troublesome during the Civil War, when Gen. James H. Carleton, head of the California Column of Volunteers, directed Army operations in New Mexico. The tribes seized the opportunity offered by the Confederate attack on New Mexico to step up their raiding. New Mexico and California Volunteers under Col. "Kit" Carson, an experienced Indian fighter, conducted three major campaigns: against the Mescalero Apaches (1862–63), Navajos (1863–64), and Kiowas and Comanches (1864–65).

The Army faced severe logistical problems in supplying troops dispersed at western posts. Pictured here from Harper's Weekly *(April 24, 1858) is an Army wagon train crossing the Plains.*

Fort Union Regulars, who replaced the Volunteers after the Civil War, along with troops from other New Mexico posts, took part in the final wars against the southern Plains tribes: General Sheridan's 1868–69 campaign, and the Red River War (1874–75). These campaigns ended the fort's participation in the Indian wars. In 1879 the arrival of the Santa Fe Railway largely ended its usefulness as a supply depot, but it was not abandoned until 1891.

Rising sharply and starkly from the plains, the history-shrouded adobe ruins of Fort Union, stabilized to arrest erosion, are reminders of a vanished frontier. Sprawling north nearly half a mile from the visitor center are a few chimneys and the outlines of melted walls of corrals, stables, hospital, barracks, officers' quarters, and large warehouses that made up Fort Union in the years 1863–91. Adjacent to this post was the massive star fort (1861–62). Ruins of the arsenal from the 1863–91 complex lie across the valley to the west, on the same site as the original log fort (1851–62), most traces of which have long since disappeared. Exceptional trail ruts of the Santa Fe Trail are readily identifiable in the vicinity and may be followed for miles. A museum and a visitor center interpret the history of the fort, and a self-guiding tour leads through the remains.

Fort Wingate, New Mexico ⊗

Location: McKinley County, in the town of Fort Wingate.

This is the second site of Fort Wingate. The first fort (1862–68) was located at El Gallo, 65 miles to the southeast. Col. "Kit" Carson founded it along with Fort Canby, Ariz. (1863–64), for his 1863–64 campaign against the Navajos. After they were confined to the Bosque Redondo Reservation, adjacent to Fort Sumner, N. Mex., troops from the fort patrolled for stragglers and raiders. In a commanding position on the Albuquerque-Fort Defiance (Ariz.) Road, it also protected miners en route to the Arizona goldfields, and in 1864 took part in the Apache campaign along the Gila and San Carlos Rivers.

In 1868, when the Navajos returned to their homeland, the Army relocated Fort Wingate to its second site. This one was

234

nearer the new Navajo Reservation, administered by the Fort Defiance Indian Agency. The site had previously been occupied by Fort Fauntleroy, or Lyon (1860–61), whose mission had also been Navajo control but which had been evacuated before the Confederate invasion of New Mexico from Texas. Besides policing the reservation, the garrison of the new fort participated in the Apache campaigns to the south. The Army withdrew in 1910, but in 1918 reactivated the fort as the Wingate Ordnance Depot. The depot moved in 1925 closer to the railroad, and a Navajo school took over the buildings.

Until its razing in the early 1960's and replacement with modern structures and school facilities, the fort was one of the best preserved frontier posts in the Southwest. A two-story barracks, rebuilt following a fire in 1896, is the only surviving major building. Constructed of stone, it has a two-level frame porch. No remains are extant of the first Fort Wingate. Its site is just off N. Mex. 53, about a mile west of San Rafael, in Valencia County.

St. Catherine's Indian School, New Mexico ⊗

Location: Santa Fe County, Griffin Street, west of Rosario Chapel, across from the Rosario and National Cemeteries, Santa Fe.

This school commemorates Catholic missionary efforts in the Southwest, particularly the humanitarianism of Mother Katharine. A Philadelphia banking heiress, Katharine Drexel (1858–1955) became a nun in 1889, and 2 years later founded the Order of the Sisters of the Blessed Sacrament for Indians and Colored People. Acquiring an interest in helping the Indians during her western travels in the 1880's, she had given liberal financial aid to the Bureau of Catholic Indian Missions, including money for St. Catherine's Indian School, built in 1886 and dedicated the next year. Catholic personnel operated the institution, supported by a Government subsidy, until 1893. The following year, Mother Katharine and nine members of her order arrived at Santa Fe from Philadelphia to manage the school. It served mainly the Pueblo Indians, but Navajos, Pimas, and Papagos also attended. Another institution Mother Katharine originated and financed,

235

Modern view of St. Catherine's Indian School.

among the Navajos in 1902, was St. Michael's Indian School, just west of Window Rock, Ariz.

Both schools are still directed by the Sisters of the Blessed Sacrament. St. Catherine's has an enrollment of about 200. Structures dating from its early years, in use today, include the 3½-story main classroom building, of adobe, and two other structures. St. Michael's, one of the largest Indian boarding schools in the Nation, has an attendance of about 400 Navajos, Hopis, Apaches, and Pueblos. A group of pitched-roof buildings from the 1910 era are the core of the modern school.

Big Mound Battlefield, North Dakota ⊗

> *Location: Kidder County, on an unimproved road, about 10 miles north of Tappen.*

The Battle of Big Mound was one of the key engagements in Gen. Henry Hastings Sibley's 1863 expedition from Fort Ridgely,

Minn., against the Santee Sioux who had sparked the uprising in the Minnesota River Valley the previous year. Eluding his troops, they had fled to Dakota and joined forces with the Tetons. On July 24 Sibley surprised about 3,000 Sioux, consisting of friendly Sissetons and Inkpaduta's hostiles, who were hunting buffalo near Big Mound. During a parley one of Inkpaduta's warriors shot and killed a military surgeon, Dr. Joseph Weiser. In a running battle the Indians fought tenaciously to protect the retreat of their families but 13 died. Following this victory, Sibley and General Sully won a series of triumphs over the Sioux.

This 50-acre site, also known as the Burman and Camp Whitney sites, is used for ranching. It is all in private hands except for a small tract owned by the State. The slightly rolling terrain, covered with prairie grass and dotted with lakes, is but slightly impaired. A stone marker, on a cairn of rocks, indicates the spot of Dr. Weiser's death and the beginning of the battle.

Fort Abercrombie, North Dakota ⊗
Location: Richland County, just off U.S. 81, eastern edge of Abercrombie.

Fort Abercrombie (1858–77) was the first Army post in present North Dakota and one of the earliest in the region. Situated on the west bank of the Red River at the head of navigation, it protected river traffic, travelers, and settlers. Logistical gateway to the largely unexplored plains of the old Northwest, it was the jumping-off place for prospectors proceeding over the northern route to the Montana and Idaho goldfields, as well as emigrants and troops. The main road was the Fort Totten Trail, pioneered in 1862–63 by Capt. James L. Fisk and extending from Fort Snelling, Minn., via the North Dakota forts of Abercrombie, Totten, Stevenson, and Buford to Fort Benton, Mont.

Fort Abercrombie also played a peripheral role in the Santee Sioux uprising of 1862, which spilled over from Minnesota into the Dakotas. In the latter part of August the Sioux attacked settlers in the Red River Valley and many of them took refuge at the fort. On September 3–6 several hundred warriors besieged it, and on September 26 reinforcements from Fort Snelling helped the garrison of Minnesota Volunteers beat off another assault. The 1862–64 campaigns of Generals Sully and Sibley in Minnesota and the Dakotas quelled the rebellion and encouraged the spread of settlement in the area.

Fort Abercrombie State Historic Park includes a small museum. A paved highway bisects the parade ground and divides the park into two tracts. The only original remaining structure is the frame guardhouse. The palisaded stockade and other buildings, built of wood except for the brick magazines, have long since disappeared. A large stockade and three blockhouses have been reconstructed. A marker near the guardhouse indicates the site of a barracks.

Fort Abraham Lincoln, North Dakota ⊗

Location: Morton County, on N. Dak. 80, about 4 miles southeast of Mandan.

Lt. Col. George A. Custer commanded this post in the years 1873–76. It was the base for his 1874 expedition into the Black Hills, in the wake of which miners poured into the region and inflamed the Sioux. In the ensuing campaign against them. he and the 7th Cavalry set out from the fort with Brig. Gen. Alfred H.

Fort Abraham Lincoln in the 1870's.

*Officers of the 7th Cavalry and their ladies at Fort
Abraham Lincoln shortly before the regiment
departed for the Little Bighorn campaign. Custer
is third from the left, and his wife is the first lady
from the left on the lower step.*

Terry's column in 1876 on their ill-fated expedition to the Little
Bighorn. After the debacle, Terry returned to it, as did also the
wounded survivors of Custer's regiment in the steamer *Far West*.

The predecessor of the fort was a stockaded infantry post called
Fort McKeen, founded in June of 1872 on the west bank of the
Missouri across from the site of Bismarck, N. Dak., and moved in
August about 5 miles to the south on the river bluffs. In November Fort Abraham Lincoln, a cavalry base activated on the plain
to the southeast, absorbed Fort McKeen. In time it grew into a
major Army post. Its troops accompanied the Yellowstone Survey
Expedition of 1873, the last of three expeditions surveying the
route of the Northern Pacific Railroad; and later protected construction workers.

During 1877 the garrison participated in the Montana campaign against the Nez Perces. When they surrendered in October, 239

it helped escort them from Fort Keogh, Mont., to Bismarck, N. Dak., en route to Fort Leavenworth, Kans. By the end of the 1880's the railroad had been completed, most of the Indians had been confined to reservations, and local settlers were numerous. The Army evacuated the fort in 1891, by which time it was already falling into ruins and being dismantled by settlers.

Fort Abraham Lincoln State Park includes the sites of the two forts and several restored Mandan Indian earth lodges. The locations of numerous buildings have been marked. Three blockhouses at Fort McKeen have been reconstructed. The original flagpole of Fort Abraham Lincoln stands in front of the Custer House marker. Only the foundations remain of this 10-room home, where Custer lived while commanding the post. A museum interprets the fort's history

Fort Buford, North Dakota ⊗

Location: Williams County, on an unimproved road, about 1 mile southwest of Buford.

Barely able to cope with Indian depredations along the Bozeman Trail, in 1866–68 the Army established a chain of forts along the Missouri River, the other major route to the newly discovered Montana goldfields. One of the new posts was Fort Buford, founded in 1866 near the confluence of the Yellowstone and Missouri Rivers in hostile Indian territory. A leading Army bastion in the Dakotas and the northern Plains region, it was a supply center and base for campaigns against the Indians in the area. Its troops also settled many of them on reservations, distributed annuities, and policed the region to restrain traders illegally bartering ammunition and whisky with the Indians for pelts. Prominent Army officers who visited the fort at one time or another include Sherman, Sheridan, Custer, Miles, and Pershing.

In 1866, while Red Cloud was plaguing the Bozeman Trail in Wyoming and Montana, Sitting Bull harassed the troops who were hastily constructing Fort Buford, a one-company post, enlarged the next year to a five-company installation with materials salvaged from the nearby Fort Union trading post. Although Buford was never directly assaulted and suffered few casualties, for the first 4 years it was under continual siege. The Indians raided woodcutting, hunting, and haying parties; rustled livestock; and attacked mail coaches running between the post and Fort Stevenson, N. Dak.

Fort Buford figured prominently in the northern Plains campaigns of the 1870's and 1880's. A main logistical base for the campaigns against the Sioux and Cheyennes in Wyoming and Montana that followed the Custer defeat in 1876, it handled many of the men and supplies shipped up the Yellowstone and Missouri via wagon trains and boats.

The nontreaty Nez Perces, defeated in the Battle of Bear Paw Mountains, Mont., in 1877, following their exodus from Idaho, passed through Fort Buford en route from Fort Keogh, Mont., to Fort Leavenworth, Kans. The post was also the scene of the surrender of Sitting Bull and his followers. After they had crushed Custer's force, they had sworn they would never accept reservation restraints and had eluded the Army and escaped to Canada. Prevented from crossing the international boundary to hunt buffalo by U.S. patrols, unwanted by Canadian authorities, and suffering from the severe cold, the hungry and tired group, reduced in number by defections to about 1,300, straggled into Fort Buford in the spring and summer of 1881. From there they were moved to Fort Yates, N. Dak. Sitting Bull was escorted from there to Fort Randall, S. Dak., and imprisoned for 2 years.

Until the post's inactivation in 1895 the garrison kept busy sending out routine patrols, policing the international border to stop Indian movements in either direction, and furnishing troops to guard railroad construction workers. The fort buildings were sold at public auction and many of them were used in constructing the present town of Buford.

About 36 acres of the Fort Buford reservation are maintained as a State historic site, and an additional 160 acres are in non-State ownership. Two of the buildings have survived in their original location. One is a frame officers' quarters, which today serves as a museum. The other is the stone powder magazine, whose roof the State restored after a fire destroyed it. Some buildings have been shifted in location and altered for modern use. These include the morgue, until recently a farm residence; and a row of frame stable sheds, apparently constructed from materials in the old barracks and used in modern times as a barn and granary. Some foundations, possibly those of the hospital, are visible not far from the powder magazine. The soldier graves in the rehabilitated cemetery, south of the fort, have been moved and only civilian graves remain.

Fort Rice, North Dakota ⊗

Location: Morton County, on an unimproved road, about 1 mile south of the town of Fort Rice.

Among the earliest of numerous Missouri River posts and the first on the river in North Dakota, this fort was founded in the summer of 1864 as a stockaded supply base by Brig. Gen. Alfred Sully during his 1863–64 expedition into the Dakotas against the Sioux who had been responsible for the 1862 Minnesota uprising. He used it again in his campaign the next year into the same region. Subsequently the primary mission of the fort was protection of river navigation, though in July 1868 it was the scene of the signing by some of the upper Missouri chiefs or their emissaries of the

Fort Rice in 1864.

Fort Laramie Treaty (1868). Sitting Bull, who sent his chief lieutenant, Gall, and other chiefs refused to attend. Father Pierre Jean De Smet, special representative of the Peace Commission that negotiated the Fort Laramie Treaty, who had met with various chiefs of the region the previous year on behalf of the Government at Forts Rice, Sully, and Berthold, had persuaded the Indians to attend the 1868 council at Fort Rice. The three Yellowstone Expeditions of the 1870's (1871, 1872, and 1873), which escorted parties surveying the Northern Pacific Railroad, organized at the fort. The establishment in the early 1870's of Fort Yates, some 32 miles to the south, and Fort Abraham Lincoln, 25 miles to the north, brought about the inactivation of Fort Rice in 1878.

Fort Rice State Historic Site, comprising 7 acres, embraces a large portion of the fort area. The foundations of many of the original buildings, log and frame except for the stone magazine, have been marked. Two restored blockhouses stand on opposite corners of the parade ground.

Fort Totten, North Dakota ⊗

Location: Benson County, on the Fort Totten Indian Reservation, near N. Dak. 57, just south of the agency town of Fort Totten.

Located on the southeastern shore of giant Devils Lake, this fort (1867–90) was one of a group founded to protect the overland route extending across Dakota Territory from southern Minnesota to the goldfields of western Montana. Its second major mission was control of the surrounding reservation, formally established for the Cut Head, Wahpeton, and Sisseton Sioux in 1878 in accordance with an 1867 treaty. When the Army departed, the U.S. Government acquired the fort and adjacent lands, and used the buildings for an Indian boarding school into the modern period. In 1960 the Bureau of Indian Affairs transferred the bulk of the fort site to the State for historical purposes.

Fort Totten State Historic Park consists of the well-preserved post, almost unchanged since its establishment a century ago. Practically all of the brick buildings of the 1870's, numbering 15,

Officers' row, Fort Totten, as it appears today.

remain. Although altered somewhat, mainly in the interiors, they are in excellent condition. They include officers' row, two-story duplex and multiplex family units; barracks; commissary store-houses; and bakery. A museum is in the hospital building.

Fort Union Trading Post National Historic Site, North Dakota-Montana ⊠

> *Location: Williams County, N. Dak., and Roosevelt County, Mont., on an unimproved road, about 1½ miles west of Buford, N. Dak.; address: c/o Theodore Roosevelt National Memorial Park, Medora, N. Dak. 58645.*

The dominant historical values of Fort Union Trading Post, like Bent's Old Fort, Colo., derive from its significance in the fur trade, but both forts were also important centers of cultural trans-mission where the Indians received their first substantial view of the alien culture that was soon to overwhelm them. Fort Union played a leading role in the growth of the upper Missouri basin for four decades, from 1829 until 1867; was a social rendezvous for explorers, fur traders, mountain men, surveyors, artists, naturalists, and other travelers; and in 1864–65 served as a temporary military post.

On the north bank of the Missouri River only a few miles from the mouth of the Yellowstone and commanding the main water route into the region of the interior fur trade, the post was a natural meetingplace for the routes of travel to and from all parts of the territory beyond. Founded by John Jacob Astor's American Fur Co. in 1829 and later taken over by other entrepreneurs, the post was the principal fur trading depot in the upper Missouri River region and monopolized the rich trade with the Plains and mountain tribes roaming the region now encompassing Montana, North Dakota, and part of Wyoming.

A formidable structure and the best built fur post on the Missouri, Fort Union was a conventional stockaded fort. It sometimes employed more than 100 people, many of foreign extraction and including artisans of all types. Many of them were married to Indian women. Self-sufficient, except for the annual receipt of basic supplies and trade goods by steamboat, the post maintained a garden and a herd of cattle and swine to supplement the meat its hunters procured.

Karl Bodmer's lithograph of Fort Union Trading Post in 1833.

The Indians bartered furs for the trade goods that so vitally influenced their material culture and upon which they became so dependent. At the same time, they received an introduction to alcohol and white men's diseases, which brought demoralization and debilitation. No matter how much some traders and companies lamented the use of alcohol as a trade item, it came to be an indispensable weapon of competition. But for many years the Government's attempts to enforce the prohibition laws were almost completely ineffective. A year or so after the passage of the stringent prohibition law of 1832, which forbade the shipment of liquor into Indian country but said nothing about its manufacture, Kenneth McKenzie, the American Fur Co. *bourgeois* at Fort Union, installed a distillery to produce corn whisky. This stirred a storm of denunciation from competitors, almost cost McKenzie his job, and nearly resulted in the company losing its license. Thereafter the traders resorted to the old smuggling methods.

Diseases also took a terrible toll. The most destructive to reach the tribes through Fort Union was smallpox, which came up the river on the company's annual supply boat in 1837. The Indians could not be prevented from coming to the fort to trade, and the quick-spreading epidemic devastated the Blackfeet, Crows, Assiniboins, Mandans, Minitaris, and Arikaras. About 15,000 of them died.

The Government, early recognizing the importance of Fort Union as a focal point in dealing with the Indian tribes on the upper Missouri and the Yellowstone, from the 1830's through the 1860's used it as an annuity distribution point for some of the tribes in the region.

Changes in the fur market and the widespread unrest among the Indians on the upper Missouri resulting from the Sioux uprising in Minnesota in 1862 all adversely affected the fur trade at Fort Union. As time went on, its condition deteriorated. When Gen. Alfred Sully campaigned through western Dakota against the Sioux in 1864–65, he found it in a dilapidated condition. But he left a company of troops there to police the region over the winter of 1864–65, replaced the next summer by another company. In 1867, when Fort Buford, N. Dak., 3 miles eastward, was enlarged from a one-company to a five-company post, the Army purchased Fort Union and dismantled it for building materials.

Fort Union Trading Post National Historic Site was authorized by Congress in 1966. In 1968 a comprehensive program of archeological excavation was initiated. At that time, the foundations of the southwestern bastion could be seen, but no surface remains of the stockades or buildings were visible. A flagpole, since fallen down, stood in the center of the site. Some ground depressions indicated the location of cellars. The integrity of the natural scene was marred only by evidences of gravel operations, the existence of cultivated fields on three sides, and a railroad line nearby. Archeologists subsequently uncovered the foundations of the northeastern bastion, the *bourgeois'* house, and the powder magazine. They also discovered differences in the sizes of several structures from those reported in historical sources. The National Park Service plans to continue the archeological program. Historical and archeological research will provide the basis for a reconstruction and development program.

Fort Yates and Standing Rock Agency, North Dakota ⊗
Location: Sioux County, town of Fort Yates.

Standing Rock Agency (Grand River Agency II) was founded in 1873 near the sacred "standing rock" of the Sioux. It was the successor of Grand River Agency I (1868–73), located farther down the Missouri close to the mouth of the Grand River. Roughly the southern half of the Standing Rock Reservation, extending a few miles below the Grand River, was in north-central South Dakota. Adjoining it on the south was the Cheyenne River Reservation, S. Dak. Established in 1868 and guarded by Fort Bennett (1870–91), the latter stretched west of the Missouri River as far south as the Cheyenne River.

Fort Yates, N. Dak. (1874–1903), protected the Standing Rock Reservation, home of the Hunkpapa, Yankton, and Blackfeet Sioux. Together with the Cheyenne River (S. Dak.), Red Cloud (Nebr.), and Spotted Tail (Nebr.) Reservations, Standing Rock was a center of unrest during the Sioux troubles of the 1870's; in 1876 it furnished men and supplies to Sitting Bull's hostiles. In October 1876, following the Custer disaster and well before Sitting Bull departed for Canada, Brig. Gen. Alfred H. Terry   247

Inspection at Fort Yates. Date unknown.

marched down from Fort Abraham Lincoln, N. Dak., with a force of 1,200 men and disarmed and dismounted the reservation Indians at Standing Rock, as well as at the Cheyenne River Agency. As the fugitive Sioux capitulated, the Hunkpapas among them were sent to Standing Rock.

After Sitting Bull's 2-year imprisonment at Fort Randall, S. Dak., following his surrender with his band in 1881 at Fort Buford, N. Dak., he returned to live with his people at Standing Rock Agency near his birthplace on the Grand River of South Dakota, about 40 miles south of Fort Yates and the Standing Rock Agency. Throughout the 1880's he resisted the efforts of the Indian Bureau to make farmers of his people and strip him of his authority. The Ghost Dance movement of 1890, in which he was a leading spirit, was strong on the Standing Rock Reservation but the Indian agent controlled it well. Nevertheless, at the peak of the Ghost Dance rebellion, Maj. Gen. Nelson A. Miles decided to arrest certain ringleaders. Accordingly, on December 15, 1890, James McLaughlin, the Standing Rock Indian agent, dispatched

a detachment of 39 Indian police and four volunteers to appre-
hend Sitting Bull at his home. At first he submitted but then responded to his followers' opposition and resisted. One of his band
shot a policeman and set off a scuffle, in which six of the police
and eight Indians died, among them Sitting Bull and one of his
sons. When cavalry reinforcements arrived to quiet the infuriated
Hunkpapas, many of them fled southward toward the Cheyenne
River and set off the grim chain of events that ended in the Battle
of Wounded Knee.

No historic structures have survived at Fort Yates or Standing
Rock Agency, around which the town of Fort Yates has grown up.
Although Standing Rock is still a Sioux agency, the old frame
buildings have given way to modern buildings. The sacred "standing rock" of the Sioux stands on a bluff above the Missouri at the
northern end of town. The Indian police who died at the same
time as Sitting Bull are buried in the town's Catholic Cemetery.
Sitting Bull was buried in the post cemetery until 1954, when his
body was moved to a Sitting Bull memorial overlooking the Oahe
Reservoir near Mobridge, S. Dak. The reservoir has inundated
the sites of the Cheyenne River Agency and Fort Bennett.

Indian police at Standing Rock Reservation about
1890. Red Tomahawk, front center, killed Sitting Bull.

249

Killdeer Mountain Battlefield, North Dakota ⊗

Location: Dunn County, on an unimproved road, about 11 miles northwest of Killdeer.

At this site in the summer of 1864 Brig. Gen. Alfred Sully culminated his campaign against the Sioux who had been responsible for the uprising in Minnesota 2 years earlier and inflicted a final defeat on the fleeing Chief Inkpaduta. After his victory at Whitestone Hill, N. Dak., in September 1863, Sully wintered on the Missouri River near present Pierre, S. Dak., where reinforcements from Fort Ridgely, Minn., and Wisconsin increased his command to 2,200. On July 28 at the southern base of Killdeer Mountain, his troops engaged 1,600 Santees and Tetons, killed and wounded about 100 of them, and burned their village.

The State owns 1 acre of the battlefield, on which stand a large marker and the gravestones of two soldiers killed in the battle. The rest of the site, except for a few cultivated patches and an artificial lake, is privately owned ranchland. Ranch buildings and corrals occupy the site of the Sioux camp.

Gen. Alfred Sully mounted campaigns against the Sioux in 1863–65 and won notable victories in North Dakota in the Battles of Whitestone Hill and Killdeer Mountain.

Whitestone Hill Battlefield, North Dakota ⊗

Location: Dickey County, on an unimproved road, about 5 miles southwest of Merricourt.

In the Battle of Whitestone Hill (September 3, 1863), the first of General Sully's two decisive victories in his 1863–64 Sioux campaign following the 1862 revolt in Minnesota, he dealt a heavy blow to Chief Inkpaduta. Surrounding Sully's advance guard, 4,000 Sioux confidently took advantage of the opportunity and applied battle paint. Sully used the time to bring up his troops. Some 300 braves died, and the troops captured 250 women and children. Army casualties were 22 deaths and 50 wounded.

Whitestone Hill Battlefield State Historic Site commemorates the battle. The natural terrain, low hills covered with prairie grass, has been only slightly disturbed. Around a monument in the center of the battlefield are 22 markers, each listing the name of a soldier who died. A small exhibit at a picnic shelter interprets the battle.

Anadarko (Wichita) Agency, Oklahoma ⊗

Location: Caddo County, northern edge of Anadarko.

The Wichita Agency, which had been attached to the Kiowa-Comanche Agency at Fort Sill, Okla., was reestablished in 1871 on the north bank of the Washita River across from the site of the city of Anadarko. Only 3 years later, it was the scene of the first battle in the Red River War (1874–75). In August 1874 troops from Fort Sill and the infantry guard at the agency defended it and the relatively peaceful Wichitas from a raid by Kiowas and Comanches. Six civilians died and four soldiers suffered wounds before the raiders fled to the Staked Plains and western Indian Territory.

In 1878 the Kiowa-Comanche Agency at Fort Sill was consolidated with the Wichita Agency at Anadarko, and in the fall of 1879 the Kiowas, Comanches, and Kiowa-Apaches at Fort Sill moved there. The new agency, known as the Kiowa-Comanche Agency and relocated to the south bank of the river, administered nine tribes. The agency in 1895 moved into new buildings constructed on an adjoining site to the west. The opening of the Kiowa-Comanche Reservation to settlement in 1901 resulted in the last great Oklahoma land boom and the city of Anadarko grew up nearby.

Nothing remains of the Wichita Agency or the first Kiowa-Comanche Agency. Nearly all the buildings of the second Kiowa-Comanche Agency are still standing. These include about 15 frame residences of agency employees, the old brick agency headquarters, a two-story office building, the stone jail, a brick blacksmith shop, and two frame warehouses. In 1958 the Bureau of Indian Affairs transferred these structures to the Kiowa, Comanche, Arapaho, and other local tribes.

Armstrong Academy, Oklahoma ⊗

Location: Bryan County, on a secondary road, about 3 miles northeast of Bokchito.

Founded in 1843 as a unit of the Choctaw school system, this academy was the result of cooperation between the Choctaw Nation and Baptist missionaries, who supervised it. Although essentially a boarding school for boys, it also provided adult education. In 1861, at the beginning of the Civil War, it closed. Two years later the building became the Choctaw national capitol, as well as the capitol for members of the Civilized Tribes supporting the Confederacy. Practically the entire Choctaw, Chickasaw, and Seminole Nations sided with it, whereas the Creek and Cherokee Nations split. In 1883 the Choctaws moved the national capitol to Tuskahoma, Okla. That same year Presbyterian missionaries reopened the academy under contract with the Choctaw Nation. Serving as a school for orphaned Choctaw boys, it offered academic, agricultural, and manual instruction until fire destroyed it in 1921.

Ruins of the two-story brick academy building may still be seen.

Camp Nichols, Oklahoma △

Location: Cimarron County, on an unimproved road, about 3 miles northwest of Wheeless.

During the critical summer of 1865 troops from this temporary camp, in Comanche and Kiowa country at the very western tip of the Oklahoma Panhandle, escorted wagon trains across the dangerous and desolate Cimarron Cutoff of the Santa Fe Trail. Since the previous year the Kiowas and Comanches had sporadically raided the cutoff. Fearing a full-scale Plains war, Gen. James H. Carleton, commanding the Department of New Mexico, ordered Col. "Kit" Carson to establish a camp about halfway between Fort Union, N. Mex., and the Cimarron Crossing of the Arkansas and provide escorts for wagon trains.

Carson and three companies of New Mexico and California Volunteers founded the camp in June on a low ridge. Breastworks of stone and earth enclosed the camp, about 200 feet square. Other defenses consisted of mountain howitzers at the corners. Inside and outside the fortifications were tents, stone dugouts with dirt roofs supported by logs, and other stone buildings. The post was continually on the alert, and every night mounted pickets supplemented the sentries.

Carson never had a chance to accomplish his second assignment of attempting negotiations with the Kiowas and Comanches. After only 2 weeks he was called to Santa Fe to testify before a joint Congressional committee investigating Indian affairs, and he never returned. But his second-in-command carried on with the escort program. Trains from New Mexico assembled at the camp and were escorted by 50-man detachments to the Arkansas River. This system was a major improvement over the one used the previous summer, when small bands of troops, dispatched along the cutoff, served as roving escorts. Under the new system, troops had orders to stay with corralled trains under attack rather than to pursue war parties. In the event of a major Indian assault, the fortified camp was to be a rallying point for troops and wagon trains. But by September the southern Plains tribes had decreased their raids, and the Army inactivated Camp Nichols.

The lonely ruins of the camp, remains of the only manmade structures ever built on the Cimarron Cutoff during its active years, are situated on a high point of land between two ravines cut by the two forks of South Carrizozo Creek. The broken and wild setting, on private ranchland, is almost completely free of modern intrusions. Few sites evoke for the modern visitor such a

253

feeling of trail territory, such a feeling of walking in the past. Low stone walls, 2 to 3 feet high, outline the breastworks and foundations and walls of the officers' quarters, commissary, and hospital. In the center of the enclosure is a flagstone area about 20 feet wide by 100 feet long, where the tie rack for the horseherd was located. One-quarter mile west of the ruins, along the left fork of South Carrizozo Creek, is Cedar Spring, whose pools stretch along the creek for 200 to 300 yards. These furnished water to the camp and passing wagon trains. The route of the Santa Fe Trail passes about half a mile south of the camp. Trail remains in the area, unusually good in both directions for miles, are among the most impressive along the entire trail.

Camp Supply, Oklahoma ⊗

Location: Woodward County, on U.S. 270, about 1 mile east of the town of Fort Supply.

Lt. Cols. Alfred Sully and George A. Custer, commanding the main column in General Sheridan's 1868–69 campaign, on November 18, 1868, established this camp near the junction of Wolf Creek with the North Canadian River as an advance base in northwestern Indian Territory. On November 23, under orders from General Sheridan, Custer pushed southward, 4 days later won the Battle of the Washita, Okla., and returned with the captives to Camp Supply. Although in time expanded into a modern post and not abandoned by the Army until 1895, Camp Supply was never considered a permanent base, even after it was redesignated as a fort in 1878. Its garrison took part in the Red River War (1874–75). In 1903 Oklahoma Territory acquired the fort and utilized it for a hospital, still active today as the Western State Hospital.

Buildings remaining from the Army era are mostly of the late period. Included are the brick guardhouse, with barred windows, now used as a storehouse; a log fire station; a frame recreation building; a vertical log structure that was probably a family officers' quarters, presently occupied by the hospital chaplain; a teamster's cabin; and a large two-story framehouse, with columned porch.

(Cherokee National Capitol, today the Cherokee County Courthouse.

(Cherokee National Capitol, Oklahoma ⚠

> *Location: Cherokee County, Courthouse Square, Tahlequah.*

1This structure commemorates the achievements of the Cherokee Indians in overcoming the hardships of removal to Indian Territory from the Southeastern United States, merging their tribal factions into a unified nation, and assuming a prominent position among the Five Civilized Tribes.

Between 1808 and 1817 some 2,000 Cherokees, disturbed by the pressure of settlers, voluntarily moved from the Southeast to a reservation in northwestern Arkansas. In 1817 another group of about 4,000 ceded their lands to the U.S. Government and within 2 years joined their brethren in Arkansas. Removed from much contact with the whites, these Western Cherokees tended to resist change, and their way of life and political institutions remained

255

static. Living a simple agrarian life, they paid little heed to educational and cultural refinements. Governed by three chiefs and a council, they lacked a written constitution and had few written laws. The council met informally several times each year to elect chiefs, councilmen, judges, and policemen.

Before long the Western Cherokees felt the pressure of the frontier's advance. As the years passed after Arkansas became a Territory in 1819, settlers began to petition Congress for their removal. Finally, in 1828 they agreed with the U.S. Government to exchange their lands in Arkansas for new ones in Indian Territory (Oklahoma). Within a year all of them had emigrated.

In contrast to the Western Cherokees, the less isolated Eastern Cherokees, those originally living mostly in Georgia but also in North Carolina, Alabama, and Tennessee, had an advanced agrarian economy and were more commercially oriented. Some of them

John Mix Stanley's on-the-spot painting of the grand Cherokee council of 1843 at Tahlequah, Okla. Attended by thousands of representatives from the Five Civilized Tribes and the Plains Indians, it resolved intertribal differences.

were wealthy and influential, owning large tracts of land and numerous slaves. They had produced many outstanding statesmen, literary figures, and educators. Although they retained a principal chief as titular head of their nation, they utilized a bicameral elective legislature and a supreme court. Their codified laws and written constitution were based on those of the United States. Following Sequoyah's invention of the Cherokee syllabary in 1821, most of them learned to read and write; in 1828 the tribe began publishing at its capital of New Echota, Ga., a national newspaper, the *Cherokee Phoenix.*

In 1835 a small group of Eastern Cherokees negotiated in secret a treaty with the U.S. Government illegally ceding all Cherokee lands east of the Mississippi and agreeing to move to Indian Territory. Known as the Treaty Party, this group managed to persuade some 2,000 of their tribesmen to emigrate between 1835 and 1838. Remaining behind were about 15,000 people, most of them strongly opposed to removal. In 1838–39 the U.S. Government forced them to march over the "Trail of Tears" to Indian Territory. Many of them died resisting removal or along the way. Only about 11,000 to 13,000 safely reached their destinations.

Conflicts inevitably arose between the two major Cherokee factions in Indian Territory. The Western Cherokees did not want to share their land, nor did they wish to change their system of government or way of life. The Eastern Cherokees, who felt their political system and culture to be superior and who were far larger in number, refused to compromise. Complicating matters was the hostility of the Treaty Party, which had formed an alliance with the Western Cherokees, toward the eastern group.

The first meeting between the eastern and western factions, in June 1839 at Takattokah (Double Springs), failed dismally. The next month more than 2,000 Cherokees gathered at a campground near Park Hill Mission. On July 12 the Chief of the Eastern Cherokees, John Ross, adopted an Act of Union uniting the two groups, though only one of the three western chiefs signed the act and few of the western braves were present. In September at another council Ross was able to win enough Western Cherokees over to his side to initiate a government. The conferees elected him as their principal chief and a Western Cherokee as assistant, or second, chief; adopted a constitution based on that of the Eastern Cherokees; and elected governmental officials from both factions. Ross chose the site of Tahlequah as the capital of the United Cherokee Nation. A minority group of Western and Treaty Cherokees remained hostile and refused to acknowledge the new government.

Chief John Ross immediately began to reconcile intertribal and tribal differences. In June 1843 he held a grand council at Tahlequah, in which delegates from a large number of tribes living in or adjacent to Indian Territory participated. Within 30 days the delegates settled major intertribal conflicts and agreed to live peaceably and end devastating border wars. Ross also spent considerable time in Washington trying to gain recognition of his government as the official government of the Cherokee Nation, as well as obtain redress for the grievances of the various factions. In 1846 he was instrumental in the defeat of a congressional bill dividing the Cherokee Nation into two separate nations and in negotiating a treaty with the U.S. Government. Signed by a delegation representing all three factions, it guaranteed the Cherokees, as a unified nation, patent to their land in Indian Territory and com-

John Ross, father of the United Cherokee Nation.

pensated all of them for losses of land and property and other inconveniences incurred during the removal.

This treaty did much to resolve factional differences. From that time on, except during the Civil War, when the tribe once again split into factions, the Cherokee Nation prospered. Other tribes especially the Creeks, often called upon it to participate in intertribal councils and to make major policy decisions affecting the lives of all Indians in Indian Territory. Because of their printing facilities, the Cherokees were also often the spokesmen for the other tribes.

For 4 years after Tahlequah became the permanent Cherokee capital in 1839, it was merely a campground where delegates met to conduct governmental business. In 1843, however, the tribe platted the town and built three log cabins for governmental purposes. In 1845, on the southeastern corner of the town square, a two-story brick building was erected for the supreme court. Fire razed it in 1874, but it was rebuilt, utilizing the surviving walls. The Supreme Court Building housed the printing press of the *Cherokee Advocate,* official publication of the Cherokee Nation and the first newspaper in Oklahoma. The Capitol, a two-story brick structure completed in 1869, occupied the center of the town square. It accommodated executive and legislative offices until 1906, the year before Oklahoma became a State, when the Five Civilized Tribes began abolishing their tribal governments in accordance with the Curtis Act (1898).

The Cherokee Capitol serves today as the county courthouse of Cherokee County. Although the interior has been altered, the exterior retains its 1869 appearance and the building is in good condition. The Supreme Court Building serves as an office building.

Chilocco Indian School, Oklahoma ⊗

Location: Kay County, on an unimproved road, about 8 miles north of Newkirk.

The Chilocco Indian School was one of the off-reservation boarding schools established on the pattern of the Carlisle Indian School, Pa. The Government founded it in 1883 to serve the children of the Plains tribes residing in western Indian Territory.

them for lsses of land and property and other in-
ncurred duing the removal.
did much to solve factional differences. From that
ot during th :ivil War, when the tribe once again
ons, the Cherokee Nation prospered. Other tribes
Creeks, ofte alled upon it to participate in inter-
♦ and to mac major policy decisions affecting the
lians in Indu Territory. Because of their printing
Cherokees c e also often the spokesmen for the

after Tahlqt ah became the permanent Cherokee
), it was mezly a campground where delegates met
)vernmentally isiness. In 1843, however, the tribe
vn and built three log cabins for governmental pur-
), on the soul eastern corner of the town square, a
k building w erected for the supreme court. Fire
74, but it wi rebuilt, utilizing the surviving walls.
e Court Buili ig housed the printing press of the
vocate, offici ublication of the Cherokee Nation
newspaper i)klahoma. The Capitol, a two-story
re completec in 1869, occupied the center of the
It accommd: ted executive and legislative offices
he year befor)klahoma became a State, when the
l Tribes begn abolishing their tribal governments
: with the Cusi Act (1898).
kee Capitol si es today as the county courthouse of
unty. Although the interior has been altered, the ex-
its 1869 appei ince and the building is in good con-
Supreme Cout Building serves as an office building.

dian School klahoma ⊗
cation: Kay Cu ty, on an unimproved road, about 8
les north of Novirk.

o Indian Schol was one of the off-reservation board-
established o the pattern of the Carlisle Indian
The Governmet founded it in 19 to serve the
Plains tribes esiding in we   ndian T

Later the Five Civilized Tribes sent many students to the school after the breakup of their tribal governments and the dissolution of their educational systems around the time of statehood. Still active today, the school stresses secondary level education, emphasizing home economics for girls and industrial art for boys.

The original structure, a four-story brick building constructed in 1884, is used today for dormitories and is designated as Home No. 2. Mingling with modern structures around the quadrangle are other older ones of limestone.

Creek National Capitol, Oklahoma ⚠

> Location: Okmulgee County, 6th and Morton Streets, Okmulgee.

This building symbolizes the successful acculturation and political evolution of the Creek Indians, one of the Five Civilized Tribes, following their removal from the Southeastern United States to Indian Territory.

Between 1827 and 1830 some 2,000 to 3,000 Creeks moved voluntarily to Indian Territory, but the majority, opposing removal, remained in Alabama and Georgia. Between 1834 and 1838 the U.S. Government forcibly relocated those Creeks. Not long after the removal, the Upper and Lower Creeks united in name but in actuality remained separate. Each group had its own council, principal and second chiefs, and town chiefs. The town chiefs and the two principal chiefs, elected for life, met annually in a General Council, which enacted tribal laws. Town officials administered them.

Embittered, impoverished, and suffering from factionalism, most of the Creeks, who had emigrated emptyhanded and who failed to receive promised supplies and implements from the U.S. Government, found it difficult to adjust to their strange surroundings. Many who had lived comfortably in the East had to resort to primitive methods to build shelters and clear and cultivate land. Also feeling threatened by warlike tribes in the area, they clung to their traditional ways. The chiefs, who opposed Christian missionaries and education, penalized Creek converts heavily. Not until 1848 did the General Council approve missionary work. An

260

Creek National Capitol.

exception to the general pattern of Creek life was one wealthy group, which patterned itself after the southern planter class and held vast acreages and large numbers of slaves.

In 1859 the Creeks began to reorganize their government. They held a democratic election to replace the two principal chiefs, who retired that year, and adopted a written constitution. Perhaps they might have undertaken more reforms had it not been for the Civil War, which created serious strife between the fullbloods and the mixed bloods; resulted in the battles of Round Mountain, Chusto-Talasah, and Chustenahlah; and hopelessly widened the division between the Upper and Lower Creeks.

After the war, in 1867, the Creeks united into a single "Muskogee Nation," and adopted a written constitution and code of laws based on the Government of the United States. Every 4 years the

anches. A group of the ter, however, were discussing peace at
ort Arbuckle and wer emporarily camped at nearby Rush
prings in the fall of 188 when the Wichita Expedition from
ort Belknap, Tex., bivoa ked at Camp Radziminski, Okla., 55
iles to the west. attacke hem. Before the Civil War, the post
as irregularly garrisone During the war, Confederate troops,
cluding the Chickasaw ttalion, replaced Federal troops, who
id not return until late n 1866. The founding of Fort Sill,
)kla., 3 years later. causd the termination of the post the next
ear. The Chickasaw Nat acquired it in an 1866 treaty.

The site is on the lawn of a private ranch. Employee residences
re grouped around the ade ground. The only visible remind-
rs of the log fort are two stone chimneys of an officers' quarters.

'ort Cobb, Oklahoma ×

*Locat   ('lc   ants, astern edge of the town of Fort
Cobb.*

n existence but a decade om 1859 until 1869, this fort on the
Vashita River nevertheless ad a colorful history. It and the adja-
ent Wichita Indian Ager were established to receive Indians
elocated from 'exas rese tions, to protect them and the local
Vichitas from the Kiowas d Comanches, and to restrain the lat-
r from raiding in exa When the post and the agency were
nly 2 years old, the Unio abandoned them and the Confeder-
tes used the post spasmod lly until the Indians drove them out
nd burned it. To clear th vay for his 1868–69 offensive against
e southern Plains tribe eneral Sheridan ordered it reacti-
ated in 1868 and the Fo obb Reservation (Kiowa-Comanche
nd Wichita Agencies cret d as a refuge for all Indians in the
rea of the offensive who c ned to be peaceful, as well as for the
Vichitas and the Texas tri that had returned from their tempo-
ary haven in Kansas. In De mber 1868, the month after Custer's
ictory in the Battle of the Vashita, General Sheridan moved his
eadquarters to Fort Cob. To hasten the capitulation of the
Kiowas, he seized and thretened to hang Chiefs Satanta and Lone
Wolf. The next March he c ivated Fort Sill to replace Fort Cobb
nd transferred the Kiowa- manche Agency to the new fort.

263

people were to elect a principal and second chief. The legislature, called the National Council, which was to meet annually in regular sessions, consisted of a House of Kings (comparable to the U.S. Senate) and a House of Warriors (resembling the U.S. House of Representatives). The National Council was charged with appointing members of the supreme court for 4-year terms. Other provisions of the constitution provided for district judges, attorneys, and policemen. That same year the tribe designated Okmulgee as its permanent capital and it remained so until about 1906, the year that the Curtis Act (1898) required the dissolution of tribal governments by the Five Civilized Tribes. The following year Oklahoma became a State.

An interesting sidelight of Creek political activity was the tribe's leadership in intertribal affairs among the Five Civilized Tribes and other tribes in Indian Territory. Before the Civil War, it had often called intertribal councils to discuss matters of common interest. In 1870, at one of these councils, delegates of the Five Civilized Tribes strengthened their 1843 Tahlequah compact, and formulated a plan to create a federal union in Indian Territory, similar to that of the United States. Although the U.S. Congress never approved this proposal, the council met annually for 5 years and solved many intertribal problems.

The first Creek capitol, erected at Okmulgee in 1868, was a two-story log structure that housed the legislature and the supreme court. In 1878 a new capitol, a native brown sandstone building of modified Victorian architectural style, replaced the log structure. From 1907 until 1916 the capitol served as the Okmulgee County Courthouse. Today owned and administered by the Creek Indian Memorial Association and in good condition, it features a museum of Creek history.

Fort Arbuckle, Oklahoma ⊗

Location: Garvin County, on an unimproved road, about 7 miles west of Davis.

The prime mission of Fort Arbuckle (1851–70) was shielding the relocated Chickasaws and Choctaws from the Plains tribes. It also watched over emigrants and dealt with the raids of Texas Comanches. A group of the latter, however, were discussing peace at Fort Arbuckle and were temporarily camped at nearby Rush Springs in the fall of 1858 when the Wichita Expedition from Fort Belknap, Tex., bivouacked at Camp Radziminski, Okla., 55 miles to the west, attacked them. Before the Civil War, the post was irregularly garrisoned. During the war, Confederate troops, including the Chickasaw Battalion, replaced Federal troops, who did not return until late in 1866. The founding of Fort Sill, Okla., 3 years later, caused the termination of the post the next year. The Chickasaw Nation acquired it in an 1866 treaty.

The site is on the lawn of a private ranch. Employee residences are grouped around the parade ground. The only visible reminders of the log fort are two stone chimneys of an officers' quarters.

Fort Cobb, Oklahoma ⊗

Location: Caddo County, eastern edge of the town of Fort Cobb.

In existence but a decade, from 1859 until 1869, this fort on the Washita River nevertheless had a colorful history. It and the adjacent Wichita Indian Agency were established to receive Indians relocated from Texas reservations, to protect them and the local Wichitas from the Kiowas and Comanches, and to restrain the latter from raiding in Texas. When the post and the agency were only 2 years old, the Union abandoned them and the Confederates used the post spasmodically until the Indians drove them out and burned it. To clear the way for his 1868–69 offensive against the southern Plains tribes, General Sheridan ordered it reactivated in 1868 and the Fort Cobb Reservation (Kiowa-Comanche and Wichita Agencies) created as a refuge for all Indians in the area of the offensive who claimed to be peaceful, as well as for the Wichitas and the Texas tribes that had returned from their temporary haven in Kansas. In December 1868, the month after Custer's victory in the Battle of the Washita, General Sheridan moved his headquarters to Fort Cobb. To hasten the capitulation of the Kiowas, he seized and threatened to hang Chiefs Satanta and Lone Wolf. The next March he activated Fort Sill to replace Fort Cobb and transferred the Kiowa-Comanche Agency to the new fort.

263

There are no surface remains of the log-sod fort, on private property, but the cottonwood-lined site is comparatively undisturbed. A State marker is located one-half mile to the southwest.

Fort Gibson, Oklahoma △

Location: Muskogee County, northern edge of the town of Fort Gibson.

Fort Gibson was one of the most important of the posts on the "Permanent Indian Frontier." The first fort established in Indian Territory, it was actively involved in the problems associated with the relocation there of the Five Civilized Tribes from the Southeast. A frontier hub of commerce and military activity, it was a key transportation point and a testing place for such newly activated organizations as the Ranger units and Dragoon Regiments.

Established in 1824 by Col. Matthew Arbuckle on the east bank of the Grand River just above its confluence with the Verdigris and Arkansas Rivers, the fort was responsible for keeping peace between the Osages, who opposed any intrusion into their territory, and the Cherokees, who were already filtering into Indian Territory. The post replaced Fort Smith, which had been too far south to control the Osages effectively and was to remain inactive, except for several months, until 1839. During the period of Indian removal, in the 1830's and 1840's, the Fort Gibson garrison helped receive, care for, settle, and enforce peace among immigrant Cherokees, Creeks, Choctaws, Seminoles, and Chickasaws, as well as attempted to protect them from the Plains Indians. Troops provided escorts for surveyors marking the boundaries of Indian lands; established other posts in Indian Territory, such as Forts Coffee and Wayne and Camp Holmes; laid out a network of military roads; and tried to control the illegal liquor traffic.

In 1834 the fort was the base for the Dragoon Expedition, originally under the command of Col. Henry Leavenworth, who died of fever en route. His successor, Col. Henry Dodge, met with some of the southern Plains tribes at the north fork of the Red River and persuaded them to send delegates to Fort Gibson for negotiations. As a result, in 1835 the tribes made their first treaties with the U.S. Government at Camp Holmes, Okla.

Reconstructed Fort Gibson.

Fort Gibson was also a center of trade and travel. Located at a point beyond which river navigation was virtually impossible, it was a supply depot for a large area. Keelboats and later river steamers came up the Arkansas to the fort a few months each year, and unloaded passengers, military stores, and Indian trade goods. Traders furnished return cargoes. The Texas Road, which ran from north to south and linked the growing American settlements in Texas with the Missouri River Valley, passed by the fort, which became a way station for emigrants, freighters, and traders. The troops also provided escorts for road traffic. The fort continued to be a transportation and freighting center until the arrival in the region of the Missouri, Kansas, and Texas Railroad in 1872.

Originally a four-company post, the fort was expanded in 1831 to accommodate a regiment and it became the district headquarters, which overtaxed its limited capacity. Situated on low ground, it was also subject to flooding and threatened by malaria. In 1846 construction began of a new post on the hill overlooking the old site. But the project proceeded slowly and by 1857 only one stone building, the commissary storehouse, had been finished. That year, because the Cherokees had been requesting that the fort be evacuated and because the frontier had moved westward, the Army abandoned it and the tribe took possession.

At the outbreak of the Civil War the Confederates occupied the fort, but in 1863 Union forces made it a Federal stronghold in

Indian Territory and sought to strengthen the loyal element of the Cherokees. Regular troops replaced the Volunteers in 1866 and garrisoned the post until 1890. During this period the fort on the hill was completed; it consisted of seven large stone buildings and 10 frame ones.

Although the original fort has long since disappeared, the State of Oklahoma, under a Works Progress Administration (WPA) grant, completed in 1936 on a 55-acre tract a reconstruction of the original log stockade and a number of outlying log buildings almost on the original site. Except for the use of more durable materials, especially pine timber and lime chinking, the reconstruction is faithful to the original. Interpretive markers guide the visitor. On the ridge to the east overlooking the reconstructed stockade is the second fort site. Stone buildings, some now private homes, survive in various stages of repair, together with some ruins. A two-story stone barracks, which has porches running its length on both levels, is the most imposing structure and is in good condition. Owned by the State historical society, it is a private residence. One mile east of the town of Fort Gibson is the Fort Gibson National Cemetery. Many of the soldiers buried there were removed from Oklahoma Forts Towson, Arbuckle, and Washita.

Fort Reno and Darlington Agency, Oklahoma ⊗

> *Location: Canadian County. The Fort Reno site is located about 6 miles northwest of El Reno on an unimproved road at the Fort Reno U.S. Livestock Research Station. The Darlington Agency site lies 1½ miles northeast of Fort Reno, along an unimproved road, on the Darlington State Game Farm.*

Across the North Canadian River from the Darlington Agency in the center of Indian Territory, Fort Reno (1874–1949) guarded the inhabitants of the huge Cheyenne-Arapaho Reservation, whose agency had been established on the north bank of the river in 1869. The U.S. Government founded the reservation and the adjacent Kiowa-Comanche Reservation during Sheridan's successful 1868–69 campaign. Brinton Darlington, a Quaker representing President Grant's Peace Policy, was the first agent at the agency

*Darlington Agency in foreground, and Fort Reno
at distant right. This photograph was probably
taken in the 1890's.*

that came to bear his name. He served until 1872, at which time
John D. Miles replaced him and remained at the post for 12 years.

In 1874, after troops from Forts Leavenworth, Kans., and Sill,
Okla., put down a Cheyenne uprising at the Darlington Agency
and the Wichita Agency, 30 miles to the south, the Army activated Fort Reno to maintain the peace. By the middle of the next
year the last dissidents had surrendered and the leaders had been
sent to Fort Marion, Fla., along with those captured in the Red
River War (1874–75), in which the Fort Reno garrison participated. In 1877, the year following Custer's defeat at the Little
Bighorn, Dull Knife and more than 900 Cheyennes arrived under
escort at the Darlington Agency. The next year Dull Knife and
many of them escaped and headed for their northern homeland;
troops from Fort Reno and other posts pursued and captured
most of them near Fort Robinson, Nebr., and returned them to
the Darlington Agency.

The fort also settled intertribal disputes and ejected trespassing
white "Boomers" and ranchers illegally grazing cattle on reservation lands. In 1889, when the Oklahoma District was opened to
settlement, the garrison guarded the border against the "Sooners,"
rushing in before the official opening date, and helped supervise
the land rush. Three years later, yielding to insistent settler demand, the Government opened the Indian reservation to white
settlement, and the Indians each received 160 acres of land. In
1908, the year before the agency was moved 2 miles to the north,
Fort Reno became an Army remount depot; in 1938 a quarter-

master depot; and in World War II a German prisoner-of-war camp. The U.S. Department of Agriculture acquired it in 1949 for use as a livestock research station.

The Darlington Agency site has been obscured by modern structures at the Darlington State Game Farm. Sixteen of Fort Reno's brick and stone buildings, built between 1876 and 1890, remodeled or repaired, are grouped around the parade ground and used by the U.S. Livestock Research Station, operated in conjunction with the Oklahoma State University of Agriculture and Applied Sciences. These include a magazine; commissary building, now a grain storehouse; warehouse, a modern storage building; five noncommissioned officers' and six officers' quarters, presently employee residences; and two latrines. The adjacent Fort Reno National Cemetery contains the graves of soldier dead of the Indian and other wars. The only surviving building of the fort's original log structures is a two-room picket type, one of whose residents may have been General Sheridan. It has been moved to the western edge of El Reno, on the north side of U.S. 66, where it has been restored and refurnished.

Fort Sill, Oklahoma ⛁

> Location: Comanche County, on U.S. 62–277–281, near the Key Gate entrance of modern Fort Sill, about 3 miles north of Lawton.

Founded in conjunction with a new Kiowa-Comanche Indian Agency near the base of the Wichita Mountains in March 1869 by General Sheridan during his 1868–69 campaign, Fort Sill played a significant part in the pacification of the southern Plains tribes and is still a major Army post today. Believing that the relocation of the fort and agency farther south on reservation lands and closer to the Texas frontier would facilitate Indian management, Sheridan founded the two installations to replace Fort Cobb and the Fort Cobb Agency, Okla., about 30 miles to the north. Later in the year the Kiowa-Comanche Agency absorbed the Wichita Agency, which had been located at Fort Cobb.

Duress soon yielded to humanitarianism. That same summer, Fort Sill was the site of an experiment in Indian management, a part of President Grant's Peace Policy. Grant inaugurated the policy in reaction to the cries of eastern reformers over the brutality of the Battle of the Washita, Okla., and other examples of Indian mistreatment. Hoping to end corruption on the reservations and to provide the Indians with examples of morality, he decided to appoint church-nominated men as Indian agents. Quakers, representing the denomination that responded most enthusiastically, were soon on reservation duty. The southern Plains, where the gentle Friends fell heir to some of the fiercest tribes in the West, became a testing ground for the "Quaker Policy."

Illustrating the problems the Quakers faced was the experience of Quaker Agent Lawrie Tatum. Arriving in July 1869 to take over the Fort Sill Indian Agency, he attempted immediately to transform his recalcitrant wards into peaceful farmers. Construing his solicitude as weakness, however, they continued their forays into Texas. They had little fear of punishment, for the Peace Policy forbade military interference on reservations unless requested by the agent. And, because Tatum refused to believe his charges

Sherman House, Fort Sill.

269

guilty, the Fort Sill Reservation offered a refuge after each escapade. Their boldness growing in proportion to their success, they defied the Army to stop them. But in 1871 an unexpected turn of events dampened their ardor.

In May of that year a Kiowa war party from the Fort Sill Reservation, led by Satanta, Big Tree, and Satank, wiped out a wagon train near Jacksboro and Fort Richardson, Tex. Gen. William T. Sherman, inspecting Texas forts, narrowly missed a similar fate at the hands of the same party. Determined to put an end to Kiowa and Comanche hostilities, he moved on to Fort Sill. There he learned the Kiowa chiefs had bragged of their exploits on their return to the reservation. He had them arrested and sent to Fort Richardson, Tex., for incarceration pending an unprecedented civil trial. Satank, seeking to escape, was shot and killed en route. Satanta and Big Tree, serving only 2 years in prison, returned to Fort Sill late in 1873. The Kiowas lost no time in resuming their raids.

Their Comanche friends had not curtailed their activities. They continued to plague Texas until even Agent Tatum was forced to acknowledge their guilt. He reluctantly called on the Army to punish them, but in so doing incurred the displeasure of his more idealistic superiors. Discouraged, he resigned in March 1873. The Army welcomed an opportunity to chastise the Indians, but its small force could only show them that the Fort Sill Reservation was no longer a haven. The Indians were incensed over the loss of the lands they had ceded in treaties and the devastation wrought by the buffalo hunters, whisky peddlers, and horse thieves.

The failure of the Peace Policy to protect Texas settlers prompted the Army to revert to sterner measures. The Red River War (1874–75), against the Arapahos, Kiowa-Apaches, Comanches, Cheyennes, part of the Kiowas, and lesser tribes, was fought mainly in the Staked Plains of the Texas Panhandle and in Indian Territory (Oklahoma). Fort Sill was one of the major bases. The month after the Kiowas and Comanches attacked a group of buffalo hunters at Adobe Walls, Tex., General Sheridan ordered all professedly friendly Indians in the region to report to their agencies for registration. A severe drought delayed his operational plans until late summer, when 46 companies of infantry

Old Guardhouse, Fort Sill.

and cavalry took to the field. Columns from Fort Union, N. Mex., Fort Sill and Camp Supply, Okla., and Forts Concho and Griffin, Tex., gradually closed in on the Staked Plains, which became a haven for fugitive bands.

Although among the most comprehensive campaigns ever prosecuted against the Indians, the casualties on both sides were few. Involved was the sort of campaigning that General Sheridan viewed as the most effective and humane—relentless pursuit that kept the enemy always off balance, always on the move, always tormented by insecurity. Such tactics so damaged morale that surrender was but a question of time. The last fugitives gave up in the spring of 1875. The Army transported more than 70 Indian ringleaders from Fort Sill to Florida for imprisonment and placed their people back on the reservations. That same year Satanta was again sent to the Huntsville penitentiary in Texas, where he later committed suicide. Except for occasional raids by stray bands, the Red River War brought permanent peace to the southern Plains.

Fort Sill continued nevertheless as an active post. In 1894 Geronimo, his Chiricahua Apaches, and some of their Warm Springs kin, after their exile in Florida, were settled on the Fort Sill Military Reservation. Officially Geronimo was carried on the Army rolls as a scout, but he actually spent most of his time in retirement until his death in 1909. Four years later, 187 of the Chiricahuas were permitted to return to the Mescalero Reservation, N. Mex., and the rest stayed at Fort Sill. In 1905 the Army had extensively rebuilt the fort and expanded it into an artillery training and command center, which it has remained to the present.

The historic area of Fort Sill is open to the public. Nearly all the old stone buildings, built in the 1870's and 1880's and located to the east of today's main post, have survived and most are still in use. The U. S. Army Field Artillery Center Museum utilizes many of them. Only the cavalry stables have been torn down to make way for new construction. Of particular interest and dating to the 1870's are the headquarters building, used in that capacity until 1911; Sherman House, home of the post commandant and scene of the confrontation between Sherman and the Kiowa chiefs; the guardhouse, today a museum devoted to the military-Indian phase of history; and the chapel, the oldest house of worship in the State in continuous use since its founding. The old stone corral, a loopholed stockade built in 1870 to the southeast of the old post, used to protect the fort's livestock and as a potential refuge in the event of Indian attack, now contains frontier transportation exhibits. Prominent Kiowa, Comanche, and Apache chiefs buried at the fort include Geronimo, Satank, Satanta, and Quanah Parker.

Fort Towson, Oklahoma ⊗

Location: Choctaw County, on an unimproved road, about 1 mile northeast of the town of Fort Towson.

In 1824 troops from Fort Jesup, La., built this fort on the east bank of Gates Creek about 6 miles north of the Red River. It was the second post in Indian Territory, the first being Fort Gibson, lying to the north. One of the chain of posts guarding the "Permanent Indian Frontier," Fort Towson also helped control marauding outlaws and Indian bands along the Red River, then the international boundary between the United States and Mexico. In June 1829 the Army abandoned the post, but in November 1830 rebuilt it at a new location immediately south of Gates Creek as a permanent fort to protect the Choctaws, whom the U.S. Government relocated from Mississippi to Indian Territory in the 1830's. Throughout the decade, Fort Towson was an important link in the frontier defense system and was a marshaling point during the War with Mexico (1846–48). The Army abandoned it in 1854. Prior to the Civil War, during which Confederate forces occupied the site, it served as the Choctaw Indian Agency.

Over the years settlers dismantled or fire destroyed the fort buildings, which once made up what was considered to be one of the best built and maintained Army posts in the West. The scattered ruins of several stone buildings, overgrown by vegetation, are all that remain. Nearby, occasional ruts mark the old road to Fort Smith, Ark. The site is privately owned.

Fort Washita, Oklahoma ⚠

Location: Bryan County, on Okla. 199 just east of the Lake Texhoma Bridge, about 11 miles northwest of Durant.

The history of this fort differs considerably from that of most others on the frontier. Founded at the request of the Indians, it usually protected rather than fought them. It was also established much later and had a lesser role in Indian affairs than the majority of its counterparts.

Although the post was one of those on the "Permanent Indian Frontier," it was not activated until April 1842, long after all the others except Fort Scott, established the following month. Representing an advance from the Fort Gibson-Fort Towson line, it was founded by Fort Towson troops on the Washita River about 20 miles above its confluence with the Red River in response to Choctaw and Chickasaw demands for the security guaranteed them in their relocation treaties. Two of the Five Civilized Tribes, in the 1830's they had been removed from their homelands in Alabama and Mississippi to southeastern Indian Territory. There they had settled in the fertile valleys of the Blue, Washita, and Boggy Rivers. But they had grown fearful because of the continual raids of Plains Indians; the Kickapoos, Delawares, Osages, and Pawnees, whom they had replaced; and irate Texas settlers and roving outlaws.

As soon as the fort was constructed, traders began operating in the area, and before long steamers were running from the Fort Towson landing up the Red and Washita Rivers to within a mile of Fort Washita. The tempo of life at the post accelerated during the Mexican War (1846–48), during which it served as a staging area and communications link. Another stimulus came in 1849, when Capt. Randolph B. Marcy, from his base at Fort Smith, Ark., pioneered the Fort Smith-El Paso Route. Replacing in importance the Fort Smith-Santa Fe segment of the Southern Overland Trail, it came to be crowded by gold seekers on their way to California. Fort Washita was a way station and outfitting point for emigrants, stage operators, and freighters. Further enhancing its eminence as a transportation center was its location in southeastern Indian Territory at the crossroads to Texas and the Plains and not far from the Texas Road, which connected the Missouri River Valley and Texas.

By 1858 a network of forts farther west had been activated and the frontier had bypassed the fort, in a dilapidated condition and manned by a skeleton force. But in December that year increasing North-South tensions caused its regarrisoning. In the spring of 1861 the Army considered concentrating forces there to repel a threatened invasion of the area from Texas, but the pro-Southern sympathies of the Choctaws and Chickasaws and the fort's isolation from other posts and supply centers made the plan untenable. In April 1861 Federal troops departed, never to return. Moving in the next day, the Confederates used the fort as a headquarters, supply depot, and refugee camp for displaced Indians. After the war, settlers apparently burned the buildings to deny them to bandits. In 1870 the military reservation reverted to the Chickasaw Nation. Eventually vandals made off with most of the buildings and the surrounding wall, leaving only desolate ruins, later used as cattle pens.

The Oklahoma Historical Society, aided by private contributions, purchased the 115-acre site in 1962 and appointed the Fort Washita Commission to maintain it. The commission has stabilized and partially restored the ruins, erected markers to identify sites, and removed excess timber to restore the historical prairie environment. Extant are the remains of 48 shell limestone buildings, which replaced the original log and frame structures. They date back as far as the 1850's, when the stone wall was erected around the post. Included are the officers' quarters and adjoining utility structures, the west and south barracks, the commissary warehouse, and the quartermaster stables. The restored eastern end of the south barracks serves as a visitor center. Gravel pathways lead to the post cemetery, the well, an old log cabin reputedly the post-Civil War home of the Confederate Gen. Douglas H. Cooper, the Confederate cemetery, a spring, and the ruins of the ghost town of Hatsboro.

Park Hill Mission and Cherokee Female Seminary, Oklahoma ⊗

Location: Cherokee County, near the junction of U.S. 62 and Okla. 82, about 3 miles south of Tahlequah.

Park Hill Mission, the "Athens of Indian Territory" until destroyed during the Civil War, was founded along the Illinois River by the Presbyterian missionary Rev. Samuel A. Worcester in 1836, the year after he had begun work among the Cherokees at Dwight and Union Missions, Okla. Park Hill became the religious, educational, and cultural center of the Cherokee Nation, whose capital of Tahlequah was created in 1839 about 4 miles to the north. Worcester built homes for missionaries and teachers, a boarding hall, and a gristmill. Beginning in 1837, utilizing the printing press he brought from Union Mission, he set up the Park Hill Press. It printed in English and the Cherokee language, employing Sequoyah's alphabet, parts of the Bible, the *Cherokee Almanac*, textbooks, and various tracts and works in the Creek and Choctaw languages.

In 1846 the Cherokee National Council authorized the founding of two high school seminaries, one for each sex. They opened in 1851, the Male Seminary just southwest of Tahlequah and the Female Seminary adjacent to Park Hill. They were housed in three-story Classical brick structures with impressive columned porticoes. The Cherokee Nation recruited many of the teachers from leading eastern colleges. The schools, whose operations suffered only a brief hiatus in the Civil War years, attained an academic excellence unparalleled among western educational institutions. In 1887 fire destroyed the Female Seminary; the following year workmen rebuilt it on the site of the future Northeastern State College, in northwestern Tahlequah, where it serves today as the Administration Building. When fire decimated the Male Seminary, too, in 1910, it was merged with the Female Seminary to create Northeastern State College.

Nothing remains of Park Hill Mission except for several old cemeteries, in one of which Reverend Worcester and his wife are buried. The nearby Murrell Mansion, a handsome two-story frame structure built in the mid-1840's that was closely associated with the mission's social life, has been restored to its original appearance and is owned by the State. Of the Female Seminary, only vine-covered columns and overgrown wall and foundation remains are extant. Nothing survives from the Male Seminary. At the entrance to Northeastern State College are two memorial columns constructed of bricks from the original seminaries.

Peace-on-the-Plains Site and Soldier Spring Battlefield, Oklahoma ⊗

Location: Kiowa County. The first site is about 5 miles southeast of the junction of U.S. 283 and Okla. 44; the second is 2 miles to the east of the first. They are accessible only by foot from Quartz Mountain State Park. Make local inquiry.

At the Peace-on-the-Plains Site, the location of the Wichita Indian villages on the north fork of the Red River, occurred the first important peace conference between U.S. officers and representatives of the southern Plains Indians. Seeking to insure unmolested travel on the Santa Fe Trail and security for the Five Civilized Tribes, with whom other tribes had been warring, the Dragoon Expedition (1834) had moved west from Fort Gibson, Okla., under Col. Henry Leavenworth. When he died of fever, Col. Henry Dodge succeeded him. Dodge held conferences at the Peace-on-the-Plains Site with chiefs of the Wichitas, Comanches, and allied bands. As a result, the next year the southern Plains tribes concluded their first treaties with the U.S. Government.

At Soldier Spring Battlefield on Christmas Day 1868, about a month after the Custer victory in the Battle of the Washita, Okla., some 40 miles to the north, Maj. Andrew W. Evans' 3d Cavalry, operating out of Fort Bascom, N. Mex., in General Sheridan's 1868–69 campaign, smashed a Comanche village.

The Peace-on-the-Plains Site, privately owned farmland, is at the mouth of Devil's Canyon where it joins the north fork of the Red River. A state historical marker is located at the junction of U.S. 283 and Okla. 44, about 5 miles to the northwest. The site is accessible only by way of the town of Lugert and Quartz Mountain State Park, which overlooks the canyon. A hike is necessary to reach its mouth. Two miles to the east, below the mouth of the canyon on the north fork of the Red River, is Soldier Spring Battlefield, also on a farm.

Rush Springs Battlefield, Oklahoma ⊗

Location: Grady County, just east of U.S. 81, about 5 miles southeast of the town of Rush Springs.

At dawn on October 1, 1858, the 2d Cavalry and Indian allies of Capt. Earl Van Dorn's Wichita Expedition from Fort Belknap, Tex., destroyed Buffalo Hump's camp of Comanches at this site and killed 83 people. Five soldiers died and Van Dorn received severe wounds. The expedition had marched 55 miles eastward from its advance base, Camp Radziminski, Okla., after a patrol had discovered the Indian camp. The battle was particularly tragic because Buffalo Hump had come north from Texas to discuss peace with the military authorities at Fort Arbuckle, Okla., and was temporarily camped at Rush Springs. The fort commander, however, had neglected to inform Van Dorn of the chief's peaceful intentions.

The battle site, partly in pasture and partly in cultivation, is on a private farm.

Sequoyah's Cabin, Oklahoma ⌂

Location: Sequoyah County, on Okla. 101, about 10 miles northeast of Sallisaw.

This cabin commemorates the accomplishments of Sequoyah, the famous Cherokee teacher and scholar whose invention of the

Cherokee syllabary gave that tribe and, by example, all the Five Civilized Tribes, the civilizing gift of literacy. Before the syllabary, the Cherokees had viewed the white man's written records as witchcraft; after the syllabary, they were able to codify their laws, adopt a written constitution, better govern and educate themselves, and express their viewpoints in print. Once they became literate in their own language, they could more easily grasp English. Shortly after they adopted Sequoyah's syllabary, the other Five Civilized Tribes began to formulate their own and before long all of them could read and write. The syllabaries provided Christian missionaries a means of written communication with the Indians through books, pamphlets, and other religious and educational materials and was a catalyst that hastened the acculturation of all five tribes. Beyond its direct benefits, the syllabary made possible the preservation of a mass of Cherokee lore in print. Of special interest to ethnologists are the writings of the Cherokee shamans, which provide an unparalleled body of information on an aboriginal religion that was unobtainable from any other U.S. tribe.

Little accurate information is available concerning the life of Sequoyah, sometimes known as George Gist (or Guess or other variants). Born in the 1760's or 1770's, probably in Tennessee, he was the son of a Cherokee woman and a white or halfbreed trader. Reared by his mother in the traditional tribal manner and becoming a silversmith or blacksmith, he never learned English, but around 1809 became interested in writing and printing, which he recognized as a powerful civilizing force. He spent years experimenting with symbols to decipher the Cherokee language. Finally, in 1821 he completed a syllabary, consisting of 84 characters, each of which represented a syllable. Because it was a phonetic rendition of the language, the syllabary could be learned in a short period of time. Within a few months after the Eastern Cherokees endorsed the syllabary, thousands of Indians had mastered it and were learning to read and write. In 1822 Sequoyah traveled to Arkansas to introduce the syllabary to the Western Cherokees. The following year he settled in Arkansas, and in 1828–29 moved with the Western Cherokees to Indian Territory, where he lived for most of the rest of his life. He died in 1843 or 1844, probably in Mexico, while searching for a band of Chero-

278

Sequoyah, creator of the Cherokee syllabary. Lithograph by an unknown artist, probably from a painting by Charles Bird King.

kees who, according to tribal lore, had migrated to the West in 1721.

As early as 1824 the Eastern Cherokees printed portions of the Bible. Four years later, at their capital in New Echota, Ga., they began publishing the first Indian newspaper, the *Cherokee Phoenix,* a weekly in Cherokee and English. This technique made news and literature available to the older generation, most of whom were fluent only in the native tongue, as well as to youths, many of whom had been schooled in English. In 1837 at Park

279

Sequoyah's Cabin.

Hill Mission, in Indian Territory, the Rev. Samuel A. Worcester
began printing in the Cherokee, Creek, Choctaw, and English languages. Other mission presses printed in the languages of the
other Five Civilized Tribes, using their syllabaries.

Sequoyah's contribution to the Cherokee Nation has been recognized in many ways. During his lifetime the U.S. Government
honored him with a monetary award, and the Cherokees granted
him a pension and medal. His name is immortalized in the giant
Sequoia trees of California and with the world's other great alphabet inventors on the bronze doors of the Library of Congress. Finally, his statue is in Statuary Hall in the U.S. Capitol.

Sequoyah's Cabin State Park preserves on its original site the
cabin constructed by Sequoyah in 1829. A typical one-room frontier home of hewn logs with stone chimney and fireplace, the
cabin has undergone minor restoration. It is enclosed in a stone
shelter, which features relics and documents associated with Se-

quoyah's life. Near the shelter stands a relocated log structure, dating from 1855, that once adjoined the cabin.

Skullyville, Fort Coffee, and New Hope Seminary, Oklahoma ⊗

Location: Le Flore County. The site of Fort Coffee is on an unimproved road, about 5 miles northeast of Spiro. The sites of New Hope Seminary and Skullyville are on U.S. 271, about 3 miles east of Spiro.

The village of Skullyville, though not officially so named until 1860, originated in 1832 as the agency for the Choctaws, being removed from the East to Indian Territory. Some of them settled around the agency, where they received annuities. In 1858 the village became a station on the Butterfield Overland Mail route. In the pre-Civil War years it was the headquarters of the Moshulatubbe District of the Choctaw Nation. The Federal troops who occupied it in 1863 left it in ruins when they departed at war's end.

Short-lived Fort Coffee (1834–38), a crude log post atop a high bluff at the Skullyville boat landing along the south bank of the Arkansas River about 3 miles north of the village, kept peace on the Choctaw lands and patrolled river traffic to prevent illegal trading. From 1843 until the outbreak of the Civil War, Fort Coffee Academy, a school for Choctaw boys financed by the Choctaw Nation and administered by the Methodist Episcopal Church, occupied the fort buildings. Confederate troops moved into them in the Civil War and stayed until 1863, when Federal troops captured and burned them.

New Hope Seminary, a boarding school founded at Skullyville in 1844 and administered by the same church, became the leading educational institution for Choctaw girls. It, too, closed during the Civil War, but was rebuilt and reopened in 1870 and continued to operate until fire destroyed it in 1897.

Skullyville is almost completely deserted today. Only foundation ruins of the agency building and those of New Hope Seminary remain. The town cemetery contains the graves of many prominent Choctaws. At the site of Fort Coffee stands a barn constructed from its logs. Building outlines are also visible.

281

Union Mission, Oklahoma ⊗

Location: Mayes County, on an unimproved road, about 5 miles southeast of Chouteau. Make local inquiry.

Established in 1820 by the Presbyterian Epaphras Chapman, in cooperation with the United Foreign Missionary Society, this mission opened a school for the Osage Indians the following year and served them primarily until 1833. They were then relocated to the west to make room for incoming Cherokees, awarded the land in the Cherokee-Osage treaty of 1828. In 1835 another Presbyterian missionary, Rev. Samuel A. Worcester, founder the next year of Park Hill Mission, Okla., came from Dwight Mission, about 50 miles to the southeast, and temporarily reopened Union Mission to accommodate the Cherokees. Utilizing equipment he had brought with him from Georgia, he set up the first printing press in Oklahoma. It printed textbooks and religious tracts in the Creek language, including the first book printed in Oklahoma, *The Child's Book* (1835).

The site is indicated by a stone marker. Only the cemetery and a few foundation stones remain.

Washita Battlefield, Oklahoma ⚠

Location: Roger Mills County, embracing a 6-square-mile area extending west and northwest from Cheyenne.

The battle fought at this site on November 27, 1868, was the major engagement in General Sheridan's winter campaign of 1868–69 against the southern Plains tribes. Involving a lamentable loss of Indian life, it also incited controversy between humanitarians and frontiersmen.

On November 18 Sheridan's main column, from Fort Dodge, Kans., founded Camp Supply, Okla., near the junction of Wolf Creek and the North Canadian River. On his arrival there, General Sheridan replaced Lt. Col. Alfred Sully, the commander of the column, with Lt. Col. George A. Custer. On November 23, eager for action, Custer's 7th Cavalry and a few Osage scouts set out southward despite a raging blizzard. On the morning of the 26th in the area of the South Canadian River scouts discovered a fresh Indian trail. Pursuing it all day, during the night the column came upon an Indian camp along the Washita River. Custer, viewing the outlines of the village from a crest of a ridge, could not determine its size. He decided nevertheless to make a surprise attack at dawn, and divided his 800-man command into four groups. Under the cover of darkness, they moved into position around the camp.

At daylight, to the sound of their band playing the regimental song, the troops swooped down on the sleeping village—occupied by the peacefully inclined Black Kettle, who had witnessed a similar scene at Sand Creek, Colo., 4 years earlier. His startled Cheyennes, not all of whom were innocent of depredations, poured forth from their lodges only to meet the fire of cavalry carbines. When the firing ceased, Black Kettle and more than 100 of his people were dead and many more were wounded. The rest fled, except for 53 women and children whom the troops captured. They also burned the village and destroyed the pony herd.

As the day wore on, large numbers of Cheyennes, Arapahos, Kiowas, Kiowa-Apaches, and Comanches began to assemble on the adjacent hills. Custer learned that Indian villages lined the Washita for 10 miles. When night fell, though Maj. Joel H. Elliott and a 16-man detachment were unaccounted for, Custer made a feint and hastily withdrew with his captives to Camp Supply. It was learned later that the Elliott detachment had been annihilated. Other Army casualties were comparatively light, four dead and 14 wounded.

The Battle of the Washita, coupled with another Army victory on Christmas Day by the Fort Bascom, N. Mex., column at Soldier Spring, Okla., demoralized the Indians. Many fled to the Staked Plains or other less remote areas, but Sheridan's troops pursued them vigorously throughout the winter. By the spring of 1869 the bulk of them had been rounded up and placed on reservations.

The battlefield lies in the verdant Washita River Valley, sheltered by surrounding hills. Aside from some agricultural activity in the bottom land, the site retains a high degree of integrity. Except for a few farmhouses on its edge, the town of Cheyenne does not intrude. A little-used and inconspicuous railroad track runs along the periphery of the battlefield south of the river. A granite monument commemorating the site, erected by the State of Oklahoma, overlooks the valley.

Wheelock Academy, Oklahoma ⚠

Location: McCurtain County, on a secondary road, about 1½ miles east of Millerton.

Wheelock Academy was the archetype for the tribal school system of the Five Civilized Tribes. As the first national academy founded under the Choctaw Nation's Education Act of 1842, it set a precedent for some 35 academies and seminaries financed and controlled by the five tribes. Unique in U.S. history, these schools were not mission or Government schools, though missionaries administered many of them under contract. They represented the commitment of the five tribes to self-education and were basic tools of their acculturation.

At a time when the typical mission or Government Indian school concentrated on rudimentary literacy and simple vocational skills, the more liberally endowed tribal schools attained a high degree of academic excellence. They attracted teachers from leading eastern colleges and offered secondary and classical courses as well as vocational training. Tribal Councils provided financial assistance to the more promising graduates who wished to enter eastern colleges. Much of the success of the Five Civilized Tribes in becoming leading citizens of Oklahoma may be traced to their educational achievements through their tribal school systems.

The antecedent of Wheelock Academy was a mission school established in 1832 by Rev. Alfred Wright, representing the American Board of Commissioners for Foreign Missions, among the Choctaw Indians during their removal to Indian Territory from the Southeastern United States in 1831–34. As missionary to the Choctaws from 1820 until 1853, he helped them formulate an alphabet and published 60 books in their language. In 1842 the tribe passed an Education Act that provided for a system of academies and seminaries financed and maintained by the tribe but administered by missionaries under contract.

The tribe chose the Wheelock school because it was already flourishing; it had been so successful that in 1839 Wright had built a two-story frame dormitory to accommodate the influx of boarding students. The tribe hired Wright to run the school and recruit teachers. He held the position until his death in 1853. Wheelock Academy was one of several boarding schools for girls established by the Choctaws, who set up other boarding institutions for boys. The school became a model of Indian education, its curriculum providing a judicious blend of cultural enlightenment and practical skills. The other Civilized Tribes soon adopted similar programs. All of them based theirs on missionary cooperation except the Cherokees, who decided upon direct administration.

During the Civil War, which disrupted Indian Territory, Wheelock Academy suffered a temporary eclipse. Reinstituted after the war, it was all but destroyed by fire in 1869. For years instruction took place in a gutted stone church built by the Choctaws in 1845–46, and in the few fire-damaged buildings. In 1880–84, aided by the Southern Presbyterian Church, the Choctaws rebuilt the academy. During the ensuing years, despite changes in administration, they retained control until 1932, the centennial anniversary of the school's founding. That year it became a U.S. Indian school. In 1955, after serving the Choctaw people for 123 years, it closed.

The academy is owned and administered by the Choctaw Nation. The main historic building, the Old Seminary, a two-story frame structure built in the early 1880's, is basically sound but is in poor condition. Scores of other structures are of historical interest. A custodian in the employ of the Bureau of Indian Affairs maintains the grounds. About 200 yards from the academy are the original stone church and a cemetery, both owned by the Southern Presbyterian Church and still in use. The cemetery contains the graves of several students and teachers, including Reverend Wright.

Fort Dalles, Oregon ⊗

Location: Wasco County, 15th and Garrison Streets and 14th and Trevitt Streets, The Dalles.

Fort Dalles (1850–67) was strategically located at the Dalles of the Columbia. Troops from Columbia Barracks (Fort Vancouver) founded it, utilizing a temporary stockade that had been erected near abandoned mission buildings just before the beginning of the Cayuse War (1848). By 1852 a town had grown up around the fort. Headquarters for central and eastern Oregon, the fort protected the Oregon Trail and served as a key outpost and supply base during the Indian troubles of the 1850's, especially the Yakima War (1855–56), in eastern Washington. Resenting the invasion of settlers and miners into the region that followed the cession of a large part of their lands to the U.S. Government in 1855, the Yakimas and allied tribes, spurred by the Yakima chieftain Kamiakin, disavowed the treaties and retaliated. Col. George Wright's campaign with a force of infantry Regulars brought the war to an end. Some troops stayed at Fort Dalles in the Civil War era, but they marched out in August 1866. Others returned temporarily in December and remained until the next July, during which time Crook's troops used the post for his Snake campaign (1866–68).

The only surviving building, at the southwest corner of 15th and Garrison Streets, is the frame surgeon's quarters (1857), an excellent example of Gothic Revival architecture. Owned by the Oregon Historical Society, it is operated as a museum by the Wasco County-Dalles City Museum Commission. The parade ground is located on the site of a private school at 14th and Trevitt Streets.

Surgeon's quarters, Fort Dalles.

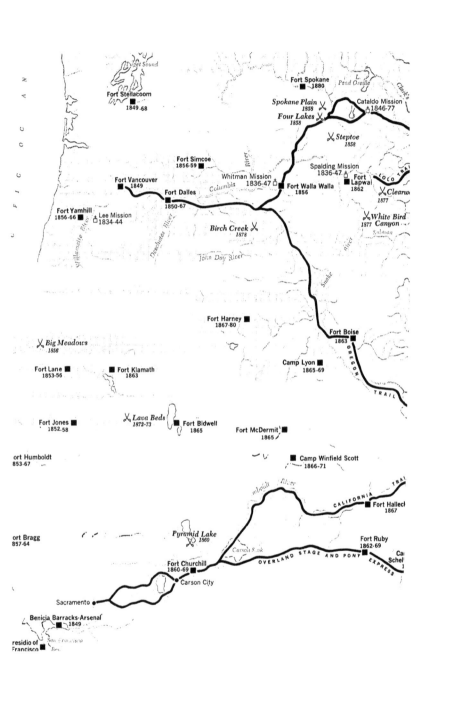

Fort Stellacoom
1849-68

Fort Spokane
1880

Spokane Plain ✗
1858
Four Lakes ✗
1858

Cataldo Mission
⚓ 1846-77

✗ Steptoe
1858

Fort Simcoe
1856-59 ■

Whitman Mission
1836-47 ⚓

Spalding Mission
1836-47 ⚓ Fort
Lapwai
1862

Fort Vancouver
■ 1849

Fort Dalles
1850-67

Fort Walla Walla
1856

✗ Clearw
1877

Fort Yamhill
1856-66 ■

Lee Mission
⚓ 1834-44

✗ White Bird
1877 Canyon
Salmon

Birch Creek ✗
1878

John Day River

Fort Harney
1867-80 ■

Big Meadows
1856

Fort Boise
1863

Fort Lane ■
1853-56

Fort Klamath
1863

Camp Lyon ■
1865-69

Fort Jones ■
1852-58

Lava Beds ✗
1872-73

Fort Bidwell ■
1865

Fort McDermit ■
1865

ort Humboldt
853-67

Camp Winfield Scott
■ 1866-71

Fort Hallecl
1867

ort Bragg
857-64

Pyramid Lake
✗ 1860

Fort Churchill
1860-69

Carson City

Fort Ruby
1862-69

Ca
Schell

Sacramento ●

Benicia Barracks-Arsenal
■ 1849

residio of
Francisco ■

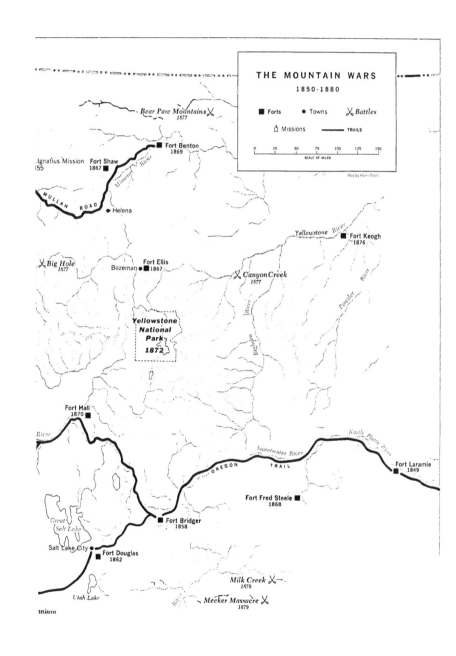

THE MOUNTAIN WARS
1850-1880

■ Forts   ● Towns   ✕ Battles
⌂ Missions   ▬▬▬ TRAILS

0   25   50   75   100   125   150
SCALE OF MILES

Map by Harry Scott

Bear Paw Mountains ✕
1877

Fort Benton
1869

.Ignatius Mission   Fort Shaw
:55   1867 ■

Missouri River

MULLAN   ROAD

● Helena

Yellowstone River   ■ Fort Keogh
1876

✕ Big Hole   Fort Ellis
1877   Bozeman ● ■ 1867

✕ Canyon Creek
1877

Powder River

Bighorn River

Yellowstone
National
Park
1872

Fort Hall
1870 ■

River

North Platte River

Sweetwater River

OREGON   TRAIL   ■ Fort Laramie
1849

Great
Salt Lake

Fort Bridger
1858 ■

Fort Fred Steele ■
1868

Salt Lake City ●   ■ Fort Douglas
1862

Utah Lake

Milk Creek ✕
1879

Meeker Massacre ✕
1879

nison

Fort Harney, Oregon ⊗

Location: Harney County, on an unimproved road, about 16 miles northeast of Burns.

Founded in 1867 in southeastern Oregon by General Crook as a temporary base during his 1866–68 Snake campaign and the scene of the treaty-signing ending it, this fort later became a permanent fortification to protect settlers from Indians. It provided minor support during the Modoc War (1872–73) and was a base and refuge for settlers during the Bannock War (1878), which spilled over from Idaho into Oregon. More than 500 Indians were imprisoned at the fort prior to being moved to a reservation in January 1879. The last troops left the next year.

Nothing remains of the log and frame fort except the cemetery, on privately owned property. It now contains only two civilian graves. The ghost town of Harney City, 2 miles to the south, also in private ownership, had boomed after the fort was inactivated.

Fort Hoskins, Oregon ⊗

Location: Benton County, on an unimproved road, adjacent to Hoskins.

This small post (1856–65) was established in west-central Oregon at the eastern entrance to the Siletz Indian Reservation, where the U.S. Government concentrated the Rogue River Indians at the end of the second Rogue River War (1855–56). With nearby Fort Yamhill, it guarded the reservation and protected settlers from further depredations. To provide security for the Indian agency, the fort commander built and garrisoned a blockhouse adjacent to it. A road, built under the supervision of Lt. Philip H. Sheridan, connected the fort and blockhouse. During the Civil War, California Volunteers replaced Regular troops.

The fort site, on privately owned property, is on a slight plateau on the edge of Hoskins. Of the original structures, the only ones remaining are the blacksmith shop and the extensively altered hospital.

287

Fort Klamath, Oregon ⊗

Location: Klamath County, on Oreg. 62, at the edge of the town of Fort Klamath.

Protection of settlers in the Klamath Basin from Modoc, Klamath, and Shasta Indians was the reason for founding this fort (1863–89). Some of these Indians allied with the Northern Paiutes (Snakes), against whom Crook campaigned in 1866–68. The fort played a major role in the Modoc War (1872–73). The troops that sparked the war by trying to force the Modoc leader Captain Jack and his band back onto the Klamath Indian Reservation, Oreg., set out from Fort Klamath. During the ensuing engagements, it was the principal supply and replacement depot and medical receiving station. After his surrender in June 1873, Captain Jack and his followers were imprisoned in a specially constructed stockade at the fort, where he was tried and hanged in October along with three of his lieutenants.

All traces of the fort have disappeared. The site, now part of a ranch, is marked by a stone monument.

Fort Lane, Oregon ⊗

Location: Jackson County, on Gold Ray Dam Road, about 9 miles northwest of Medford.

In the shadow of majestic Lower Table Rock on the south bank of the Rogue River, this small fort was founded at the conclusion of the first Rogue River War (1853) and figured prominently in the second (1855–56). Near Lower Table Rock, in August 1853, troops won the final victory of the first war; a few weeks later, near the rock, the peace treaty was signed. The second war, like the first, was predominantly a Volunteer effort against elements of the Rogue River, Shasta, Umpqua, and other tribes. Resenting the intrusion of settlers and miners, they had strayed from the Table Rock (Rogue River) Reservation, to which they had been assigned at the end of the first war, and had aroused the wrath of settlers. During the ensuing hostilities, the handful of dragoons at Fort Lane were too few to offer much help to the Volunteers and Regulars under Maj. Robert C. Buchanan that General Wool fielded in March 1856. Many nonparticipating Indians took refuge at Fort Lane. At war's end, the captives and their kinsmen were gathered there and most of them shipped to the Siletz Indian Reservation, Oreg. The fort's short history came to an end.

No remains of the log and mud post have survived. The site, on privately owned pastureland, is indicated by a stone marker, about 200 yards away.

The Dalles (Wascopam) Mission, Oregon ⊗

Location: Wasco County, in the vicinity of 12th and Court Streets, The Dalles.

This mission, founded among the Wascopam Indians in 1838 by the Reverends Daniel Lee and H. K. W. Perkins, was the second Methodist and the fourth Protestant mission in Oregon country. Its predecessor was the Willamette (Lee) Mission, founded by Jason and Daniel Lee 4 years earlier. The new site was located along the Oregon Trail on the south bank of the Columbia River at the western end of the Dalles, a series of falls and rapids interrupting river navigation. This spot was an old rendezvous for traders and Indians. Until 1846 it was a major stopping place at which wagon trains transferred to rafts to continue downriver. After the completion of the Barlow Road that year, most of the emigrants shifted to it and the Dalles declined in importance.

*The Dalles (Wascopam) Mission in 1849, some
2 years after its abandonment. Painting by
William H. Tappan.*

The missionaries at first preached from what came to be known as Pulpit Rock. The rock was near a spring, rich soil, and abundant timber. Adjacent to the rock the missionaries constructed several log buildings, including a dwelling house; three more structures, one used as a school; and outbuildings. Three years later a Catholic mission opened close by. As in the Willamette Valley, the Methodist efforts at the Dalles failed because of the disinterest of the local Indians in Christianity. In 1847 the Methodist Mission Society sold The Dalles Mission, its last active post in the Oregon country, to the American Board of Commissioners for Foreign Missions. Dr. Marcus Whitman, representing the board, placed his nephew, Perrin B. Whitman, in charge of The Dalles Mission, but he departed in December, the month after the Waiilatpu Massacre. That same month Volunteer troops occupied the site. During the Cayuse War (1848), they constructed a stockade. In 1850 the Army utilized it to found Fort Dalles. By that time the Catholic mission had also been vacated. The settlement of The Dalles soon grew up around the fort.

Although nothing remains of The Dalles Mission, Pulpit Rock, at 12th and Court Streets, is a well-known natural feature. A granite marker, in a triangular plot at 6th and Trevitt Streets, commemorates the mission.

Willamette (Lee) Mission, Oregon ⊗
Location: Marion County, Salem.

In October 1834 the Methodist ministers Jason Lee and his nephew Daniel Lee founded this mission, the first established by any denomination in the Oregon country. It was originally located on the east bank of the Willamette River near the agricultural settlement of French Prairie, founded by ex-Hudson's Bay Co. employees. The Lees made little progress in educating and converting the local Indians, who were plagued with sickness and disease. Undaunted and envisioning an extensive missionary-colonization program in Oregon, in 1838 Jason sent Daniel and another missionary to found The Dalles branch mission and returned to the East to collect funds and recruit missionaries and settlers.

In 1840 Jason moved the Willamette Mission to a more favor-

Willamette (Lee) Mission, at its first location (1834–40), in 1841. Lithograph by one of the artists on the Charles Wilkes Expedition (1838–42).

able location 10 miles to the south, at the site of Salem, where waterpower was available. Shortly thereafter, 50 recruits arrived. Most of them stayed in the vicinity of the mission, but concentrated on farming rather than trying to further the mission's cause. A few left, however, to establish branches at Willamette Falls, Clatsop Plains, and Fort Nisqually. By 1842 the party had completed a gristmill, sawmill, home for Jason Lee, Indian school, and parsonage to house teachers. Despite this progress, word of Lee's failure among the Indians reached the Methodist

Jason Lee House, now being restored.

Mission Society, which in 1843 suspended him. The next spring he returned East. That same year the society sold its property at both sites to settlers. A prosperous agricultural settlement called Chemeketa, later Salem, soon grew up at the second site.

The site of the first Willamette Mission, of which nothing remains, is today a Marion County park, located a half mile south of the Wheatland Ferry. A bronze plaque mounted on a large boulder marks the general location of the mission. Of the second mission, two 2½-story frame structures, built in 1841–42, are extant in Salem. The mission parsonage, not at its original location, is temporarily located on 13th Street. Jason Lee's home, 960 Broadway, is privately owned and has been extensively altered.

Carlisle Indian School, Pennsylvania ⚠

Location: Cumberland County, on U.S. 11, at Carlisle Barracks, northeastern edge of Carlisle.

As the first of the off-reservation boarding schools and the model for scores of others, the Carlisle Indian School commemorates the efforts of the 19th-century reformers who attempted to improve conditions among the Indians. In its almost four decades of existence, from 1879 until 1918, the Government-operated institution

Group of Sioux on arrival at Carlisle Indian School.

292

Richard H. Pratt, founder
of Carlisle Indian School.

provided thousands of students with an elementary and practical education.

Richard H. Pratt, Civil War officer and later cavalry officer in Indian Territory (Oklahoma) and Texas, conceived the idea of the school. Between 1875 and 1878 he had been in charge of a group of Indian prisoners at Fort Marion, Fla., and had evolved an educational program for the younger ones. In 1878, when the prisoners gained their freedom, Pratt arranged for some of the young men and a group of western Indians to attend the black school at Hampton, Va. Stimulated by the success of that program, Pratt persuaded the Army to turn over the cavalry post at Carlisle Barracks, inactivated that same year, to the Indian Bureau for a school. The Army authorized Pratt to serve there. Beginning with 136 boys and girls the first year, the school grew rapidly. Pratt, who rose in rank from lieutenant to colonel while superintendent, retired from the Army as a colonel in 1903 and the following year was awarded a brigadier general's star.

Although a popular misconception exists that the school had the status of a university—thanks to its athletic achievements in collegiate competition—it actually offered only a limited elemen-

Superintendent's quarters, Carlisle Indian School,
now occupied by Army War College commandant.

tary education and instruction in mechanical arts, agriculture, and home economics. The length of the term was first 3 and later 5 years. As he had done at Fort Marion, Pratt ran the school on a semimilitary basis. Male students drilled and wore surplus Civil War uniforms. A unique feature of the instruction was the "outing" system, under which selected boys and girls lived with nearby white families and gained practical experience in farming and domestic arts. This program helped each race know the other better. Students from tribes that were traditionally enemies lived and worked together amicably.

The athletic program, notably "Pop" Warner's excellent football teams, won the school much fame. Outstanding among a number of eminent Carlisle athletes was Jim Thorpe, the Sauk-Fox Indian who was an All-American football player and excelled in the decathlon and pentathlon during the 1912 Olympics. Sportswriters voted him the outstanding U.S. athlete of the first half of the 20th century.

A number of buildings of the Indian school era are grouped in close proximity near the western limits of the present military reservation. One is the commandant's quarters, once occupied by

Pratt and today the home of the commandant of the Army War College, which now has jurisdiction over Carlisle Barracks. Thorpe Hall was the school gymnasium, a role it still fulfills for Army personnel. The Coren Apartments, built immediately after the destruction of Carlisle Barracks by fire in 1863, was a girls' dormitory and is currently an officers' quarters. Armstrong Hall, at present containing the post headquarters offices, served as the school laundry. Quarters No. 2, home of the deputy commandant of the war college, was erected in 1887 as the residence of the school's assistant superintendent. Washington Hall, another survivor of the school, is a guesthouse. On the eastern side of the post is located a small cemetery where Indian students are buried. Visitors may obtain permission from military policemen to visit the historic buildings and cemetery.

Fort Meade, South Dakota ⊗

> *Location: Meade County, on S. Dak. 34, about 2 miles east of Sturgis.*

Control of the Sioux and protection of the Black Hills mining district were the responsibilities of this fort (1878–1944), founded about 14 miles northeast of Deadwood, S. Dak. It replaced a tem-

Officers' row, Fort Meade, in 1889.

295

porary camp known as Camp Sturgis, established 2 months earlier about 5 miles to the northeast. In 1890–91 Fort Meade was a key headquarters during the Sioux unrest that culminated in the Battle of Wounded Knee, in which the fort's troops participated.

Fort Meade has been a Veterans' Administration Hospital since 1944. Most of the original buildings have given way to modern ones, but the officers' quarters, dating from the late 1880's, are basically unchanged. Comanche, the horse that survived the Custer battle, was quartered at the stables from 1879 to 1887, when the 7th Cavalry made up the garrison. A military cemetery overlooks the site from an adjacent hill. All that remains of Camp Sturgis, on S. Dak. 79, are slight indentations along Spring Creek marking the site of huts dug under canvas tops. A highway marker identifies the site.

Fort Randall, South Dakota ⊗

Location: Gregory County, just off U.S. 18, on the west bank of the Missouri River, below the southwestern corner of the Fort Randall Dam, across from Pickstown.

This strategic Missouri River fort (1856–92), almost astride the South Dakota-Nebraska boundary and not far west of Iowa and Minnesota, played an outstanding role in many of the events on the northern Plains in the last half of the 19th century. Its activities ran a broad gamut: Indian control and protection of settlers, keeping the peace between warring tribes and factions occupying the various reservations in the area, and the supply of posts on and policing of the upper Missouri River. The fort hosted such prominent Indian fighters as Custer, Sheridan, Sully, Sherman, and Terry. It was also a base for Brig. Gen. Alfred Sully's expeditions in 1863–65 against the Sioux in the Dakotas following the 1862 uprising in Minnesota. And in the years 1881–83 Sitting Bull was imprisoned at the fort, to which he was transported by steamer from Fort Yates following his surrender at Fort Buford, N. Dak.

The wide-ranging activities of the garrison reflected the fort's diverse responsibilities and involved participation in such endeavors as: the reprisals against Chief Inkpaduta following the Spirit

*Sitting Bull, with two of his wives and some of his
children, while imprisoned at Fort Randall.*

Lake Massacre, Iowa (1857); the Mormon Expedition (1857–58),
to Utah; the Corps of Engineers expedition (1859), under Capt.
William F. Raynolds, that explored the Yellowstone River and its
tributaries; the Yellowstone Survey Expeditions of 1872 and 1873,
surveying the route of the Northern Pacific Railroad; the attempts to exclude miners from the Black Hills after Custer's reconnaissance in 1874; the warfare that subsequently broke out
with the Sioux and Cheyennes because of the illegal violation by

miners of the Great Sioux Reservation; and, with the remaining units of the 7th Cavalry, the disarming of the Hunkpapa Sioux at the Standing Rock Reservation, N. Dak.-S. Dak., in September 1876 after the Custer disaster.

Fort Randall, whose site is under the jurisdiction of the U.S. Army Corps of Engineers, is one of the few of the large number of prehistoric and historic sites in the area running upriver along the Missouri to Big Bend spared by the waters of the Fort Randall Reservoir. The only surviving remain above ground is the roofless and windowless cross-shaped chapel, Christ Church (1875), which also served as a library and lodge meeting hall. Its unstabilized and still-impressive cut-stone native masonry ruins, of interesting architectural design, have somehow survived vandalism and years of exposure to the elements. A few ancient and battered cottonwood trees grow along the parade ground, which is outlined by crumbling and brush-covered masonry foundations and cellar walls. The post cemetery, on a nearby hillside, today contains only a few civilian burials.

Fort Sisseton, South Dakota ⊗

Location: Marshall County, on an unimproved road, about 6 miles northwest of Eden.

Founded in 1864 by Wisconsin and Minnesota Volunteers during the Civil War not far west of the Minnesota boundary in the northeastern corner of South Dakota, this fort was known as Fort Wadsworth until 1876. The Army established it to assure settlers, fearful even though the campaigns of Sibley and Sully in 1863–64 had pacified most of the Sioux in the region. The local Sisseton and Wahpeton Sioux were friendly; and on the basis of an 1867 treaty agreement, in the 1870's they were placed on a reservation adjacent to the fort. Besides controlling the Indians, it protected emigrants traveling the wagon routes to the Idaho and Montana goldfields; aided railroad surveyors; and, a hub of civilization on the frontier and a policing agency before the establishment of civil courts, was a stabilizing influence on settlement. In 1889 the Army transferred the fort to the State.

The State has carried on the restoration and repair program in-

Modern appearance of Fort Sisseton. Clockwise, adjutant's office, commanding officer's quarters, doctor's quarters, and hospital.

augurated in 1932 by a local citizens' group to replace buildings that had been torn down or fallen into ruins during the previous four decades, when it had been leased to ranchers and sportsmen. In the years 1935–39, utilizing **Works** Progress Administration (WPA) labor, the National Park Service continued the project. As a result of all these efforts, Fort Sisseton State Park contains an extensive and architecturally interesting complex of 16 major stone and brick buildings, which over the years had replaced the original log structures. Now in varying stages of restoration and repair, they suffer from few modern intrusions.

Pine Ridge Agency, South Dakota ⊗
Location: Shannon County, town of Pine Ridge.

This agency was the focal point of the Sioux Ghost Dance rebellion in 1890 and the ensuing military operations. These culminated in the Battle of Wounded Knee, in which the Army crushed the Sioux. Following the Battle of the Little Bighorn, the Army launched a series of drives in Wyoming and Montana and in 1876–77 forced practically all the hostile Sioux onto the Great Sioux Reservation. In 1876 their more peaceful reservation breth-

Troops from Camp Cheyenne, S. Dak., mingling with Miniconjou Ghost Dancers in the autumn of 1890.

ren, in the Black Hills Treaty, had ceded to the United States the Powder River hunting grounds of Wyoming and Montana; the Black Hills; and the rest of the western part of the Great Sioux Reservation, which under the Fort Laramie Treaty (1868) had embraced roughly the entire western half of South Dakota. The Indians also agreed to relinquish all land outside the Great Sioux Reservation; included were their two agencies in Nebraska.

As a result, in 1877 the Indian Bureau relocated the Red Cloud and Spotted Tail Agencies from northwestern Nebraska to sites along the Missouri River in South Dakota, the Red Cloud Agency a few miles north of its junction with the White River and the Spotted Tail Agency just north of the Nebraska boundary. About 800 of the 13,000 Indians on the march escaped to Canada and the rest refused to travel as far as the new agencies. The Oglalas of the Red Cloud Agency chose to settle along White Clay Creek, S. Dak., and the Upper Brûlés of Spotted Tail Agency just to the east along the east fork of the White River. The next year, 1878, the Indian Bureau bowed to Indian intransigence and relocated the agencies westward to the area in which the tribes resided and renamed them, respectively, Pine Ridge and Rosebud. As part of the same overall consolidation of the Sioux in 1876–78, the Miniconjous were settled on the Cheyenne River Reservation, S. Dak.; and the Hunkpapa, Yankton, and Blackfeet Sioux at the Standing

*General Miles and staff viewing Indian encampment
near Pine Ridge Agency in January 1891.*

Rock Reservation, N. Dak.-S. Dak., adjoining the Cheyenne River Reservation on the north.

All the Sioux, nomadic tribes who found adjustment to an alien civilization in the harsh reservation system exceedingly difficult, began to dream of a miraculous return to their former way of life. They were thus receptive to the Ghost Dance religion of the Nevada Paiute Wovoka. In the winter of 1889–90, 11 Sioux delegates—eight from Pine Ridge; two from Rosebud, one of whom was Short Bull; and one, Kicking Bear, from the Cheyenne River Reservation—visited Wovoka in the Mason Valley of Nevada. They returned to their reservation in the spring with glowing reports of the new religion. But the Indian agents at Pine Ridge and Rosebud repressed their attempts to introduce it among their tribesmen, and those at the Standing Rock and Cheyenne River Reservations at the time evinced slight interest in Wovoka's doctrines.

By summer, conditions at the reservations had so worsened that they presented a fertile environment for the religion's spread. Indian grievances included a large reduction in the Great Sioux Reservation in 1889; hunger, resulting from a curtailment of Government rations caused by a cut in appropriations; a drought in the summer of 1890; the onslaught of measles and other diseases highly fatal among the children; and the corruption or ineffectiveness of some Indian agents, who had continual jurisdictional disputes with the Army.

Thus, in itself the Sioux adoption of the essentially pacifistic Ghost Dance religion would probably not have generated the conflagration that ensued. The problem was that it was in reality a symptom of profound unrest stemming from tangible complaints. In their bitterness, the Sioux added to it militance and hatred of the whites. The displays of unbridled emotions expressed in the wild dance, which climaxed in ecstatic illusionary trances, alarmed the Indian agents and settlers in the region. The Sioux responded to the repressive measures of the agents by arming themselves against possible intervention and launching a vigorous defense of the religion that turned into a virtual holy crusade. Religious fanaticism made peaceful control of the restless warriors difficult and a few clashes resulted. By September and October many Indians on the Cheyenne River, Standing Rock, Rosebud, and Pine Ridge Reservations were in a state of wild excitement and rebelliousness. The apprehensive Indian agents and settlers in the region began to request military aid.

At Pine Ridge, particularly, conditions were chaotic. There the lot of the Sioux had long been especially unhappy and relations with the Indian Bureau had been characterized by dissension and animosity. In the years 1879–86 Indian Agent Valentine T. McGillicuddy and the Oglala Chief Red Cloud had clashed regularly. The chief strenuously resisted the educational program in

Lt. John J. ("Black Jack") Pershing and troop of Oglala scouts at Pine Ridge Reservation in 1891. Pershing later won fame in World War I.

farming, attempts to diminish the paramount position of tribal chiefs, and the imposition of the scores of other social and religious changes that spelled doom to the old way of life. Relations were smoother during Hugh D. Gallagher's regime (1886–90), but resentment continued, and in 1890 the reservation became a center of the Ghost Dance religion. On October 9, at a time when the religious frenzy of the Oglalas and Brûlés was at a peak, a new and inexperienced agent, Daniel F. Royer, replaced Gallagher. Royer proved to be the catalyst. Frightened and completely unable to cope with the situation, 4 days after his arrival he dispatched a frantic plea for military protection.

On November 20 the first contingents of troops, from Omaha and Forts Robinson and Niobrara, Nebr., arrived at the Pine Ridge and Rosebud Reservations. By the end of the month thousands more from all the surrounding States had arrived on the scene—nearly half the Army's infantry and cavalry and some artillery, the largest concentration of troops anywhere in the United States between the Civil War and the Spanish-American War and one of the largest ever assembled in one place to confront Indians. At Pine Ridge, Maj. Gen. Nelson A. Miles, commanding the operation, converged his greatest force, which totaled about 3,000 and included the entire 7th Cavalry Regiment, under Col. James W. Forsyth.

At the appearance of the troops, Kicking Bear and Short Bull and 3,000 Ghost Dancers fled to the badlands about 50 miles north-

These infantrymen at Pine Ridge were part of the force that massed in the region prior to the Battle of Wounded Knee.

Part of the artillery detachment that took part in
the Battle of Wounded Knee at Pine Ridge in
January 1891, a month after the battle. The Hotchkiss
guns had rained deadly fire on the Indians.

west of the Pine Ridge Agency, at the northwest corner of the
Pine Ridge Reservation. Although this action was not hostile,
General Miles decided to remove from the reservations and incar-
cerate the most conspicuous agitators. Prominent among them was
Sitting Bull, Custer's nemesis, who allegedly was fomenting a rebellion at his camp on the Standing Rock Reservation. His death
while resisting arrest on December 15, and the flight of his followers southward contributed to the events that led, 2 weeks later, to
the Battle of Wounded Knee.

Pine Ridge is still the agency of the Oglalas. Although a few of
the buildings date from the turn of the century, most are of recent origin.

Rosebud Agency, South Dakota ⊗
Location: Todd County, town of Rosebud.

The successor of Spotted Tail Agency in controlling the Brûlé
Sioux, this agency originated at the same time and for the same
reasons as Pine Ridge, which adjoined it on the west. Although
conditions on the Rosebud Reservation were not much better

than at the other Sioux reservations, Rosebud experienced less strife than most of them and certainly less than Pine Ridge. The main reason was that the Brûlés had no strong leader; in 1881 another Indian had killed Chief Spotted Tail. But the competition among those who sought to succeed him sometimes resulted in near-anarchy. Many of the Brûlés became Ghost Dancers in 1890, but they participated chiefly at the Pine Ridge Reservation, the center of the religion and the scene of its subsequent military repression.

The Brûlé agency is still headquartered in the town of Rosebud, whose buildings are nearly all of 20th-century origin.

Slim Buttes Battlefield, South Dakota ⊗

Location: Harding County, on S. Dak. 20, about 2 miles west of Reva.

At this site north of the Black Hills the Sioux suffered one of their first setbacks in the wake of their defeat of Custer in June 1876. Brig. Gen. George Crook's force, after separating from Terry's command in August, was en route to the hills to obtain supplies. On September 8 Capt. Anson Mills, leading the advance guard, came upon a band of Sioux under American Horse camped at Rabbit Creek near Slim Buttes. Although greatly outnumbered, the troops charged, captured the village, and held out until the main body came to their aid. Crazy Horse and his braves, not far away, tried to help American Horse, but they arrived too late. American Horse and several of his men, trapped in a cave, surrendered when the chief received mortal wounds. Casualties were not great on either side. But the Army continued its pursuit of the survivors and other fugitives. In the autumn many of them, tired of the pursuit and facing the rigors of winter, slipped back to the agencies to surrender. The others were to endure months of insecurity as soldiers braved winter perils to pursue them.

The site is located on an unbroken prairie surrounded by pine-dotted hills. A monument and several markers stand on a small hill near the highway.

Wounded Knee Battlefield, South Dakota ⚠

Location: Shannon County, on a secondary road, about 16 miles northeast of the town of Pine Ridge.

The regrettable and tragic clash of arms at this site on December 29, 1890, the last significant engagement between Indians and soldiers on the North American Continent, ended nearly four centuries of warfare between westward-wending Americans and the indigenous peoples. Although the majority of the participants on both sides had not intended to use their arms—precipitated by individual indiscretion in a tense and confused situation rather than by organized premeditation—and although the haze of gunsmoke that hung over the battlefield has obscured some of the facts, the action more resembles a massacre than a battle. For 20th-century America, it serves as an example of national guilt for the mistreatment of the Indians.

The arrival of troops on the Pine Ridge Reservation, S. Dak., to quiet the Ghost Dance disorders of 1890 provided the climate for the battle. After Indian police killed Chief Sitting Bull while trying to arrest him on December 15 on the Standing Rock Reservation, his Hunkpapas grew agitated and troop reinforcements arrived. When 200 of the Indians fled southward to the Cheyenne River, military officials feared a Hunkpapa-Miniconjou coalition. Most of the Standing Rock fugitives allied for a time with the Miniconjou Chief Hump and his 400 followers before joining them in surrendering at Fort Bennett, S. Dak.

About 38 of the Hunkpapas joined a more militant group of 350 or so Miniconjou Ghost Dancers led by Big Foot. After a few days of defiance, Big Foot, ill with pneumonia, informed military authorities he would capitulate. When he failed to do so at the appointed time and place, General Miles ordered his arrest. On December 28 a 7th Cavalry detachment under Maj. Samuel M. Whitside intercepted him and his band southwest of the badlands at Porcupine Creek and escorted them about 5 miles westward to Wounded Knee Creek, the place where Big Foot-said he would surrender peacefully. Early that night, Col. James W. Forsyth arrived to supervise the operation and the movement of the captives by train to Omaha via Pine Ridge Agency. His force, totaling more than 500 men, included the entire 7th Cavalry Regiment, a company of Oglala scouts, and an artillery detachment.

The disarming occurred the next day. It was not a wise decision, for the Indians had shown no inclination to fight and regarded their guns as cherished possessions and means of livelihood. Between the tepees and the soldiers' tents·was the council ring. On a nearby low hill a Hotchkiss battery had its guns trained directly on the Indian camp. The troops, in two cordons, surrounded the council ring.

The warriors did not comply readily with the request to yield their weapons, so a detachment of troops went through the tepees and uncovered about 40 rifles. Tension mounted, for the soldiers had upset the tepees and disturbed women and children; and the officers feared the Indians were still concealing firearms. Meanwhile, the militant medicine man Yellow Bird had circulated

Modern view of Wounded Knee Battlefield, looking northward. Before artillery drove them out of the ravine in the foreground, the Indians inflicted heavy casualties on the troops. The Hotchkiss guns, located near the present Sacred Heart Church, raked the Indian village, in the coulee near the modern windmill.

among the men urging resistance and reminding them that their ghost-shirts made them invulnerable. The troops attempted to search the warriors and the rifle of one, Black Coyote, considered by many members of his tribe to be crazy, apparently discharged accidentally when he resisted. Yellow Bird gave a signal for retaliation, and several warriors leveled their rifles at the troops, and may even have fired them. The soldiers, reacting to what they deemed to be treachery, sent a volley into the Indian ranks. In a brief but frightful struggle, the combatants ferociously wielded rifle, knife, revolver, and war club.

Soon the Hotchkiss guns opened fire from the hill, indiscriminately mowing down some of the women and children who had gathered to watch the proceedings. Within minutes the field was littered with Indian dead and wounded; tepees were burning; and Indian survivors were scrambling in panic to the shelter of nearby ravines, pursued by the soldiers and raked with fire from the Hotchkiss guns. The bodies of men, women, and children were found scattered for a distance of 2 miles from the scene of the first encounter. Because of the frenzy of the struggle and the density of the participants, coupled with poor visibility from gunsmoke, many Indian innocents met death accidentally. In the confusion, both soldiers and Indians undoubtedly took the lives of some of their own groups.

Of the 230 Indian women and children and 120 men at the camp, 153 were counted dead and 44 wounded, but many of the wounded probably escaped and relatives quickly removed a large number of the dead. Army casualties were 25 dead and 39 wounded. The total casualties were probably the highest in Plains Indian warfare except for the Battle of the Little Bighorn. The battle aroused the Brûlés and Oglalas on the Pine Ridge and Rosebud Reservations, but by January 16, 1891, troops had rounded up the last of the hostiles, who recognized the futility of further opposition.

Although a comparatively small number of Sioux died at Wounded Knee, the Sioux Nation died there too. By that time its people fully realized the totality of the white conquest. Before, despite more than a decade of restricted reservation life, they had dreamed of liberation and of a return to the life mode of their fathers—a sentiment strongly manifested in the Ghost Dance religion. But the nightmare of Wounded Knee jolted them from their sleep. They and all the other Indians knew that the end had finally come and that conformance to the white men's ways was the price of survival. It was perhaps not purely coincidental that the same year as Wounded Knee the U.S. Census Bureau noted the passing of the frontier.

The battlefield, though scarred by modern intrusions and fragmented by a road system, remains an impressive reminder of the last major military-Indian clash. It is located on the Pine Ridge Indian Reservation. On the site of the 1890 troop positions are the Wounded Knee store, post office, a privately operated museum displaying battlefield relics, and other modern structures. Dominating the pleasant pastoral scene is the modern church of the Sacred Heart Mission, a simple white frame structure. It stands atop a low hill on the approximate site of the Hotchkiss battery. Behind the church, in the cemetery, is the mass grave of the Indians who died in the battle and the Big Foot Massacre Memorial, erected by the Sioux Indians in 1903. Below, on the site of the Indian camp, where the main fighting took place, the State historical society and the Sioux have placed a series of markers. Practically all the sites, as well as the surrounding lands embracing Wounded Knee Creek and the ravines that figured in the pursuit, are in private and tribal ownership.

Adobe Walls Battlefield, Texas ⊗

Location: Hutchinson County, on an unimproved road, about 17 miles northeast of Stinnett. Make local inquiry.

This site on the Canadian River in the Texas Panhandle, where William Bent had built an adobe trading post in the 1840's but soon abandoned it because of Indian hostility, was twice a battleground. The first engagement, between Col. Christopher ("Kit") Carson's command and a force of Kiowas, occurred late in November 1864. Carson, fresh from victories over the Apaches and Navajos of New Mexico, was leading an expedition sent out by Brig. Gen. James H. Carleton, Federal commander at Santa Fe, to punish the Kiowas and Comanches for raiding the Santa Fe Trail. Carson's 336 California and New Mexico Volunteers and 75 Ute

*Nick Eggenhoffer's painting of the first Battle of
Adobe Walls, Tex., hangs at Fort Union
National Monument, N. Mex.*

and Jicarilla Apache auxiliaries discovered Chief Little Mountain's village of Kiowas at the Adobe Walls site. A conflict ensued
with 1,000 warriors. The attackers became the besieged, however,
when Kiowas and Comanches from other camps joined in the
fight. The battle raged on, but Carson's two mountain howitzers
saved the day. At dusk the troops burned one of the camps and
retreated to their base at Fort Bascom, N. Mex. Three of Carson's
men died and 15 received wounds. Indian casualties totaled 60.

The second battle at the site, late in June 1874, was one of the
causes of the Red River War (1874–75). The Kiowas and Comanches, prodded by some Southern Cheyennes, were attempting
to rid the Texas Panhandle of white buffalo hunters. A large group
attacked 28 hunters, camped about a mile from the scene of the
Carson fight at a trading center established earlier the same year
by Dodge City merchants. The hunters took refuge in two stores
and a saloon. They withstood the assault for several days with re-
markably accurate fire until reinforcements arrived from other
hunting parties in the area and helped rout the Indians.

The site is owned by the Panhandle-Plains Historical Society of
Canyon (Tex.), which has erected a marker. The remains of the
buildings, however, have disappeared.

Big Bend National Park, Texas ⊠

Location: Brewster County; park headquarters located at the southern terminus of U.S. 385; address: Big Bend National Park, Tex. 79834.

Stretching along the United States-Mexico border in the cradle of the Big Bend of the Rio Grande, this giant park presents a panorama of rugged and spectacular river, mountain, canyon, and desert scenery; unusual geological features; and unique plant and wildlife. The magnificent Chisos Mountains soar 4,000 feet above the desert floor in the center of the park. Although primarily significant for its natural and scenic qualities, the park has associations with the phases of history treated in this volume.

The majority of early Spanish soldiers, explorers, and missionaries who passed through the region skirted the park area, whose brooding canyons were hospitable only to scattered Indian bands. A particular scourge to the Spanish and Mexican (after 1821) frontiers were the nomadic Comanches, some of whom frequented the Big Bend region, especially the Chisos Mountains. Early adopting the Spanish-introduced horse, they swept down from their home in the Oklahoma-Texas Panhandles over the Great Comanche War Trail, which passed through the park, and spread devastation as far south as Durango, Mexico. To counter these raids, the Spaniards founded a series of presidios. One of these, maintained in the 1780's and 1790's, was the Presidio of San Vicente, established across the Rio Grande from today's park in Mexico to guard a key ford.

In 1845 the United States annexed Texas, which 9 years earlier had won its freedom from Mexico. By the outbreak of the Civil War, Texas Rangers and U.S. troops had begun the difficult task of pacifying the Indians of western Texas. During the period of Confederate occupation of Fort Davis, Chief Nicolás' band of Southern Mescaleros, who had been raiding the San Antonio-El Paso Road, killed two herders while rustling cattle at the fort. In the Big Bend country, within the present park, the Indians annihilated Lt. Reuben E. Mays' pursuing detachment of 14 men. Only one Mexican scout survived. After the war, in 1871, Lt. Col. William R. Shafter, Fort Davis commander, led a small expedition into the Big Bend region to intimidate the Apaches lurking

there. Meeting none but finding abundant evidence of their presence, he demonstrated to the Indians that the mountains of the Big Bend were no longer a haven.

Many of the Indians, feeling the pressure of white settlements and often being divided by factional quarrels, resisted Army attempts to force them onto reservations. Seeking refuge in the Big Bend area or pausing there on raids, they readily slipped into Mexico when the intensity of the pursuit mounted. The Army's post-Civil War drive against them culminated in the 1880's. The death of the Apache Chief Alsate in his Chisos stronghold in 1882 marked the end of Indian troubles in the Big Bend region. During the decade, railroads and large numbers of cattlemen penetrated the trans-Pecos region and inaugurated the modern era.

The array of park interpretive services—such as self-guiding trails, marked drives, roadside exhibits, evening campfire talks, and guided hikes—emphasize the park's geology, prehistory, and plant and wildlife but include a coverage of the history. All extant historical structures in the park pertain to themes outside the scope of this volume: the growth of ranching, farming, and mining in the area; and diplomatic, economic, and military relations with Mexico in the 20th century.

The Chisos Mountains of Big Bend National Park.

Camp Cooper, Texas ⊗

*Location: Throckmorton County, on a privately owned
ranch, in the vicinity of Fort Griffin State Park, which is
on U.S. 283. Accessible by foot only. Make local inquiry.*

A collection of tents and makeshift buildings of mud, stone, and
wood, this short-lived camp (1856–61) protected settlers and controlled the 400 or so Comanches living on the nearby Comanche
Indian Reservation. Robert E. Lee served at the camp as a junior
officer in 1856–57. It was the base of numerous expeditions and
patrols against the Indians until the Civil War began and the
commander surrendered to Texas troops. During the post-Civil
War period, State militia and Texas Rangers occasionally used the
camp.

A building dating from the early 1850's, probably constructed
with fragments of post structures, stands in the vicinity of the
southern edge of the parade ground. The present ranchhouse, a
mile to the east, contains stones and glass from the camp. Permission to visit the site, which involves wading across the hip-deep
Clear Fork of the Brazos River, should be obtained from the
ranch owners.

Camp Hudson, Texas ⊗

*Location: Val Verde County, on Tex. 163, about 20 miles
north of Comstock.*

Camp Hudson (1857–68), located in the wild and remote Devil's
River region of western Texas, guarded the lower San Antonio-El
Paso Road. In 1859 its troops participated in the Army's camel experiment by accompanying a caravan on a 75-day patrol through
the area. The following year another caravan passed by the camp
on its way to Fort Stockton, Tex. At the outbreak of the Civil
War, Federal troops evacuated Camp Hudson, and the Texas
Mounted Rifles occupied it until U.S. soldiers returned after the
war.

The site is located in a desolate rock-strewn field. A State marker and a small gravestone are the only memorials.

Camp Verde, Texas ⊗

Location: Kerr County, on County 689, about 2 miles
north of the town of Camp Verde.

This camp (1856–69) was one of a chain of forts protecting Texas
settlers and did its share of Comanche fighting, but it won its
major distinction as headquarters of the Army's camel experiment. This project was the brainchild of Edward F. Beale, Superintendent of Indian Affairs for California and Nevada, who persuaded Secretary of War Jefferson Davis to test camels in trans-
porting personnel and freight in arid country. At his urging,
Congress in 1855 appropriated $30,000 to conduct the experiment.
More than 70 camels, acquired by the War Department in the
Mediterranean area, and a few herders arrived on Navy ships at
Indianola, Tex., in 1856–57 and were then herded to Camp
Verde. A specially erected caravansary, or khan, modeled after
one in North Africa, accommodated them. In 1857 Beale took
about 25 of them to Fort Tejon, Calif., while surveying a pro-
posed road across the Southwest.

Those based at Camp Verde were tested under field conditions
in various parts of western Texas. Lt. Col. Robert E. Lee was in
charge of the experiment. The Confederates acquired the camels
when they took over Camp Verde in 1861 and they were still on
hand when Federal troops reoccupied it in 1866. Three years later
the Army relinquished Camp Verde and sold the herd to a private
entrepreneur in San Antonio. Although the camels had demonstrated their superiority over mules, after the war any project associated with Confederate President Jefferson Davis was discredited.
This and other factors brought about the end of the program.

. The site is marked. Remaining are only two stucco buildings,
much altered and probably dating from the 1850's, used today by
the ranch owners as guesthouses. One of these is a linear barracks
building, a composite of three original structures. The other
building, the officers' quarters, has a rear wing. Mounds of earth
reveal the site of the caravansary. The parade ground is distin-
guishable.

Fort Belknap, Texas △

Location: Young County, at the terminus of Tex. 251, about 3 miles south of Newcastle.

Founded in 1851 to safeguard settlers and emigrants in the Red River area, Fort Belknap was both a base for military operations against the Indians and a peacemaking center, but did not excel in the latter role.

Following the U.S. annexation of Texas (1845) and the Mexican War (1846–48), Texas frontier settlers began to demand protection against Kiowa and Comanche raids from the north and west. The Army set up a string of forts: Martin Scott, in 1848; and Worth, Gates, Graham, Croghan, Duncan, and Lincoln, the following year. But the rapidly advancing line of settlement soon brought new outcries from the frontiersmen. Another system of forts came into being: Forts Belknap and Phantom Hill, in 1851; and Forts Chadbourne, McKavett, and Clark, the next year. The northern anchor, Belknap, on the Brazos River, was the nearest to the dangerous Kiowa and Comanche country. Besides watching out for settlers, Forts Belknap and Phantom Hill guarded the Fort Smith-El Paso Road, a major link in the transcontinental route pioneered in 1849 by Capt. Randolph B. Marcy.

In the early 1850's large numbers of Regulars, often bolstered by Texas Rangers and State troops, did their best to deal with Kiowa and Comanche raids. More successful was Col. Albert S. Johnston's newly organized 2d Cavalry Regiment, which arrived in December 1855 in Texas and dispersed among the forts in the chain.

The major offensive involving Fort Belknap troops was Capt. Earl Van Dorn's 1858–59 Wichita Expedition, a march into Indian Territory to retaliate for raids into Texas. Van Dorn led 250 of the garrison's cavalrymen and infantrymen and 135 Indian allies northward; founded Camp Radziminski, Okla., as an advance base; and won victories against the Comanches in the Battles of Rush Springs, Okla. (October 1, 1858) and Crooked Creek, Kans. (May 13, 1859), near present Dodge City, Kans. These aggressive measures caused the Comanches to divide into smaller bands. Many fled to the Staked Plains of eastern New Mexico and the Texas Panhandle, while those remaining near the

315

more populated areas of Texas curtailed their activities. The next year a regiment of State troops organized at Fort Belknap and pushed north as far as Kansas, but took part in no engagements.

Fort Belknap had also been the base of the expedition of Captain Marcy and Lt. George B. McClellan in 1852. This was Marcy's third. The first two had originated at Fort Smith, Ark. Marcy and McClellan explored the Canadian River and discovered the headwaters of the Red River, the last segment of the southern Plains to be explored.

Marcy returned to Fort Belknap in 1854 to help Indian Agent Robert S. Neighbors survey and establish two Indian reservations. The State authorized them in response to Neighbors' humanitarian efforts, which had begun as early as 1845 and included the negotiation of peace treaties between Indians and whites. In 1854–55 he and Marcy founded the Brazos Agency, a few miles south of Fort Belknap; and the Comanche Reservation (Comanche Reserve), 45 miles to the west, guarded by Camp Cooper. Within 3 years more than 1,100 peaceful Indians from various small tribes had settled around the Brazos Agency, but only 400 Comanches moved onto the Comanche Reservation.

Under Neighbors' tutelage the reservation Indians relinquished their nomadism and took up agriculture. Bitter area settlers, however, blamed them for depredations committed by nonreservation Indians. In July 1859, after Neighbors and Fort Belknap troops had repulsed a mob of settlers intent on murdering the reservation inhabitants, he realized the only solution was abandonment of the two reservations. A squadron of cavalry moved a caravan of Indians to a spot on the Washita River 12 miles west of the newly established Wichita Agency, Okla., protected by Fort Cobb. Upon his return, Neighbors was assassinated by a disgruntled settler in the town of Belknap, founded in 1856 near the fort. Between 1858 and 1861 Belknap was a station on the Butterfield Overland Mail.

Meantime, in 1859, because of lack of water, a problem that in 1851 had necessitated a 2-mile move downriver from the original location, Federal troops had abandoned Fort Belknap and transferred to Camp Cooper. During the Civil War, Confederates of the Texas Frontier Regiment used it for a base against hostile Indians and for the protection of settlers, but the inexperienced troops

Restored Fort Belknap.

could not stop Indian raids. For a short time in 1867, U.S. troops returned to the fort and even began to restore its buildings, but abandoned it because of the poor water supply and because the frontier had moved westward. Forts Richardson, to the northeast, and Griffin, to the southwest, replaced Belknap in the frontier defense system. Detachments were occasionally stationed there to watch over the mail road or to control Indian uprisings, but after the subjugation of the southern Plains tribes in the Red River War (1874–75) the fort fell into ruins and settlers dismantled it.

In 1936 the State of Texas, using supplemental Federal funds, began to restore the fort. At that time only the magazine and part of the cornhouse were standing. The State restored these structures and reconstructed the commissary, a kitchen, two two-story barracks, and the well. All of these are on the original foundations except the kitchen, constructed between the barracks. The buildings are of stone construction and have shingled roofs. The 20-acre site is a county park. The Fort Belknap Society adminis-

317

ters museums in the commissary and cornhouse; and, jointly with Texas Wesleyan College, the Fort Belknap Archives of Western America, located in one of the barracks. In the town of Belknap is a monument to Indian Agent Neighbors.

Fort Bliss, Texas ⊗

Location: El Paso County, various locations in and near El Paso. See following account.

Since its creation in 1848 this post has been located at five different places, all in the city limits of El Paso except the present one, and sometimes its garrison was billeted in the city. Over the years the post has had almost as many variant names as sites: Post of El Paso and Post at Smith's Ranch, at Smith's Ranch (1849–51); Fort Bliss, at Magoffinsville (1854–68, including Confederate occupation in 1861–62); Camp Concordia and Fort Bliss, at Concordia Ranch (1868–77); and Fort Bliss, at Hart's Mill and the current location (1878–present).

The fort was founded across the Rio Grande from El Paso del Norte (Ciudad Juárez), Mexico, to establish and maintain U.S. authoriy in the area acquired in the War with Mexico (1846–48), to defend the El Paso area from Indian depredations, and to protect the Southern Transcontinental Trail to California. The fort logistically supported and its garrison participated in various Apache campaigns in Texas and New Mexico, in 1857 and in the 1870's and 1880's. But the troops spent even more time controlling local lawless elements and arbitrating border conflicts. Activities at the fort peaked in World Wars I and II, and it is now the Army Air Defense Center.

Nothing has survived of the first three posts (Smith's Ranch, Magoffinsville, and Concordia Ranch. At the Hart's Mill site (1878–93), on the western edge of El Paso at the intersection of U.S. 80 (Alternate) overpass and Doniphan Street, are several officers' quarters, now used as apartments, and an adobe barracks. At modern Fort Bliss (1893–present), on the northeastern edge of the city, is an adobe replica of the Magoffinsville fort, donated by the El Paso Chamber of Commerce. It now serves as a chapel and museum. Other buildings of interest at the modern post include the old brick messhall, remodeled and serving as the post ex-

318

change; 14 sets of officers' quarters, still in use; and 2 original barracks buildings, on either side of the old messhall, housing administrative offices.

Fort Chadbourne, Texas ⊗

Location: Coke County, just off U.S. 277, about 2½ miles north of its junction with Tex. 70, some 4 miles northeast of the town of Fort Chadbourne.

Fort Chadbourne (1852–67) was one of the outer ring of posts founded in the early 1850's to protect the Texas frontier from plundering Kiowas and Comanches. Other forts in the ring were Belknap, Phantom Hill, McKavett, and Clark. From 1858 until 1861 Fort Chadbourne was division headquarters for the Butterfield Overland Mail. During the Civil War, Confederate troops periodically occupied the fort. Union troops returned in May 1867 but remained only until December, when Fort Concho was established not far to the south. Fort Chadbourne, however, continued to serve as a station on the San Antonio-El Paso stageline and the Army sometimes used it as a subpost.

A State marker indicates the privately owned site, which is not open to the public. The ruins are part of the headquarters of a cattle ranch, and the parade ground is a grazing area. The walls of four limestone buildings, two barracks and two officers' quarters, stand in their entirety, as well as several partial walls. Piles of stone rubble outline other structures. One of the barracks has been reroofed and is used as a cattle barn.

Fort Clark, Texas ⊗

Location: Kinney County, southern edge of Brackettville.

Unlike many other forts prominent in the Indian wars, this fort in south-central Texas remained an active post through World War II. It was founded in 1852 and inactivated in the mid–1940's. Southern anchor of the Texas defense line in the 1850's, it guarded the San Antonio-El Paso Road and policed the Mexican border. In 1861 the Confederates moved in, but Union troops returned 5 years later. The fort was the headquarters of Col. Ranald

319

S. Mackenzie in 1873 when he created an international incident by crossing the border and attacking Kickapoo and Lipan Apache raiders who were using Mexico as a sanctuary. Troops from the fort played a small role in the Red River War (1874–75). After the 1880's, the Indians in the region subdued, the fort remained active as an infantry and cavalry post and was a cavalry training center during World War II.

Approximately 25 to 30 buildings dating from the 19th century have survived amid later military construction. At least three of them, two sets of officers' quarters and one other building, all of vertical log construction, probably date from the early 1850's. The remainder, of stone construction, were constructed in the later 1850's or the 1880's. They include officers' quarters, barracks, commanding officer's house, quartermaster storehouse, and guardhouse. Most of the buildings have been altered, and are used by the privately owned guest ranch that occupies the site.

Fort Concho, Texas △

> Location: Tom Green County; the general area bounded by Avenues "B" and "E," Rust Street, and South Oakes Street; San Angelo.

Fort Concho (1867–89) was one of a series of posts guarding the Texas frontier during the post-Civil War era. After the war, the Army reconstituted and reoccupied most of the antebellum posts in western Texas guarding the San Antonio-El Paso Road—Stockton, Davis, Quitman, and Bliss. In addition, it constructed a new group of posts—Richardson, Griffin, and Concho. With Forts McKavett and Clark, they formed an irregular line running from El Paso to the northeastern border of Texas and separated Indian country from settlements. At the very center of the line was Fort Concho, at the confluence of the North and South Concho Rivers, where a number of east-west trails converged to avoid the Staked Plains to the north and a semidesert area to the south, both infested with Indians. Deep in Kiowa and Comanche country, for more than two decades it was the headquarters of such noted Indian fighters as Ranald S. Mackenzie, William R. Shafter, Wesley Merritt, Anson Mills, and Benjamin H. Grierson. Situated on the Goodnight-Loving Cattle Trail (1860–1880's) and the upper branch of the San Antonio-El Paso Road, part of the Southern Transcontinental Trail, the fort was also a way station for travelers, emigrants, and cattlemen.

The garrison took part in no campaigns during the first few years of the fort's existence. In 1869, however, it clashed with Indians on two occasions on the Salt Fork of the Brazos River, and it patrolled regularly to stem the forays of Kiowas and Comanches from their "sanctuary" at Fort Sill, Indian Territory. Between 1870 and 1875 the troops accompanied Col. Ranald S. Mackenzie on several arduous campaigns. One of them, in 1873, in the pursuit of Lipan and Kickapoo raiders into Mexico, created an international incident. The garrison also participated in the Red River War (1874–75), including Mackenzie's victory at the Battle of Palo Duro Canyon (September 27, 1874), the turning point in the war. The last major campaign involving Concho forces was that against Victorio (1879–80).

Barracks at Fort Concho.

In 1930 a group of San Angelo citizens acquired the old administration building of Fort Concho to house the West Texas Museum, later renamed the Fort Concho Museum, and spearheaded a drive to acquire the rest of the fort, which had passed into private hands in 1889, and develop it as a historic site. By mid-1969 the city had acquired the entire property except for a couple of small residential tracts and two large industrial sites. The complex, consisting of about 15 acres, is owned by the city and administered by the Fort Concho Museum Board.

An outstanding collection of stone buildings may be viewed. The main structure is the administration, or headquarters, building (1876), which today serves as a visitor center and houses a museum of Texas history. Other structures include nine sets of officers' quarters; the restored chapel, which also served as a schoolhouse; two barracks, reconstructed from the original stones, now housing museum exhibits; and the powder magazine, which has been moved stone by stone from its original site near the river and rebuilt behind the barrracks.

Fort Davis National Historic Site, Texas ☒

Location: Jeff Davis County, on Tex. 17, just north of the town of Fort Davis; address: P.O. Box 785, Fort Davis, Tex. 79734.

The picturesque remains of Fort Davis, more extensive and impressive than those of any other southwestern fort, are a vivid modern reminder of a colorful chapter in western history. They also stand as a tribute to the courage of frontier soldiers, black and white, and their tenacious Indian opponents. A key post in the western Texas defensive system, Fort Davis was one of the most active in the West during the Indian wars, especially the 1879–80 campaign against the Apache Victorio. As Fort Bowie, Ariz., spearheaded the campaign against the Chiricahua Apaches, so did Fort Davis against the Warm Springs and Mescaleros. Forts Bowie and Davis also both protected transcontinental emigrant, freight, and stage routes.

The mounting tide of westward travel in the 1850's, generated by the California gold rush and the newfound interest of settlers

322

Fort Davis about 1885.

in the vast territory the United States acquired from Mexico in the Mexican War (1846–48) and the Gadsden Purchase (1853), swelled traffic over the transcontinental trails. To avoid the winter snows and mountains of the central routes to the goldfields or to seek their fortune in the newly acquired Southwest, thousands of gold seekers and emigrants pushed along the southern route. A vital segment was the San Antonio-El Paso Road, opened in 1849, which also carried a large volume of traffic between the two cities and Santa Fe, N. Mex., and Chihuahua, Mexico.

The road presented rich opportunities for plunder to Kiowa, Comanche, and Mescalero Apache raiders. Intersecting it were the trails of marauding Indians who had long swept down from the north and devastated the isolated villages and haciendas of northern Mexico. West of the Davis Mountains, foraying Mescaleros of New Mexico crossed the road. East of the mountains, the Great Comanche War Trail bisected its lower branch at Comanche Springs.

Inevitably the Indians paused to assail travelers on the San Antonio-El Paso Road. As depredations mounted, a finger of military outposts pointed west into the trans-Pecos region. Forts Hudson, 323

Lancaster, Stockton, Davis, Quitman, and Bliss extended military protection from the outer ring of defensive posts all the way to El Paso.

Of these, Fort Davis was the largest and most important. Lt. Col. Washington Seawell and 8th Infantry troops from Fort Ringgold, Tex., founded it in 1854 near a site known as Painted Comanche Camp. At the eastern edge of the Davis Mountains north of the Big Bend of the Rio Grande, the new fort was situated in a small box canyon, lined by low basaltic ridges, just south of Limpia Canyon. Strategically located in relation to emigrant and Indian trails and on the San Antonio-El Paso Road, it also afforded an adequate water supply, mandatory in the arid region, from nearby Limpia Creek; a good timber supply, for fuel and construction, in the Davis Mountains; and a salubrious climate. Seawell never built the more permanent post he envisioned to the east at the mouth of the canyon. Instead, in time a motley collection of tent-like structures and thatch-roofed buildings of log, picket, frame, and stone straggled along the length of the canyon.

In the pre-Civil War years the garrison patrolled regularly, guarded mail relay stations, escorted mail and freight trains, and fought occasional skirmishes with the Kiowas, Comanches, and Apaches. The troops made little progress, however, in pacifying the Indians in the region. Tempting targets to the warriors were the mail-carrying stagecoaches that operated on a local and interregional basis in the 1854–61 period through Fort Davis over the San Antonio-El Paso Road and offered connections with St. Louis, Santa Fe, and California: the George H. Giddings (1854–57) and James Birch (1857–61) lines, and the Butterfield Overland Mail (1859–61).

One of the few diversions of the fort's troops, whose duties were alternately grueling and boring, was watching the camels of the Army's experimental corps that occasionally lumbered in. Edward F. Beale's herd of 25 en route in 1857 from the Camp Verde camel base to Fort Tejon, Calif., passed by. In 1859 and 1860 Texas military authorities utilized some of the Camp Verde animals in an attempt to blaze a shorter route from San Antonio and the Pecos to Fort Davis and to compare their efficiency with mules. Although the camels proved superior, the camel project ultimately came to naught.

Lt. Col. Wesley Merritt and his black 9th Cavalry troops reactivated Fort Davis in 1867. He later won distinction during the northern Plains campaigns.

The Union evacuated its forts in western Texas in 1861, when Texas joined the Confederacy. The Confederates took over Fort Davis in 1861–62, but withdrew upon their failure to conquer New Mexico and the approach of General Carleton's California Volunteers. Meantime the men in grey had enjoyed no immunity from the Apaches, who wiped out a detachment of 14 of them deep in the Big Bend country. Wrecked by Apaches, Fort Davis lay deserted for 5 years.

Federal soldiers, under Lt. Col. Wesley Merritt, did not return until the summer of 1867, but when they did their color had changed. Between then and 1885, elements of all the Army's post-Civil War black regiments, composed largely of ex-slaves and commanded by white officers, were stationed at the fort at one time or another along with various white regiments. The black units were the 9th and 10th Cavalry and the 24th and 25th Infantry, all of which served with notable distinction not only at Fort Davis but throughout the West during the Indian wars.

Rather than trying to rebuild the old fort, which had been vulnerable to Apache attacks from closeby ridges, Merritt fulfilled

325

Barracks at Fort Davis. Top, in 1875; center, 2 years before the National Park Service began restoration; and bottom, following restoration in 1965–66.

Seawell's dream by beginning the erection of a new fort at the mouth of the canyon. Of more substantial stone and adobe, it was not completed until the 1880's. Meantime Fort Davis had resumed its role of protecting western Texas. Highlighting the achievements of the fort's black troops, as well as those from other Texas forts, was participation in the Victorio campaign (1879–80). As many as 1,000 troops, a large number of them black, at various times tramped 135,000 miles in the arduous but frustrating pursuit of Victorio's tiny group of some 100 Warm Springs and Mescalero Apaches.

In the spring of 1879 Victorio, who for 2 years had resisted the efforts of Indian agents to move his band to the San Carlos Reservation, Ariz., recruited some of the discontented Mescaleros at the Fort Stanton Reservation, N. Mex., who had been raiding in Texas themselves. The new allies, outrunning pursuing troops, fled into Mexico. For 2 years, employing clever guerrilla tactics, they wreaked havoc on both sides of the Rio Grande and struck repeatedly in New Mexico, western Texas, and Chihuahua (Mexico). When cornered, they skirmished with soldiers, Texas Rangers, and citizens' posses, but always managed to escape. In September 1879 and January 1880 Victorio returned to New Mexico. On the latter occasion, New Mexico and Texas troops attempted to disarm the Mescaleros at Fort Stanton Reservation before Victorio could recruit them. But 50 of them escaped and joined Victorio, who returned to Mexico.

Knowing that Victorio would appear again but preferring to stop him in Texas rather than sending troops to New Mexico, Col. Benjamin H. Grierson in the summer of 1880 established the headquarters of his black 10th Cavalry at Fort Davis; dispersed troops all along the arid country from there to El Paso; sharpened patrol actions; set up subposts along the Rio Grande at Viejo Pass, Eagle Springs, and Fort Quitman; and carefully watched the waterholes Victorio would need to rely on to cross the inhospitable country.

Finally, in the vicinity of present Van Horn, Tex., Grierson and his men defeated Victorio in two battles in July and August and forced him back into Mexico. Two months later Mexican soldiers killed him. A remnant of his band, under the aged Warm Springs leader Nana, escaped to the Sierra Madre, where they

Col. Benjamin H. Grierson, commander of the black 10th Cavalry. Fort Davis was a key base in his vigorous 1879–80 campaign against the Warm Springs Apache Victorio.

later joined forces with another wily Apache leader, Geronimo. But Victorio's death ended the era of Indian warfare in Texas.

In the 1880's large numbers of cattlemen settled in the area of the fort. The routine was punctuated only by occasional tours of escort duty for railroad builders, bandit-chasing expeditions, and border-patrol actions. The routes of the Texas Pacific and Southern Pacific Railroads, which pushed through western Texas in the 1880's, bypassed the fort. The last troops left in 1891.

In 1963 Fort Davis came into the National Park System. A program was immediately launched to save the remaining buildings, begin restoring some of them, and interpret the story of the fort to the public. Of the more than 50 adobe and stone buildings that constituted the second Fort Davis at the time of its abandonment, visitors today may inspect 16 officers' residences, two sets of barracks, warehouses, a magazine, the hospital, and other structures. Stone foundations mark the sites of other buildings. Archeologists have recently uncovered the foundations of many structures of the first fort (1854–61), in the canyon west of the second. The site of the Butterfield stage station, a half mile northeast of the first fort, has also been identified. The National Park Service presents a unique sound program of special interest to the visitor. He may

328

hear a bugle, echoing from the nearby hills, peal out the various orders of the day. Another interesting sound presentation is a formal retreat ceremony.

Fort Duncan, Texas ⊗

Location: Maverick County, Fort Duncan Park, city of Eagle Pass.

Fort Duncan (1849–83), commanding strategic Eagle Pass, was located on the east bank of the Rio Grande. Like Fort McIntosh and other posts along the river, it guarded the international boundary, scrutinized the traders crossing it, and protected settlers and emigrants. It was evacuated in 1859, reoccupied the following year, abandoned again in 1861, and occupied by the Confederates in 1862–64. In 1864 Union troops attacked it and Fort McIntosh. (Eagle Pass was a Confederate center for trade with Europe by way of Mexico.) The fort was occupied by Federal troops in 1868. Another military post, known as Camp at Eagle Pass (1886–1927), succeeded Fort Duncan on its site.

The dozen buildings from the old fort remaining in Fort Duncan Park, a city recreational park, include a stone magazine (1849), in excellent condition; stone stables; and an adobe officers' quarters.

Fort Griffin, Texas ⊗

Location: Shackelford County, on U.S. 283, about 15 miles north of Albany.

During the years 1867–81 this fort, which helped assume the mission of the inactivated Fort Belknap, protected settlers from Comanche and Kiowa hostilities; escorted mail riders, surveyors, and cattle drovers; served as a communication link on the Fort Concho-Fort Richardson Military Road; and, as Col. Ranald S. Mackenzie's main supply depot, played a major part in the Red River War (1874–75). The wild town of Fort Griffin, or The Flat, which grew up at the bottom of the hill north of the fort, was a supply and shipping center for buffalo hide hunters and a major stop on the Western Cattle Trail. As the buffalo hunters completed their slaughter and the troops from the fort pacified the Plains, the cattlemen pushed their holdings and their drives northwest from the town which declined.

Fort Griffin State Park, on a flat hilltop overlooking the valley of the Clear Fork of the Brazos River, preserves the stone remains of several buildings. Included are those of the powder magazine, bakery, administration building, and sutler's store. The sites of some other buildings are marked. A 40-ton granite shaft, erected by the State, stands in the center of the parade ground. One false-front building is located at the privately owned site of The Flat.

Fort Lancaster, Texas ⊗

Location: Crockett County, just off U.S. 290, about 10 miles east of Sheffield.

For the 6 years (1855–61) Fort Lancaster was active, its garrison pursued Comanches and Mescalero Apaches and guarded the Pecos crossing of the San Antonio-El Paso Road. Federal troops abandoned it in 1861, never to return permanently. The Confederates sporadically occupied it. After the war it was frequently a subpost and remained a stopping off place for travelers, attracted by the water supply.

The extensive stone ruins of the fort, visible from the State marker on U.S. 290, reveal the location of practically every building. The vegetation-covered ruins, of which those of the barracks stand out, consist of foundations; partial stone walls, some rising 6 to 8 feet; chimneys and fireplaces; and piles of rubble. In 1965 the owners donated the 39-acre site to the county for preservation as a historic site.

Fort McIntosh, Texas ⊗

Location: Webb County, on Fort McIntosh Reservation, about 15 blocks west of downtown Laredo, via Victoria Street.

This was one of the few frontier forts whose history extended into the modern period, until 1946. Founded on the banks of the Rio Grande at Laredo in 1849, right after the Mexican War, it policed the international boundary and defended settlers from hostile Apaches and Comanches. During the Civil War, Confederates garrisoned the post, a star fort of earth and stone, and withstood an 1864 Union raid. In 1865 reoccupying U.S. forces relocated the fort a half mile down the river and erected a more conventional frontier post.

The fort's complex of stone, brick, and frame buildings, modern and old, is used by Laredo Junior College and various Government agencies. The newer buildings and the parade ground are near the entrance. Brick and frame officers' quarters line two sides of the parade ground, and two-story brick barracks a third. The older buildings are north of the parade ground. The guardhouse is now a warehouse, and the U.S. Border Patrol occupies the headquarters building. All that remains of the first fort, in the northwestern corner of the Fort McIntosh Reservation, are mounds of earth.

Fort McKavett, Texas ⊗

Location: Menard County, town of Fort McKavett.

Fort McKavett (1852–83), perched atop a high bluff overlooking the San Saba River, was part of a system of forts established in the 1850's to guard the Texas frontier. It was evacuated in 1859 and not reoccupied until 1868, though the Confederates used it intermittently during the Civil War. In the intervening years the stone post had fallen into ruins, and only one building was habitable. In 1869 Col. Ranald S. Mackenzie made it his headquarters and launched a major repair and expansion program. The garrison participated in the Red River War (1874–75) and the Victorio campaign (1879–80).

Impressive stone remains stand today in Fort McKavett State Historic Park. Most of the original structures have survived, and many of them are residences or business places. Scattered among the inhabited buildings are stone walls and vacant, crumbling buildings, overgrown with weeds.

331

Fort Phantom Hill, Texas ⊗

Location: Jones County, on an unimproved road, about 14 miles north of Abilene.

A hardship post frequently harassed by Indians, Fort Phantom Hill (1851–54) existed for just a few years. Located on the Clear Fork of the Brazos River, it served as a link in the Texas defense system and watched over the Fort Smith-Santa Fe emigrant road. Between 1858 and 1861 the site of Fort Phantom Hill was a stage station on the Butterfield Overland Mail, and after 1867 was sometimes utilized by patrols operating out of Forts Griffin and Richardson.

The privately owned site is commemorated by a State marker, but is heavily covered with underbrush. The magazine and guard-house, two of the few stone buildings at the fort, remain intact. A large number of stone chimneys of the log buildings are extant.

Fort Richardson, Texas ⚠

Location: Jack County, on U.S. 281, southern edge of Jacksboro.

This fort, the most northerly in a line of Texas forts and one of the most important in the region during the post-Civil War era, helped replace prewar Fort Belknap. Founded in 1867 not far below the boundary of Indian Territory (Oklahoma), Fort Richardson was a key defense bastion against the Kiowa and Comanche raiders who swept eastward from the Staked Plains and southward from their reservations in Indian Territory to prey on Texas settlers. It also guarded the stagelines running westward to El Paso over the old Butterfield route. In time, with Fort Sill, Okla., and other forts, Fort Richardson ended the Indian threat on the southern Plains.

As raids into Texas from Indian Territory accelerated in the early 1870's, mainly because of the launching of President Grant's Peace Policy at the Oklahoma reservations, the wrath of settlers mounted. Yet Fort Richardson's busy garrison, whom the Peace Policy prevented from pursuing marauding Indians beyond the Red River boundary, could only rely on such defensive measures

The hospital, one of the surviving buildings at Fort Richardson.

as providing escorts for travelers and sending out large scouting parties.

In 1871 the settlers gained a chance to vent their emotions. At Fort Sill General Sherman arrested the Kiowa chiefs Satank, Satanta, and Big Tree, who in May had led a war party that had wiped out a wagon train near Fort Richardson and the adjacent town of Jacksboro, and took the unprecedented step of sending them to Fort Richardson for imprisonment pending a civil trial in Jacksboro. Satank was shot en route while trying to escape. The trial demonstrated the wide variance in attitudes of frontiersmen and eastern humanitarians and attracted national attention. To frontiersmen, it marked perhaps the first instance of Indians being tried by a civil court and implied that in the future they might be judged for their crimes by the white man's standards rather than their own.

At the end of the trial the judge sentenced the two chiefs to death by hanging. Federal officials, however, influenced by humanitarian agitation, first pressured the Governor of Texas into commuting the sentences to life imprisonment at the Huntsville, Tex., penitentiary; and, after the chiefs had served only 2 years, into freeing them. On their return to the Fort Sill Reservation, the Kiowas and Comanches intensified their raiding.

Yet the Texas settlers had gained some revenge in the trial and imprisonment. The Government in Washington, which had been convinced the Peace Policy was working and had usually ignored pleas for help from military officials and settlers, was also probably better aware of their need for protection. And General Sherman had begun a series of aggressive campaigns that would before long reverse the Peace Policy, subdue the Kiowas and Comanches, and open western Texas to full-scale settlement. Col. Ranald S. Mackenzie's 4th Cavalry, assigned to Fort Richardson, began the punitive actions with an 1871–72 campaign onto the Staked Plains. The final thrust came in the Red River War (1874–75), in which the fort served as a troop depot and its garrison participated in many engagements, including Mackenzie's victory at the Battle of Palo Duro Canyon. Following the war, the need for Fort Richardson declined. For a few uneventful years, its troops patrolled along the Red River and escorted cattle drives northward. In May 1878 they abandoned the post, which then served for a short time as an Indian school.

Fort Richardson is now a 41-acre State historical reserve, administered by the city and the Jack County Historical Society. Although urban and industrial development have encroached on the site, seven original buildings remain in various stages of restoration, reconstruction, and repair. The hospital building, built of native sandstone, is the central feature. It houses a museum, the historical society offices, and an archives room. Other stone structures are the morgue, where Satanta and Big Tree were confined awaiting trial; bakery; guardhouse; and powder magazine. One frame officers' quarters, 1½ stories in height with dormered windows and wide porch, has been restored. A sandstone commissary warehouse, originally connected with another by a frame shed and now an abandoned ruin, is separated from the restored fort by a railroad track.

Fort Stockton, Texas ⊗

Location: Pecos County, on Spring Drive between Second and Fifth Streets, town of Fort Stockton.

Part of the frontier defenses of western Texas, Fort Stockton (1858–86) was established at Comanche Springs, a strategic watering place on the Great Comanche War Trail. Its mission was protection of local and transcontinental traffic on the San Antonio-El Paso Road, which passed by the springs. U.S. troops evacuated the fort at the beginning of the Civil War and did not return until 1867. They took part in the Victorio campaign (1879–80). The subsequent bypassing of the fort by the railroad, which ended the requirement to protect the mail, emigrants, and stages, caused its inactivation.

The site, indicated by a State marker on the courthouse grounds of the town, borders James Rooney Park, surrounding Comanche Springs. Four buildings remain: a stone guardhouse, unoccupied; and three adobe officers' quarters, remodeled and used as residences. The Chamber of Commerce has marked these buildings, as well as other historic structures in the town.

Fort Terrett, Texas ⊗

Location: Sutton County, on an unimproved road about 1 mile north of U.S. 290, about 32 miles southeast of Sonora.

One of the less important Texas forts and active only in the years 1852–54, this hardship post was surrounded by numerous others. Its infantrymen guarded settlements along the old San Antonio Road from Comanche attacks. Reasons for abandonment, beyond its limited strategic significance, were the sickness rate and low morale.

A privately owned ranch occupies the site, marked by the State. Remaining are two remodeled stone buildings: a barracks, used as a garage; and the commanding officer's home, now a residence. Foundations trace other buildings, and the parade ground is ascertainable.

Guadalupe Mountains National Park, Texas ⊞

Location: Culberson and Hudspeth Counties, on U.S. 62–180, just northwest of the town of Signal Peak; address: c/o Carlsbad Caverns National Park, P.O. Box 1598, Carlsbad, N. Mex. 88220.

The lofty peaks identifying this new national park, notable primarily for its natural features and geological phenomena, rise dramatically from the desert floor. Although the greater part of the Guadalupe Mountains lie in New Mexico, the highest peaks, those comprising the national park, are in Texas. Indeed, they are the highest in the State. Historically, the mountains were a stronghold of the Mescalero Apaches.

In 1849, by the time of the California gold rush, western Texas was a vast stretch of wilderness that few Americans had seen. West of San Antonio, the barren and rocky desert, broken only by a series of rugged mountains, was inhabited mainly by Lipan and Mescalero Apaches. For two decades other Indians, bands of Mescaleros from New Mexico and Kiowas and Comanches from Indian Territory, had traversed the area on forays into Mexico to obtain food. This pattern prevailed until the 1850's.

After the discovery of gold in California, gold seekers poured over the upper and lower branches of the San Antonio-El Paso Road, surveyed in 1849. But lightning-like Mescalero raids hampered travel over both routes. In 1854, to guard the lower branch, which passed through the Davis Mountains, the Army established Fort Davis, Tex., but left the upper road, which ran along the southern end of the Guadalupe Mountains, unguarded. In 1855, while the Fort Davis garrison gave the Mescaleros no surcease, New Mexico troops campaigned against them in the Sacramento and Capitan Mountains of New Mexico. As a result, most of them settled on a reservation near Fort Stanton, N. Mex. A few bands continued to live in the Guadalupe and Davis Mountains and in the Chisos Mountains of the Big Bend. These groups resumed raiding roads in Texas and villages in Mexico, sometimes with the aid of their kinsmen from the reservation.

The Butterfield Overland Mail in 1858 won a Government contract to deliver mail from St. Louis to San Francisco. The company chose a southern route, a portion of which followed the upper branch of the San Antonio-El Paso Road. In a pass at the foot of the Guadalupes, a stage station was erected and called Pine Springs (Pinery). The next year, however, seeking the protection of Fort Davis, the Butterfield line moved to the lower branch. In 1861, when the Army evacuated Fort Davis and the other forts in western Texas, the company abandoned the southern route altogether in favor of a central one. The roads lay at the mercy of the Indians.

El Capitan, Guadalupe Mountains National Park.

The Army reactivated Fort Davis in 1867 and renewed its efforts to curb Mescalero raids. These had increased because in 1865 the Mescaleros had fled a new reservation in eastern New Mexico, near Fort Sumner, where they had been confined in 1862–63. They continued to use the Guadalupes and their other mountain haunts to regroup and resupply for their forays into Mexico. To patrol such a large area more effectively, Fort Davis set up a number of subposts at the more important waterholes. One of these subposts was Pine Springs, the old Butterfield stage station.

In 1869 Col. Edward Hatch took over command of Fort Davis. The next year, determined to curb the Mescaleros once and for all, he launched an offensive, supported by other Texas and New Mexico posts. He led three patrols from Fort Davis northward into the Guadalupes. Only once did his men make contact with the Indians, in January, when a group of them surprised and inflicted severe casualties on an Apache camp. This action convinced the Mescaleros that the Guadalupes were not as safe as they had believed. Late in 1871 the principal bands reported to the Fort Stanton Reservation. But the calm was of short duration.

In the last half of the 1870's the Mescaleros erupted again, leaving the reservation and returning to the remote canyons of the Guadalupes and other ranges in the trans-Pecos region. They resumed raiding in Texas and Mexico. The reasons for the new unrest included the pressure of white settlement around the Fort Stanton Reservation, the unsettling influence of the cattlemen's war in Lincoln County, N. Mex. (1878), and the growth of factionalism among the reservation Mescaleros.

Many of the Mescaleros joined the Warm Springs Apache Victorio, whose band roved back and forth between Mexico, Texas, and New Mexico and terrorized the borderland in 1879–80. To little avail, troops in the Victorio campaign often scoured the Guadalupe and Sacramento Mountains looking for the adversary. During the summer of 1880 the Army repelled Victorio in the Battles of Tinaja de las Palmas and Rattlesnake Springs, Tex. The latter battle was fought within sight of the mighty peaks of the Guadalupe Mountains, for which the Indians were heading and from which a group of Mescaleros had been riding to reinforce Victorio when troops intercepted them. Soon thereafter Mexican troops killed Victorio, whose death marked the end of the Mescalero insurgency and the Indian wars in Texas.

Guadalupe Mountains National Park, authorized in 1966, is a new National Park Service area. An interpretive program was being formulated for the park when this volume went to press. Traces of the dry-masonry stone walls of the Pine Springs stage station and military subpost remain on U.S. 62–180 at the base of the landmark known as El Capitan. Behind the ruins are a weed-choked well.

Palo Duro Canyon Battlefield, Texas ⊗

> *Location: Armstrong County, about 20 miles southeast of the town of Canyon. Accessible by foot only. Make local inquiry.*

In this colorful and jagged canyon on the Staked Plains of the Texas Panhandle, Col. Ranald S. Mackenzie's 4th Cavalry, operating out of Fort Concho, Tex., dealt a severe blow to the Co-

Col. Ranald S. Mackenzie, noted Indian fighter, won a resounding victory at the Battle of Palo Duro Canyon.

manches and hastened the end of the Red River War (1874–75). On September 27, 1874, Mackenzie discovered a sizable camp in the canyon, a favorite Comanche campsite and refuge. He descended and attacked. The Indians scattered in the rough terrain and fought so fiercely from shelters along the canyon slopes that the troops had to retreat. The Indians suffered few casualties, but Mackenzie captured and destroyed their pony herd, numbering 1,400 head. This deprived them of sustenance, hampered their mobility and morale, and contributed significantly to their ultimate surrender.

Part of Palo Duro Canyon, formed by the Prairie Dog Town Fork of the Red River, is now a State park. The battle site, however, is down the canyon from the park. It is inaccessible by wheeled vehicle but may be viewed from the south rim of the canyon at a point about 10 miles northwest of the village of Wayside. At this overlook a trail, the only one on the south rim for miles and the one used by Mackenzie, leads into the canyon.

Tinaja de las Palmas Battle Site, Texas ⊗

Location: Hudspeth County, on an unimproved road, about 15 miles southeast of the town of Sierra Blanca.

The defeat inflicted by Col. Benjamin H. Grierson's black troops on the Warm Springs Apache Victorio and his followers at this

339

site climaxed the Army's 1879–80 campaign against them and ended their forays in the Southwest. In the summer of 1880 Grierson, anticipating another raid by the group across the Rio Grande into Texas and New Mexico, established his headquarters at Fort Davis and intensified defensive measures. On July 29, while on an inspection trip with eight men, he was near the Eagle Mountains when he learned Victorio had crossed the Rio Grande in the vicinity. Sending for reinforcements from nearby Eagle Springs and Fort Quitman, Grierson supervised the erection of two small stone barricades along narrow Devil Ridge, which overlooked a waterhole west of the Eagle Mountains known as *Tinaja de las Palmas*. It was the only source of water in the arid valley that Victorio had to follow to pass around the mountains.

Engaging Victorio and his party the next morning when they arrived at the waterhole, Grierson and his handful of men held them off until reinforcements arrived. Seven of Victorio's men died and many more suffered wounds. The soldiers counted only one dead and two wounded. Victorio retreated to Mexico. A few days later, on August 6, to the northeast of *Tinaja de las Palmas* near Rattlesnake Springs, on the east side of the Sierra Diablo, Grierson's command once again repulsed him. Thwarted in reaching New Mexico, he had to move back across the Rio Grande, where 2 months later Mexican soldiers killed him and many of his followers.

No marker is located at the site, on the east side of the road, but the State has erected one in front of the courthouse at the nearby town of Van Horn. Permission must be obtained from the rancher who owns the Tinaja de las Palmas site before it may be visited. The natural scene is almost completely unimpaired. On the southern end of Devil Ridge are the remains of the two stone barricades. A linear indention marking the route of the San Antonio-El Paso Road is visible across the valley for miles.

Cove Fort, Utah ⊗
Location: Millard County, town of Cove Fort.

Built in 1867 by order of Brigham Young with church funds, Cove Fort provided a refuge for settlers during the Ute Black

Hawk War and was a way station for travelers between Salt Lake City and Mormon settlements in the Virgin River Valley and in southern Nevada and California. The site was a favorite camping place of Young, who made frequent trips to southwestern Utah. The builder of the fort, Ira N. Hinckley, maintained it as a residence until 1877. One of its 12 original rooms housed a telegraph station on the Mormon line. Fortunately Indians never attacked or besieged the fort, for its water supply was poor. An earlier fort, known as Willden's Fort, consisting of three rooms and a dugout, had been built on the site in 1861.

Although privately owned, Cove Fort is open to the public. Constructed of blocks of basalt laid with lime mortar, it consists of two one-story rows of six rooms each that face each other across a courtyard and form the north and south walls of a 100-foot square fortification. Each room has a door and window to the court and door connecting with adjacent rooms, but the exterior walls have no openings. The south range is original, and the north range was restored in 1917. The courtyard is walled at each end with the same type of masonry, and in each wall is a large

Cove Fort, Utah.

gate of heavy planks. Just above the tops of the gates and running the full length of each end wall is a wooden catwalk to enable defenders to use the upper portion of the wall for protection while shooting through firing ports. The exterior walls of the rooms also served as parapets.

Fort Deseret, Utah ⊗

Location: Millard County, on Utah 257, about 1 mile south of Deseret.

Fort Deseret was one of many built by the Mormons to protect settlers and serve as way stations for travelers. Although the Indians never attacked the post, local residents found it a welcome refuge when hostilities threatened. Constructed in 1866 of mud and straw, it had two corner bastions and was approximately 550 feet square. Most of the 10-foot walls have fallen down. The corners, two bastions, and most of the east wall still stand in an undeveloped State park.

Fort Douglas, Utah ⊗

Location: Salt Lake County, on the Fort Douglas Military Reservation, northeastern edge of Salt Lake City.

This fort was founded in 1862 in the foothills of the Wasatch Mountains on a rise overlooking Salt Lake City by Col. Patrick E. Connor and his California Volunteers. Commanding the Military District of Utah, Colonel Connor supervised Army operations in Utah, Nevada, and part of Wyoming. The garrison protected the overland mail and transcontinental telegraph lines from the Indians; kept the Mormons under surveillance; guarded the transportation routes crossing Utah in all directions; and aided road-surveying parties. One of the few instances in which the troops saw action in the Indian campaigns was Colonel Connor's 300-man campaign in the fall and winter of 1862–63 against marauding Shoshonis, Snakes, and Bannocks, in northern Utah; in January 1863 he dealt a severe defeat to the Shoshoni Chief Bear Hunter in the Battle of Bear River. Once the Civil War ended, Regulars replaced the Volunteers. The Army inactivated the post in 1967, but retained about 100 acres for Reserve training and the Deseret

Officers' quarters at Fort Douglas in the 1890's.

Test Center headquarters. The State of Utah has since acquired a large portion of the remainder of the acreage.

The modern military installation of Fort Douglas grew up around the old fort and has changed its historical appearance. Remaining stone structures, which replaced the original log and frame buildings and date from the 1880's, are grouped around the parade ground. They consist of a number of officers' quarters, the old headquarters building, post office, stables, and chapel. The post cemetery includes the bodies of soldiers killed in the Battle of Bear River.

Gunnison Massacre Site, Utah ⊗

> *Location: Millard County, on an unimproved road, about 9 miles southwest of Deseret.*

At this site a band of Ute Indians massacred Capt. John W. Gunnison's Pacific Railroad Survey party, one of several sponsored by the War Department's Corps of Topographical Engineers. Una-

343

*Gen. Patrick E. Connor,
commander in Utah and
the Great Plains during
the Civil War years.*

ware that the Walker War had broken out between the Ute Indians of central Utah and the Mormons, Gunnison and seven men set out on October 21, 1853, from their camp at Cedar Springs, just west of Fillmore, Utah, to explore the Sevier Lake country, in the area of Indian hostilities. Four days later a band of Utes massacred the party. Searchers found the bodies and buried them at the site. The massacre halted surveying activities in Utah until the following year, when Ute hostilities ended. Lt. Edward G. Beckwith resumed the survey and completed it to the Pacific. A monument marks the massacre site, relatively undisturbed.

Hampton Institute, Virginia ⊗
Location: Just off I–64 (U.S. 60), Hampton.

This private school is primarily significant in the growth of black education and culture in the United States, a topic treated in other volumes of this series, but for many years it also educated small groups of Indians. Founded as the Hampton Normal and Industrial Institute in 1868 by Gen. Samuel C. Armstrong, a white whose interest in black education was stimulated while leading a colored regiment during the Civil War, it became a model for the numerous black normal and industrial schools subsequently established. It also influenced Lt. Richard H. Pratt in his founding of Carlisle Indian School, Pa.

In 1878 a group of about 17 young Indians who had been released as prisoners of war from Fort Marion, Fla., began to attend Hampton, the only school that had responded to Pratt's appeal for their further education under Government auspices. That same year Pratt recruited 49 additional Indians in the West, including 9 girls. Indians attended the school until 1923, though the Government discontinued appropriations in 1912. Hampton's distinguished alumnus Booker T. Washington returned to his alma mater in 1879–81 as secretary to Armstrong, and among his duties in 1880 took charge of the Indian dormitory.

Numerous buildings on the campus date from the 19th century. Pertinent to Indian education is the Wigwam, erected in 1878 to house the students from Fort Marion. A museum in the Administration Building is devoted to Indian cultural displays, contributed mainly by ex-students.

The "Wigwam," Hampton Institute.

Gen. Patrick E. Connor, commander in Utah and the Civil War years.

... ... between the Ute Indi-
... ... and seven men
... ... Cedar Springs,
... Lake country, in
... ... were a band of Utes mas-
... ... them and burned them at
... activities in Utah until
... ended Lt. Edward G.
... ... to the Pacific. A

....

... in the growth of black
... ... a topic treated in
... ... years it also educated
... Hampton Normal and
... C. Armstrong, a
... ... stimulated while
... ... became a

r the numerous blck normal and industrial schools sub-
 established. It als nfluenced Lt. Richard H. Pratt in
ling of Carlisle Inian School, Pa.

3 a group of about/ young Indians who had been re-
prisoners of war frm Fort Marion, Fla., began to attend
i, the only school tht had responded to Pratt's appeal for
ther education uncr Government auspices. That same
t recruited 49 addicnal Indians in the West, including
ndians attended th school until 1923, though the Gov-
discontinued apprp iations in 1912. Hampton's distin-
lumnus Booker 7 Washington returned to his alma
1879-81 as secretar to Armstrong, and among his duties
ok charge of the Irlian dormitory.

ous buildings on th ampus date from the 19th century.
to Indian educatin is the Wigwam, erected in 1878 to
students frcm For Marion. A museum in the Adminis-
uilding is devotedt Indian cultural displays, contrib-
ly by ex-students.

wam," Hampton Inif ite.

Coulee Dam National Recreation Area, Washington ⊠

Location: Parts of Douglas, Ferry, Grant, Lincoln, Okano-
gan, and Stevens Counties, in the environs of Grand Cou-
lee Dam and Franklin D. Roosevelt Lake, in the northeast-
ern part of the State. The Fort Spokane site, focus of
historical interest, is located on Wash. 25, near the southern
shore of the Spokane River arm of Roosevelt Lake. Ad-
dress: P.O. Box 37, Coulee Dam, Wash. 99116.

The 660 miles of shoreline along Franklin D. Roosevelt Lake not
only provide extensive recreational facilities and a scenic wonderland, but also have considerable historical significance. Thirteen
Indian tribes, seminomadic hunters and fishers of Salishan stock
speaking the same language, originally inhabited the northeastern
part of present Washington. The first Europeans to penetrate the
region were fur trappers of the Canada-based North West Co.,
which between 1807 and 1821 monopolized fur trapping and the
Indian trade in the Columbia Basin. In 1821 the North West Co.
merged with the Hudson's Bay Co., which maintained the mo-
nopoly into the 1840's and 1850's—even after 1846, when Britain
recognized U.S. sovereignty over the area. In 1855–56 a minor
gold rush to the Colville River caused the Indians to begin a
series of retaliations, and U.S. settlers did not move into the
Columbia Basin until 1858, after the Army brought the Indians
under control.

In 1872 the U. S. Government created the Colville Indian Reservation and concentrated there several thousand members of 10
tribes inhabiting northeastern Washington—joined in 1885 by
some of the nontreaty Nez Perces returning to the Pacific Northwest from Indian Territory, where they had been confined after
their defeat in 1877. In 1881 the Army set up the Spokane Reservation, directly to the east of the southern part of the Colville Reservation.

The year before, though the reservation Indians were peaceful,
to quiet settlers' fears of further hostilities, Gen. Oliver O. Howard had activated Fort Spokane, on the south bank of the Spokane
River about a mile above its junction with the Columbia. Inactivated in 1899, its history was rather uneventful. It served as an
Indian school until 1914 and an Indian hospital until 1929.

Fort Spokane during its active years.

The National Park Service administers Coulee Dam National Recreation Area in cooperation with the Bureaus of Reclamation and Indian Affairs. The three buildings that are extant from Fort Spokane—the brick guardhouse, brick magazine, and large frame stables—have been restored. Ruins of the brick granary have been stabilized, and the foundations and sites of other buildings, all of which were frame, have been marked. The visitor center, in the guardhouse, interprets the history of the fort and region.

Fort Simcoe, Washington ⊗

Location: Yakima County, at the western terminus of Wash. 220, about 5 miles southwest of White Swan.

This short-lived fort (1856–59) was founded in south-central Washington at the end of the Yakima War (1855–56) to prevent any further uprisings of the Yakimas, command the central Washington trails, and prevent settlers from trespassing on Indian lands. Its major activity, apart from constructing and improving a road to Fort Dalles, Oreg., was participation in Col. George Wright's 1858 campaign against the eastern Washington tribes. Wright, operating out of Fort Walla Walla, Wash., conducted operations in the area east of the Columbia River; and Maj. Robert

347

okane during its active years.

National Park Service administers Coulee Dam National
tion Area in cooperation with the Bureaus of Reclamation
dian Affairs. The three buildings that are extant from Fort
e—the brick guardhouse, brick magazine, and large frame
—have been restored. Ruins of the brick granary have been
ed, and the foundations and sites of other buildings, all of
were frame, have been marked. The visitor center, in the
ouse, interprets the history of the fort and region.

mcoe, Washington ⊗

*Location: Yakima County, at the western terminus of Wash.
220, about 5 miles southwest of White Swan.*

iort-lived fort (1856–59) was founded in south-central
gton at the end of the Yakima War (1855–56) to prevent
her uprisings of the Yakimas, command the central Wash-
trails, and prevent settlers from trespassing on Indian
s major activity, apart from constructing and improving a
Fort Dalles, Org., was participation in C
s 1858 campaign against the   Was
operating out of brt Wall
in the area east of the C   J. B   47

S. Garnett from Fort Simcoe, in the area north and west. Garnett and his men, numbering 300, one of whom was a young lieutenant named George Crook, went into the field for 44 days. Covering 700 miles, rounding up some Indians, and executing 10 for killing miners, they took part in no major engagements.

When early the next year the Government opened the area east of the Cascades to settlement, the Army transferred the Fort Simcoe garrison to Fort Colville, Wash., turning over the vacated post to the Indian Bureau for use as the Fort Simcoe (Yakima) Agency. Under Rev. James H. Wilbur, an Episcopalian priest, it became a model for Indian administration in the Northwest. In 1922 it was moved to Toppenish. In 1953 the State leased the 140-acre Fort Simcoe tract from the Yakima Nation and began restoration.

Fort Simcoe State Park, in an attractive rural setting on the Yakima Reservation, contains five log and frame buildings: three one-story officers' quarters (1857–58), one of the four original blockhouses (1856), and the two-story commandant's house (1857–58). The latter, once also used by the Indian agency, represents an excellent example of Gothic Revival architecture in pioneer Washington and has been refurnished to the era of the 1860's. The park includes a museum.

Commandant's house, Fort Simcoe.

*Col. George Wright led
the forces that triumphed
in 1858 over the Indians
of eastern Washington.*

Fort Steilacoom, Washington ⊗

> *Location: Pierce County, on Steilacoom Boulevard, about
> 3 miles east of Steilacoom.*

This fort was activated in 1849 at the southern end of Puget
Sound, 6 miles from the original site of Fort Nisqually, the Hudson's Bay Co. farming center. The latter, which the Indians had
attacked earlier in the year, was the nucleus of settlement in the
area. During the Indian uprisings in western Washington in
1855–56 that culminated in an assault on Seattle, warriors attacked and almost captured the fort, the major operational base
during the uprisings. The Army abandoned it in 1868, and 6
years later Washington Territory gained possession of part of the
military reservation.

Western State Hospital, a psychiatric institution, now occupies
the site. Four of the officers' quarters have survived, serving today
as doctors' residences.

349

Fort Walla Walla, Washington ⊗

Location: Walla Walla County, on the Veterans' Administration Hospital grounds, southwestern part of Walla Walla.

Soldiers from this fort took part in most of the Indian wars of the Northwest: the 1858 campaign in eastern Washington, the Modoc War (1872–73), the Nez Perce War (1877), and the Bannock War (1878). First situated north of Mill Creek and in the spring of 1858 moved southward 1½ miles to its present location, Fort Walla Walla (1856–1911) was founded during a series of Indian outbreaks about 30 miles east of the Hudson's Bay Co. trading post of the same name. In 1855 most of the tribes of Washington had ceded the majority of their lands to the U.S. Government, retaining only enough for reservations. But the subsequent influx of miners and settlers inflamed them, as did reports of U.S. Government plans to construct a railroad from the Missouri River to the Columbia. The coastal tribes went on the warpath in 1855–56, attacking Seattle before being pacified. Some of the tribes of central Washington expressed their aggressions in the Yakima War (1855–56).

Fort Walla Walla in 1857, at its first location.
Drawing by Edward Del Girardin.

*Second Cavalry troops on parade in 1887 at Fort
Walla Walla.*

Two years later the Spokans, Coeur d'Alenes, and the Palouses
of eastern Washington, irritated by a trickle of miners moving to
the Colville mining district in 1855–56, began what is sometimes
called the Spokane, or Coeur d'Alene, War (1858) by defeating
Maj. Edward J. Steptoe's force from Fort Walla Walla near present Rosalia, Wash. Fort Walla Walla subsequently became Col.
George Wright's base, supported by Fort Simcoe. In September he
won major victories in the Battles of Four Lakes and Spokane
Plain, Wash. That same fall the opening of the Walla Walla Valley to settlement created new friction with the Indians, and the
garrison kept busy maintaining the peace. Beginning the next
year and until 1862, it also helped protect crews constructing the
Mullan Road.

Numerous historic buildings remain amid modern structures.
They are in excellent condition, though the Veterans' Administration has modified many of them. Rows of officers' quarters and
barracks run along opposite sides of the parade ground. To the
rear of the barracks are the stables. The post cemetery, where military burials from the Nez Perce War are consolidated, is within a
city park, immediately south of the hospital. The Daughters of

the American Revolution has placed a marker at the first site of the fort, on Main Street between First Avenue and Spokane Street.

Four Lakes Battlefield, Washington ⊗
Location: Spokane County, town of Four Lakes.

The clash at this site on September 1, 1858, marked the beginning of a running engagement that culminated 4 days later in the Battle of Spokane Plain. In these battles, Col. George Wright revenged the victory of the Spokans, Palouses, and Coeur d'Alenes of eastern Washington over Major Steptoe in May about 25 miles to the southeast of the Four Lakes Battlefield. Wright's 600 cavalry men and infantry men, equipped with the new 1855 long-range rifle-muskets, whipped an equal-sized Indian force, emboldened by its triumph over Steptoe. The troops, who did not have a single casualty, killed 60 Indians and wounded many others.

An arrow-shaped stone pyramid in the town of Four Lakes marks the site of the battle.

Spokane Plain Battlefield, Washington ⊗
Location: Spokane County, marker on U.S. 2, about 10 miles west of Spokane.

In the wake of the Battle of Four Lakes, the Battle of Spokane Plain was the last in Colonel Wright's 1858 campaign in eastern Washington. Ranging over 25 miles and testing the endurance of the participants, it resulted in another Army victory. After the battle, shrugging off peace overtures, Wright marched through Indian country singling out the fomentors of the war and destroying the horseherds. The Yakima chieftain Kamiakin again made good his escape. But, before returning to Fort Walla Walla, Wright hanged 15 war leaders and placed others in chains. Like the Rogue River Indians of Oregon, the tribes he campaigned against in 1858 never again tried to stem the flow of settlers by force of arms.

A large stone pyramid in a 1-acre State park commemorates the battle.

Gustav Sohon's drawing of the Battle of Spokane Plain.

Steptoe Battlefield, Washington ⊗

Location: Whitman County, on U.S. 195, about 1 mile southeast of Rosalia.

The 1858 campaign against the Indians of eastern Washington that culminated in Army victories in September in the Battles of Four Lakes and Spokane Plain began at this site. On May 18 about 1,000 Spokans, Coeur d'Alenes, and Palouses attacked Maj. Edward ɪ. Steptoe and his force of 164 men, who were investigating reported Indian depredations and seeking to awe the Indians on a march from Fort Walla Walla, Wash., to the Colville mining district. Severe fighting lasted all day. During the night, Steptoe broke contact and made a forced 85-mile march from the knoll on which he had taken refuge to the Snake River, where some friendly Nez Perces helped the troops cross and find safety on the other side.

The knoll is commemorated by a 4-acre State memorial park. It features a 25-foot granite shaft erected by the Daughters of the American Revolution, which deeded the site to the State. Listed on the shaft are the names of the soldiers who lost their lives and the Nez Perces who aided the retreating troops. The running battle took place in Pine Creek Valley for a distance of 4 miles upstream to the north from the knoll. Except for agricultural use,

353

*The 1858 Steptoe disaster, pictured here by Gustav
Sohon, spurred Army retaliation.*

the landscape is little altered. On the basis of a mistaken identification with Steptoe Butte, a natural landmark about 30 miles to the south, Steptoe Battlefield is sometimes incorrectly called Steptoe Butte Battlefield.

Tshimakain Mission, Washington ⊗

*Location: Stevens County, on Wash. 231, about 7 miles
northeast of Ford.*

In 1838 the interdenominational American Board of Commissioners for Foreign Missions sent a small group of reinforcements to join Dr. Marcus Whitman and Rev. Henry H. Spalding in the Oregon country. Part of the group were two Congregational ministers and their wives: Elkanah and Mary Walker and Cushing and Myra Eells. After spending the winter at Whitman Mission, Walker and Eells moved north in the spring of 1839, and at a site in a pleasant valley north of the Spokane River that the Spokan Indians called *Tshimakain* ("Place of the Springs") established a mission. About 25 miles northwest of the site of the city of Spokane, it was the farthest north of the American Board establish-

354

*Tshimakain Mission in 1853. Tinted lithograph
by John Mix Stanley.*

ments. Its nearest non-Indian neighbors were at the Hudson's Bay
Co. post of Fort Colville, 50 miles farther north. The missionaries
had only limited success with the Spokans. When the Cayuses attacked Whitman Mission in the fall of 1847, the Walkers and
Eellses fled to Fort Colville and in the spring of 1848 to the Willamette Valley. Tshimakain Mission never reopened.

No remains have survived, and a modern farmhouse occupies
the site. The spring that provided the missionaries with water still
flows through the farmyard. A State marker stands on the east side
of Wash. 231 directly in front of the site. The valley itself is virtually unchanged except for occasional fences.

Vancouver Barracks, Washington ⊗

> *Location: Clark County, east of the Vancouver Freeway,
> bounded on the south by East 5th Street and on the north
> by East Evergreen Boulevard, adjacent to Fort Vancouver
> National Historic Site, Vancouver.*

Known at various times as Camp Vancouver (1849–50), Columbia
Barracks (1850–53), Fort Vancouver (1853–79), and Vancouver

355

Barracks (1879–present), this base was a key military headquarters and supply depot through World War II. Strategically located about 100 miles up the Columbia River, it was the nerve center of the campaigns against the Indians in the Pacific Northwest, highlighted by those in the 1850's and the Nez Perce War (1877). A troop-marshaling point and major command post, it was the headquarters in 1850–51 of the 11th Military District and for most of the period 1866–1920 of the Department of the Columbia. During the Spanish-American War and World Wars I and II, it was a mobilization and training center. Famed officers who served there in the course of their careers include Ulysses S. Grant, Philip H. Sheridan, George Crook, Oliver O. Howard, Nelson A. Miles, and George C. Marshall.

Like the second Fort Kearny, Nebr. (1848), Fort Laramie, Wyo. (1849), and Cantonment Loring, Idaho (1849), the post was founded to protect the Oregon Trail. In 1849, some 3 years after the United States gained full title to the region south of the 49th parallel from Great Britain, the Regiment of Mounted Riflemen and troops who had come by sea around Cape Horn estab-

Gustav Sohon's tinted lithograph (1853) shows Vancouver Barracks on the hill at the left, and the Hudson's Bay Company post of Fort Vancouver on the right.

356

lished the fort adjacent to the Hudson's Bay Co. fur trading-agricultural post known as Fort Vancouver. From the time of its founding, at another nearby site, in 1824, the company post had been the economic, political, social, and cultural hub of the Oregon country and nucleus of U.S. settlement there, especially because of the aid extended to emigrants by Dr. John McLoughlin, chief factor during the years 1824–46.

Hudson's Bay Co. officials, hoping the Army's presence would reduce the pressure on its possessions exerted by U.S. settlers, welcomed the troops. In time, however, friction mounted between the Americans and the British, the fur trade declined, and the Hudson's Bay Co. landholdings and livestock dwindled. Finally, in 1860, the company evacuated the post and turned over the buildings and land to the U.S. Army. But within 6 years, fire destroyed all the buildings.

By 1946 the Vancouver Barracks Military Reservation consisted of 640 acres. In that year the Army inactivated it as a Regular post, but retained 64 acres for Reserve training. The city of Vancouver, the Washington National Guard, and the National Park Service acquired the rest of the reservation. The National Park Service's 98 acres, utilized for the establishment of Fort Vancou-

Headquarters building (1849), Vancouver Barracks.

357

ver National Historic Site, included the Vancouver Barracks parade ground and the site of the Hudson's Bay Co. post.

The structures at Vancouver Barracks are predominantly modern, but most of a row of 19th-century officers' quarters are still intact. Originally constructed of logs, they are all now clapboarded and painted white. In the center of the row, at 1106 East Evergreen Boulevard, stands an imposing two-story structure, probably erected in 1849. It was the headquarters building and the home of the commanding officer until 1887 and was then utilized for a number of years as an officers' mess. Owned by Vancouver School District #1, it houses the Ulysses S. Grant Museum, operated by the Soroptimist Club of Vancouver in recognition of Grant's tour of duty at the post as a young officer. Part of the clapboard has been removed to reveal the original log buildings, an excellent and well-preserved example of dovetailed-joint log construction. A short distance to the southeast, on the eastern end of the parade ground, is located the visitor center of Fort Vancouver National Historic Site. The national historic site commemorates the Hudson's Bay Co. post, part of which has been reconstructed southwest of the visitor center, but it also interprets the history of Vancouver Barracks.

Whitman Mission National Historic Site, Washington ⊠

Location: Walla Walla County, on a short connecting road leading south from U.S. 12, about 7 miles west of Walla Walla; address: Route 2, Walla Walla, Wash. 99362.

This national historic site preserves the remains of the Whitman, or Waiilatpu, Mission (1836–47), the second Protestant mission in the Oregon country. Enduring wilderness hardships and dangers, Dr. Marcus and Narcissa Whitman worked among the Cayuse Indians. In the 1840's their mission became a haven for Oregon Trail emigrants. The invasion of emigrant-settlers and Indian-missionary misunderstandings brought about the tragic death of the Whitmans at the hands of the Cayuses only 11 years after the founding of the mission.

Early in the 19th century, stirred by accounts of explorers and traders, missionaries began to turn their gaze toward the Oregon

Visitors at Whitman Mission National Historic Site view the Great Grave and monument to William H. Gray, also buried at the site. On the hilltop is the Whitman Memorial Shaft.

country. As early as the 1820's the interdenominational American Board of Commissioners for Foreign Missions began to consider a program there, but was discouraged by its remoteness. Finally, in 1835, spurred by reports that a Nez Perce and Flathead delegation had visited governmental officials at St. Louis seeking to learn of the white man's religion, the board sent the Reverend Samuel Parker and Dr. Marcus Whitman westward to investigate the possibilities. In Missouri the two men joined a fur caravan heading for the fur traders' rendezvous along Wyoming's Green River. Talks with the Flatheads and Nez Perces spawned an enthusiasm on the part of the two men for missionary work in the Northwest. Separating, Parker pushed on to Oregon, wintering at the Hudson's Bay Co. post of Fort Vancouver, Wash., and investigating mission sites before returning to the East by ship the next spring. Whitman immediately returned there to recruit missionaries.

In April 1836 Whitman's party set out from Liberty, Mo. It

consisted of himself; his recent bride, Narcissa; the Reverend Henry H. Spalding and his wife, Eliza; and the mechanic-carpenter William H. Gray. In May they overtook an American Fur Co. caravan near the junction of the Platte River and the Loup Fork, in Nebraska. Traveling via Fort Laramie, Wyo., and across South Pass, they arrived at the Green River Rendezvous in July. Escorted by two Hudson's Bay Co. traders, the party then set out on a long journey via Fort Hall to Fort Vancouver, where it arrived in September. The two wives were the first American women to travel across the continent.

The men soon retraced their steps up the Columbia River to choose mission sites, while the women enjoyed the hospitality of Chief Factor John McLoughlin. Whitman chose a spot in southeastern Washington on Mill Creek on the north bank of the Walla Walla River, 22 miles above its junction with the Columbia and the Hudson's Bay Co. post of Fort Walla Walla. The local Indians, the Cayuses, called the spot *Waiilatpu* ("Place of the Rye Grass"). Spalding chose a site 110 miles farther east, where he founded among the Nez Perce Indians what came to be known as the Spalding Mission, Idaho.

The next March Mrs. Whitman gave birth to a daughter, Alice Clarissa, the first American child born in the Pacific Northwest; 2 years later the child died in a tragic drowning accident. In 1838 missionary reinforcements arrived. Among them were the Reverends Elkanah Walker and Cushing Eells and their wives, who the next year founded the Tshimakain Mission about 135 miles to the north. That same year the Reverend Asa B. Smith established among the Nez Perces the Kamiah Mission, Idaho, about 50 miles up the Clearwater River from the Spalding Mission; he maintained the mission only 2 years, abandoning it because of disillusionment and a sick wife.

Meantime, construction of the Whitman Mission, informal headquarters of the mission field, had begun. In time it included a large adobe mission house; Gray's adobe residence, in later years a shelter for emigrants; a gristmill; a blacksmith shop; and a sawmill, 22 miles away. Yet, despite Whitman's energy and devotion, progress in educating and converting the Cayuses was slow. Rejecting his plea to become farmers, most of them continued their nomadic way of life. They were also less eager to learn than Whitman had anticipated and were indifferent to Christianity. Furthermore, he and the Indians were unable to understand each other's customs. In addition, he and all the missionaries at the other mission stations quarreled continually. Reports of this dissension and budgetary problems caused the American Board in 1842 to order that the Whitman and Spalding Missions be closed. It directed the Spaldings to return to the East, and the Whitmans to move to the Tshimakain Mission. The missionaries ignored these instructions. To plead their case before the board, Whitman returned to Boston in a harrowing winter journey in 1842–43. After listening to his arguments, the board rescinded its original orders.

On the return trip, at Independence, Mo., Whitman in May 1843 intercepted a huge wagon train of about 1,000 emigrants, the largest wagon train to that time on the Oregon Trail. As the expedition's physician and part-time guide, he accompanied it to his mission. There the members rested and replenished their supplies, as had another expedition the previous year. From then on, Waiilatpu was a major way station on the trail. Even though the main trail soon bypassed it, sick and destitute emigrants headed there and received kind and generous treatment.

After Whitman's return to Waiilatpu in 1843, relations among the missionaries improved somewhat. Those between the Indians and the missionaries, however, further deteriorated. The increasing numbers of emigrants frightened the Cayuses, who were aware that they were taking over Indian lands elsewhere and were bringing measles epidemics that decimated entire tribes. Whitman was also devoting more and more time to caring for emigrants and less to them. Anyway, they were rapidly losing faith in the missionaries. Their growing resentment was heightened in the autumn of 1847 when a measles epidemic spread from the wagon trains to their villages and within 2 months killed about half of them. Because Whitman was unable to check the epidemic, some of the Indians came to believe he was poisoning them to make way for settlers.

On November 29 a small group of Cayuses assaulted the mission, at the time sheltering 74 people, most of them emigrants. The attackers killed 13 people, including Marcus and Narcissa Whitman. A few of the survivors escaped. The Indians captured

49 people, mostly women and children. Two of the young girls died; and the next month Peter Skene Ogden, a Hudson's Bay Co. official, ransomed the rest. The massacre, which set off the Cayuse War (1848), temporarily ended Protestant missionary efforts in the Oregon country. In 1848 emissaries of Oregon's provisional legislature, which had been seeking Territorial status, carried news of the tragedy and petitions to Washington, D.C. Congress reacted by creating the Oregon Territory, the first one west of the Rockies.

Whitman Mission National Historic Site preserves the foundation ruins of the mission buildings and the restored irrigation ditch, millpond, and orchard. The Great Grave contains the remains of the 1847 massacre victims. A marble slab, placed over the grave in 1897 to commemorate the 50th anniversary of the massacre, is inscribed with their names. On a nearby hill stands a 27-foot-high memorial shaft, dedicated in 1897. The visitor center houses artifacts uncovered by archeologists and interprets the history of the mission and missionary efforts in the Oregon country.

Bighorn Canyon National Recreation Area, Wyoming-Montana ⊞

Location: Big Horn County, Wyo., and Big Horn and Carbon Counties, Mont., accessible via U.S. 14A or Mont. 313; address: P.O. Box 458YRS, Hardin, Mont. 59035.

Bighorn Canyon National Recreation Area, including the 71-mile-long Bighorn Lake Reservoir, created by the giant Yellowtail Dam, extends more than 40 miles through the spectacular Bighorn Canyon. Outstanding attractions are recreational facilities, spectacular wilderness scenery, geologic wonders, and varied wildlife. The recreation area's historical significance relates to the Bozeman Trail. Associated with the trail are the sites of Fort C. F. Smith and the Hayfield Fight, in the northeastern fringes of the recreation area, in Montana.

The Crow Indians, whose modern reservation partially surrounds the recreation area in Montana, were among the earliest residents of the area. Charles François Larocque, a French-Canadian trapper, encountered the tribe in 1805. The next year Capt.

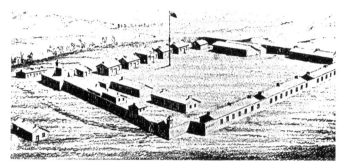

Fort C. F. Smith in 1867. Sketch by Capt. I. D'Isay
after Anton Schonborn's drawing.

William Clark passed by the mouth of the Bighorn River, and fur traders followed him.

The Army activated Fort C. F. Smith, Mont. (1866–68), at the upper Bighorn Crossing of the Bozeman Trail, as the northernmost of three forts protecting travelers en route to Montana goldfields from Sioux and Cheyenne attacks. Red Cloud's warriors kept it and Forts Phil Kearny and Reno, Wyo., under continual siege for 2 years.

Indicative of the heat of the conflict was the Hayfield Fight. Early in the summer of 1867 the Sioux and Cheyennes agreed to a joint effort to wipe out Forts Phil Kearny and C. F. Smith, but a disagreement divided their formidable numbers into two factions, each to attack the fort of its choice. On August 1, 1867, one faction, made up of 500 to 1,000 Cheyennes and Sioux, fell upon a detail of a lieutenant, 19 soldiers, and six civilians working in a hayfield 2½ miles from Fort C. F. Smith. Taking refuge in a log and brush corral, the intended victims withstood the attack all day long. When Lt. Sigismund Sternberg lost his life, one of the civilians, Al Colvin, who had been an officer during the Civil War, assumed command. The Indians, launching fierce assaults, suffered heavy casualties, but even fire arrows failed to dislodge the defenders. The Indians withdrew late in the afternoon, having killed three whites and wounded four. The next day, the other faction—Sioux led by Red Cloud—clashed with Fort Phil Kearny troops in the Wagon Box Fight.

When the garrisons of the three Bozeman Trail forts withdrew in 1868, in accordance with the Fort Laramie Treaty, the Indians burned all the posts. In time, the Indians in the Bighorn region were pacified and confined to reservations. As the gold fever subsided, ranchers moved into the area.

Bighorn Canyon National Recreation Area, established in 1966, is administered by the National Park Service through agreement with the Bureau of Reclamation. Mounds of earth tracing the foundations of the log and adobe buildings are all that remain of Fort C. F. Smith. A stone monument, erected by a local historical society, is located near the fort site, which is not impaired by any modern intrusions of consequence. Another stone marker stands at the nearby site of the Hayfield Fight. Wagon ruts from the Bozeman Trail, which forded the Bighorn River about 2 miles below the modern dam, are visible on both sides of the stream, especially the western side. A visitor center near the dam features historical displays and audiovisual programs showing construction of the dam.

Dull Knife Battlefield, Wyoming ⊗

Location: Johnson County, just off an unimproved road, about 23 miles west of Kaycee. Make local inquiry.

At this site on the Red Fork of the Powder River in the winter of 1876 the Army defeated Dull Knife and his Cheyennes, who had helped whip Custer the previous summer. Beginning the retaliatory campaigns, Crook marched from Fort Fetterman back into the Powder River country. At dawn on November 25, 1876, Col. Ranald S. Mackenzie's 4th Cavalry surprised Dull Knife's winter camp. Indian casualties were light, 25 deaths, but the troops destroyed the bulk of the Indians' shelter, food, and clothing. Most of the survivors, recognizing the futility of holding out any longer, surrendered in the spring at Fort Robinson, Nebr., along with Crazy Horse and his people.

The battlefield, in a picturesque setting among rugged hills on a privately owned ranch, is marked by a stone monument, on the side of a hill. A ranch headquarters at the upper end of the canyon and a hay meadow downstream do not appreciably alter the natural scene.

Fort Bridger, Wyoming ⊗

Location: Uinta County, just south of I–80, adjacent to the town of Fort Bridger.

This fort's rich history spans practically all phases of western development except the fur trade. The first Fort Bridger was a mud and pole trading post, founded in 1842 or 1843 on Black's Fork of the Green River by the mountain man Jim Bridger and his partner, Luis Vásquez, to trade with Indians and emigrants. A significant landmark on the Oregon-California Trail, it was the second major stopping place on one of the two major routes west of Fort Laramie, Wyo., and second only to it as a supply point. In 1853 a group of Mormons, who earlier in the year has set up a rival post, Fort Supply, 12 miles to the south, bought or forced Bridger out. At his post they erected several stone houses within a huge stone wall. In 1857, just before U.S. troops arrived en route to the Utah, or Mormon, War (1857–58), the Mormons put the torch to Forts Bridger and Supply. The troops wintered nearby at a temporary camp of mud and skin lean-tos. In the spring the bulk of them proceeded to Salt Lake City, but some remained to begin rebuilding a permanent fort of log and stone.

During the Civil War, the garrison dwindled in numbers, but Regular troops returned in 1866. A base of operations for southwestern Wyoming and northeastern Utah, the post guarded stage routes and the transcontinental telegraph line, accommodated a Pony Express station, patrolled emigrant trails, took action against Indian raids, guarded the miners who moved into the South Pass and Sweetwater region, and protected and supplied workers building the Union Pacific Railroad not far to the north. Treaties were signed at the fort with the friendly Shoshonis in 1863 and 1868, the second creating a reservation east of the Wind River Mountains. Although strategically located, the fort never served as a base for any of the major military expeditions of the 1870's against the Indians in the region, but some of the garrison was reassigned for fighting purposes. Temporarily abandoned in 1878, reactivated in 1880, the post was finally evacuated in 1890.

Acquired in 1928 by the State and today a State historical park, the site contains a group of well-preserved and maintained struc-

Jim Bridger, ex-mountain man, founded the trading post in southwestern Wyoming that was the predecessor of the Army's Fort Bridger.

*Fort Bridger in 1889, the year before
the last troops left.*

tures, amid a heavy overgrowth of vegetation and trees. Some restoration has been accomplished, and the State has extensive developmental plans. The 1884 barracks building has been completely reconstructed and houses a museum. Crumbling ruins of the commissary building and the old guardhouse, both built in 1858, are visible. In better condition are the new guardhouse (1884), sentry box (1858), officers' quarters (1858), sutler's store, Pony Express stables, post office, a group of lesser buildings, and a portion of the wall constructed by the Mormons. The foundations of other buildings are marked. Interred in the cemetery are Bridger's daughter and Judge W. A. Carter, pioneer rancher in the area. Portions of the original fort grounds and some buildings are located on privately owned property outside the State-owned area.

Fort Casper and Platte Bridge Fight Site, Wyoming ⊗
Location: Natrona County, Casper and vicinity.

The predecessor of Fort Casper (1865–67) was Platte Bridge Station, established in 1858 as one of a series of fortified stations on the Oregon-California Trail. Located on the south side of the North Platte River at a crossing point and emigrant campground, the Platte Bridge post protected wagon trains, mail stages, and the supply-communication lines of the Mormon Expedition to Utah

367

*Fort Casper and Platte Bridge. Artist and date
of lithograph unknown.*

(1857–58). Adjacent to the fort, at a place known as Mormon
Ferry, emigrants crossed the river by ferry, operated by some Mormons in the years 1847–50 and thereafter by a private company.
Regular troops abandoned the station in 1859, the same year a
1,000-foot toll bridge was completed across the river. This bridge
supplemented one a few miles to the east, built in 1853.

In 1862, during the Civil War, to counter increased Indian hos-
tilities along the Oregon-California Trail and to guard the telegraph lines, Volunteers reoccupied Platte Bridge Station. The
Indian threat reached a peak in the summer of 1865, when 3,000
Sioux, Cheyennes, and Arapahos descended on the trail from the
Powder River country. On July 26, on the north side of the
North Platte River, they ambushed a detachment of Kansas cavalry under Lt. Caspar W. Collins riding out from Platte Bridge
Station to escort an eastward-bound Army wagon train, guarded
by Sgt. Amos J. Custard and 24 men. The troops managed to fight
their way back to the bridge, but Collins and four men lost their
lives. The Indians then attacked the wagon train, killing Custard
and 19 other soldiers. Through an error, the Army renamed
Platte Bridge Station as Fort Casper, the spelling adopted by the
city that grew up adjacent to it. Troops enlarged and rebuilt the
fort in 1866, but the following year evacuated it and moved to
Fort Fetterman, Wyo. Almost immediately the Indians burned
the buildings and the bridge.

A replica of Fort Casper at the southwestern edge of Casper marks the site of the original log fort. Constructed in the 1930's, it is owned by the city and administered by the Fort Caspar Commission. The Fort Casper Museum, West 13th Street, interprets the history of the fort and station, including the ambush and the attack on the wagon train.

Fort D. A. Russell, Wyoming ⊗

Location: Laramie County, at the end of Randall Avenue, Francis E. Warren Air Force Base, Cheyenne. The main gate of the Air Force base is about 1 mile northwest of the State Capitol.

A prominent Army installation from the time of the Indian wars through World War II, this post is today the jet-age Francis E. Warren Air Force Base. Its history has always been closely related to that of Cheyenne, the State capital. The base and an associated quartermaster depot known as Camp Carlin (1867–88) were founded in 1867 to protect crews constructing the Union Pacific Railroad, railroad property, and lines of travel to Denver and

With the passage of time, frontier troops enjoyed more of the amenities. Squadroom at Fort D. A. Russell in the 1880's.

369

*Fort Casper and Platte Bridge. Artist and dat.
of lithograph unknown.*

(1857–58). Adjacent to the fort, at a pice known as Mormon Ferry, emigrants crossed the river by ferry operated by some Mormons in the years 1847–50 and thereaft by a private company. Regular troops abandoned the station u 1859, the same year a 1,000-foot toll bridge was completed acr¤ the river. This bridge supplemented one a few miles to the east, uilt in 1853.

In 1862, during the Civil War, to cou er increased Indian hostilities along the Oregon-California Tr i and to guard the telegraph lines. Volunteers reoccupied Pl te Bridge Station. The Indian threat reached a peak in the su mer of 1865, when 3,000 Sioux, Cheyennes, and Arapahos descer ed on the trail from the Powder River country. On July 26, ᵢ the nort h side of the North Platte River, they ambushed a ltachment of Kansas cavalry under Lt. Caspar W. Collins ridi ᵢ out from Platte Bridge Station to escort an eastward-bound Army wagon train, guarded by Sgt. Amos J. Custard and 24 men. 1b troops managed to fight their way back to the bridge, but Coll s and four men lost their lives. The Indians then attacked the w 9on train, killing Custard and 19 other soldiers. Through an rot, the Army renamed Platte Bridge Station as Fort Casper, th spelling adopted by the city that grew up adjacent to it. Troop nlarged and rebuilt the fort in 1866, but the following year cuated it and moved to Fort Fetterman, Wyo. Almost immediately the Indians burned the buildings and the bridge.

A replica of Fort Caspr at the southwestern edge of Casper marks the site of the origir l log fort. Constructed in the 1930's, it is owned by the city and administered by the Fort Caspar Commission. The Fort Caspe Museum, West 13th Street, interprets the history of the fort and station, including the ambush and the attack on the wagon train

Fort D. A. Russell, Wyoming ⊗

Location: Laramie County, at the end of Randall Avenue, Francis E Warn Air Force Base. Cheyenne. The main gate of the Air b ce base is about 1 mile northwest of the State Capitol.

A prominent Army installat on from the time of the Indian wars through World War II, the post is today the jet-age Francis E. Warren Air Force Base. Its history has always been closely related to that of Cheyenne, the state capital. The base and an associated quartermaster depot known as Camp Carlin (1867–88) were founded in 1867 to protect crews constructing the Union Pacific Railroad, railroad property and lines of travel to Denver and

With the passage of time, frontier troops enjoyed more of the amenities. Squar om at Fort D. A. Russell in the 1880's.

*Fort Casper and Platte Bridge. Artist and date
of lithograph unknown.*

(1857–58). Adjacent to the fort, at a ace known as Mormon Ferry, emigrants crossed the river by fer operated by some Mormons in the years 1847–50 and thereaf e by a private company. Regular troops abandoned the station i 1859, the same year a 1,000-foot toll bridge was completed acss the river. This bridge supplemented one a few miles to the eas built in 1853.

In 1862, during the Civil War, to co er increased Indian hostilities along the Oregon-California Tl and to guard the telegraph lines. Volunteers reoccupied Platte Bridge Station. The Indian threat reached a peak in the summer of 1865, when 3,000 Sioux, Cheyennes, and Arapahos desce ied on the trail from the Powder River country. On July 26, o the north side of the North Platte River, they ambushed a etachment of Kansas cavalry under Lt. Caspar W. Collins rid g out from Platte Bridge Station to escort an eastward-bound my wagon train, guarded by Sgt. Amos J. Custard and 24 men. Te troops managed to fight their way back to the bridge, but Collis and four men lost their lives. The Indians then attacked the wgon train, killing Custard and 19 other soldiers. Through an ror, the Army renamed Platte Bridge Station as Fort Casper, e spelling adopted by the city that grew up adjacent to it. Troc p enlarged and rebuilt fort in 1866, but the following year acuated it and Fort Fetterman, Wyo. Almost immetely the the buildings and the bridge.

368

A replica of Fort Casper at the southwestern edge of
marks the site of the original log fort. Constructed in the 1936, s
is owned by the city and administered by the Fort Caspe
mission. The Fort Caspe Museum, West 13th Street, _____
the history of the fort an station, including the ambush and
attack on the wagon train

Fort D. A. Russell, Wyming ⊗

Location: Larani County, at the end of Randall A__
Francis E. Warr. Air Force Base, Cheyenne. The
gate of the Air orce base is about 1 mile northeast of ___
State Capitol.

A prominent Army installtion from the time of the Indian war
through World War II, is post is today the jet-age Francis I
Warren Air Force Base. I history has always been closely relate
to that of Cheyenne, the tate capital. The base and an associate
quartermaster depot known as Camp Carlin (1867-88, was
founded in 1867 to protet crews constructing the Union Pacific
Railroad, railroad propey, and lines of travel to Denver and

With the passage of time, fro.ier troops enjoyed
more of the amenities. Squaroom at Fort D. A.
Russell in the 1880's.

Laramie. Cheyenne soon grew up as a railroad division point a short distance to the southeast.

The strategically situated fort and camp provided extensive logistical support to the major Indian campaigns on the northern Plains in the late 1860's and 1870's; and operated mule and pack trains as far west as Fort Douglas, Utah, and Fort Hall, Idaho. Renamed Fort Francis E. Warren in 1929, the fort remained an important training center through World War II and since 1948 has been an Air Force base.

Visitors may obtain passes to visit the historic area. A large number of brick buildings, which in the 1880's replaced the frame and adobe structures, are extant among modern structures and most of them are still in use. They include the hospital, administration building, commanding officer's house, and several officers' quarters. One of the latter was the residence of Brig. Gen. John J. Pershing when he served at the fort in 1912. A plaque on a boulder marks the old main gate, at the end of Randall Avenue near the unusual diamond-shaped parade ground. The site of Camp Carlin, of which no remains are extant but which is marked by a granite monument, is located on First Street near the railroad crossing.

Fort Fetterman, Wyoming ⊗

Location: Converse County, on the Orpha Cutoff, accessible via I-25, about 11 miles northwest of Douglas.

Figuring notably in the campaigns of the late 1860's and 1870's against the northern Plains tribes, this fort was founded in the summer of 1867 on the Bozeman Trail about 80 miles northwest of Fort Laramie. Along the south bank of the North Platte River, the post was an intermediate base between Fort Laramie and Forts Reno, Phil Kearny, and C. F. Smith. The latter three forts had been established the previous summer to guard the trail but had been under continual siege. By the time Fort Fetterman was activated, the Sioux and Cheyennes had halted traffic over the trail. When the Government, as a concession to the Indians, abandoned the three forts in the summer of 1868, isolated Fort Fetterman assumed major importance as a supply base, headquarters, and marshaling point for expeditions into the hostile Powder River country. The post also protected the nearby routes of the Union Pacific Railroad and the Oregon-California Trail.

Fort Fetterman was the base for General Crook's three expeditions in 1876 into the Powder River area: in March, culminating in the Battle of Powder River, Mont.; in May-June, ending in the Battle of the Rosebud, Mont.; and in November, highlighted by the defeat of Dull Knife's Cheyennes along the Powder River. The latter expedition, combined with others in 1876–77, ended the major phase of Army-Indian conflict on the northern Plains. The Indians confined to reservations, Fort Fetterman was abandoned in 1882. But "Fetterman City," a wild town that was the prototype for "Drybone" in Owen Wister's western novels, grew up at the fort, an outfitting point for wagon trains. In 1886, however, when Douglas replaced "Fetterman City," most of the fort buildings were sold, dismantled, and moved to other locations.

Part of the site is in private ownership, but since 1962 the State has owned most of it and is developing a State historical park. Prior to 1962, vandals had caused much damage. The State has restored the two remaining original buildings: a log and adobe duplex officers' quarters, today housing a small museum, open in the summer, and caretaker's quarters; and a rammed-earth ordnance warehouse. Foundations of other buildings may be viewed. The setting is unchanged except for agricultural operations. Ruts, apparently from the Bozeman Trail, are visible in the vicinity.

Fort Fred Steele, Wyoming ⊗

Location: Carbon County, about 2 miles north of I-80 and 15 miles east of Rawlins, in the community of Fort Fred Steele.

Like Forts Bridger, Sanders, and D. A. Russell, Wyo., Fort Fred Steele protected workers building the Union Pacific Railroad through Indian country. The fort also partially filled the void created north of the North Platte River by the abandonment of Forts Phil Kearny, Reno, and C. F. Smith in the summer of 1868. Col. Richard I. Dodge's command founded Fort Fred Steele that

371

same summer on the west bank of the North Platte River just opposite a new trestle bridge. Once the construction crews moved
westward, the troops forwarded rail supplies and guarded part of
the Wyoming stretch of track, maintained law and order among
the settlers, chased cattle rustlers and outlaws, watched over the
nearby Oregon-California Trail, and supported military operations against the Indians in the region.

The fort figured prominently in the Ute uprising of 1879 in
Colorado, when Indians at the White River Agency went on a
rampage. In response to Agent Nathan C. Meeker's request for
aid, Maj. Thomas T. Thornburgh organized an expedition from
Fort Fred Steele but met disaster in the Battle of Milk Creek,
Colo. A relief expedition under Col. Wesley Merritt proceeded
from Fort D. A. Russell via Fort Fred Steele to the White River
Agency to put down the rebellion and remained over the winter.
In January 1880 General Crook used the fort to direct logistical
support of the operations at the agency. After its abandonment in
1886, local residents occupied it.

Ownership of the site is divided among the Union Pacific Railroad, whose tracks traverse the central part of the site atop a high
earth grade, and various private individuals. Existing buildings
are in fair condition despite weathering, neglect, vandalization,

*Fort Fred Steele was one of the posts founded to
guard crews constructing the Union Pacific Railroad.
The railroad station is pictured here in 1886, the
same year the fort was abandoned and long
after the railroad had moved west.*

and in numerous instances postmilitary occupation. They include the commanding officer's quarters, two large warehouses, barracks, stone powder magazine, and some smaller structures. Foundations and earth mounds mark the location of other structures. Soldier grave markers are extant in the cemetery, on a small hillock overlooking the fort site, though the Army has relocated the bodies. Civilian burials date from 1868.

Fort Laramie National Historic Site, Wyoming ☒

Location: Goshen County, on a county road off U.S. 26, about 3 miles southwest of the town of Fort Laramie; address: Fort Laramie, Wyo. 82212.

Fort Laramie, situated amid the rolling prairie of eastern Wyoming near where the Laramie River blends into the North Platte, was of outstanding significance in the history of the Rocky Mountain region and the West. From 1834 until 1890, it was a center of trade, supply-transportation, warfare, and diplomacy on the northern Plains. Its long and varied history epitomizes the successive stages by which Americans conquered and settled the immense territory stretching from the Missouri River to the Pacific. Through its gates passed trappers, traders, mountain men, overland emigrants, missionaries, adventurers, explorers, homesteaders, Mormons, forty-niners, and soldiers.

Frederick Piercy's sketch of Fort Laramie in 1853.

373

Fort Laramie in 1876, at time of maximum occupation.

Located in the buffalo country of the Sioux, during the period 1834–49 the fort was a major fur trading post and Indian-trader rendezvous. In the years 1834–41, it was also known as Fort William and Fort Lucien, a log stockade; and in 1841–49 as Fort John, an adobe, walled fort. From the 1840's until 1869, when completion of the Union Pacific Railroad augured the end of the covered wagon migrations, Fort Laramie was a key landmark and stopping point on the Oregon-California Trail; a division point on transcontinental stage and mail routes; a base for civil and Army freighters; and for a time a Pony Express relay station. As a military post during the period 1849–90, it protected emigrants and was closely associated with some of the treaties and many of the campaigns designed to pacify the northern Plains tribes. Its role in the fur trade, transportation-communications, and the overland migrations will be treated in detail in the appropriate volumes of this series. The following discussion is limited to the last phase of the fort's history.

One of the largest posts in the West, Fort Laramie was active longer than most. Its strategic location made it an effective command headquarters and logistical-transport center for the many forts farther West and the troops that funneled in to man them or participate in the various campaigns. The fort originated as one of the first three posts founded by the Regiment of Mounted Riflemen to guard the Oregon-California Trail, the other two being the second Fort Kearny, Nebr. (1848–71), and Cantonment Loring, Idaho (1849–50). The increase in travel over the trail had demonstrated the need for military bases to serve as supply centers and provide protection from the Indians, who were venting their alarm over the stream of westbound caravans and the disappearance of grass and game from the vicinity of the trail by occasionally raiding wagon trains. As soon as the Mounted Riflemen purchased Fort Laramie from the American Fur Co. in 1849, the garrison inaugurated a building program, temporarily utilizing the existing adobe post. Within a decade, Fort Laramie became a sprawling military installation.

For the first half of that decade the Indians were relatively quiet, particularly after the Fort Laramie Treaty (1851), comparable to the Fort Atkinson Treaty (1853) with the southern Plains tribes. In the summer of 1851 one of the largest assemblages of Indians in the history of the West gathered around Fort Laramie—9,000 Sioux, Cheyennes, Arapahos, and Crows. Because of the better forage along Horse Creek, 35 miles to the east, the councils were held there. The Indians, in exchange for annuities, agreed not to raid the Oregon-California Trail or to war with one another and promised to permit the construction of military posts and roads. .

An incident in the summer of 1854 shattered the comparative peace and marked the beginning of 3½ decades of warfare between the Plains Indians and the Army. Not far from Fort Laramie, the Sioux reacted to the rashness of Lt. John L. Grattan, trying to arrest one of them for a minor offense, by annihilating his detachment and going on the warpath. Although seriously undermanned, the fort was not attacked by the Sioux and allied Cheyennes, who focused on stagelines and emigrant trains.

The tempo of assaults accelerated during the Civil War, when the fort's Regular garrison was withdrawn and the men available sometimes numbered less than 100. In the years 1864–67 the post commander maintained a small stockaded subpost, Fort Mitchell (Camp Shuman), Nebr., about 50 miles down the North Platte River just above Scotts Bluff. In the first half of 1865 the Sioux and Cheyennes launched a string of attacks on the Oregon-California Trail northwest of Fort Laramie.

The decade following the Civil War was a critical one. The campaigns of Generals Sibley and Sully in the years 1863–65 had inflamed the Sioux, Cheyennes, and Arapahos west of the Missouri

Fort Laramie in 1876, at time of maximum occupation.

Located in the buffalo country of the Sioux, during the period
1834–49 the fort was a major fur trading post and Indian-trader
rendezvous. In the years 1834–41, it was also known as Fort William and Fort Lucien, a log stockade; and in 1841–49 as Fort
John, an adobe, walled fort. From the 1840's until 1869, when
completion of the Union Pacific Railroad augured the end of the
covered wagon migrations, Fort Laramie was a key landmark and
stopping point on the Oregon-California Trail; a division point
on transcontinental stage and mail routes; a base for civil and
Army freighters; and for a time a Pony Express relay station. As a
military post during the period 1849–0, it protected emigrants
and was closely associated with some of the treaties and many of
the campaigns designed to pacify the northern Plains tribes. Its
role in the fur trade, transportation communications, and the
overland migrations will be treated in detail in the appropriate
volumes of this series. The following discussion is limited to the
last phase of the fort's history.

One of the largest posts in the West, Fort Laramie was active
longer than most. Its strategic location made it an effective command headquarters and logistical-transport center for the many
forts farther West and the troops that funneled in to man them or
participate in the various campaigns. The fort originated as one
of the first three posts founded by the Regiment of Mounted Riflemen to guard the Oregon-California Trail, the other two being
the second Fort Kearny, Nebr. (1848–1), and Cantonment Loring, Idaho (1849–50). The increase in travel over the

demonstrated the need for military bases to serve as [...] and provide protection from the Indians, who were in alarm over the stream of westbound caravans and [...] ance of grass and game from the vicinity of the trails [...] raiding wagon trains. As soon as the Mounted Riflemen [...] Fort Laramie from the American Fur Co. in 1849 [...] inaugurated a building program, temporarily utilizing [...] adobe post. Within a decade, Fort Laramie became a [...] military installation.

For the first half of the decade the Indians were [...] quiet, particularly after the Fort Laramie Treaty [...] rable to the Fort Atkinson Treaty (1853) with the [...] Plains tribes. In the summer of 1851 one of the largest [...] of Indians in the history of the West gathered around [...] mie—9,000 Sioux, Cheyenes, Arapahos, and Crows [...] the better forage along Horse Creek, 35 miles to the [...] councils were held there. The Indians, in exchange f [...] agreed not to raid the Oregon-California Trail or to war [...] another and promised to permit the construction of [...] and roads.

An incident in the summer of 1854 shattered the [...] peace and marked the beginning of 3½ decades of war [...] tween the Plains Indians and the Army. Not far from F[...] mie, the Sioux reacted to the rashness of Lt. John L. Gra[...] ing to arrest one of them for a minor offense, by annihilat[...] detachment and going on the warpath. Although seriously [...] manned, the fort was not attacked by the Sioux and allied [...] ennes, who focused on stagelines and emigrant trains.

The tempo of assaults accelerated during the Civil War w[...] the fort's Regular garrison was withdrawn and the men and [...] sometimes numbered less than 100. In the years 1864-67 t[...] commander maintained a small stockaded subpost, Fort M[...] (Camp Shuman), Nebr., about 50 miles down the North [...] River just above Scotts Bluff. In the first half of 1865 th[...] and Cheyennes launched a string of attacks on the Ore[...] fornia Trail northwest of Fort Laramie.

River. Further aggravating them, in the summer of 1865 Brig. Gen. Patrick E. Connor led a 2,600-man force in three columns from Fort Laramie and Omaha into the Powder River country of Wyoming, partly in an attempt to still the public clamor for better protection of the Bozeman Trail. The Powder River Expedition marched long distances and endured many hardships. On the headwaters of the Tongue River one of the columns surprised and wiped out an Arapaho village. Otherwise, because of lack of coordination between the columns, the campaign failed dismally. By annoying but not intimidating the Indians, it aroused them to strike back.

The Bozeman Trail proved a tempting target, on which the Oglala Red Cloud and his allies intensified their assaults. In the summer of 1866 Red Cloud stormed out of a conference at Fort Laramie concerning use of the trail when troops marched in on their way to build a chain of protecting forts. Devastation followed in the region for 2 years, during which time Fort Laramie provided logistical and personnel support to the beleaguered Bozeman Trail forts of Phil Kearny, Reno, and C. F. Smith; and dispatched a relief expedition to Fort Phil Kearny after the Feterman Disaster (December 1866).

The Fort Laramie Treaty (1868) ended hostilities for a time. Actually a series of generally similar but separate treaties with the

The Fort Laramie post trader's store, hub of social and business activity, about 1875.

northern Plains tribes, it was negotiated by the same Peace Commission that the previous October had concluded the Medicine Lodge Peace Treaties with the southern Plains Indians. Various northern Indian groups signed the treaty at Fort Laramie in April and May 1868, and those of the upper Missouri at Fort Rice, N. Dak., in July. But, frustrating the commissioners, Red Cloud did not sign until November, the month following the commission's disbandment, by which time the treaty's provisions had already been put into effect.

In the Fort Laramie treaties the U.S. Government and the northern Plains tribes declared peace. In the treaty with the Sioux the Government bowed to the demands of Red Cloud and other chiefs and agreed to close to white occupation and travel the Bozeman Trail region and the rest of an area designated for an indefinite period as "unceded Indian Territory." This territory embraced the area north of the North Platte River, east of the summits of the Bighorn Mountains, and in effect extending as far north as the Yellowstone River. The United States also granted the Sioux hunting privileges for an unspecified time in the region along the Republican Fork of the Smoky Hill River, in the lands north of the North Platte River, and in essence reaching northward to the Yellowstone River. In the hunting grounds the Sioux agreed not to obstruct white settlement, railroad construction, travel, or military operations.

Finally, the Government created for exclusive Sioux use in perpetuity the Great Sioux Reservation, roughly the western half of South Dakota beyond the Missouri River; and agreed to provide varied medical, educational, agricultural, and other facilities, as well as annuities and food. Relinquishing all claims to lands outside the Great Sioux Reservation, the Sioux agreed in time to settle down on it and live by agriculture rather than by hunting. The treaties with the Northern Cheyennes, Crows, and Northern Arapahos created reservations for each tribe or allowed its members to utilize existing reservations; and specified hunting grounds.

On the southern Plains the tribes initiated hostilities within a year of their signing the treaties of Medicine Lodge, but the Fort Laramie treaties brought for a time a considerable degree of peace on the northern Plains. It lasted until the 1875–76 mining inva-

377

Fort Laramie today. "Old Bedlam" dominates the scene.

sion of the Black Hills, in the Great Sioux Reservation, infuriated the Sioux and Cheyennes and set off a war that lasted until 1877. During the Black Hills rush, hundreds of prospectors en route to the goldfields stopped at Fort Laramie, for a time a station on the Deadwood-Cheyenne stageline. In the extensive campaigns of 1876–77 the fort was a major base.

During the 1870's and 1880's ranchers began occupying the surrounding country and the post's mission changed. The garrison, helping to maintain law and order, apprehended cattle rustlers and highwaymen and escorted stages. Appropriately enough, the same year Fort Laramie was inactivated, 1890, the Census Bureau noted the passing of the frontier and the Army smashed the last Indian hopes for freedom in the Battle of Wounded Knee, S. Dak.

Fort Laramie National Historic Site preserves the surviving features of the military fort, and carries out restoration and archeological programs. The remains of 21 buildings and ruins may be seen. Some of the buildings have been restored or partially restored and many are furnished in the styles of different periods in the fort's history. Interpretive markers tell the story of extant buildings or foundations and indicate the sites of others.

The most historic building is the frame officers' quarters known as "Old Bedlam" (1849), which has been restored in its entirety, including the kitchen wings. The first military structure and the oldest standing military building in Wyoming, it was the scene of many gala affairs and long the administrative and social center of the post. Also significant is the post trader's store. It consists of adobe, stone, and lime-concrete sections, built between 1849 and 1883, and served at various times as a store, sutler's office, post office, officers' club, and enlisted men's bar. Other especially interesting structures are the lime-concrete lieutenant colonel's quarters (1884), two frame double officers' quarters (1870 and 1875), and the stone guardhouse (1866).

No remains have survived of Fort Laramie's subpost, Fort Mitchell, Nebr., but a marker is located on the west side of a secondary road about 1 mile south of Nebr. 92 some 3 miles northwest of the headquarters of Scotts Bluff National Monument, Nebr., and outside its boundaries. The actual site is on the east side of the road about where a ranchhouse now stands.

Archeological excavation has revealed the site of the Fort John fur post, but not that of the earlier Fort William.

Fort Phil Kearny and Related Sites, Wyoming ⚠

Location: Johnson and Sheridan Counties. The fort site and those of the Fetterman Disaster and Wagon Box Fight lie within a few miles of one another just off I-90 in the vicinity of Story. The fort and Wagon Box sites are located on secondary roads, and the Fetterman Disaster site is on U.S. 87. Follow road markers.

The tragic events associated with Fort Phil Kearny, the Fetterman Disaster, and the Wagon Box Fight form one of the most dramatic chapters in the history of the Indian wars: the bloody 2 years of warfare in 1866–68 sparked by bitter Sioux opposition to the invasion of their hunting grounds by prospectors bound over the Bozeman Trail to the Montana goldfields. In one of the few instances during the Indian wars when the Army was forced to abandon a region it had occupied, the Sioux triumphed and the forts were evacuated. But the conflict foreshadowed the final dis-

1884), two frame double officers' quarters (1870 and 1875), the stone guardhous 1866

remains have survived of Fort Laramie's subpost, Fort Mitchell, Nebr. It is located on the west side of a secondary road about 1 mile south of Nebr. 92 some 3 miles north of the headquarters of Scotts Bluff National Monument, and outside its boundaries. The actual site is on the east the road about which a ranchhouse now stands.

Archeological excavation has revealed the site of the Fort John but, but not that of the earlier Fort William.

Phil Kearny and Associated Sites, Wyoming ⚠

Location: Johnson and Sheridan Counties. The fort site and those of the Fetterman Disaster and Wagon Box Fight lie within a few miles of one another just off I-90 in the vicinity of Story. The fort and Wagon Box sites are located on secondary road, and the Fetterman Disaster site is on U.S. 87. Follow marked markers.

Tragic events associated with Fort Phil Kearny, the Fetterman Massacre, and the Wagon Box Fight form one of the most dramatic chapters in the history of the Indian wars: the bloody 2 years of warfare in 1866–68 sparked by bitter Sioux opposition to the invasion of their hunting grounds by prospectors bound over the Bozeman Trail to the Montana goldfields. In one of the few instances during the Indian wars when the Army was forced to abandon a region it had occupied, the Sioux triumphed and the forts were evacuated. But the conflict ... final dis

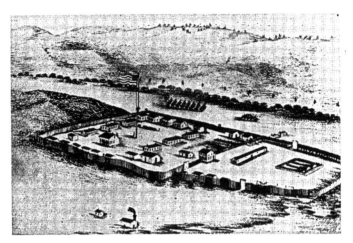

*Fort Phil Kearny, from a sketch by Bugler Antonio
Nicoli, 2d Cavalry, in 1867.*

astrous confrontation between frontiersman and Indian that ensued on the northern Plains as the westward movement accelerated after the Civil War.

Strikes in 1862 by Idaho prospectors in the mountains of western Montana triggered a rush to the diggings at Bannack and subsequently to Virginia City. The next spring John M. Bozeman
and John M. Jacobs blazed the Bozeman Trail. Running north
from the Oregon-California Trail along the eastern flank of the
Bighorn Mountains and then westward, it linked Forts Sedgwick,
Colo., and Laramie, Wyo., and the Oregon-California Trail with
Virginia City. Spared the circuitous route through Salt Lake City,
gold seekers soon poured over the trail, which crossed the heart of
the hunting grounds the hostile Sioux had recently seized from
the Crows. The Sioux, taking advantage of the absence of Regular
troops in the Civil War, quickly unleashed their fury.

In 1865, at Fort Sully, S. Dak., the Government concluded treaties with a few Sioux chiefs. In return for the promise of annuities, they agreed to withdraw from the vicinity of emigrant routes
and not to attack them. The commissioners, however, had dealt
with only unimportant leaders of the bands along the Missouri
River—not the people who really mattered. Red Cloud, Man-

Afraid-of-His-Horses, and other chiefs who roamed the Powder and Bighorn country to the west vowed to let no travelers pass unmolested.

In the late spring and summer of 1866 a U.S. commission met with these leaders at Fort Laramie, Wyo. In the midst of the council, Col. Henry B. Carrington and 700 men of the 18th Infantry marched into the fort. When Red Cloud and the other chiefs learned that their mission was the construction of forts along the Bozeman Trail, they stalked out of the conference and declared war on all invaders of their country. That summer and fall Carrington strengthened and garrisoned Fort Reno and erected Forts Phil Kearny and C. F. Smith. Nevertheless, by winter Sioux, Arapaho, and Northern Cheyenne warriors had all but closed the trail. Between August 1 and December 31 they killed 154 persons in the vicinity of Fort Phil Kearny, wounded 20 more, regularly attacked emigrants, and destroyed or captured more than 750 head of livestock. Even heavily guarded supply trains had to fight their way over the trail. The forts endured continual harassment, and wagon trains hauling wood for fuel and construction had to ward off assaults.

Sioux efforts focused on Carrington's headquarters, Fort Phil Kearny, situated between the Big and Little Piney Forks of the Powder River on a plateau rising 50 to 60 feet above the valley floor. The largest of the three posts guarding the Bozeman Trail, it was one of the best fortified western forts of the time. It ultimately consisted of 42 log and frame buildings within a 600 by 800 foot stockade of heavy pine timber 11 feet high, and had blockhouses at diagonal corners. A company of the 2d Cavalry reinforced Carrington's infantry.

Strong defenses were necessary. The warnings of Red Cloud had not prevented the fort's establishment, but he soon put it under virtual siege. Carrington, saddled with 21 women and children dependents who had accompanied him from Fort Kearny, Nebr., maintained a defensive stance. A clique of his younger and more impetuous officers, who disliked him and resisted his attempts to impose discipline, were contemptuous. Prominent among them was Capt. William J. Fetterman, who boasted that he and 80 men could ride through the whole Sioux Nation.

On December 21, 1866, a small war party, in a feint, made a

typical attack on a wood train returning eastward from Piney Island to the fort. To relieve the train, Carrington sent out Fetterman, two other officers, 48 infantrymen, 28 cavalrymen, and two civilians—81 men in all. Although warned not to cross Lodge Trail Ridge, where he would be out of sight of the fort, Fetterman let a small party of warriors decoy him northward well beyond the ridge and into a carefully rehearsed ambush prepared by Red Cloud. Within half an hour, at high noon, hundreds of Sioux, Cheyenne, and Arapaho warriors annihilated the small force to the last man. Relief columns from the fort, which scattered the Indians, were too late to rescue Fetterman and his men. They had suffered the worst defeat inflicted by the Plains Indians on the Army until that time and one that vied with subsequent debacles, such as the Battle of the Little Bighorn.

Following the Fetterman Disaster, Carrington hired civilians John "Portugee" Phillips and Daniel Dixon to carry a message for Omaha headquarters concerning the disaster and a plea for rein-

Diorama of the Wagon Box Fight.

Artist's version of the Fetterman Disaster. Harper's Weekly *(March 23, 1867)*.

forcements to the telegraph station at Horseshoe Bend, near Fort Laramie. Phillips continued on through a snowstorm to Fort Laramie on a 236-mile ride, honored in the annals of Wyoming history. Carrington was replaced in January 1867.

By that summer the Indians had closed the Bozeman Trail to all but heavily guarded military convoys, but the troops won two victories. The Sioux and Cheyennes agreed to pool their resources and wipe out Forts Phil Kearny and C. F. Smith. One faction, in the Hayfield Fight, attacked a haying party near Fort C. F. Smith on August 1, but suffered heavy casualties. The next day the other group, 1,500 to 2,500 Sioux and Cheyennes led by Red Cloud, set upon a detachment of 28 infantrymen guarding civilian woodcutters a few miles west of Fort Phil Kearny. Most of the civilians succeeded in safely reaching the post, but four were trapped with the soldiers in an oval barricade that had been formed earlier as a defensive fortification from the overturned boxes of 14 wood-hauling wagons that had been removed from the running gears. The troops were armed with newly issued breech-loading Springfield rifles—a costly surprise for the Sioux. Six times in 4 hours

383

they charged the wagon boxes, but each time were thrown back with severe casualties. Reinforcements finally arrived from the fort with a mountain howitzer and quickly dispersed the opposition. The Army reported only about three dead and two wounded, but the Indians claimed the figures were at least 60 and 120, respectively.

The Hayfield and Wagon Box Fights exacted a modicum of revenge for the Fetterman Disaster, but they did not deter hostilities. Forays increased steadily until the next year, when the Government was forced to come to terms with the Indians. In the Treaty of Fort Laramie (1868), in return for certain Indian concessions, it bowed to Red Cloud's demands and agreed to close the Bozeman Trail and abandon the three forts protecting it. As soon as this occurred, in July and August, the Sioux, unknowingly celebrating the zenith of their power on the northern Plains, jubilantly burned them to the ground.

The basically unaltered natural scene of the sites of Fort Phil Kearny, the Fetterman Disaster, and the Wagon Box Fight, despite surrounding ranch operations, are marred by but few modern intrusions. Picturesquely located at the foot of the Bighorn Mountains, they permit ready historical visualization. Nothing remains of the fort, whose approximate location is about 1 mile west of U.S. 87 and 2½ miles southeast of Story. The site is marked by one side of a stockade, all that survives from a Works Progress Administration (WPA) reconstruction in the 1930's, and a log cabin erected by the Boy Scouts. The State owns 3 acres of the probable 25-acre site. About 5 miles to its north, along U.S. 87 and about 1½ miles northeast of Story, is the spur ridge east of Peno Creek, and the route of the Bozeman Trail, along which Fetterman and his men retreated southward. At the southern end of the estimated 60 privately owned acres embracing the battlefield, at the point where most of the bodies were found, stands a War Department monument on a tiny tract of Federal land on the east side of the highway. The only modern intrusion of consequence is the highway. Another monument, lying in an upland prairie some 1½ miles southwest of Story, marks the location of the Wagon Box Fight, 1 acre of which is State owned out of an estimated 40-acre total.

Fort Reno (Fort Connor), Wyoming ⊗

Location: Johnson County, about 27 miles northeast of Kaycee, approximately 1 mile east of an unimproved road at a point some 10 miles from its junction with a paved road some one-half mile northwest of Sussex. Make local inquiry.

Brig. Gen. Patrick E. Connor founded Fort Connor in the summer of 1865 on the north bank of the Powder River about 180 miles northwest of Fort Laramie, Wyo., in hostile Sioux country as a temporary base for his Powder River Expedition. In November the Army renamed the post Fort Reno. The following summer Col. Henry B. Carrington, laying out the Bozeman Trail defense line, added blockhouses and bastions at two corners of the cottonwood stockade and strengthened the garrison. For 2 years Fort Reno, as well as newly founded Forts C. F. Smith and Phil Kearny, Wyo., protected the trail as best it could from the continual attacks of the Sioux Red Cloud and his Cheyenne and Arapaho allies. In 1868 the Indians burned all three forts when the Army evacuated them in accordance with the Fort Laramie Treaty.

This site should not be confused with that of Cantonment Reno (Fort McKinney No. 1) (1876–78), a temporary supply base General Crook's men built of dugouts and a few cottonwood huts about 3 miles to the north during the 1876 offensive that followed Custer's defeat. In 1878 the Army relocated this post, subsequently known as Fort McKinney No. 2, about 40 miles to the northwest on the north bank of the Clear Fork of the Powder River. It was inactivated in 1894.

The Fort Reno (Connor) site, occasionally flooded by the Powder River, is in private ownership and is indicated by a granite marker. Mounds of earth apparently trace the outline of the stockade and blockhouses. Bits of debris may be the result of ranch operations rather than fort remains. The Cantonment Reno (Fort McKinney No. 1) site, about 3 miles northward on the same side of the Powder River nearly opposite the mouth of the Dry Fork, also in private ownership, is not marked and is almost impossible to find without a local guide. Surface evidence is fairly extensive. The Fort McKinney No. 2 site, on U.S. 16, some 3 miles west of

385

Buffalo, Wyo., is occupied today by the Wyoming Soldiers' and Sailors' Home. The old fort hospital, moved from its original location, is today the visitors' house of the home. All that otherwise remains of the post are old mule and cavalry stables, the latter now used as a garage, as well as some cellar ruins of other buildings.

Fort Washakie, Wyoming ⊗
Location: Fremont County, town of Fort Washakie.

This fort, whose history provides a notable example of amicable Indian-white relations on the frontier, is one of the few named for an Indian. The distinguished Shoshoni leader Washakie was a friend of the white man and kept his tribe at peace throughout the Indian wars. He and many of his people served with distinction as Army scouts, joining cause with the Crows against the Sioux, Cheyennes, and Arapahos. Still on the Army rolls at the time of his death in 1900, apparently at the age of 102, he was the only full-blooded Indian ever to have been buried with military honors. A Christian, he had been baptized in 1897.

Fort Washakie (1869–1909) was located at two different sites. The first (1869–71), when the fort was a subpost of Fort Bridger, was along the Popo Agie River on the site of Lander, Wyo. The second was at the junction of the north and south forks of the Little Wind River. The post's major mission was protecting the Shoshonis on the Wind River Reservation, created in 1868, from their wandering Indian enemies. The post also guarded miners in the nearby Sweetwater region until Camp Stambaugh (1870–78) was established to the south between Atlantic City and Miners Delight. During the 1870's and 1880's, Fort Washakie also served as a supply base and springboard for expeditions entering Yellowstone National Park, established in 1872, and for gold seekers and others heading into the Bighorn country.

Since the Army departed, the fort has been the agency headquarters for the Wind River Indian Reservation, occupied since 1877 by Arapahos as well as Shoshonis. Many of the old fort buildings, constructed of adobe, frame, and stone and including the old frame barracks and adobe guardhouse, are still used by the agency and are intermingled with modern structures. Chief Wash-

Shoshoni Chief Washakie. He and his people were friends of the white man.

Wyo., is occupied today by the Wyoming Soldiers' and Home. The old fort hospital, moved from its original loca-today the visitors' house of the home. All that otherwise of the post are old mule and cavalry stables, the latter now a garage, as well as some cellar ruins of other buildings.

Washakie, Wyoming ⊗

...of Fort Washakie.

..., whose history provides a notable example of amicable ...white relations on the frontie... is one of the few named for ...leader Washakie was a ...of the white man and kept h... tribe at peace throughout ...wars. He and many of h... people served with distinc-...Army scouts, joining cause with the Crows against the ...Cheyennes, and Arapahos. S... on the Army rolls at the ...of his death in 1900, apparentl... the age of 102, he was the ...half-blooded Indian ever to h... been buried with military ...A Christian, he had been ba... in 1897.

...Washakie (1869-1909) was located at two different sites. ...(1869-78), when the fort w... a subpost of Fort Bridger, ...the Popo Agie River on t... site of Lander, Wyo. The ...was at the junction of the n... and south forks of the Lit-...Wind River. The post's majo... mission was protecting the ...on the Wind River Reser... ation, created in 1868, from ...wandering Indian enemies. T... post also guarded miners in region until Camp Stambaugh (1870-78) ...established to the south betw... Atlantic City and Miners ...During the 1870's and 18... , Fort Washakie also served ...supply base and springboard f... expeditions entering Yellow-...National Park, established in ... 172, and for gold seekers and ...heading into the Bighorn country.

...the Army departed, the f... has been the agency head-...for the Wind River India... Reservation, occupied since ...by Arapahos as well as Sh... abnis. Many of the old fort ...constructed of adobe, f... be, and stone and including ...frame barracks and adobe guardhouse, are still used by the ...with modern structures. Chief Wash-

Shoshoni Chief Washakie. He and his people were friends of the white man.

akie's grave is in the former military cemetery about 4 miles south of the fort. A marker in downtown Lander indicates the location of the first fort, when it was known as Camp C. C. Augur and Camp Brown.

Grattan Fight Site, Wyoming ⊗

Location: Goshen County, between an unimproved road and the North Platte River, about 3 miles west of Lingle.

Only slightly more than a century ago an incident occurred at this site that marked the beginning of 3½ decades of intermittent warfare on the northern Plains. On a summer afternoon in 1854 a young lieutenant, belligerently seeking to arrest a Sioux Indian for a trivial offense, forced a fight. By sundown all the troops but one were dead. An enraged American public, unaware of the actual circumstances, demanded action. The Sioux and other northern tribes, with whom relations rapidly deteriorated, made numerous raids along the Oregon-California Trail. The next year Col. William S. Harney led a punitive expedition (1855–56) onto the Plains from Fort Kearny, Nebr. The Indian wars, a bitter, generation-long struggle, had begun.

During the years just preceding the Grattan Fight, despite the waves of settlers passing west over the trail, the northern Plains Indians had been relatively peaceful. In July and early August 1854 about 600 lodges of Brûlé, Miniconjou, and Oglala Sioux, as well as those of a few Northern Cheyennes, dotted the North Platte River Valley for several miles east of Fort Laramie. This large concentration of Indians, which could easily have overwhelmed the fort's feeble garrison, was impatiently awaiting the delayed annuity issue to which they were entitled by the Fort Laramie Treaty (1851). On August 18 a Miniconjou named High Forehead, visiting Conquering Bear's Brûlé camp, shot and ate a cow belonging to a Mormon emigrant.

That same day Conquering Bear visited Fort Laramie's commanding officer, Lt. Hugh B. Fleming, and offered to make amends. Rejecting these overtures, he decided to arrest High Forehead, an act in violation of existing treaties. The commander assigned the mission to John L. Grattan, a rash 24-year-old lieutenant fresh out of West Point, and gave him broad discretionary powers.

The next afternoon Grattan, an interpreter named Lucien Auguste, and 29 infantrymen set out with a wagon and two small artillery pieces. They stopped first at the Gratiot Houses fur trading post and then at James Bordeaux' trading post, 300 yards from the Brûlé camp and 8 miles southeast of Fort Laramie. Over Grattan's protests, at both places the interpreter, who had become intoxicated, abused and threatened loitering Indians.

A series of conferences between Grattan and Conquering Bear and other chiefs culminated in front of High Forehead's lodge, where Grattan finally moved his troops despite the warnings of the alarmed Bordeaux. The chiefs made new offers to pay for the cow, pleaded with the unyielding Grattan to postpone action until the Indian agent arrived, and continued to urge the obstinate High Forehead to surrender. Conquering Bear explained that High Forehead was a guest in his village and was not subject to his authority. Aggravating matters was the arrival of some impetuous young Oglala warriors, who in defiance of Grattan's orders had hurried down from their village. Distrusting Auguste's translation of what was being said and seeking to avoid a clash, Conquering Bear tried but failed to obtain the translation services of Bordeaux. As the situation became more tense, the Brûlé women and children fled from the camp toward the river.

At some point a few shots were fired and an Indian fell, but the chiefs cautioned the warriors not to reciprocate. Convinced nevertheless of the need for an even greater show of force, Grattan ordered his men to fire a volley. Conquering Bear slumped to the ground mortally wounded. Arrows flew. Once Grattan fell, his command panicked and fought a running battle back along the Oregon-California Trail. Finally the mounted Indians, forcing the foot soldiers onto level ground, overwhelmed them. All died except for one mortally wounded man who managed to make it back to Fort Laramie.

The Indian chiefs, feeling that the Great White Father would realize that the soldiers had been partly at fault and would forgive the Indians for the battle but not an attack on Fort Laramie, restrained their warriors. Within a few days they did, however, ransack Gratiot Houses of its goods as a substitute for their annuities and then departed from the North Platte River Valley. Life at the fort slowly settled into the familiar routine, but the old security was gone.

The site, privately owned and used for ranch operations, is marked by a stone monument, on the north side of the road. Extensive modern alterations of the terrain for irrigation purposes prevent the identification of the exact positions of the participants in the fight. The site of the cairn, where the enlisted men are buried, is about 200 yards west of the probable site of the Bordeaux trading post, marked by ground debris. Grattan's body is interred at Fort Leavenworth, Kans. The likely site of Gratiot Houses, also debris covered, is located a few rods from the river about a quarter mile east of the headgates of the Gratiot Irrigation Ditch.

ATHEARN, ROBERT G. *William Tecumseh Sherman and the Settlement of the West.* Norman, Okla., 1956.

BERTHRONG, DONALD J. *The Southern Cheyennes.* Norman, 1963.

BOURKE, JOHN G. *On the Border with Crook.* New York, 1891.

CARLEY, KENNETH. *The Sioux Uprising of 1862.* Publications of the Minnesota Historical Society, Russell W. Fridley, Director and Editor. St. Paul, 1961.

CATLIN, GEORGE. *Episodes From Life Among the Indians, and Last Rambles,* ed. by Marvin C. Ross. Norman, 1959.

CHITTENDEN, HIRAM M. *The American Fur Trade of the Far West.* 3 vols. New York, 1902; several reprintings.

CROOK, GEORGE. *General George Crook: His Autobiography,* ed. by Martin F. Schmitt. Norman, 1946.

DALE, EDWARD E. *The Indians of the Southwest: A Century of Development Under the United States.* Norman, 1949.

DEBO, ANGIE. *The Road to Disappearance.* Norman, 1941.

DOWNEY, FAIRFAX D. *Indian-Fighting Army.* New York, 1941.

DUNN, JACOB P., JR. *Massacres of the Mountains: A History of the Indian Wars of the Far West, 1815–1875.* New York, 1886; reprinted, New York, 1958.

FEY, HAROLD E., and D'ARCY MCNICKLE. *Indians and Other Americans: Two Ways of Life Meet.* New York, 1959.

FOREMAN, GRANT. *The Five Civilized Tribes.* Norman, 1934.

FRAZER, ROBERT W. *Forts of the West: Military Forts and Presidios and Posts Commonly Called Forts West of the Mississippi River to 1898.* Norman, 1965.

FRITZ, HENRY. *The Movement for Indian Assimilation, 1860–1890.* Philadelphia, 1963.

GLASSLEY, RAY H. *Pacific Northwest Indian Wars.* Portland, Oreg., 1953.

GRINNELL, GEORGE B. *The Fighting Cheyennes.* New York, 1915; other eds., New Haven, 1926, Norman, 1956.

HAGAN, WILLIAM T. *American Indians.* Chicago, 1961.

HAINES, FRANCIS. *The Nez Percés, Tribesmen of the Columbia Plateau.* Norman, 1955.

HALEY, J. EVETTS. *Fort Concho and the Texas Frontier.* San Angelo, Tex., 1952.

HALLOWELL, A. IRVING. "The Backwash of the Frontier: The Impact of the Indian on American Culture." *Smithsonian Institution Annual Report for 1958.* Washington, 1959.

HART, HERBERT M. *Old Forts of the Far West.* Seattle, 1965.

———. *Old Forts of the Northwest.* Seattle, 1963.

———. *Old Forts of the Southwest.* Seattle, 1964.

———. *Pioneer Forts of the West.* Seattle, 1967.

HERR, JOHN K., and EDWARD S. WALLACE. *The Story of the U.S. Cavalry, 1775–1942.* Boston, 1953.

HYDE, GEORGE E. *Red Cloud's Folk: A History of the Oglala Sioux Indians.* Norman, 1937; 2d ed., Norman, 1957.

JOSEPHY, ALVIN M., JR., ed. *The American Heritage Book of Indians.* New York, 1961.

LA FARGE, OLIVER. *A Pictorial History of the American Indian.* New York, 1956.

LAVENDER, DAVID. *Bent's Fort.* Garden City, N.Y., 1954.

LECKIE, WILLIAM H. *The Military Conquest of the Southern Plains.* Norman, 1963.

LINTON, RALPH, ed. *Acculturation in Seven American Indian Tribes.* New York, 1940.

LOCKWOOD, FRANK C. *The Apache Indians.* New York, 1938.

LOWIE, ROBERT H. *Indians of the Plains.* New York, 1954.

MCNICKLE, D'ARCY. *They Came Here First: The Epic of the American Indian.* Philadelphia, 1949.

MATTES, MERRILL J. *Indians, Infants, and Infantry: Andrew and Elizabeth Burt on the Frontier.* Denver, 1960.

NYE, WILBUR S. *Carbine and Lance: The Story of Old Fort Sill.* Norman, 1938; other eds., Norman, 1942, 1969.

OLSON, JAMES C. *Red Cloud and the Sioux Problem.* Lincoln, Nebr., 1965.

POTOMAC CORRAL OF WESTERNERS. *Great Western Indian Fights.* Garden City, 1960.

PRIEST, LORING B. *Uncle Sam's Stepchildren: The Reformation of United States Indian Policy, 1865–1887.* New Brunswick, N.J., 1942.

PRUCHA, FRANCIS P. *A Guide to the Military Posts of the United States, 1789–1895.* Madison, 1964.

RADIN, PAUL. *The Story of the American Indian.* New York, 1934; rev. ed., New York, 1944.

RICHARDSON, RUPERT N. *The Comanche Barrier to South Plains Settlement.* Glendale, Calif., 1933.

RISTER, CARL C. *Border Command: General Phil Sheridan in the West.* Norman, 1944.

RUTH, KENT. *Great Day in the West: Forts, Posts, and Rendezvous Beyond the Mississippi.* Norman, 1963.

SANDOZ, MARI. *Crazy Horse, the Strange Man of the Oglalas.* New York, 1942.

SCHMITT, MARTIN F., and DEE BROWN. *Fighting Indians of the West.* New York, 1948.

SEYMOUR, FLORA W. *Indian Agents of the Old Frontier.* New York, 1941.

SPICER, EDWARD H. *Cycles of Conquest: The Impact of Spain, Mexico, and the United States on the Indians of the Southwest, 1553–1960.* Tucson, 1962.

STEWART, EDGAR I. *Custer's Luck.* Norman, 1955.

STIRLING, MATTHEW W., et al. *National Geographic on Indians of the Americas.* Washington, 1955.

THRAPP, DAN L. *The Conquest of Apacheria.* Norman, 1967.

UNDERHILL, RUTH M. *The Navajos.* Norman, 1956; rev. ed., Norman, 1967.

———. *Red Man's America: A History of Indians in the United States.* Chicago, 1953.

UTLEY, ROBERT M. *Frontiersmen in Blue: The United States Army and the Indian, 1848–1865.* New York, 1967.

———. *The Last Days of the Sioux Nation.* New Haven, 1963.

WEBB, WALTER P. *The Great Plains.* Boston, 1931.

WELLMAN, PAUL I. *Death on Horseback: Seventy Years of War for the American West.* Philadelphia, 1947.

WINTHER, OSCAR O. *The Great Northwest.* New York, 1947.

WISSLER, CLARK. *Indians of the United States: Four Centuries of Their History and Culture.* New York, 1940.

———. *Indian Cavalcade, or Life on the Old-Time Indian Reservations.* New York, 1938.

GLASSLEY, RAY H. *Pacific Northwest Indian Wars*. Portland, Oreg
1953.

GRINNELL, GEORGE B. *The Fighting Cheyennes*. New York, 1915
other eds., New Haven, 1926. Norman, 1956.

HAGAN, WILLIAM T. *American Indians.*Chicago, 1961.

HAINES, FRANCIS. *The Nez Percés, Tribesmen of the Columbia
Plateau*. Norman, 1955.

HALEY, J. EVETTS. *Fort Concho and the Texas Frontier*. San
Angelo, Tex., 1952.

HALLOWELL, A. IRVING. "The Backwash of the Frontier: The
Impact of the Indian on American Culture."
Smithsonian Institution Annual Report for 1958.
Washington, 1959.

HART, HERBERT M. *Old Forts of the Far West*. Seattle, 1965.
Old Forts of the Northwest. Seattle, 1963.
Old Forts of the Southwest. Seattle, 1964.
Pioneer Forts of the West. Seattle 1967.

HERR, JOHN K., and EDWARD S. WALLACE. *The Story of the U.S.
Cavalry, 1775-1942*. Boston, 1953.

HYDE, GEORGE E. *Red Cloud's Folk: A History of the Oglala
Sioux Indians*. Norman 1937; 2d ed., Norman,
1957.

JOSEPHY, ALVIN M., JR., ed. *The American Heritage Book of
Indians*. New York, 1961.

LA FARGE, OLIVER. *A Pictorial History of the American Indian*.
New York, 1956.

LAVENDER, DAVID. *Bent's Fort*. Garden City, N.Y., 1954.

LECKIE, WILLIAM H. *The Military Conquest of the Southern Plains*.
Norman, 1963.

LINTON, RALPH. ed. *Acculturation : Seven American Indian
Tribes*. New York, 1941.

LOCKWOOD, FRANK C. *The Apache Indians*. New York, 1938.

LOWIE, ROBERT H. *Indians of the Plains*. New York, 1954.

MCNICKLE, D'ARCY. *They Came Here First: The Epic of the
American Indian*. Philadelphia, 1949.

MATTES, MERRILL J. *Indians, Infant and Infantry: Andrew and
Elizabeth Burt on the Frontier*. Denver, 1960.

NYE, WILBUR S. *Carbine and Lance: The Story of Old Fort Sill*.
Norman, 1938; other eds., Norman, 1942, 1969.

OLSON, JAMES C. *Red Cloud and the Sioux Problem*. Lincoln,
Nebr., 1965.

PRIEST, LORING B. *Uncle Sam's Stepchildren: The United States Indian Policy* [...] wick, N. J. 1942

PRUCHA, FRANCIS P. *A Guide to the Military [...] State. 17[...] 1895.* Madison, 1964.

RADIN, PAUL. *The Story of the American Indian.* rev. ed. New York, 1944

RICHARDSON, RUPERT N. *The Comanche Barrier [...] Settlement.* Glendale, Calif. 1933.

RISTER, CARL C. *Border Command: General Phil. [...] West.* Norman, 1944

RUTH, KENT. *Great Days in the West: Forts, Posts [...] Beyond the Mississippi.* Norman, 19[...]

SANDOZ, MARI. *Crazy Horse, the Strange Man of the [...]* York. 194[...]

SCHMITT, MARTIN F. and DEE BROWN. *Fighting Indians.* New York, 1948.

SEYMOUR, FLORA W. *Indian Agents of the Old Frontier.* York, 194[...]

SPICER, EDWARD H. *Cycles of Conquest: The Impact [...] Mexico and the United States on the [...] the Southwest, 1533-1960.* Tucson, 1962.

STEWART, EDGAR I. *Custer's Luck.* Norman, 1955.

STIRLING, MATTHEW W., et al. *National Geographic on [...] the Americas.* Washington, 1955.

THRAPP, DAN L. *The Conquest of Apacheria.* Norman, 196[...]

UNDERHILL, RUTH M. *The Navajos.* Norman, 1956 [...] Norman, 967.

——— *Red Man's America: A History of Indians in the [...] States.* Chicago. 1953.

UTLEY, ROBERT M. *Frontiersmen in Blue: The United [...] Army and the Indian, 1848-1865.* New York.

———. *The Last Days of the Sioux Nation.* New Haven, 19[...]

WEBB, WALTER P. *The Great Plains.* Boston, 1931.

WELLMAN, PAUL I. *Death on Horseback: Seventy Years of [...] the American West.* Philadelphia, 1947.

WINTHER, OSCAR O. *The Great Northwest.* New York, 19[...]

WISSLER, CLARK. *Indians of the United States: Four [...] Their History and Culture.* New York [...]

———. *Indian Cavalcade or Life on the Old-Time [...] vations.* New York, 1938.

CRITERIA FOR SELECTION
OF HISTORIC SITES
OF NATIONAL SIGNIFICANCE

A. National significance is ascribed to buildings, sites, objects, or districts which possess exceptional value or quality in illustrating or interpreting the historical (history and archeology) heritage of our Nation, such as:

1. Structures or sites at which events occurred that have made a significant contribution to, and are identified prominently with, or which outstandingly represent, the broad cultural, political, economic, military, or social history of the Nation, and from which an understanding and appreciation of the larger patterns of our American heritage may be gained.

2. Structures or sites associated importantly with the lives of persons nationally significant in the history of the United States.

3. Structures or sites associated significantly with an important event that outstandingly represents some great idea or ideal of the American people.

4. Structures that embody the distinguishing characteristics of an architectural type specimen, exceptionally valuable for a study of a period, style, or method of construction; or a notable structure representing the work of a master builder, designer, or architect.

5. Objects that figured prominently in nationally significant events; or that were prominently associated with nationally significant persons; or that outstandingly represent some great idea or ideal of the American people; or that embody distinguishing characteristics of a type specimen, exceptionally valuable for a study of a period, style, or method of construction; or that are notable as representations of the work of master workers or designers.

6. Archeological sites that have produced information of a major scientific importance by revealing new cultures, or by shedding light upon periods of occupation over large areas of the United States. Such sites are those which have produced, or which may reasonably be expected to produce, data affecting theories, concepts, and ideas to a major degree.

7. When preserved or restored as integral parts of the environment, historic buildings not sufficiently significant individually by reason of historical association or architectural merit to warrant recognition may collectively compose a "historic district" that is of historical significance to the Nation in commemorating or illustrating a way of life in its developing culture.

B. To possess national significance, a historic or prehistoric structure, district, site, or object must possess integrity. For a historic or prehistoric *site*, integrity requires original location and intangible elements of feeling and association. The site of a structure no longer standing may possess national significance if the person or event associated with the structure was of transcendent importance in the Nation's history and the association consequential.

For a historic or prehistoric *structure*, integrity is a composite quality derived from original workmanship, original location, and intangible elements of feeling and association. A structure no longer on the original site may possess national significance if the person or event associated with it was of transcendent importance in the Nation's history and the association consequential.

For a historic *district*, integrity is a composite quality derived from original workmanship, original location, and intangible elements of feeling and association inherent in an ensemble of historic buildings having visual architectural unity.

For a historic *object*, integrity requires basic original workmanship.

C. Structures or sites which are primarily of significance in the field of religion or to religious bodies but are not of national importance in other fields of the history of the United

States, such as political, military, or architectural history, will not be eligible for consideration.

D. Birthplaces, graves, burials, and cemeteries, as a general rule, are not eligible for consideration and recognition except in cases of historical figures of transcendent importance. Historic sites associated with the actual careers and contributions of outstanding historical personages usually are more important than their birthplaces and burial places.

E. Structures, sites, and objects achieving historical importance within the past 50 years will not as a general rule be considered unless associated with persons or events of transcendent significance.

ACKNOWLEDGMENTS

Advisory Board on National Parks, Historic Sites, Buildings, and Monuments (1969–70)

Durward L. Allen, Purdue University.
Anthony A. Buford, Clayton, Mo.
Loren C. Eiseley, University of Pennsylvania.
Joe B. Frantz, University of Texas.
Emil W. Haury, University of Arizona.
Mrs. Lyndon B. Johnson, Stonewall, Tex.
Peter C. Murphy, Jr., Eugene, Oreg.
Nathaniel A. Owings, San Francisco, Calif.
Melvin M. Payne, National Geographic Society.
Elisha Walker, Jr., New York, N.Y.
James W. Whittaker, Seattle, Wash.

Consulting Committee for the National Survey of Historic Sites and Buildings (1969–70)

Edward P. Alexander, Colonial Williamsburg, Inc.
The Reverend John F. Bannon, S.J., St. Louis University.
James Biddle, National Trust for Historic Preservation.
J. O. Brew, Harvard University.
Richard H. Howland, Smithsonian Institution.
Herbert E. Kahler, Eastern National Park and Monument Association.
Charles E. Lee, South Carolina Department of Archives and History.
Henry A. Millon, Massachusetts Institute of Technology.
Frederick D. Nichols, University of Virginia.
Donald Robertson, Tulane University.

399

National Park Service

Roy E. Appleman, Chief (retired), Branch of Park History, Division of History.

Edwin C. Bearss, Historian, Division of History.

Roy F. Beasley, Historian, Fort Union National Monument, N. Mex.

Frederick R. Bell, Picture Librarian, Office of Information.

Elroy W. Bohlin, Management Assistant, Big Hole National Battlefield, Mont.

Lenard E. Brown, Historian, Division of History.

John D. Caldwell, Student Research Assistant (Northeastern University), Division of History.

George S. Cattanach, Jr., Archeologist, Division of History.

Thomas N. Crellin, Chief, Office of History and Historic Architecture, Eastern Service Center, Washington, D.C.

Bobby L. Crisman, Park Ranger, Fort Davis National Historic Site, Tex.

Robert J. Gamer, Park Ranger, Fort Bowie National Historic Site, Ariz.

Vincent L. Gleason, Chief, Division of Publications.

John A. Hussey, Historian, Office of History and Historic Architecture, Western Service Center, San Francisco.

Ronald F. Lee, Special Assistant to the Director.

Benjamin Levy, Historian, Division of History.

Mrs. Thelma Lund, Park Aide, Hubbell Trading Post National Historic Site, Ariz.

Douglas C. McChristian, Historian, Fort Larned National Historic Site, Kans.

John D. McDermott, Historian, Division of History.

Merrill J. Mattes, Chief, Office of History and Historic Architecture, Western Service Center, San Francisco.

Thomas W. Mullen, Student Research Assistant (Northeastern University), Division of History.

Thomas A. Munson, Management Assistant, Fort Larned National Historic Site, Kans.

Albert H. Schroeder, Archeologist, Southwest Regional Office, Santa Fe.

James W. Sheire, Historian, Division of History.

Charles W. Snell, Historian, Division of History.

Franklin G. Smith, Superintendent, Fort Davis National Historic Site, Tex.

L. Clifford Soubier, Historian, Custer Battlefield National Monument, Mont.

David G. Stimson, Superintendent, Chiricahua National Monument, Ariz.

Erwin N. Thompson, Historian, Division of History.

Bernard G. Tracy, Superintendent, Hubbell Trading Post National Historic Site, Ariz.

Thomas E. White, Historian, Fort Laramie National Historic Site, Wyo.

Other Individuals

Bill Barnhart, Historian, Wyoming Recreation Commission, Cheyenne.

Mrs. Clara S. Beatty, former Director, Nevada Historical Society, Reno.

Jack K. Boyer, Director, Kit Carson Home and Museum, Taos, N. Mex.

Joe R. Brankley, Assistant Director of Public Relations, Hampton Institute, Hampton, Va.

Sidney Brinckerhoff, Curator, Arizona Pioneers' Historical Society, Tucson.

Mrs. W. Neil Clark, Supervisor, Municipal Museums, Greeley, Colo.

Donn M. Coddington, Historic Sites Supervisor, Minnesota Historical Society, St. Paul.

Mrs. Mary K. Dains, Research Assistant, State Historical Society of Missouri, Columbia.

Jeff C. Dykes, College Park, Md.

Russell W. Fridley, Director, Minnesota Historical Society, St. Paul.

Mrs. Barbara S. Friedman, Photograph Librarian, Oregon Historical Society, Portland.

Maurice Frink, former Executive Director, State Historical Society of Colorado, Denver.

Miss Mildred Goosman, Curator, Western Collections, Joslyn Art Museum, Omaha.

Gillett Griswold, Director, U.S. Army Field Artillery Center Museum, Fort Sill, Okla.

Miss Lola Homsher, former Executive Secretary, Wyoming State Historical Society, Cheyenne.

Mrs. R. J. Hubbell, Ganado, Ariz.

Miss Lila Johnson, Chief, Audiovisual Library, Minnesota Historical Society, St. Paul.

Robert N. Killen, Historic Sites Specialist, Nebraska Game and Parks Commission, Lincoln.

Bruce Le Roy, Director, Washington State Historical Society, Tacoma.

C. Boone McClure, Director, Panhandle-Plains Historical Museum, Canyon, Tex.

Neal E. Miller, Director, Wyoming State Archives and Historical Department, Cheyenne.

Nyle H. Miller, Executive Secretary, Kansas State Historical Society, Topeka.

Patrick Patterson, Director, Woolaroc Museum, Bartlesville, Okla.

Robert A. Pike, Assistant Director, Division of Recreation and State Parks, Oklahoma Industrial Development and Park Department, Oklahoma City.

Richard H. Randall, Jr., Director, Walters Art Gallery, Baltimore.

F. G. Renner, Washington, D.C.

Don Rickey, Jr., Assistant Director, Military History Research Collections, U.S. Army War College, Carlisle Barracks, Pa.

Paul A. Rossi, Director, Gilcrease Institute of American History and Art, Tulsa.

Paul E. Schulz, Interpretive Specialist, Nevada State Park System, Carson City.

Barry Scobee, President, Fort Davis Historical Society, Fort Davis, Tex.

Joseph W. Snell, Assistant State Archivist, Kansas State Historical Society, Topeka.

James E. Sperry, Superintendent, State Historical Society of North Dakota, Bismarck.

K. Ross Toole, former Director, Montana Historical Society, Helena.

Mrs. Donna H. Traxler, Chief, Reference Service Branch, U.S. Army Photographic Agency, Washington, D.C.

Thomas Vaughan, Director, Oregon Historical Society, Portland.

Merle W. Wells, Director, Idaho Historical Society, Boise.

Miss Muriel H. Wright, Secretary, Oklahoma Historical Society, Oklahoma City.

Mrs. Arthur Young, Clerk-Stenographer, Department of Public Relations, Union Pacific Railroad, Omaha.

PICTURE CREDITS

The National Park Service gratefully acknowledges the assistance of agencies and individuals furnishing illustrations and granting permission to reproduce them. Where available, names of photographers are indicated in parentheses following page numbers.

AMON CARTER MUSEUM OF WESTERN ART: 10

ARIZONA PIONEERS' HISTORICAL SOCIETY: 51, 60, 70, 178, 224

BANCROFT LIBRARY, UNIVERSITY OF CALIFORNIA: 289, 291 top, 355, 356

BUREAU OF OUTDOOR RECREATION (DEPARTMENT OF THE INTERIOR) : 129
(Jonathan Blair)

CALIFORNIA HISTORICAL SOCIETY: 82

COLORADO HISTORICAL SOCIETY: 23, 104, 108, 113, 116, 201

COWBOY HALL OF FAME: 183

CREEK INDIAN MEMORIAL ASSOCIATION: 261 (Kent Spring)

DENVER PUBLIC LIBRARY WESTERN COLLECTION: 20, 52 (C. S. Fly), 59,
105, 111 (W. G. Chamberlain), 115, 192, 209, 220, 233, 248
(David F. Barry), 302, 303, 383

DYKES, JEFF C.: 101

EASTERN NATIONAL PARK AND MONUMENT ASSOCIATION: Frontispiece
(color separations)

FORT CONCHO (TEX.) MUSEUM BOARD: 321

GILCREASE INSTITUTE OF AMERICAN HISTORY AND ART: Frontispiece, 11
bottom, 29

GREELEY (COLO.) MUNICIPAL MUSEUMS DEPARTMENT: 112

HAMPTON INSTITUTE: 345

JACK COUNTY (TEX.) HISTORICAL SOCIETY: 333 (Russell Jones)

KANSAS HISTORICAL SOCIETY: 141, 156, 328, 366

KIT CARSON MEMORIAL FOUNDATION, INC.: 221

LIBRARY OF CONGRESS: 9, 12 top, 19 right, 25 top left, 26 top left, 26

PICTURE CREDITS

The National Park Service gratefully acknowledges the assistance of agencies and individuals furnishing illustrations and granting permission to reproduce them. Where available, names of photographers are given within parentheses following page numbers.

AMON CARTER MUSEUM OF WESTERN ART: 10

ARIZONA PIONEERS' HISTORICAL SOCIETY: 51, 60, 70, 178, 224

BANCROFT LIBRARY, UNIVERSITY OF CALIFORNIA: 289, 291 top, 355, 356

BUREAU OF OUTDOOR RECREATION (DEPARTMENT OF THE INTERIOR): 129 (Jonathan Blair)

CALIFORNIA HISTORICAL SOCIETY: 82

COLORADO HISTORICAL SOCIETY: 3, 104, 108, 113, 116, 201

COWBOY HALL OF FAME: 183

CREEK INDIAN MEMORIAL ASSOCIATION: 261 (Kent Spring)

DENVER PUBLIC LIBRARY WESTERN COLLECTION: 20, 52 (C. S. Fly), 59, 105, 111 (W. G. Chamberlin), 115, 192, 209, 220, 233, 248 (David F. Barry), 302, 383

DYKES, JEFF C.: 101

EASTERN NATIONAL PARK AND MONUMENT ASSOCIATION: Frontispiece (color separations)

FORT CONCHO (TEX.) MUSEUM BOARD: 321

GILCREASE INSTITUTE OF AMERICAN HISTORY AND ART: Frontispiece, 11 bottom, 29

GREELEY (COLO.) MUNICIPAL MUSEUMS DEPARTMENT: 112

HAMPTON INSTITUTE: 345

JACK COUNTY (TEX.) HISTORICAL SOCIETY: 33 (Russe   )

KANSAS HISTORICAL SOCIETY: 13, 366

KIT CARSON MEMORIAL FOUNDATION: 221

LIBRARY OF CONGRESS: 9, 1

405

bottom left, 35, 40 (J. A. Anderson), 69 bottom, 86, 97 bottom, 122, 157, 166, 225 (Matthew B. Brady), 292, 295 (John C. H. Grabill), 300 (John C. H. Grabill), 301 (John C. H. Grabill), 304 (John C. H. Grabill), 354

LOUISIANA STATE PARKS AND RECREATION COMMISSION: 163

MINNESOTA HISTORICAL SOCIETY: 22, 170, 171, 173 (E. D. Becker), 238, 242, 250

MISSOURI COMMERCE AND INDUSTRIAL DEVELOPMENT DEPARTMENT: 176 (Gerald Massie)

MONTANA HISTORICAL SOCIETY: 28

MUSEUM OF NEW MEXICO: 16 bottom right, 77 (Ben Wittick)

NATIONAL ARCHIVES: 12 bottom, 14, 17 top left (William S. Soule), 17 bottom left (William S. Soule), 17 bottom right, 25 bottom left, 25 bottom right, 26 top right, 26 bottom right, 27, 32, 38 (A. J. McDonald), 39, 58, 61, 63, 68, 69 top, 72 (Baker and Johnston), 95, 97 top, 118, 126, 134, 148, 186, 193, 195, 196, 197, 228, 245, 267, 323, 325 (Matthew B. Brady), 326 top, 339 (Matthew B. Brady), 343, 344 (Matthew B. Brady), 347, 349, 350, 351, 363, 367, 368, 369, 374, 380

NATIONAL PARK SERVICE: Rear endpaper, 11 top, 25 top right, 34, 53 (Fred Mang, Jr.), 56 (H. Parent), 65, 75, 79, 84, 88, 90 (Charles W. Snell), 91 (Charles W. Snell), 107 (Robert M. Utley), 119, 124, 135, 137, 143, 151 (Margaret Mercer), 154, 160 (Jackson W. Moore, Jr.), 179 (Charles W. Snell), 181 (M. W. Williams), 184 (Bill Keller), 189 (Jack Boucher), 211, 231 (Laura Gilpin), 236, 239, 265, 286, 291 bottom, 307 (George Grant), 310, 312 (George Grant), 317, 326 middle and bottom, 337, 341, 348, 357, 359, 373, 376, 378 (Ray M. Littler), 382

NEVADA STATE PARK SYSTEM: 213

NORTH DAKOTA HISTORICAL SOCIETY: 244

NORTHERN NATURAL GAS COMPANY COLLECTION, JOSLYN ART MUSEUM: Front endpaper

OKLAHOMA INDUSTRIAL DEVELOPMENT AND PARK DEPARTMENT: 280

OREGON HISTORICAL SOCIETY: 19 left

RENNER, F. G.: 10, 28, 183

SMITHSONIAN INSTITUTION (BUREAU OF AMERICAN ETHNOLOGY): 15, 16 top left (Charles M. Bell), 16 top right (A. Frank Randall), 16 bottom left (David F. Barry), 17 top right (William S. Soule), 31 (L. Heller), 36 (C. S. Fly), 73, 167 (A. Zeno Shindler), 218 (James Mooney), 249 (David F. Barry), 256, 258 (A. Zeno Shindler), 279, 297, 353, 387 (Baker and Johnston)

SOUTH DAKOTA DIVISION OF PARKS AND RECREATION: 299

TAHLEQUAH (OKLA.) CHAMBER OF COMMERCE: 255
UNION PACIFIC RAILROAD MUSEUM COLLECTION: 24 (A. J. Russell), 372
U.S. ARMY (DEPARTMENT OF DEFENSE) : 100, 146 top and bottom, 269, 271, 294
UTAH HISTORICAL SOCIETY: 5, 206
WALTERS ART GALLERY: 6
WOOLAROC MUSEUM: 21, 188
YALE UNIVERSITY LIBRARY: 42, 293

bottom left, 35, 40 (J. A. Anderson), 9 bottom, 86, 97 b
122, 157, 166, 225 (Matthew B. Brady), 292, 295 (John
Grabill), 300 (John C. H. Grabill), 30 (John C. H. Grabill
(John C. H. Grabill), 354

5–

75

57,

ak.)

ney-
14,
05,

INDEX

Ash Hollow, Battle of, and Ash Hollow Battlefield, see Blue Water Creek

Ashley, William H., fur trader, 205

Assimilation, cultural, see Culture

Assiniboin Indians, 246

Astor, John Jacob, fur entrepreneur, 245

Astoria, Astorians, and Fort Astoria (trading post), 130, 176

Athletics, 155, 159, 178, 195, 196, 293, 294, 295

Atkinson, Henry, Army officer, 179, 204, 205

Atlantic City, Wyo., 386

Atrocities and brutality, 22, 109, 115–116, 269

Attorney General, U.S., see United States Attorney General

Attorneys, see Courts

Audiovisual presentations, see specific sites

Auguste, Lucien, interpreter, 389

Authors, see Literature

Auxiliaries, Army, see Reserves; Scouts; Volunteers

Balloon school (Army), 208

Band (Army), 69

Bandits, see Crime

Bank Building, Army, Kans., 148

Banking, see Commerce

Bannack, Mont., 193, 380

Bannock Indians and Bannock War, 4, 33, 92, 125, 127–128, 194, 215, 287, 350

Baptist Church, 252

Barlow and Sanderson stageline, 106

Barlow Road, 289

Bascom, George N., Army officer, see Apache Pass

Baseball, 178

Basketmaker culture, 53

Battle Ridge (Mont.), 191

Battles and battlefields: major sites of, identified, 46; specific, see under name of battle and see maps

Bayou Pierre, 163, 164

Beale, Edward F., career of, 94–95, 314. See also Camel experiment.

Beale's Crossing, Ariz., 73

Bear Hunter, Shoshoni chief, 342

Bear Paw Mountains, Battle of Bear Paw Mountains, Bear Paw Mountains Battlefield, and Bear Paw Mountains State Monument, Mont., 35, 130, 133, *182–183*, 185, 196, 241

Bear River, Battle of, Utah, 342, 343

Beaver, see Fur trade

Becknell, William, Army officer, 177

Beckwith, Edward G., Army officer, 344

Beckwourth, Jim, mountain man, 204

Beecher, Frederick W., Army officer, Beecher's Island (natural feature and town), Battle of Beecher's Island, and Beecher's Island Battlefield, Colo., *101–102*, 153

Belknap, Tex., 316, 318

Belle Point (*Belle Pointe, La*) (Ark.), 86, 89

Benét, James W., Army officer, 90

Benét, Stephen Vincent, poet, 90

Benét, William Rose, poet, 90

Benicia (city), Calif., 89–91

Benicia Barracks and Arsenal, Calif., *89–91*, 94

Bent, Charles, fur trader and Governor, 103, 105, 106, 221

Bent, William, fur trader, 102–107, 309

Bent, St. Vrain, and Co., 103–107

Bent Masonic Lodge #42, 222

Benteen, Frederick W., Army officer, 186–191

Benton, Senator Thomas Hart, 182

Bent's Fort, see Bent's Old Fort

Bent's New Fort, Colo., *102–103*, 106, 108

Bent's Old Fort (Fort William; Bent's Fort) and Bent's Old Fort National Historic Site, Colo., 6, 46, 102, *103–106*, 126, 244

Berkeley, Bishop, and westward expansion, 182

Bible, see Christianity

Bicameral legislature, 257

Big Bend (Missouri River), see Missouri River

411

413

415

418

and training centers and schools
Curtis Act (*1898*) , 259, 262
Custard, Amos J., Army sergeant, 368
Custer, George A., Army officer,
frontispiece, 28–29, 32, 140, 141, 142,
149, 153, 186, 187, 238, 239, 240,
254, 263, 276, *282–283*, 296, 297.
See also Custer Battlefield National
Monument.
Custer, Mrs. George A. (Elizabeth B.) ,
153, 239
Custer Battlefield National Cemetery,
Mont., 189, 191
Custer Battlefield National Monument
(Battle of the Little Bighorn) ,
Mont., 33, 34, *186–191*, 194, 195,
196, 198, 199, 201, 202, 210, 212,
239, 247, 267, 296, 298, 299, 304,
305, 308, 364, 382, 385. *See also*
Custer, George A.
Custer Hill (Mont.) , 191
Custer House site, N. Dak., 240
"Custer's Last Stand," *see* Custer
Battlefield National Monument
Cut Head Sioux Indians, 243. *See
also* Sioux Indians.

Dakota, Dakotas, and Dakota Territory (region and Territory) : history of and historic sites in, 21–22,
32, 46, 165–169, 171, 188–189, 206,
236–251, 295–309. *See also* North
Dakota; South Dakota.
Dakota, Department of (Army) , 171,
188–189
Dalles, The (city, natural feature, and
mission) , *see The Dalles* entries
Dams, *see* Floods
Darlington, Brinton, Indian agent,
266–267
Darlington Agency, *see* Fort Reno and
Darlington Agency
Darlington State Game Farm, Okla.,
268
Daughters of the American Revolution,
93, 106, 174, 192, 194, 197, 226,
351–352, 353
Davis, Jefferson, Army officer, Secretary
of War, and Confederate president,
179, 314

Davis Mountains, 323, 324, 336
Dawes Act (*1887*), 41
Dead Buffalo Lake, Battle of, N.
Dak., 22, 168
Deadwood, S. Dak., 295, 378
Deadwood (S. Dak.) -Cheyenne
(Wyo.) stageline, 378
Declaration of Independence (U.S.) ,
40
Delaware Indians, 273
Democracy, *see* Politics
Denver, Colo., 110, 116, 140, 149, 232,
369
Departments: Military (Army) , *see*
Headquarters *and specific depart-
ments under regional, State, or
numerical designation;* of U.S. Gov-
ernment, *see specific departments
prefixed by United States*
Deputy marshals, U.S., *see* United
States deputy marshals
Deseret Test Center (Army) , Utah,
342
Deserts, *see* Aridity
De Smet, Father Pierre Jean, mis-
sionary, 19, 121–123, 126, 243
Desmet (town) , Idaho, 123
Desperadoes, *see* Crime
Devil Ridge, 340
Devil's Canyon, 277
Devils Lake, 243
Devil's River region of Tex., 313
Diplomacy, U.S., *see* United States Gov-
ernment; *and specific countries*
Disciplinary Barracks, U.S. (Army) ,
Kans., 148
Diseases, sickness, and medical treat-
ment: among emigrants, 361;
among Indians, 6, 77, 106, 155,
158, 229, 246, 290, 301, 361, 377;
in Army, 71, 223, 237, 265, 288,
335. For Army, Indian, and other
hospitals, *see specific sites.*
District of Columbia, *see* Washington,
D.C.
Districts and Divisions, Military
(Army), *see* Headquarters; *and
specific districts and divisions
under regional, State. or numerical designation*

419

Dixon, Daniel, courier, 382
Doctors, *see* Diseases; *and specific doctors*
Dodge, Henry, Army officer, 105, 147, 177, 264, 276
Dodge, Richard I., Army officer, 371
Dodge City, Kans., 138, 140, 310, 315
"Dog Soldiers," 117
Dogs, war (Army), 211
"Domestic dependent nations," 8
Dominguez-Escalante Expedition (*1776*), 78
Dormitories, *see* Education
Dos Cabezas Mountains, 61–62
Double Springs (Takattokah), Okla., 257
Douglas, Wyo., 371
Dragoon Mountains, 55, 56, 62, 63
Dragoons, Dragoon Regiments, and Dragoon Expedition (*1834*), 105, 145, 147, 150, 152, 177, 203, 222, 231, 264, 276, 288. *See also* Cavalry.
Dred Scott case, 182
Drexel, Katharine (Mother Katharine), Catholic superior, 235–236
Drought, *see* Aridity
Drum Barracks (Camp Drum), Calif., 94
Dry Fork (Powder River), 385
"Drybone" (town), 371
Dull Knife, Cheyenne chief, 202, 210, 267, 364, 371
Dull Knife, Battle of, and Dull Knife Battlefield, Wyo., *364–365*, 371
Durango, Mexico, 311
Dwight Mission, Okla., 275, 282

Eagle Mountains, 340
Eagle Pass, 329
Eagle Springs, 327, 340
Earth lodges, 240
Earthquakes, 99
East Building, Kans., 161–162
East Kamiah site, Idaho, 133
Eastern Cherokee Indians, *see* Cherokee Indians
Eastern Sioux Indians, *see* Santee Sioux Indians
Eastern United States: and Camp Grant Massacre, 67; and "factories,"

175; and Johnson, 161; and Meeker, 111–112; Army fights Indians in, 13; Cherokee lands in, 257; Civil War in, *see* Civil War; colleges in, 275, 284; emigration from, *see* Trails *and* Westward movement; Indians in, 3, 4, 260, 284; Indians relocated from, *see* Removal *and* relocation of Indians; Indians relocated from, area occupied by, mapped, 8–9; land patterns in, 42; meets West, 180; mining in, 7; missionaries return to, 290, 292, 359, 360, 361; steamboats in, 180. *See also* Northern United States; Southeastern United States; Southern United States.
Economic conditions: among Indians, 4, 6, 15, 19–20, 40, 41–42, 76–78, 154, 219, 256–257, 259, 261; among whites, *see* Commerce
Education Act of 1842 (Choctaw Nation), 284
Education and schools: for blacks, 119, 293, 344–345; for Indians, 41–42, 60, 68, 92, 94, 114, 117–120, 131, 136–138, 154–156, 158, 159–162, 198, 201–202, 215, 235–236, 243, 252, 256, 257, 259–260, 275–282, 284–285, 290–295, 302, 344–346, 377; for whites, 106, 111, 161, 195, 199, 211, 276, 286, 318, 331; in Army, *see* Induction and training centers and schools
Eells, Rev. Cushing and Myra, missionaries, 354–355, 360
18th Infantry Regiment, 381
8th Infantry Regiment, 210, 324
El Camino Real, 227
El Capitan (natural feature), Tex., 337, 338
El Gallo, N. Mex., 234
El Paso, Tex., 15, 87, 318–320, 324, 327, 332. *See also entries immediately following.*
El Paso (Tex.) Chamber of Commerce, 318
El Paso del Norte (Ciudad Juárez), Mexico, 318
El Paso (Tex.) -Fort Smith (Ark.)

422

433

copal Church, and Methodist Mission Society, 136–138, 160, 161, 162, 281, 289–292

Métis, 170

Mexican War, 7, 37, 98, 105, 136, 145, 147, 150, 164, 178, 230, 232, 273, 274, 315, 318, 323, 331

Mexico: border of, U.S. forts patrol conflicts and outlaws along, 163–164, 226, 227, 272, 318, 319, 328; border of, U.S. park along, 311; commerce of, 103, 223, 227, 323, 329; controls parts of present U.S. and cedes to Tex. and U.S., 7, 37, 55, 61, 67, 68, 82, 98, 99, 100, 164, 230, 232, 311, 318, 323; diplomatic, military, and economic relations of, with U.S., 37, 62, 64, 83, 312, 319–321; emigration to U.S. from, 83; scout from, 311; Sequoyah in, 278; Spanish presidio in, 311; U.S. Indians in and campaigns against, 14, 15, 35–38, 57, 58, 60, 64, 65, 69–71, 226, 228, 229, 272, 312, 320, 321, 323, 327, 336, 337, 338, 340; wars with U.S., *see* Mexican War

Midwestern (Middle West) United States, 178

Migration: Indian, forced, *see* Removal and relocation of Indians; Indian, seasonal, 9; national, *see* Westward movement

Miles, John D., Indian agent, 267

Miles, Nelson A., Army officer, 25, 30–35 *passim,* 38, 61, 65, 70, 81, 101, 140, 183, 196, 197, 199, 202, 240, 248, 301, 303–304, 306, 356

Military Departments, Districts, and Divisions (Army), *see* Headquarters; *and specific departments, districts, and divisions under regional, State, or numerical designation*

Military Post Opposite El Paso, *see* Fort Bliss

Military reservations, *see specific camps, forts, and military installations*

Military topics, *see various entries throughout this Index*

Militia, State, *see* Volunteers

Milk Creek, Battle of Milk Creek, and Milk Creek Battlefield, Colo., 35, *114,* 372

Mill Creek, 350, 360

Mills, Anson, Army officer, 305, 320

Miners: historic remains of, 45; Indians hostile to and Army protects, 9–10, 13, 18, 24, 30 (*and see specific sites*); invade West, 20, 24 (*and see various regions, Territories, and States*); laws among, 124; supplied, 180–181, 193–194, 216 (*and see* Commerce)

Miners Delight (town), Wyo., 386

Miniconjou Sioux Indians, 199, 300, 306, 388. *See also* Sioux Indians.

Minitari Indians, 246

Minneapolis, Minn., 174

Minnesota (State), Minnesota River, Minnesota River Valley, and Minnesota Sioux uprising (1862): history of and historic sites associated with, 12, 20–22, *164–174,* 236–238, 242–243, 246, 250, 251, 296, 298 (*and see maps*)

Minnesota Historical Society, 169, 171, 172

Minnesota Volunteers, 238

Missions and missionaries: activities and achievements of, 19, 41, 46, 77, 82, 121–123, 130–138, 155, 159–162, 172–173, 180, 201–202, 235–236, 252, 257, 260, 275–276, 278, 282, 284–285, 289–292, 311, 348, 354–355, 358–362, 373; missions mapped, 286–287. *See also* Christianity.

Mississippi (State), 273

Mississippi River and Mississippi River Valley, 7, 45, 86, 145, 169–170, 172, 174, 175, 177, 178, 180, 182, 203

Missouri, Department of the (Army), 139

Missouri, Division of the (Army), 188

Missouri (Territory and State): history of and historic sites in, 86, 105, 106, 109, 145, 150–151, 155, 160, 161, 162, *175–182,* 220,

described individually, 47–379 *passim*; areas in, mapped, 46–47, 190–191; historical and archeological programs of, 46–49 (*and see specific sites*)

National Register of Historic Places, 48

National significance of historic sites and buildings, *see* National Historic Landmarks

National Survey of Historic Sites and Buildings, 47–49, 399. *See also* National Historic Landmarks.

Native Sons of Kansas City (Mo.), 177

Naturalists, 244

Navajo Indians, Navajo (Fort Defiance) Agency, and Navajo Reservation, Ariz., 4, 15, 18, 21, 29–30, 53–54, 68, 74–79, 222, 224, 225, 228, 229, 230, 233, 234–236, 309

Navy, U.S., *see* United States Navy

Nebraska (State): history of and historic sites in, 7, 145, 147, 157, 176, *203–212*, 247, 296, 300, 303, 306, 356, 360, 364, 374, 375, 376, 379, 381, 382, 388

Nebraska, University of, 211

Nebraska City, Nebr., 206, 207

Nebraska State Historical Society, 205, 211

Negroes, *see* Blacks

Neighbors, Robert S., Indian agent, 316, 318

Neosho River, 136, 137, 138

Nevada (region, Territory, and State): history of and historic sites in, 21, 24, 92, 94, *212–219*, 301, 314, 341, 342 (*and see maps*)

Nevada Volunteers, 214, 216

New Camp Grant, *see* Fort Grant

New Echota, Ga., 257, 279

New England, 125

New Hope Seminary, Okla., *281*

New Mexico, Department of (Army), 222, 225, 253

New Mexico (region, Territory, and State): history of and historic sites in, 3, 9–10, 21, 30, 36–38, 54, 55, 57, 62, 63, 64, 65, 66, 68, 76, 82, 103, 105–106, 107, 108–109,

137, 138, 139, 140, 143, 147, 150, *220–236*, 253, 271, 272, 277, 283, 309, 310, 318, 323, 325, 327, 336–338, 340 (*and see maps*). *See also* Santa Fe Trail.

New Mexico Volunteers, 21, 220, 222, 227, 228, 233, 253, 309

New Orleans, La., 180

New Post of Fort Omaha, *see* Fort Crook

New Ulm (town), *see* Fort Ridgely

New York (State), 112, 150, 204

New York Tribune, 112

Newspapers, *see* Books

Nez Perce Buffalo Road, *see* Lolo Trail

Nez Perce Indians, Nez Perce War, Nez Perce Agency/Reservation, and Nez Perce National Historical Park, Idaho, 4, 17, 33–35, 92, 121, *128–135*, 182–184, 196, 197, 198, 214, 239–240, 241, 346, 350, 351, 353, 359, 360

Nez Perce Tribal Executive Committee, 133

Nicolás, Apache chief, 311

19th century, *see various topics throughout this Index*

9th Cavalry Regiment, 210, 325

Nixon (town), Nev., 217

Nomadism, Indian, 4, 40, 59, 123, 131, 155, 232, 301, 311, 316, 346, 360

Nonreservation Indian schools, *see* Education

Nontreaty Nez Perce Indians, *see* Nez Perce Indians

Nordyke (town) and Nordyke Ranch, Nev., 219

Normal schools, *see* Education

North, Frank and Luther, Army officers, 117

North (U.S.), *see* Civil War; Slaves; Union

North Africa, 314

North American Continent, 43, 75, 187, 306, 360

North Building, Kans., 160–162

North Canadian River, 110, 254, 266, 282. *See also* Canadian River.

North Carolina (State), 256

437

Ordnance Department and arsenal-armory system (Army), 89–91, 147–148, 178–179, 207, 231, 235, 371. *See also* Guns.

Oregon and Oregon country (region, Territory, and State): history of and historic sites in, 7, 9–10, 18, 21, 30, 92, 93, 96, 120, 121, 123, 124, 125, 126, 127, 128, 131, 181, 217, *285–292*, 352, 354 *(and see maps)*. *See also* Northwestern United States (present); Oregon-California Trail; Pacific coast; Washington (region, Territory, and State).

Oregon-California Trail: and Bozeman Trail, 380; Indians and Indian hostilities along and Army protection of, 9–10, 14, 45–46, 123, 126–127, 147, 149, 150, 206–207, 208, 286, 356, 358–362, 367, 368, 371, 372, 374–375, 388–389; mapped, 138–139, 168–·169, 286–287; route of and traffic and way stations on, 7, 126, 145–147, 159–160, 289, 358–362, 365, 368, 373–379; ruts of, 148. *See also* California Trail.

Oregon Historical Society, 131, 286

Ormsby, William M., Army officer, 216–217

Orphan Indian Institute, *see* Highland Mission

Orphans, Indian, 155, 252

Osage Indians, 86, 136–138, 176, 264, 273, 282

Other Sites Considered: and National Register, 48; defined, 48; described individually, 47–390 *passim*

Ouray, Ute chief, 107–108

"Outing system," 294

Outlaws, *see* Crime

Owens River Valley, 94

Owyhee Crossing-Ruby City Road, **120**

Owyhee River, 120

Ox teams, *see* Freight; Trails

Pacific, Department of the (Army), 90, 98

Pacific coast and Pacific Ocean, 1, 4, 7, 8, 18, 36, 89–101 *passim*, 129, 176, 344, 373. *See also* California; North-western United States · (present); Oregon; Washington (region, Territory, and State)

Pacific Division (Army), 90

Pacific Northwest, *see* Northwestern United States (present)

Pacific Railroad Survey, 343

Pacifism, Indian, 219, 302

Pack trains, *see* Freight; Trails

Painted Comanche Camp, Tex., 324

Paiute Indians, 4, 21, 73, 92, 120, 124, 125, 213, 214, 215, 216–219, 286, 287, 288, 301, 342

Pajarito, N. Mex., 76

Palo Duro Canyon, Battle of Palo Duro Canyon, and Palo Duro Canyon Battlefield, Tex., 32, 321, 334, *338–339*

Palouse Indians, 18, 351, 352, 353

Panhandle-Plains Historical Society, 310

Papago Indians, 66–67, 235

Paradise Valley, 212

Paris, Tex., 89

Park Hill Mission and Park Hill Press, Okla., 257, *275–276*, 279–280, 282

Parker, Judge Isaac C., 85–89

Parker, Quanah, Comanche chief, 272

Parker, Rev. ·Samuel, missionary, 359

Patented Indian lands, 41–42

Pawnee (town), Kans., 149, 161

Pawnee Indians and Pawnee Reservation, Nebr., 4, 117, 205–206, 273

Pawnee Killer, Sioux chief, 101–102

Pawnee River, 143

Peace commissions, conferences, and treaties, Indian-U.S. Government, 7, 8–9, 18, 27, 30, 32, 39, 68, 96, 97, 105, 108, 109, 136, 138, 144, 145, 147, 156–159, 160, 161, 164, 176, 187, 201, 204, 205, 208, 210, 229, 242–243, 263, 264, 270, 276, 277, 286, 287, 288, 298, 300, 315, 316, 364, 365, 374–379, 380–381, 384, 385

Peace-on-the-Plains Site, Okla., *276–277*

Peace Policy, *see* Grant, Ulysses S.

Pecos River and Pecos and trans-Pecos River region, 21, 229, 230, 312, 323, 330, 338

441

442

Second Seminole War, 117, 178
Secondary education, *see* Education
Sedentary life, Indian, 4, 18, 40, 131. *See also* Agencies.
Seminaries, *see* Education
Seminole Indians, 19–20, 117, 252, 264. *See also* Five Civilized Tribes.
Seminole War, Second, 117, 178
Senate, U.S., *see* United States Senate
Sequoia trees, 280
Sequoyah (George Gist or Guess), Sequoyah's Cabin, and Sequoyah's Cabin State Park, Okla., 257, 275, *277–281*
Settlers: and humanitarians, *see* Humanitarians; Army protects, 10, 13, 20 *(and see specific forts)*; dismantle forts, *see under* Building materials; Indians removed from areas occupied by, *see* Peace commissions; Indians resent and attack, 10, 15, 22, 27, 30, 33, 41 *(and see various sites)*; resent and attack Indians, 96, 101, 118, 139, 142, 153. *See also* Farming; Lands; Westward movement.
7th Cavalry Regiment, 140, 142, 149, 153, 158, 186–191, 238–239, 282–283, 296, 297, 303, 306
7th Infantry Regiment, 164, 184
Severalty movement, 41–43
Sevier Lake, 344
Shafter, William R., Army officer, 311–312, 320
Shaker religion, 217–219
Shamans, *see* Medicine men
Shasta Indians, 288
Shawnee Indians and Shawnee Tribal Council, 147, 159–162
Shawnee Mission (Shawnee Methodist Mission and Indian Manual Labor School; Fort Leavenworth Indian Manual Training School; Shawnee Manual Labor School), Kans., 147, *159–162*
Sheep, *see* Farming
Sheridan, Philip H., Army officer, and Sheridan's 1868–69 winter campaign, 25, 28, 30, 32, 102, 110, 116–117, 139, 140, 142, 144, 159, 179, 188, 223,

234, 240, 254, 263, 266, 268, 278, 279, 282–283, 287, 296, 356
Sheridan (city), Wyo., 189, 200
Sherman, William T., Army officer, 25, 90, 107–108, 179, 240, 269, 270, 272, 296, 333–334
Sherman Barracks, *see* Fort Omaha
Sherman House, Okla., 269, 272
Short Bull, Sioux leader, 301, 303
Shoshoni Indians, 4, 21, 127, 342, 365, 386–388
Shreveport, La., 164
Sibley, George C., factor, 176, 177
Sibley, Henry Hastings, career of, Sibley family, Sibley House, Minn., and Sibley House Association, 22, 165–169, *173–174*, 236–238, 298, 375
Sickness, *see* Diseases
Sierra Diablo, 340
Sierra Madre (Mexico): Indians take refuge in and troops pursue, 36, 37, 58, 64, 65, 70–71, 81, 327–328
Siletz Reservation, Oreg., 287, 289
Silver mining, *see* Miners
Silversmithing, *see* Craftwork
Sioux City, Iowa, 168
Sioux Indians, Great Sioux Reservation, Sioux Nation, and Sioux wars, 4, 8, 13–14, 16, 21–22, 27, 28, 32–33, 81, 101–102, 110, 113, 157, 164–174, 186–203, 205–206, 208–212, 219, 237–251 *passim*, 292, 295–309 *passim*, 363–390 *passim*; wars mapped, 168–169
Siskiyou County, Calif., 93
Sisseton Sioux Indians, 237, 243, 298. *See also* Sioux Indians.
Sisters of Providence, 202
Sisters of the Blessed Sacrament, 235–236
Sitting Bull, Sioux chief, 16, 33, 132, 187–192, 196, 199, 210, 212, 240, 241, 242, 247–249, 296, 297, 304, 306
6th Cavalry Regiment, 50, 224
6th Infantry Regiment, 204
Skating, 196
Skeleton Canyon, Ariz., 38, 65, *80–81*
Skeleton Cave, *see* Salt River
Skullyville, Okla., 281
Slaves and slavery, 12, 67, 151, 161,

67, 82, 230, 232, 311; missionaries in, 235–236; mountains in, 55; peace comes to, 81; pioneers in, 78; roads cross, 94, 314; Spain explores and controls, 55, 62, 232, 311; U.S. controls and settles, 7, 36, 55, 61, 62, 66, 67, 82, 142, 318, 323. *See also* Southern United States; Western United States; *specific regions, Territories, and States; and maps.*

Spain: and St. Louis, 180; and transmission of horses to Indians, 3–4; cedes Fla. to U.S., 117; disputes Tex. boundary with U.S., 163; explores and controls Calif. and Southwest, 3, 4, 15, 36, 54, 55, 61, 62, 68, 76, 82, 98, 99, 100, 220, 222, 311; in present Southeastern U.S., 117; influence of, with Indians, 175; wars with U.S., 90, 98, 303, 356

Spalding, Rev. and Mrs. Henry H. (Eliza), missionaries, and Spalding (Lapwai) Mission, Idaho, 19, 126, 130–131, 133, 354, 360–361

Spaniards, *see* Spain

Spanish-American War, 90, 98, 303, 356

Spanish Colonial furnishings, 222

Spider Rock (Ariz.), 53

Spirit Lake Massacre, Iowa, 165, 296–297

Spokan Indians, 18, 131, 351, 352, 353, 354, 355

Spokane (city), Wash., 123, 354

Spokane Plain, Battle of Spokane Plain, and Spokane Plain Battlefield, Wash., 18, 351, *352,* 353

Spokane Reservation, Wash., 346

Spokane River, 346, 354

Spokane (Coeur d'Alene) War, *see* Wright, George

Spotted Tail, Sioux chief, 157, 305

Spotted Tail Agency/Reservation, Nebr. and S. Dak., 209–210, 212, 247, 300, 304

Spring Creek, 296

Spring of Death, 227

Springfield rifles, *see* Guns

Squatters, *see* Farming; Land; Settlers; Westward movement

Stagecoaches, 55, 61, 62, 65, 66, 73, 76,

81–85, 94, 106, 109, 110, 120, 124, 127, 142, 214, 215–217, 274, 319, 322, 324, 328, 332, 335, 336, 337, 365, 367, 374, 375, 378; routes of, mapped, 286–287

Staked Plains: Indians take refuge on and Army pursues, 30, 251, 270, 271, 283, 315, 320, 332, 334, 338

"Standing rock," of Sioux, 249

Standing Rock Agency/Reservation, *see* Fort Yates

Star forts, 231, 234, 331

Starvation, *see* Hunger

State Industrial School, Ariz., 70

State University of Montana, 195

States (U.S.) : and historic sites, 46–48. *See also various States.*

Statuary Hall (U.S. Capitol), 280

Steamboats and riverboats, 24, 83, 145, 157, 175, 178, 180, 193–194, 237, 239, 241, 242, 244–247, 265, 274, 281, 289, 296

Steens Mountain, 120

Steptoe, Edward J., Army officer, and Steptoe Battlefield, Wash., 18, 351, 352, *353–354*

Steptoe Butte and Steptoe Butte Battlefield (erroneous designation), Wash., 354

Sternberg, Sigismund, Army officer, 363

Stevensville, Mont., 121

Stone, *see* Building materials

Stoneman, George, Army officer, 74

Stony Lake, Battle of, N. Dak., 22, 168

Stores, commercial, *see* Commerce

Story (town), Wyo., 384

Strategic Communications Command (Army), 71

Suicide, 118, 271

Suisun Bay, 89

Sully, Alfred, Army officer, 21–22, 168–169, 237, 238, 242, 246, 250, 251, 254, 282, 296, 298, 375

Sulphur Springs, Ariz., 63

Summit Springs, Battle of Summit Springs, and Summit Springs Battlefield, Colo., 29, *116–117*

Sumner, Edwin V., Army officer, 14, 109

Sun Dance, 41

447

Headquarters; created, 10; first clash of, with Sioux, 203; largest troop concentrations of, 303; last significant clash of, with Indians, 306; major defeats of, 186–187, 191, 382; responsible for Indian affairs, 8, 10–13, 161; role of, in West, 8, 10–13, 24, 30. *See also* United States Armed Forces; United States War Department; *and various sites and topics throughout this Index.*

United States Attorney General, 118

United States Border Patrol, 331

United States Bureau of Indian Affairs: acquires and relinquishes real estate, *see specific sites;* and historic sites, 47; educational and sociological programs of, 60, 154–155, 243, 251–252, 285. *See also* Agencies; United States Indian Bureau.

United States Bureau of Reclamation, 80, 85, 199, 347

United States Capitol, D.C., 280

United States Census Bureau, 309, 378

United States circuit and district courts, 85, 87–89

United States Congress: and Army, *see* United States Army; and Army camel experiment, *see* Camel experiment; and Cherokees, 258; and Creeks, 262; and "factories," 175, 177; and Fort Atkinson, 138; and Indian removal, *see* Removal and relocation of Indians; and Sand Creek Massacre, 115, 116; authorizes Dragoon Regiments, 145; authorizes national parks, 66, 133, 247; creates Oregon Territory, 362; library of, 280; regulates Indian affairs, 7, 157, 209, 253 *(and see* Peace commissions*)*. *See also* Laws; United States House of Representatives; United States Senate; *and specific Congressmen.*

United States Constitution, 20

United States Court for the Western District of Arkansas, 87–89

United States Declaration of Independence, 40

United States Department of Agricul-ture. 192, 196, 211, 216, 268. *See also various agencies.*

United States Department of the Interior, 8, 48, 96–98, 131–132, 196, 198. *See also specific agencies.*

United States deputy marshals, 85–89

United States Disciplinary Barracks, Kans., 148

United States district courts, *see* United States circuit and district courts

United States Forest Service, 128, 129, 130, 216

United States General Services Administration, 100

United States Government, *see* Union; *various United States entries; and other topics throughout this Index*

United States Government Survey Commission, 136

United States Highways, *see specific sites*

United States House of Representatives, 262. *See also* United States Congress.

United States Indian Bureau: and "factories," 175; and Indian problem, 41, 157, 188, 300; and Nez Perce War, 131; educational and sociological programs of, 161–162, 248, 293, 334; mismanaged, 13; mission of, and Army, 8, 10–13, 161, 302; real estate holdings of, *see specific sites. See also* Agencies; United States Bureau of Indian Affairs.

United States merchant marine, 229

United States Military Academy (West Point), N.Y., 191, 389

United States Navy, 110, 208, 314. *See also* United States Armed Forces.

United States peace commissions, *see* Peace commissions

United States post offices, *see* Mail service

United States Public Health Service, 74, 125, 229

United States Senate, 262. *See also* United States Congress.

United States Smithsonian Institution, 449

450

453

☆ U. S. GOVERNMENT PRINTING OFFICE : 1971 O - 397-484

Lightning Source UK Ltd.
Milton Keynes UK
UKHW02f2109170818
327336UK00009B/520/P